3-MINUTE
PRAYERS
for Difficult Times

3-MINUTE PRAYERS

PRAYERS

for Difficult Times

RAE SIMONS

BARBOUR
PUBLISHING

Published by Barbour Publishing, Inc., 1810 Barbour Drive, Uhrichsville, Ohio 44683, www.barbourbooks.com

Our mission is to inspire the world with the life-changing message of the Bible.

Member of the
Evangelical Christian
Publishers Association

Printed in the United States of America.

Introduction

Quiet down before GOD, be prayerful before him.
PSALM 37:7 MSG

These encouraging prayers are especially for those days when you are weary from life's challenges and your soul is longing for a quiet time of refreshment in the Creator's calming presence. Three minutes from your hectic day is all you'll need to fill your cup to overflowing with strength for life's difficult times.

- Minute 1: Read and reflect on God's Word.
- Minute 2: Pray, using the provided prayer to jump-start a conversation with God.
- Minute 3: Reflect on a question for further thought. You may want to come back to it throughout your day.

This book isn't meant to be a tool for deep Bible study, but each soul-stirring prayer can be a touchstone to keep you grounded and focused on the One who hears all your prayers. May this book remind you that God cares about everything that happens to you. Go on—talk to Him today about any difficulty you may be facing. He's ready and waiting to hear from you!

My Refuge in Times of Trouble

The LORD also will be a refuge for the oppressed,
a refuge in times of trouble. And they that know
thy name will put their trust in thee: for thou,
LORD, hast not forsaken them that seek thee.

PSALM 9:9-10 KJV

I feel oppressed in so many ways, Lord. I'm weighed down with such a heavy load of responsibilities that I get tired just thinking about it. On top of that, every day seems to bring some new and unexpected challenge for me to deal with. And then there's the bigger world out there, a world that is overflowing with problems, problems that are so big I can't even begin to know the solutions. But, Lord, You know the answers. And Your presence is my hiding place whenever life seems too much to handle. Teach me to truly know Your name. I'm putting my trust in You today. Show me Your presence in my life and in the world around me. I know You will never forsake me.

THINK ABOUT IT

Sometime, when we feel particularly challenged by life, we forget to seek God. How can you intentionally make time to seek His presence today?

The Riches of God's Glory

*My God will meet all your needs according
to the riches of his glory in Christ Jesus.*

PHILIPPIANS 4:19 NIV

I feel such a terrifying mixture of emotions, Lord: embarrassment, guilt, anger, shame, fear. All those feelings keep swirling around in my head. They keep me awake at night, and they're there waiting for me as soon as I wake up in the morning. I never imagined that I would find myself in such dire financial straits. I keep looking for someone to blame—but then I turn around and feel ashamed of the mistakes I made. I'm scared of what the future holds. The only place I can find rest for my thoughts is in You, God. I am so grateful that You are taking care of me even now. My financial mess is not too big for You to handle.

——————— **THINK ABOUT IT** ———————

Have you given your finances to God? Or are
you still trying to handle them yourself? What
might change in your life and in your heart if
you relied completely on God's "riches"?

A Hiding Place from Betrayal

You are my hiding place; you will protect me from
trouble and surround me with songs of deliverance.

PSALM 32:7 NIV

God, I really trusted this person. I told her my secrets. I let her see me at my worst. I thought she loved me. I thought we were friends, the kind of friends who have each other's backs. And then I found out she had gossiped about my secrets. She said unkind things about me behind my back. I feel so betrayed! How could she do this to me? Thank You, though, that I can count on You, even when people fail me. I know You understand how I feel—and I know I can hide myself in Your love. Please protect me from the damage this person has done to my reputation. Fill me with Your songs of joy, even now, when I feel so hurt and embarrassed. Help me to rest in You, confident that Your love is all I need.

THINK ABOUT IT

God is our hiding place—but we have to seek Him out. How can you hide yourself in God today? What actions might you need to take to help you feel His protection and hear His songs of deliverance?

Give Your Worry to God

Cast all your anxiety on him because he cares for you.

1 PETER 5:7 NIV

Sometimes, Lord, my mind becomes obsessed with worries. My worries are both big and small, both selfless and selfish: I worry about the health of my loved ones. I worry about my children's safety. I worry about our finances. I worry about the state of the world. I worry about my weight. I worry what people will think of me. I worry about my job. Especially at night, when I'm trying to sleep, all these worries just tumble around in my head like heavy, wet towels in a dryer. But those "towels" never get dry; they just tumble and tumble and tumble, going nowhere, spinning endlessly. So, dear Lord, I'm giving them to You. Take the whole heavy, lumpy load of worry out of my mind. Thank You for loving me so much that You're right there beside me, ready to help as soon as I let You.

THINK ABOUT IT

It's hard to control our thoughts, but with practice, we can learn to quickly turn over our worries to the God who loves us. How can you remind yourself today to stop worrying and start trusting?

A Change of Attitude

*For I consider that the sufferings of this present
time are not worthy to be compared with
the glory that is to be revealed to us.*

ROMANS 8:18 NASB

When I'm worried about money, Lord, it's so easy to lose
my sense of perspective. The tiny size of my bank account
starts to seem like the most important thing in the world.
I forget that I'm living in eternity right now, even while I'm
living in this world; I forget that You are in control of my life
and You are working even in the midst of this financial strain
I'm experiencing. Remind me, God, that in the big scheme of
things—Your scheme—my finances are a very small concern.
The financial limitation I'm experiencing now is nothing—truly
nothing!—compared to all You have in store for me. So, Lord,
I'm asking You to shift my perspective. Help me to see my life
with Your eyes. Reveal Your glory in me, I pray.

—————— **THINK ABOUT IT** ——————

Imagine the worst thing that might happen because
of your financial problems. Now imagine yourself
putting that imaginary situation in God's hands. As
you do so, open yourself to the glory of the Holy
Spirit. Can you feel the change in your attitude?

Brokenhearted Joy

So be truly glad. There is wonderful joy ahead, even though you must endure many trials for a little while.

1 PETER 1:6 NLT

God, I've always struggled with this verse, and now I'm *really* struggling. How can I be "truly glad" when my marriage has fallen apart? That just doesn't make sense to me. I feel such hurt and betrayal, such shame and failure, such sorrow and heartache. Your joy seems far, far away from my heart. Even so, Lord, I'm going to cling to this verse. I'm going to keep believing that You are working in this situation. I do not know the future, but You do, and I know that one day, one way or another, You will heal my broken heart. You will help me to be glad again. I'm trusting You.

———— THINK ABOUT IT ————

Have you confided all your deepest feelings about your broken marriage to the Lord? Set aside some time to do that as soon as you can. And then open yourself to God's joy, a joy that doesn't depend on circumstances.

Antidote for Anxiety

"Be strong and courageous! Do not be afraid or discouraged. For the LORD your God is with you wherever you go."

JOSHUA 1:9 NLT

I'm feeling spiritually weak, Lord, but also emotionally and physically weak. Anxiety is eating me up inside. It feels like an animal gnawing on my stomach, making me sick. It's hard to breathe, hard to swallow. I can't seem to get my thoughts together. My heart is constantly racing. God, I need Your help! I'm desperate. Please give me Your strength and courage. Take away my fear. Send Your Spirit to encourage me. Reveal to me Your presence at my side. I'm too weak to deal with this anxiety on my own. I need Your help.

THINK ABOUT IT

Psychologists tell us that anxiety is fear of something that's not yet real—and may never be real. It's the fear of what *might* happen. Try something different today. Whenever anxiety starts to consume you, repeat to yourself, "The Lord my God is with me wherever I go." See what happens.

Possibilities

"All things are possible for the one who believes."

MARK 9:23 NASB

I seem to have run out of hope, God. I look at my life, and I just can't imagine anything changing. Maybe I've hit rock bottom, and now there's no place to go but up—but that's not how I feel. I feel trapped, like there's no escape from the situation. I don't see a way out. I'm so discouraged that just getting up in the morning is a real effort. Lord, now, when I have nothing left to cling to, I'm turning to You. Maybe You needed to get me to this place where I had no hope left, where I've been forced to realize that I've used up all my own ideas and skills. Here, God, at the bottom of this pit of hopelessness, I choose to put my hand in Yours. I believe in You. I don't know the way out of this situation, but I believe You do. Do the impossible, the way You always do. Show me the way to go from here. Reveal to me Your possibilities.

THINK ABOUT IT

How can God use your hopelessness to get you to depend on Him in a new and fuller way?

Hopes Deferred

And we know that God causes all things to work together for good to those who love God, to those who are called according to His purpose.

ROMANS 8:28 NASB

Dear God, You know how much I want a baby. I believe You even put this longing in my heart. And yet month after month, I'm faced with the same message: yet again I've failed to get pregnant. And it does feel like a failure, as though I'm not good enough in some important way. Lord, take those feelings from me. Remind me that I am not a failure, and that in all this, You are still working. Teach me to rely only on You. Help me not to cling to what *I want* but instead to trust that You will do the exactly right thing at the exactly right time, just like You always do. I believe You have a purpose for my life. I hope that purpose includes motherhood—but I trust You to do what's best in my life. Weave together each aspect of my life, including my longing for a baby, and make something beautiful.

—————— **THINK ABOUT IT** ——————

What might God be trying to teach you from this situation? Can you trust that He has a purpose for your life?

15

The Wisdom of the Present Moment

Do not say, "Why were the old days better than these?" For it is not wise to ask such questions.

ECCLESIASTES 7:10 NIV

I'm so tired of hurting, Lord. This pain of mine never goes away. It interrupts my sleep; it cuts into my productivity during the day. It robs me of joy and peace. It even interferes with my relationships with my friends and family. I just want things to go back to the way they used to be, before this pain was eating me alive, day after day. I want my life to be the way it was when I was younger and stronger and pain-free. I know, though, that it doesn't do me any good to keep looking backward at the past. The answers to my life don't lie behind me. Instead, I'm going to look for You to reveal Yourself to me in a different way today. I give You this pain of mine—and I ask You to do something new in my life. Show me that You are here with me right now, in this very moment. Don't let this pain come between my heart and Yours.

THINK ABOUT IT

How does dwelling on the past hold you back? How can you find ways to seek God in the present moment today?

A Handle for Life

The fundamental fact of existence is that this trust in God, this faith, is the firm foundation under everything that makes life worth living. It's our handle on what we can't see.

HEBREWS 11:1 MSG

I get so caught up in anxiety, Lord, and when I do, I become blind to the world around me, not to mention the spiritual world. All I see are my imaginary fears (but they seem so real!) Strengthen my faith now, God, I pray. Make it a firm foundation under my unsteady feet. Remind me that You alone are the reason life is worth living—and nothing can ever shake or diminish Your reality. Help me to grab hold of the handle of faith so I can relax and enjoy the life You have given me.

THINK ABOUT IT

Do you think of faith as the "fundamental fact of existence"? How might your priorities need to change for your faith to become the "handle" that allows you to live with greater confidence in God's love?

Seeking God's Will

*Seek his will in all you do, and he
will show you which path to take.*

PROVERBS 3:6 NLT

Oh God, how did my finances get so bad that I'm being forced to give up my home? How could this happen? What is my family going to do now? How will this affect my children? What should I do next? I'm so confused by this situation; questions bombard me, one after another, and each one makes me cringe with fear. Lord, I really don't know what will come next, and I don't know how my family is going to handle the loss of our home. But I do know that I can trust You. I know that You have a plan for my family. You're not going to abandon us, and I can trust You to show me where to go from here, one step at a time.

—— THINK ABOUT IT ——

Take a look at your own heart: Have you been
honestly seeking God's will—or have you been trying
to figure out this situation with your own strength?

My Strength and My Shield

The LORD is my strength and my shield; my heart trusts in him, and he helps me. My heart leaps for joy, and with my song I praise him.

PSALM 28:7 NIV

I'm feeling pretty weak right now, Lord. I'm overwhelmed, and I just don't know where to find the strength to keep going. But wait a minute, that's not right! I *do* know where to find the strength I need: in the same place I've found it over and over down through the years—in *You!* Be my strength, God. Wrap Your loving arms around all that is weak in me. I know I can trust You to help me, physically, emotionally, spiritually. I know I don't need to be embarrassed to confess to You how weak I am. You have me covered.

―――――――――― **THINK ABOUT IT** ――――――――――

As you turn your attention to God and His love for you, can you also praise Him, even in the midst of your weakness?

Confident Hope

I pray that God, the source of hope, will fill you completely with joy and peace because you trust in him. Then you will overflow with confident hope through the power of the Holy Spirit.

ROMANS 15:13 NLT

When I feel like giving up hope, God, remind me that the power of Your Spirit has no limits. Even when everything else ends up being a dead end, Your path stretches into eternity. Teach me not to rely on anything but You. Sharpen my focus on Your love and energy so that I stop looking to other sources that sooner or later will let me down. Fill me with Your joy and peace. May I overflow with Your hope so that I bring hope to every situation and person I encounter today. Make me confident in You, I pray.

——————— **THINK ABOUT IT** ———————

Is God the source of your hope?
Or have you been relying on other things?

Avoid the Traffic Jams!

*"Step out of the traffic! Take a long, loving look at me,
your High God, above politics, above everything."*

PSALM 46:10 MSG

The injustice in the world is weighing heavy on my heart,
Lord. It seems like every day there's a new story about people
who are suffering and oppressed. Sometimes I just don't
want to hear anymore. I want to plug my ears and shut
my eyes so I don't have to know the terrible realities
that others are experiencing. I feel so helpless to do anything,
and so I'd rather just not know. I'm tired of all the fighting
and polarization, all the protests and politics. I'd like to
hide from them and think about something else. But I know,
God, that many people don't have the luxury of hiding;
they have to face injustice in their daily lives. And so, God,
today I'm stepping out of all the noise and arguing, the
anger and the accusations. Instead, I'm going to fix my eyes
on You. Show me Your way of justice. Reveal to me what I
am called to do to build Your kingdom.

THINK ABOUT IT

What is the "traffic" in your life that you
may need to step away from in order to
hear God's call to justice more clearly?

Building Instead of Arguing

Encourage one another and build one another up.

1 THESSALONIANS 5:11 NASB

It seems like the world is full of arguments lately, God. One side sees things one way, and they're absolutely certain they're right—and meanwhile, the other side sees things just as clearly in the exact opposite way, and they're equally positive that they're holding the correct position. It's hard not to get sucked into the arguments when they're everywhere: in social media, between friends and family, between neighbors, even within the church. We just can't seem to agree on so many important issues. Lord, we need Your help. We need to stop looking at all the ways we disagree and instead begin focusing on how we can encourage each other and build each other up. God, I ask that You help me to do my part. Help me to resist arguing so that Your love can flow through me (even to the people I disagree with).

—— THINK ABOUT IT ——

What do you think is more important— being right or being loving?

The Future Starts Now

We've been given a brand-new life and have everything to live for, including a future in heaven—and the future starts now! God is keeping careful watch over us and the future. The Day is coming when you'll have it all—life healed and whole.

1 PETER 1:3 MSG

My pain defines each day, Lord. I can't get away from it. It's always there with me, no matter what I'm doing. I try to ignore it, but it's like a nagging child, pulling at my sleeve until I pay attention to it. Teach me ways to gently tell my pain to wait so that I can take a few moments to focus on You. Thank You that the life You have planned for me isn't defined by my pain. I believe that one day You will heal me—and in the meantime, I will trust You to guard me and bless me. Even on my most painful days, give me hope in You. Remind me that my life with You begins now.

THINK ABOUT IT

Have you allowed your pain to
come between you and God?

Hope for the Future

"For I know the plans I have for you," says the
LORD. *"They are plans for good and not for*
disaster, to give you a future and a hope."
JEREMIAH 29:11 NLT

Oh God, I feel as though my life is coming to an end. All my financial hopes and plans are lying in dust around my feet. It's a hopeless situation, with no way out except bankruptcy. I'm so ashamed, so scared. I can't believe this happened to me. It's the sort of thing that happens to other people—not to me! But, Lord, even now I hear Your voice whispering to me, reminding me that You have not changed. Your plans for me are eternal. I can trust the future to You because You will lead me into something new, something far better than I could ever even imagine. And so, God, I'm trusting You. Lead me through this financial disaster. Remind me to keep my eyes fixed on You.

——————— **THINK ABOUT IT** ———————

How can you use this situation as an
opportunity to draw nearer to God?

Generous Wisdom

If you need wisdom, ask our generous God, and he will give it to you. He will not rebuke you for asking.

JAMES 1:5 NLT

God, I don't know what to do. You know I love my husband; I know You love him too. So that's why I can say to You what I'm afraid to say to anyone else: my husband hurts me. I believe my husband loves me—but he also abuses me. I've gotten to the place where I don't know how to trust myself. I'm afraid to ask advice from anyone. I just don't know what to do. Part of me feels ashamed that I even allowed myself to get into this situation. Another part of me wonders if I'm just exaggerating, if it's not really as bad as it seems. Yet another part is so scared of being hurt more that I'd do anything just to make things go back to normal. And still another part is angry, furious, that he could treat me like this. God, I bring it all to You. I know You love me, and I know You don't want me to live in danger. Show me what steps to take. I need Your wisdom and clarity.

—————————— **THINK ABOUT IT** ——————————

How have you allowed fear to control your life? Do you believe that God wants to give you a life free from fear?

Upheld!

*"Do not fear, for I am with you; Do not be afraid, for I
am your God. I will strengthen you, I will also help you,
I will also uphold you with My righteous right hand."*

ISAIAH 41:10 NASB

The thought of losing our home terrifies me, Lord. Our home is
the place where our family goes to be together, to enjoy each
other's presence, to rest, to be safe. And now our home—the
physical symbol of our family—is going to be taken away from
us. How are we going to survive? How can we ever feel safe
and secure again? Thank You, God, that *You* are our safety.
You are our home. Show us the right way to go from here. As
we find our security in You, lead us to a new physical home.
Uphold us with Your hand and take away my fear.

THINK ABOUT IT

God wants to help you with every problem
that comes your way. Have you hesitated
to ask His help with this situation?

God's Peace Guard

Don't worry about anything; instead, pray about everything. Tell God what you need, and thank him for all he has done. Then you will experience God's peace, which exceeds anything we can understand. His peace will guard your hearts and minds as you live in Christ Jesus.

PHILIPPIANS 4:6–7 NLT

God, when financial worries threaten to overwhelm my mind, remind me of all You have done for me in the past. You have never abandoned me, and I know You won't now. When I look back, I see all the ways You have provided for me and my family. Even the worst situations somehow worked out, and You were with us every step of the way. And so now, Lord, I need to spend some time praying about my finances. I'm going to go through every bill, and I'm going to put each one in Your hands.

THINK ABOUT IT

How is God's peace different from the peace that comes from knowing you have plenty of money in your bank account? Which peace would you rather have?

God Is on Your Side!

If God be for us, who can be against us?
ROMANS 8:31 KJV

I was counting on these people, Lord. I thought they respected and liked me. I was sure they would help me get ahead in life. I believed these were useful contacts You had brought into my life to help me do Your work. And now it turns out they had their own agenda. They didn't care about helping me; they only wanted to use me to help themselves. I feel embarrassed and betrayed—but even worse, I feel so disappointed. I really thought we could accomplish great things together, and now I feel as though everything I had hoped for has fallen into pieces. But now, Lord, remind me that Your will for my life won't ever be limited by anything people can do or say. You are on my side, and I am on Yours. Together we will do great things in this world, things that will bring love and healing to the people You love. Help me to put this setback behind me and move on, confident that You have everything under control.

THINK ABOUT IT

How would your attitude change if you became
convinced that God was truly on your side?

Thief-Proof

"The thief comes only to steal and kill and destroy; I came so that they would have life, and have it abundantly."

JOHN 10:10 NASB

God, I get so tired of being differently abled from the rest of the world. I'm tired of the constant challenges to live in a world that's not set up to handle my abilities. I'm tired of the pitying and curious looks people give me. And maybe most of all, I'm just plain tired of feeling like my body has stolen the life I might have had if I'd been born like everyone else. Lord, I thank You, though, that You will not let this condition destroy me. It can only steal my life from me if I let it—and I choose instead to cling to You and the abundant life You give me.

--- **THINK ABOUT IT** ---

Can you make a list of all the ways God has blessed you with abundance, in spite of—maybe even *because of*—your body's differences?

Motivation

*Let us think of ways to motivate one
another to acts of love and good works.*
HEBREWS 10:24 NLT

I'm afraid I've gotten into a rut with my family, Lord—a negative rut. Everything they do seems to irritate me. When I'm talking to them, almost every word that comes out of my mouth is a criticism. I feel like my complaints are legitimate (if they'd just listen to me, everything in our household would go so much more smoothly!), but I realize that my constant negativity has become a burden for our family. I ask for Your forgiveness, Lord. Today, help me not to notice all the things my family does wrong but to look for ways to motivate them to do better. Remind me to build them up, not tear them down.

——————— **THINK ABOUT IT** ———————

Does angry criticism motivate you to do better?
Do you think it motivates your family?

The Best, Not the Worst

You'll do best by filling your minds and meditating on things true, noble, reputable, authentic, compelling, gracious—the best, not the worst; the beautiful, not the ugly; things to praise, not things to curse.

PHILIPPIANS 4:8 MSG

Have You noticed, Lord, that lately it seems like all my husband and I do is argue? And I have to admit that I'm not talking about the sort of lively discussions that can clear the air. No, our arguments have gotten angry and hurtful. We're walking away from them wounded. I know things need to change. These constant arguments aren't getting us anywhere. So today, when I'm tempted to complain to my husband about something he's doing wrong, remind me instead to find something to appreciate about him. When I'm focusing on all the things that are wrong about my husband, remind me of all the things that are right. Remind us both of why we fell in love with each other.

THINK ABOUT IT

What are the things you love about your husband?

Prayer in the Midst of Disappointment

Be joyful in hope, patient in affliction, faithful in prayer.
ROMANS 12:12 NIV

Once again, Lord, I had my heart set on something—and then it never materialized. This time I was so sure it was actually going to happen. It didn't seem like anything could go wrong. But now here I am again, my heart aching with disappointment. Is this a definite no, Lord? Or are You asking me to wait a little longer for Your perfect timing? Either way, I'm going to need Your help with this. Give me Your joy, Your hope, I pray: a joy and hope that don't depend on circumstances, that are firmly grounded in Your unchanging love. I also ask for patience and endurance. Keep my eyes fixed on You. Remind me not to obsess about my disappointment but instead to keep bringing it to You in prayer. Thank You that You always listen, You always care.

THINK ABOUT IT

When you are disappointed, are you faithful in prayer?

Waiting upon the Lord

*They that wait upon the LORD shall renew their strength;
they shall mount up with wings as eagles; they shall run,
and not be weary; and they shall walk, and not faint.*

ISAIAH 40:31 KJV

God, I'm so exhausted. My body is tired, my mind is tired, my heart is tired. The stress of my life has sapped all my strength away, leaving me weak and vulnerable. I'm on the verge of getting sick or sinking into depression. I'm in desperate need of a dose of divine strength. Show me the practical steps I need to take to renew my energy and stamina. Let me know where I need to cut back on the things I'm doing—and then give me the strength to follow through. Remind me that only You are omnipotent; my strength will always be limited. Help me to be a good steward of the energy and skills You've given me. Most of all, Lord, lift me up on the eagle wings of Your Spirit. Draw me closer to You, the Source of all my strength. Let me always wait upon You.

THINK ABOUT IT

Can you identify two things that are consuming
your strength right now? Do you think God
might want you to cut back on anything?

Take Heart!

*"I have told you these things, so that in me you may
have peace. In this world you will have trouble.
But take heart! I have overcome the world."*

JOHN 16:33 NIV

Life seems so full of pain. Whenever I watch the news on television, my chest grows tight with anxiety; it's just one terrible story after another. And then my personal life hasn't exactly been a walk in the park lately. Every morning as I face a new day, I can't help but wonder what will go wrong. Some days it feels as though anxiety is my obligation, a heavy burden I'm duty bound to constantly carry around with me. Remind me, Lord, that anxiety is optional. As Your child, I have the choice to trust You instead. You never promised that the world wouldn't be full of trouble—but You did promise that You are greater than anything the world can throw at me. Teach me to dwell on Your Good News rather than on the nightly news. Give me Your peace, I pray.

THINK ABOUT IT

What would it take to convince you today that
your anxiety is optional? What do you need
to do to grab hold of the peace of Jesus?

God's Care for You

Give all your worries and cares
to God, for he cares about you.

1 PETER 5:7 NLT

My stomach is in knots, Lord, as I think about this legal situation. I'm scared of what might happen. I worry about the wisest course of action. Everyone in my life has their own ideas about what I should do, but I don't know who to trust. I'm so confused. Thank You, God, that I can bring this situation to You. You know all the ins and outs of my case, better even than my lawyer. You understand my feelings better than even my friends and family do. I trust You to guide me. I know I'll keep pulling my worries back out of Your hands, but I'm going to keep on giving them right back to You, no matter how many times it takes. Give my lawyer wisdom. Give the judge and everyone concerned clear eyes to see what is right. Thank You for loving me and never abandoning me, no matter what the future brings.

THINK ABOUT IT

It takes trust to work with a lawyer, allowing her to defend you in court. Can you give the same trust to God?

Self-Image

Whatever I have, wherever I am, I can make it through anything in the One who makes me who I am.

PHILIPPIANS 4:13 MSG

Jesus, losing this job has shaken me down to my toes. I loved my work; I felt as though it made me who I am. Without it, I'm aimless and adrift, unsure of my place in the world. I feel as though my value has been diminished, as though I'm no longer important—and meanwhile, life goes on without me. Remind me, my loving Friend, that it wasn't actually my job that gave me my identity; it was always You. Now, when suddenly I'm no longer as busy as I used to be, open me up to discovering more about the self You created me to be. Give me the strength to let go of the past and instead look toward the future You are creating even now. Make me willing to learn new things and have new experiences. I know that as long as I have You, I can make it through anything, even this.

THINK ABOUT IT

What is the source of your self-image? Might God be asking you to expand your sense of yourself? Maybe He wants to create a "bigger" you.

Opportunity for Joy

When troubles of any kind come your way, consider it an opportunity for great joy. For you know that when your faith is tested, your endurance has a chance to grow. So let it grow, for when your endurance is fully developed, you will be perfect and complete, needing nothing.

JAMES 1:2–4 NLT

Lord, it seems as though Your Word is always telling me the same, almost impossible thing: find joy even in the hard things. I read the words, but they don't make sense to my heart. How can *this* situation be an opportunity for joy? How can You expect me to be happy in the midst of bankruptcy? I feel like I need to be practical. I need to focus on what I have to do to recover from this financial disaster. I don't have time to be spiritual right now. God, I need Your help with my attitude. I need You to shift my perspective so that I see You at the center of this trouble. Use this crisis to make me stronger in You. Teach me that even when my finances are in shambles, I have absolutely everything I need in You.

——————— **THINK ABOUT IT** ———————

How is your faith being tested by this situation?
How might God be asking you to grow?

The "Thorn" of Weakness

I was given a thorn in my flesh. . . . Three different times I
begged the Lord to take it away. Each time he said, "My
grace is all you need. My power works best in weakness."

2 CORINTHIANS 12:7-9 NLT

I don't like feeling weak, Lord. I would much rather be strong and competent. I want to impress people with how well I do things. I don't want them to feel sorry for me because I'm too weak right now to keep up with my responsibilities. I feel so frustrated with myself! I just want You to make me strong, the way I used to be. But maybe that's not Your will for me right now. If the apostle Paul had to live with his weakness, his "thorn in the flesh" (whatever it was), then help me also to accept myself the way I am right now. Clearly, You were able to use Paul in all sorts of amazing ways, regardless of his weakness. So if that's what You want, Lord, then go ahead—use my weakness to reveal Yourself in the world. Teach me to rely on Your grace rather than my own strength.

―――――――――― **THINK ABOUT IT** ――――――――――

How might you allow God's power to
work through your weakness today?

Don't Fret!

Do not fret because of those who are evil
or be envious of those who do wrong.

PSALM 37:1 NIV

I find myself caught up in arguments so easily, Lord. Lately there are countless things to argue about: politics, health precautions, race, sex, the environment. There are so many issues, and we can't seem to agree on any of them. My own point of view truly does seem like the right one! I really believe it is—and then I get so upset with the people who don't agree with me. I feel that they're not following You the way they should. The harder I try to persuade them, the more bitter our arguments become. I find myself feeling so angry, brooding about them, wishing there was some way to convince them. God, I realize I've been letting these argument rob me of the peace You want me to have. I've been fretting when I should have been trusting You. And so, Lord, I give You all these issues. You know how strongly I feel about them; You know I truly want what's best. I put them all into Your hands. I'm not going to argue anymore.

--- **THINK ABOUT IT** ---

What are the issues you feel most passionate
about? Can you trust them to God?

It's Okay to Cry

*Weeping may last through the night,
but joy comes with the morning.*

PSALM 30:5 NLT

I have been sad for so long, Lord, longing for a baby. While everyone around me seems to be having babies, I still can't conceive. I have tried to give this sadness I feel to You; I have tried to be patient and wait on Your perfect timing. I have tried to listen to all the wise words my friends and family have told me. But today I'm sick of trying. I'm sick of smiling when a friend talks to me about her pregnancy. I am sick of being "spiritual" when people tell me to trust God. I am sick of waiting for a baby. But, Lord, I know You understand my heart. You're not asking me to pretend to feel anything but sadness. You're okay with my tears. I can vent all my sorrow and frustration into Your listening ears. Thank You, Lord, for Your assurance that it's okay to cry. And thank You for Your promise to bring joy into my life again.

THINK ABOUT IT

This season of your life is a hard one—but it will
not last forever. If you can set aside your longing
for a baby just for a moment, what other dreams do
you have for the future? Do you see God working
to bring any of those dreams into reality?

Stay Alert!

Then GOD's Message came again....."Stay alert! I am GOD,
the God of everything living. Is there anything I can't do?"

JEREMIAH 32:26 MSG

My sense of helplessness has turned into apathy, God.
There's nothing I can do to change things—so why should I
care anymore? I've been drifting through my days in a fog
of discouragement. I've given up. I just don't want to keep
trying. But, Lord, the Bible reminds me that I'm not the first
person to feel this way. Your people have always had times
of doubt and discouragement, times when they could see no
way out of their situation, when they felt completely helpless.
And yet every time, You stepped in and saved them. Down
through the centuries, no situation has ever been too hard
for You to handle. So, God, I ask You today to wake me up
out of my fog. Remind me to look around me and see what
You are already doing. Keep me expectant, eager to see
what You will do next. Remind me that even when I am
helpless, You are strong.

—————— **THINK ABOUT IT** ——————

What can you do today to "stay alert"
to what God is doing in Your life?

Absolute Trust

Though he slay me, yet will I trust in him.

JOB 13:15 KJV

I don't like to think about dying, Lord. I don't want to leave the people I love, and there are still so many things I want to accomplish in life. Worst of all, no one *really* knows what lies on the other side of death. When I think about the reality that I too must one day die (just like everyone does, either sooner or later), I feel scared. I shift my thoughts as quickly as I can to something else. But God, even though I don't know what eternity will be like, I do know *You.* I know You have never treated me unkindly, You have never shown me anything but love. When I look back at my life, I see You were always there with me, right from the beginning. And so I will trust You with my death as well. I will put my confidence in Your unfailing love. No matter what happens, I have faith in You. You will keep me safe in this world—and the next.

THINK ABOUT IT

Can you trust God with your own death? If not, what holds you back? What makes you afraid to rely on God's love to carry you into eternity?

Unconditional Love

Love never gives up, never loses faith, is always
hopeful, and endures through every circumstance.

1 Corinthians 13:7 nlt

I've messed up, God. I made mistakes that have had consequences, and now I feel like such a failure. I've let people down—and I'm disappointed in myself. But, Lord, I'm so glad that You are never disappointed in me. This Bible verse that's so often read at marriage ceremonies applies just as much to Your love for me. You never give up on me, no matter how badly I mess up. You never lose faith in me, no matter how many other people I may have disappointed. You have hope for my future, and You share that hope with me. Your love endures even when I fail. I don't have to do anything to earn Your love, because You will always love me just the way I am.

--- **THINK ABOUT IT** ---

Do you believe that God's love is unconditional?
What would it take to convince you?

Spirit Wind

Those who enter into Christ's being-here-for-us no longer have to live under a continuous, low-lying black cloud. A new power is in operation. The Spirit of life in Christ, like a strong wind, has magnificently cleared the air, freeing you from a fated lifetime of brutal tyranny at the hands of sin and death.

ROMANS 8:1–2 MSG

Our world is so full of violence, Lord. My heart aches each time I hear about another shooting, one more act of senseless rage against innocent people. The world seems to be smothering under a thick cloud of hatred and death. Thank You, God, that Your Spirit has the power to blow away the clouds. Thanks to Your presence, I can breathe in the cool, clear air of love and hope, even in the midst of this world's sin.

THINK ABOUT IT

What does the phrase "Christ's being-here-for-us" mean to you? Can you look back at the past few days and find examples when you knew Christ was with you?

Brokenhearted

*The LORD hears his people when they call to him
for help. He rescues them from all their troubles.
The LORD is close to the brokenhearted; he
rescues those whose spirits are crushed.*

PSALM 34:17-18 NLT

God, I never dreamed my husband would be unfaithful to me.
We might not have had the perfect marriage, but I still didn't
think something like this could happen to *us*. I feel as though
I was walking along, thinking I was on solid ground, and now
I've suddenly discovered there's no ground under my feet at
all. I've fallen so far and so fast that I can't seem to get my
bearings. My heart is broken, and my safe, predictable life has
been smashed to bits. I feel unloved, lonely, and desperate,
as though everything inside me has broken and there's just
nothing left I can cling to. But, God, I know that's not true. I
know that *no matter what happens*—even my husband being
unfaithful to me—Your love will hold me steady. Help me, I
pray. Rescue me. Stay close to me. I need You.

——— THINK ABOUT IT ———

Can you take comfort in God's love,
even when human love has failed you?

Little Lies

*Do not lie to each other, since you have
taken off your old self with its practices.*

COLOSSIANS 3:9 NIV

Lies slip out of my mouth so easily sometimes, Lord. Not big lies. Not lies that would hurt anyone (or at least that's what I tell myself). Just the little lies that make a conversation go a little easier—or that make a story more interesting. All people tell those sorts of lies, don't they? And yet, Lord, when I read the Bible, I can't help but notice that You take the truth seriously. Dishonesty may be common in the world, but it's not Your way. So teach me to guard my tongue. Remind me that the truth matters. Show me the ways my little lies spring from my old self, the version of me that cared more about herself than she did God or anyone else. I want to be true to You and to the person You created me to be.

THINK ABOUT IT

Why do you think honesty is so important to God?
Do even "little lies" have the potential to do harm?

All You Need

The LORD is my shepherd; I have all that I need.
PSALM 23:1 NLT

I know, God, that many people are out of work right now, but somehow, I never thought it would happen to me. Yes, I know I'll qualify for unemployment, but that income will be a fraction of what I was earning. There won't be any vacations for our family this year. There won't be many new clothes, and we won't be eating out very often. I can handle all that, but what is sending me into a panic is the fear of what will happen if the car breaks down again, one of the kids needs braces, the furnace breaks, or some other unforeseen expense comes up. There's just not enough money in our savings account to cover all the things that could happen. But wait a minute, God. I realize I'm letting my thoughts spin out of control, anticipating disasters that may never happen. Quiet my frightened heart, I pray. Remind me that You are taking care of my family and me, and You will make sure we have everything we truly need.

THINK ABOUT IT

What are the things in life that you *need* (not just want)? Can you trust that God will make sure you have those things?

Buttercups and Dandelions

*"If God gives such attention to the wildflowers, most
of them never even seen, don't you think he'll attend
to you, take pride in you, do his best for you?"*

LUKE 12:28 MSG

I know the Bible promises that You will take care of Your
people, Lord. It promises that You love me and that You will
never leave me. It promises so many wonderful things! But
right now, I'm having a hard time believing that those promises
mean anything. They seem like wishful thinking. They're too
good to be true. And then I look at the beauty of an ordinary
flower, a buttercup or a dandelion, and I see how intricate the
petals are, how perfectly designed, each one a tiny miracle
of loveliness. That flower is just one small evidence of Your
love at work in the universe. It's a reminder to me that You
are present everywhere, Your love constantly on the move
to bring beauty and hope into our world. My doubts are just
clouds in my head; they don't represent reality. You always
keep Your promises.

THINK ABOUT IT

When do doubts multiply in your mind? Is there
anything you can do that will help you remain
more confident in God's love and care?

Heavy Burdens

*"Come to Me, all who are weary and
burdened, and I will give you rest."*

MATTHEW 11:28 NASB

Oh God, my life is just so *hard* lately. Work is a constant stress,
my family has been sick, I can't seem to shake this cold, my
friend and I had an argument, and the dog ate my best pair
of shoes I was planning to wear to a wedding. All those things
may sound so small, I know, but together they pile up. They
make a heavy load on my shoulders. I'm so tired of lugging
it around. Every morning, I wish I didn't have to get up and
deal with so many challenges. I wish instead I could just curl
up and sleep a little longer. But I can't—so, Lord, help me out.
Take the many challenges of my life into Your capable hands,
I pray. Thank You that You are big enough to carry them all.

THINK ABOUT IT

Are you willing to let God carry your burdens? What
would you need to do to release them into His hands?

A Crown of Life

God blesses those who patiently endure testing and temptation. Afterward they will receive the crown of life that God has promised to those who love him.

JAMES 1:12 NLT

Thank You, loving Father, that I never have to be ashamed to bring my temptations to You. You understand that I'm weak—and You don't condemn me. You are always there at my side, waiting to help me. So once again, Lord, here I am, asking for Your help. I don't want to rely on alcohol to get me through life; I just want You. So show me how to endure the temptation to drink (without giving in to it). Remind me that I want Your crown of life far more than I want to drink.

THINK ABOUT IT

What does the phrase "crown of life" mean to you?
In what ways does God crown you with life?

Deep Security

The Lord is my light and my salvation;
whom shall I fear? the Lord is the strength
of my life; of whom shall I be afraid?

PSALM 27:1 KJV

You know my past, Lord. You know how hard it is for me to trust people. Even with the people I love most, I'm always half expecting them to let me down. I'm always waiting for the little signs that will tell me they've stabbed me in the back, in one way or another. God, I know my distrust is coming between me and the people I want to be close to. It's even coming between me and You. Deep down inside, I'm just plain scared. Remind me, I pray, that it doesn't matter what other people do—You are the One who will keep me safe. I don't need to be scared about other people letting me down, because You never will.

--- **THINK ABOUT IT** ---

If trust comes hard to you because of your past, can you
ask God to give you a deep security that's rooted in Him?

Called to Glory

The God of all grace, who called you to his eternal glory in Christ, after you have suffered a little while, will himself restore you and make you strong, firm and steadfast.

1 PETER 5:10 NIV

God of all grace, I've looked at the checklist for depression—and yes, I have to confess, I qualify as depressed. Feeling sad? Check. Loss of interest in things that once gave me pleasure? Check. Changes in my appetite? Check. Sleeping problems? Check. Loss of energy? Check. Feeling worthless? Oh yes. Difficulty concentrating? Yes. Thoughts of death or suicide? Sometimes. Lord, I understand that depression is an illness, and I know You can heal all illnesses. So I pray that You will restore my mental health. Show me what steps I need to take to participate in my healing. Give my doctor wisdom about medications. Help me to find a counselor I can relate to, one You can use to help me heal. Please make me strong again. Show me the way out of this depression. May Your glory shine through me.

THINK ABOUT IT

Do you feel guilty or ashamed about your depression?
Can you give those feelings to God, knowing
that His love understands all your pain?

God's Protection

*Even when I walk through the darkest valley, I will
not be afraid, for you are close beside me. Your
rod and your staff protect and comfort me.*

PSALM 23:4 NLT

I'm tired of being hurt, Lord. I'm sick of being criticized. I feel
so small, so broken. This man I love says he loves me, and I
believe he does—but he also hurts me. He's robbed me of my
confidence in myself. He's forced me to live a secret life, hiding
my bruises from the people who love me. I feel ashamed, afraid,
angry, and just so hurt, right down to my bones. How can the
person who says he loves me most be the person who hurts me
most? Is this my fault, God? Do I deserve his anger? But no, I
hear Your gentle voice whispering to my heart: I did nothing
to deserve this. You don't want me to be hurt like this. Oh
God, help me. I am in the darkest valley I've ever known; lead
me out into the light. I'm afraid; stay close beside me. Protect
me and guide me; show me what steps to take. Give me the
courage to walk into the freedom and safety You want for me.

THINK ABOUT IT

A shepherd's rod and staff were used to protect the sheep
from dangers. Can you imagine the Good Shepherd using
His rod and staff as you seek help for your situation?

Mercy and Comfort

*Blessed be God, even the Father of our Lord Jesus
Christ, the Father of mercies, and the God of all comfort;
who comforteth us in all our tribulation, that we may be
able to comfort them which are in any trouble, by the
comfort wherewith we ourselves are comforted of God.*

2 Corinthians 1:3–4 KJV

God, I know the temptation to rely on alcohol when I really need You. I've experienced this temptation for myself. Thank You for walking with me through that experience, for continuing to walk with me. Thank You so much for Your mercy and for Your comfort. And now, Lord, if I can be of use to someone else who is going through the same temptation, help me to do that. I don't want to be too proud to share my own weakness, not if my experiences might help someone else. Keep my ego out of the way (the part of me that wants others to be impressed with what a good person I am) so that I can reach out with Your mercy and comfort to those who are struggling with alcohol abuse.

THINK ABOUT IT

Do you think of alcohol abuse as a disease—or as
a sin? How do you think God thinks about it?

Even to the Point of Death

"Do not be afraid of what you are about to suffer.... Be faithful, even to the point of death, and I will give you life as your victor's crown."

REVELATION 2:10 NIV

I get so scared, Lord, when I think about the future. So many threats hang over our world—violence, disease, disaster—and I know I can't assume that my loved ones and I will escape them all. These aren't things that just happen to *someone else*; they could very easily happen to me or someone I care about. That terrifies me. But I know, God of love, that no matter what happens, You are with us. You will keep us safe, through violence, disease, disaster, and even death. Our bodies may suffer, but our spirits are safe with You. And so I ask, Lord, that You take my fear from me. Give me the courage to be faithful.

--- **THINK ABOUT IT** ---

Can you believe that God will keep you and your loved ones truly safe, even if you are asked to suffer in this life? What does the word *safe* mean to you?

God Never Gets Tired

The LORD is the everlasting God, the Creator of the
ends of the earth. He will not grow tired or weary, and
his understanding no one can fathom. He gives strength
to the weary and increases the power of the weak.

ISAIAH 40:28-29 NIV

I feel utterly helpless, Lord. I don't know what to do to fix this situation—and if I *did* know what to do, I'm not sure I'd have the strength to follow through. These circumstances are simply too big and too complicated for my abilities. So I'm glad, God of power and might, that I can turn to You. If You created the world, You can certainly handle the situation I'm facing. Thank You that You are never too tired to help me. Thank You that Your wisdom is infinite. Lead me, I pray. Give me the strength and insight I need to address this problem. I know I can't do it without You.

THINK ABOUT IT

When you look at creation, does that give you greater confidence in God's ability to take action on your behalf?

Inward Renewal

Therefore we do not lose heart. Though outwardly we are wasting away, yet inwardly we are being renewed day by day. For our light and momentary troubles are achieving for us an eternal glory that far outweighs them all. So we fix our eyes not on what is seen, but on what is unseen, since what is seen is temporary, but what is unseen is eternal.

2 CORINTHIANS 4:16–18 NIV

Give me eyes, Lord, to see from the perspective of eternity. Help me to see past my constant illness. Remind me that my life is bigger than what my body can contain. As hard as it is to keep going with this chronic condition that never ends, still I believe You are working in my life. Use me in whatever way You can, despite my body's weakness. Thank You that my spirit is still prospering, even as my body suffers. Teach me to take joy in You, no matter how sick I feel.

THINK ABOUT IT

How might God be renewing you
inwardly, despite your body's illness?

Enemies of Love

*For I am persuaded, that neither death, nor life,
nor angels, nor principalities, nor powers, nor things
present, nor things to come, nor height, nor depth, nor
any other creature, shall be able to separate us from
the love of God, which is in Christ Jesus our Lord.*

ROMANS 8:38–39 KJV

I took a stand for justice, Lord. I spoke out for love, and I
stood firm, believing You stood with me. But now people are
angry with me. They feel threatened by my words. They don't
like the company I keep. I've made enemies—real enemies,
who would harm me physically if they could. Their threats
scared me. But God, I know they can do nothing to separate
me from Your love. No matter what happens, my spirit is safe
with You. Your love wraps around me and holds me close.
Please continue to use me to speak Your truth.

─────── **THINK ABOUT IT** ───────

Do you trust God enough to stand
with Him even when it's dangerous?

As Above, So Below

"Our Father in heaven, reveal who you are. Set the world right; do what's best—as above, so below."

MATTHEW 6:10 MSG

I've been blessed in so many ways, Lord, but when I look around, I realize that many people are not as fortunate as I am. People are suffering injustice and oppression; the sins of hatred and division seem to grow stronger with each day. I'm tempted to throw up my hands and say, "There's nothing I can do"—and then retreat back into my own safe little world. Instead, God, give me courage to follow You. Reveal who You are through my words and actions. Use me in whatever way You can to build Your kingdom of love and justice here on earth.

——————— **THINK ABOUT IT** ———————

How might God want you to speak out
against injustice? Have you asked Him?

Less of You and More of God

"You're blessed when you're at the end of your rope.
With less of you there is more of God and his rule."

MATTHEW 5:3 MSG

Lord, You know how important it is to me to succeed—but this time, I've run out of ideas. I've run out of energy too. And most of all, I've run out of patience. I can't turn this situation around. No, I've completely and utterly failed. There's nothing else I can do. But as I think that, I hear Your Spirit whisper in my heart, *"At last! Now that you're finally ready to step back, I'll have room to get to work."* Okay, Lord. I'll stay out of Your way. Show me what You want to do.

———————— **THINK ABOUT IT** ————————

Have you ever thought that your need to
look good to others might be getting in the
way of the Spirit working through you?

Embraced by God

*"You're blessed when you feel you've lost what
is most dear to you. Only then can you be
embraced by the One most dear to you."*

MATTHEW 5:4 MSG

You know, God, how I depended on my husband. Now that our marriage has collapsed, I realize how much I took for granted all the little things—having someone to share the driving with on a trip, someone who could deal with some of our household problems, someone to eat dinner with, someone to sleep next to at night, someone to keep me from being alone. Most of all, I counted on the love we shared. And now that's gone. How do I think about our past together now? What was real that I can hold on to? How do I go on alone? Lord, thank You that You are with me through this painful experience. When I am lonely, teach me to fly into Your arms. Bring me closer to You than I ever was before.

--- **THINK ABOUT IT** ---

Can you see that the loss of your husband might make more room in your heart for God? How might God want to bless you in new ways through this experience?

Self-Acceptance

*"You're blessed when you're content with just who you are—
no more, no less. That's the moment you find yourselves
proud owners of everything that can't be bought."*

MATTHEW 5:5 MSG

I turn to drugs, God, because I can't seem to manage life on my own. Drugs help me to feel like a better person—a happier person, a stronger person, a more relaxed person, a more pain-free person. I realize that I've begun to depend on these chemicals to get me through life. Teach me that I can accept myself just as I am, even if I'm sad or stressed, hurting or bored. I don't need to get rid of those feelings with drugs; I can learn to be content with who I am, even at my worst. And when that happens, Lord, I believe You will reward me with the riches of *Your* glory, an unending universe of love.

--- **THINK ABOUT IT** ---

How might drug use be connected to your unhappiness with yourself and your feelings? Can you trust God to be a far healthier and more effective substitute for drugs?

An Appetite for God

"You're blessed when you've worked up a good appetite for God. He's food and drink in the best meal you'll ever eat."

MATTHEW 5:6 MSG

Seems like, Lord, that I'm always wanting *more*. I want more clothes in my closet, when there are plenty there already. I want second helpings (and thirds), when really, my stomach was full after the first helping. I want more household items, even though my home is already overflowing. I want so many things that are newer, bigger, better. It's like I have a hole inside me, and I'm trying to stuff it full of more and more things—when all along, the only thing that will really fill that hole is You, Holy Spirit. So, I pray, give me an appetite for You. Teach me to desire You more than anything this world can offer. I know that You alone can truly satisfy me.

THINK ABOUT IT

When you find yourself wanting *more*, can you take a moment to look inside your heart—and see if it might be God you're really wanting?

Mercy

"Blessed are the merciful, for they will receive mercy."

MATTHEW 5:7 NASB

There are some things, Lord, I just can't forgive. People who do hateful things don't deserve to be forgiven! And yet, Spirit, I hear You reminding me that You forgave me for some hateful things I did. I didn't deserve to be forgiven, and yet You did anyway. In Your mercy, You didn't hold my sins against me. Make me more like You, Lord. Give me mercy for others, even those who have done terrible things. Help me to see past their sins to the beautiful souls You created them to be. Show me how to love as You love.

THINK ABOUT IT

Why do you think you have such a hard time forgiving some people more than others? Can you ask God to make your own heart clear to you?

Mind and Heart

"You're blessed when you get your inside world—your mind and heart—put right. Then you can see God in the outside world."

MATTHEW 5:8 MSG

Doubts have been multiplying inside my head, Lord. They started out small, but they keep growing, proliferating. Now they take up so much space that every time I try to talk to You, they get in the way. When I want to feel close to You, I can't anymore. I keep asking myself if maybe I just made You up, if You're nothing more than the adult version of an imaginary friend. God, something inside me has gotten out of alignment. I can't even tell what it is exactly, but I know something feels wrong. I don't know how to fix it. So I'm asking You—in spite of all my doubts—to heal my heart and mind. I want to see Your hand at work in my life. I want to feel close to You again.

--- **THINK ABOUT IT** ---

What causes the doubts you're feeling? Can you remember when they began? Remember, God loves you, even through your doubts!

Cooperation

*"You're blessed when you can show people
how to cooperate instead of compete or fight.
That's when you discover who you really
are, and your place in God's family."*

MATTHEW 5:9 MSG

It's easy, God, just to dig in my heels and claim my position of righteous superiority. I *know* I'm right, and I *know* they're wrong. Why should I try to make peace when they won't listen to me? The more I argue with them, trying to persuade them to see the light, the angrier they get with me. You wouldn't want me to compromise my principles, would You? I didn't choose to be their enemy, but if that's what they want, I can't stop them. Oh, but God, now that I've put my feelings into words, I realize this isn't Your way. Your Word never says, "Stick to your principles at the cost of all else." Instead, it tells me to reach out my hand to my enemies, to seek common ground, to find ways we can cooperate instead of fight. Remind me to make love my priority.

—————— **THINK ABOUT IT** ——————

What might you do today to find a way to cooperate
with the people who disagree with you?

66

Persecution

"You're blessed when your commitment to God provokes persecution. The persecution drives you even deeper into God's kingdom."

MATTHEW 5:10 MSG

I don't like to offend people, Lord. I like to keep a low profile. I don't want to upset people. I especially don't want to make them angry with *me*—so when I hear people speaking in hateful ways, I just keep my mouth shut and walk away. I don't want to risk getting myself in trouble. But God, show me when You want me to speak out for Your kingdom. Don't let my fear hold me back from taking a stand against injustice. Give me the courage I need to stand firm against hate. I want my commitment to You to be greater than any discomfort I might feel. And if people don't like what I say and do—well, God, You can handle that. Just draw me closer to You.

THINK ABOUT IT

As Christ's follower, you're not likely these days to be thrown to the lions or burned at the stake—but are you willing to speak out against injustice, even if it means you will face disapproval, anger, even hatred?

Violent Words

*"Count yourselves blessed every time people put
you down or throw you out or speak lies about you
to discredit me. What it means is that the truth is too
close for comfort and they are uncomfortable."*

MATTHEW 5:11 MSG

Not all violence is physical. Sometimes violence is verbal. It's
people speaking lies about me, people rejecting me, people
insulting me and criticizing me. Lord, I ask that You cloak me
in Your love so that the violence aimed at me never reaches
my heart. Let me not hesitate to speak the truth, no matter
what is said to me. Show me how to bring Your peace to
every situation. Bless me as I take a stand for You and Your
kingdom—and use me, I pray, to bless others, even those
whose words are violent.

——————— **THINK ABOUT IT** ———————

Why do you think the truth can impel some
people to resort to violence? Does fear ever
hold you back from speaking truth?

Unbroken

We've been surrounded and battered by troubles,
but we're not demoralized; we're not sure what to do,
but we know that God knows what to do; we've been
spiritually terrorized, but God hasn't left our side;
we've been thrown down, but we haven't broken.

2 CORINTHIANS 4:8–9 MSG

Dear Jesus, help me to claim these verses as my own during this time when I'm beset with challenges. You know that I'm surrounded on all sides; You know that my heart and body feel battered and exhausted. Despite this, do not let me be demoralized, I pray. I'm confused about what to do next—but You know the way I should go. I feel spiritually oppressed, anxious, and fearful, but I feel Your presence with me. I've fallen flat on my face more than once during this time, Lord (and I probably will again), and yet You keep me whole. You have never abandoned me in the past, and I know You won't now.

THINK ABOUT IT

When we follow Jesus, He doesn't remove all challenges from our lives. Can you use these difficult times as opportunities to lean that much harder on God?

The Secret

I know what it is to be in need, and I know what it
is to have plenty. I have learned the secret of being
content in any and every situation, whether well fed
or hungry, whether living in plenty or in want. I can
do all this through him who gives me strength.

PHILIPPIANS 4:12-13 NIV

I hate sitting down to pay bills and then realizing there's not enough money in the bank account to cover them all. So this month I pay one bill, and next month I'll pay another, trying to keep my creditors happy. Somehow I make it from payday to payday. We have food to eat, a roof over our heads, and a car that runs. But, Lord, I wish we had more. I wish paying bills wasn't so stressful. I wish we had enough for extras. God, teach me the secret that the apostle Paul knew: show me how to be content with financial strain. Remind me that I am rich because I have You. Give me the strength I need to keep struggling forward, even when money is tight.

--- **THINK ABOUT IT** ---

What do you think the secret was that Paul
had learned? Have you learned it yet?

Alone Time

"When you pray, go away by yourself, shut the door behind you, and pray to your Father in private. Then your Father, who sees everything, will reward you."

MATTHEW 6:6 NLT

Lord, I've tried reasoning with my family. I've tried using honey instead of vinegar to bring about a resolution to our conflict. (And if I'm honest, I've used plenty of vinegar too!) I've talked till I'm blue in the face—and none of it has done any good. The tension between our family members is always present. So today, God, I'm taking a break from talking. In fact, I'm taking a break from my family altogether. Instead, I'm going to spend some time alone with You, praying for my family. I'm hanging a DO NOT DISTURB sign on my door, and I'm not coming out again until I've given every aspect of this situation to You.

—————————— THINK ABOUT IT ——————————

Has the time come for you to acknowledge that you can't fix your family problems without God's help? Can you step back and spend some time alone with God?

Daily Bread

Give us this day our daily bread.

I know You know what I need, Lord God—and I know You'll make sure I have it. But there are a lot of things I *want*, even though I may not *need* them. When those things evade my grasp, I feel so disappointed. There's so much I want in life that I don't have. Help me, Lord, to trust You enough that I can accept that each day You will provide me with what I need, even if I don't always get what I want. Remind me to stop thinking about what I can't have and instead focus on the many blessings You *have* given me. Today, keep my eyes open so that I can see the "daily bread" You give to me. Help me to stop wanting life's cake and candy when I have the Bread of Life.

THINK ABOUT IT

When Jesus spoke of "daily bread," do you think He meant literal bread? What else might be included in this term? What nourishment does God give to you each day?

Forgiveness

Forgive us our debts, as we forgive our debtors.
MATTHEW 6:12 KJV

A debt is something owed; thank You, Jesus, that because of You, I owe no debt for all the ways I've turned away from You and Your plan for my life. You crossed out all my debts, allowing me to walk away free. Help me now, Lord, to extend the same grace to those who have hurt me or harmed me. May I hold nothing against them, but instead, help me to set them free, the way You set me free. Give me the strength to forgive, even when it's hard. Remind me that forgiveness doesn't mean I can't protect myself from future hurts, and forgiveness doesn't mean that all consequences of wrongdoing are erased. Make me secure enough in You that I realize I can afford to forgive others. May I love the people who have hurt me, just as You love me.

--- **THINK ABOUT IT** ---

Why do you think Jesus connected God's forgiveness with ours? How might these two actions (God's and our own) flow together?

Temptation

And lead us not into temptation, but deliver us from evil.

MATTHEW 6:13 KJV

I may always be tempted to abuse drugs. Nothing guarantees that I'll ever be free from that temptation. Instead, Lord, help me to avoid the situations where I know I'm likely to be the most tempted. Teach me to recognize the settings, the emotions, the people who trigger those temptations. Give me the strength and the wisdom to make good choices *before* I'm too weak to resist temptation. Help me to care for my body, keeping myself well rested and well nourished, while I also care for my heart and soul by spending regular time with You. Make me strong enough to avoid temptation—and when I can't avoid it, make me strong enough to resist.

THINK ABOUT IT

Make a list of places, feelings, and situations where you are most tempted. What can you do either to avoid those situations or to ensure that you are at your strongest when you face them?

Get Your Priorities Straight

A soldier on duty doesn't get caught up in making deals at the marketplace. He concentrates on carrying out orders. An athlete who refuses to play by the rules will never get anywhere. It's the diligent farmer who gets the produce. Think it over. God will make it all plain.

2 TIMOTHY 2:3–5 MSG

If I let it, Lord, this court case could take up way too much space in my head. Help me to give it to You and let it go. Remind me that whether I win or lose, my goal is always to serve You. Keep my perspective clear. Keep me honest. Give me a nudge whenever I forget that You are the Alpha and the Omega, the beginning and the end, of my life. I want to be Your diligent servant, working for Your kingdom as my first priority. As I talk to my lawyer and make a plan for going forward, give me wisdom and insight. No matter what happens, may You be glorified.

THINK ABOUT IT

How might this situation be an
opportunity for you to serve God?

Mountain Walking

*The Sovereign LORD is my strength! He makes me as
surefooted as a deer, able to tread upon the heights.*

<small>HABAKKUK 3:19 NLT</small>

From the moment I get up, God, the possibility of an accident
is always there with me. I could trip on the stairs and break my
neck; I could slip on the sidewalk and break a bone; I might
get in a car accident on the way to work; the next time I take
a flight, the plane might crash. Maybe that sounds silly, to
worry about all those things—except that I know people who
have experienced each of those accidents. And then, once
I start thinking about all the accidents that *might* happen,
I work myself up so much that I'm nearly too anxious to get
out of bed in the morning. Remind me, Lord, that You are my
strength in life. With Your help, I can rise above even the most
dangerous situations. No matter how steep the mountain, I do
not need to fear, for you make me nimble and light-footed.

THINK ABOUT IT

What are the "heights" you have had to walk in life,
thanks to an accident that disrupted your life? During
that time, did you sense God's presence with you?

Change Your Focus

Search for the LORD and for his strength; continually seek him.

1 CHRONICLES 16:11 NLT

I don't have the strength to resist the temptation to abuse alcohol; I just don't, Lord. I make up my mind to quit, and then again and again, I give in. I'm so grateful, God of love, that You don't condemn me or reject me for my weakness. I don't know what the answer is, but today I'm making up my mind to do something different. Instead of focusing so hard on resisting the temptation to drink, I'm going to focus on You. Instead of searching for the strength inside me to quit drinking, I'm going to search for Your strength. I'm going to make You the continual focus of my life. I know that doesn't mean the urge to drink will automatically disappear—but I believe You have the strength and the wisdom I need to overcome this problem.

———— THINK ABOUT IT ————

What would have to change in your life if you were to replace your focus on alcohol with a focus on God?

Something New

"For I am about to do something new. See, I have already begun! Do you not see it? I will make a pathway through the wilderness. I will create rivers in the dry wasteland."

ISAIAH 43:19 NLT

Dear Jesus, I feel like I've been living in a dry wasteland for a very long time. My life has seemed barren, without meaning or hope. I've been lost in a wilderness of depression, a depression so thick and heavy that I've given up trying to find my way out. And yet, Lord, this verse promises me that You're already working in my life to create something new. I can't see behind the scenes; I can't sense that any change is on its way; but nevertheless, I trust Your Word. I'm going to start looking for the little hints that will tell me something new is coming. Reveal these glimpses of hope to me, I pray. Give me the strength to hold on a little longer. I'm waiting for You, Lord. Show me rivers running through the desert of my heart.

THINK ABOUT IT

Depression can't be dismissed as just a sad feeling, and you can't just make up your mind to "get over it." What steps might God want you to take to bring something new into your life? Have you talked to your doctor about your feelings? Have you seen a counselor?

Walls of Protection

*"Afflicted one, storm-tossed, and not comforted, behold,
I will set your stones in antimony, and I will lay your
foundations with sapphires. Moreover, I will make your
battlements of rubies, and your gates of crystal,
and your entire wall of precious stones...."*

ISAIAH 54:11–12 NASB

God, even all these years later, I'm still not the same. The abuse I experienced is like a festering wound I keep hidden out of sight. Even though others can't see it, even when I keep it pushed out of my own consciousness, it's always there. It makes me shaky when I want to be strong. I don't know how to set healthy boundaries around my heart and my life. Deep inside, I'm always afraid. But, Lord, these verses promise me a different way to live. They offer me comfort for my pain. They promise me foundations and walls that are both sturdy and beautiful, set with jewels. They show me that I can have a gate into my heart, a place where I can choose to let people in, even as I keep out any further oppression or abuse. Thank You, God, for protecting me. Teach me to trust You more.

--- **THINK ABOUT IT** ---

Can you imagine yourself with beautiful
walls of protection around you?

The Richness of the Gospel

Let the message about Christ, in all its richness, fill your lives. Teach and counsel each other with all the wisdom he gives. Sing psalms and hymns and spiritual songs to God with thankful hearts.

COLOSSIANS 3:16 NLT

I know, Lord, that church is meant to be the place where we gather to support each other in the body of Christ. Lately, though, I don't feel supported or encouraged; I just feel annoyed. People get upset about the smallest things; they backbite and gossip. Frankly, I don't even feel like going to church anymore. It's not a place where I feel close to You these days. But Jesus, I ask You to change our church. May Your message—the Good News of Your love—fill each of our gatherings. Help us to be conduits of Your wisdom, enriching one another and building each other up, rather than tearing each other down. May songs of praise replace the gossip and backbiting, and may we give thanks instead of complaints.

— THINK ABOUT IT —

What is one small thing you can do this week to communicate love, wisdom, and thanksgiving to your church body?

Trust Instead of Disappointment

*Trust in the LORD with all your heart and
do not lean on your own understanding.*

PROVERBS 3:5 NASB

I don't understand, Lord, why You keep letting me be disappointed. Why can't You answer my prayers with a yes? Why do You always say no? The things that I've asked for aren't bad things; they're things I believe would make the world a better place, things that would be a blessing. And yet You still say no. Wise Lord, help me to trust You more. Remind me that You know far more than I do; You can see the entire scope of time and eternity. You do all things at the right time. So I'll stop talking about what makes sense to me, and I'll start leaning on You more. You know how I long for wishes to come true—but I'll trust Your love to do what's right for me.

THINK ABOUT IT

How might disappointment be
connected to a lack of trust?

Strength in the Lord

*David was now in great danger because all his
men were very bitter about losing their sons and
daughters, and they began to talk of stoning him.
But David found strength in the LORD his God.*

1 SAMUEL 30:6 NLT

I'm glad, Lord, that the Bible is so full of stories to encourage
us. David's enemies kidnapped all the women and children
while the soldiers were away—and then his own men turned
on him too. I can relate to that story, for I too have made
enemies because people thought I had failed to do what I
should have. Rather than accept the situation, they blamed
me. Lord, when I find myself facing enemies, remind me of
this story. Teach me to go to You for strength, just as David
did. David sought direction from You, and You guided him
and went with him, allowing him to rescue all who had been
kidnapped. He stood up to his enemies and clung to You.
May I do the same.

—————————— **THINK ABOUT IT** ——————————

How can you find strength in the Lord today? What do
you need to do to be able to face your enemies with
the same confidence and wisdom that David did?

Saying Yes to Life

The road to life is a disciplined life.
PROVERBS 10:17 MSG

It's so easy, Lord, to give in to the temptation to use drugs. When I'm stressed, drugs offer relaxation. When I'm sad, they offer me comfort. When I'm bored, they give me pleasure. Using drugs feels like the path of least resistance. It's the road I take when I'm on autopilot. But God, I've learned that road leads nowhere. It's always just the same old dead end. So when I'm tempted to abuse drugs, please remind me that I have the power to say no. May I say no to drugs so that I can say yes to the full, rich spectrum of the life You offer me.

THINK ABOUT IT

Does the word *discipline* have negative connotations for you? Can you see that many of the good things in life require discipline (like playing a sport, learning a musical instrument, being a faithful friend)? How might saying no to drugs enrich your life, allowing you to say yes to other things instead?

Humility

Submit to one another out of reverence for Christ.
EPHESIANS 5:21 NIV

Lord, I realize that when I get caught up in arguments, it's almost always my selfish nature taking control. No matter how much I believe in my own "cause" (whatever it is), when it comes right down to it, I just want my own way. I want people to see that *I'm right*. I don't have the humility to give in or to compromise; I just dig in my heels and keep arguing. Jesus, teach me Your way instead. I want to model my life on Yours. Take away my selfishness and pride. Open my eyes to other perspectives and viewpoints. Make me willing to learn. Show me others' dignity and wisdom. May I honor You in all my interactions.

THINK ABOUT IT

What role do pride and selfishness play in your arguments? How might things look differently if you regarded others with respect and openness? How might humility be an antidote for arguments?

Words of Life

The words of the godly are a life-giving fountain;
the words of the wicked conceal violent intentions.
PROVERBS 10:11 NLT

I know I'm guilty of telling lies sometimes, Lord, but honestly, I don't have violent intentions! I only tell the sort of lies that smooth over an awkward social situation. Sometimes I lie to avoid upsetting someone, or I say what I know the other person wants to hear, even if it's not true. Can You really call that "violent"? Or am I concealing my true intentions even from myself? When I deny someone the truth, who am I caring about, really—myself or the other person? Do I really care what's best for the other person, or do I care more about making myself look good? God, help me not to make excuses for myself. May each of my words be spoken in love, with the intention of giving life.

--------- **THINK ABOUT IT** ---------

The word the Bible uses for "violent" has to do with doing damage and causing harm. How might even little "polite" lies do damage and cause harm?

Heart Healing

He heals the brokenhearted and binds up their wounds.

PSALM 147:3 NIV

My heart is broken, Lord. My husband's unfaithfulness has wounded me so deeply that I'm not sure how to go on with life. Everything I thought I could count on has suddenly been shaken. I don't know how to make plans. I can't seem to do my work anymore. My pain comes between me and everything else. Will I ever find a way to be happy again? Thank You, Lord, for Your promise to be with me, even now when I feel so abandoned and rejected. Heal my broken heart, I pray. Bandage my wounded heart. Take my pain so that I can once more enjoy the life You've given me. Thank You for being with me. Thank You that *You* will never leave me. You will never betray me, never abandon me, never stop loving me. Show me the way forward.

THINK ABOUT IT

It's never a good idea to make major decisions when your heart is breaking. Can you wait for God to bring a measure of healing to your heart before making definite decisions about the future?

Bridges of Gentleness

A gentle answer deflects anger,
but harsh words make tempers flare.

PROVERBS 15:1 NLT

I can hardly remember how this family fight began, Lord. It was probably something little, but over the years, more arguments have piled on top of it. People took sides, each side claiming to be the innocent party. Now there's so much resentment between us that I don't know how to reach past it. These are people I love, God—and yet I've allowed anger to drive us apart. Show me how to begin to heal this terrible division within our family. May I not respond to anger with more anger, adding fuel to the flame; instead, teach me gentleness. Remind me to keep a close hold on my own reactions so that I don't speak harsh words that will cause hurt and more anger. Allow me to build bridges of reconciliation.

THINK ABOUT IT

It's never too late to bring an end to a family feud.
What can you do this week to begin building
a bridge between your family factions?

Setting Healthy Boundaries

Don't be naive. There are difficult times ahead. As the end approaches, people are going to be self-absorbed, money-hungry, self-promoting, stuck-up, profane, contemptuous of parents, crude, coarse, dog-eat-dog, unbending, slanderers, impulsively wild, savage, cynical, treacherous, ruthless, bloated windbags, addicted to lust, and allergic to God. They'll make a show of religion, but behind the scenes they're animals. Stay clear of these people.

2 TIMOTHY 3:1–5 MSG

I know You want me to love everyone, Lord, but I also know You want me to steer clear of destructive relationships that can pull me down. Remind me that the qualities described in these verses may be common, but that doesn't make them *healthy*. When I encounter these behaviors and attitudes in other people, may I never dismiss them as "just the way things are." Don't let me absorb them into myself. Show me how to love people like this while still setting healthy boundaries that will protect my relationship with You.

––––––––––– **THINK ABOUT IT** –––––––––––

What boundaries do you need to set in your life to protect yourself from destructive and unhealthy influences?

Violent Deceit

He shall redeem their soul from deceit and violence.

PSALM 72:14 KJV

It's interesting, Lord, that Your Word often pairs lies with violence. Our society is quick to excuse lies as being a "necessary evil," and yet scripture indicates that dishonesty is actually a form of violence. When I look at what has wounded me most over the years, I can see that the lies people told me were truly a form of violence, for they hurt my soul. They smashed my trust. Those who lied to me never hit me or harmed me physically—and yet they harmed my heart. Thank You, God, that You have the power to heal me. You can bring me back and restore clarity and faith to my soul.

THINK ABOUT IT

The Hebrew word translated as "redeem" in this verse also implies a relationship of kinship. Can you trust in a God who loves you more than family to protect you from the violence of deceit?

Protecting the Spirit

Throw out the mocker, and fighting goes, too.
Quarrels and insults will disappear.

PROVERBS 22:10 NLT

Lord, I feel as though my group of friends has been poisoned. Ever since a certain person joined us, all we seem to do is quarrel. We insult each other, pretending to be funny, but we're wounding each other right down to the quick. The long talks we used to have about everything under the sun have turned into gossip sessions. When one of us isn't present, we gossip about that person too. Where we once used to encourage and support each other, now all we do is tear each other down. I know, God, that You exclude no one from Your love—but Your Word also has very practical advice about relationships. Give me wisdom about what to do in this situation. I want to model Your unconditional love, but I also want to restore my circle of friends to the life-giving relationship we once had together. Show me how to set healthy boundaries that will protect Your Spirit among us.

THINK ABOUT IT

The Bible makes clear that sometimes we have
to say no to certain relationships. Can you set
up boundaries to protect the Spirit's presence in
your midst while still extending love to everyone?

Trust vs. Revenge

Dear friends, never take revenge.
Leave that to the righteous anger of God.

ROMANS 12:19 NLT

Some people, Lord, deserve to suffer a little. I have an especially hard time forgiving those who have hurt people I love. Maybe I won't plot ways to get even with them (though sometimes I do!), but at the very least, I'm going to make it clear to these people that I dislike them because of what they did. I'm going to turn away when they say hello, and I'll answer their smiles with scowls. Can You really expect anything else from me, Lord, after what they did? But then I come across a verse like this one, and I know You don't approve of my desire for revenge. That's not Your way. So okay, God, I'll let my anger go. I'll surrender it into Your hands. I'll let You sort out the damage these people have done, and I'll mind my own business. I'll trust Your Spirit to work in their hearts.

THINK ABOUT IT

Does revenge ever accomplish anything?

Honoring God with Your Body

Don't you realize that your body is the temple of the Holy Spirit, who lives in you and was given to you by God? You do not belong to yourself, for God bought you with a high price. So you must honor God with your body.

1 Corinthians 6:19–20 NLT

Lord, when I'm tempted to abuse alcohol, remind me that too much alcohol can harm my body. It can increase my risk of heart attack and stroke; it can damage my liver and pancreas; it may increase my chances of getting certain cancers; and it weakens my immune system. If I drink while I drive, I may end up hurting myself and others in a car accident. God, I know my body is precious to You. It's the vehicle You've given me in this life to do Your work in the world. I don't want to do anything that might impair my ability to serve You. I want to be all that You created me to be—body, mind, and soul.

―――――――― **THINK ABOUT IT** ――――――――

Alcohol abuse can harm your body; how else might it hinder your ability to serve God?

Forgiven and Forgotten

"Their sins and lawless acts I will remember no more." And where these have been forgiven, sacrifice for sin is no longer necessary.

HEBREWS 10:17-18 NIV

I keep going over my failures, Lord. At night they haunt me. They interrupt my thoughts when I'm driving. They even distract me from my work. I'm so sorry I let You down. I wish I could go back and undo the past. I'm ashamed of myself. But Jesus, Your Word tells me I can let go of the past. You don't hold my failures against me. You don't even remember them! I don't have to keep saying I'm sorry, and I don't have to find ways to punish myself. I am truly freed from everything I did. I can serve You with a clean heart, for You have restored my innocence and made me whole. Empower me now to live for You.

--- **THINK ABOUT IT** ---

As human beings, we can forgive, but we can't usually forget. But God is not like us. What does it mean to you to have your failures not only forgiven by God but also forgotten? How does it make you feel?

Murderous Anger

"You're familiar with the command to the ancients, 'Do not murder.' I'm telling you that anyone who is so much as angry with a brother or sister is guilty of murder. Carelessly call a brother 'idiot!' and you just might find yourself hauled into court. Thoughtlessly yell 'stupid!' at a sister and you are on the brink of hellfire. The simple moral fact is that words kill."

MATTHEW 5:21-22 MSG

Lord, I've always prided myself on my good Christian family. We taught our kids to be respectful and kind. We certainly never hit each other or shove each other around. But I have to confess that we've fallen into bad habits. We're getting on each other's nerves—and we're venting our frustration and irritation on each other. We're using our words to hurt each other. Jesus, I ask for forgiveness. Teach us to curb our violent tongues. Help us to control our anger. Restore peace to our family.

THINK ABOUT IT

Why do you think Jesus said that anger can
be as dangerous and deadly as murder?

Strength to Resist

*No test or temptation that comes your way is beyond
the course of what others have had to face. All you
need to remember is that God will never let you
down; he'll never let you be pushed past your limit;
he'll always be there to help you come through it.*

1 CORINTHIANS 10:13 MSG

Oh God, I hate to confess my addiction out loud. I want
to believe that I'm too strong, too good, to be addicted to
anything. But as I look at my life, I'm forced to admit that I've
become too dependent on something. In fact, it's taken Your
place in my life. Lord, I want to do better. I want to give You
first place again—but I'm afraid I'm not strong enough to say
no to this thing I've come to love so much. Thank You that
You have promised to help me. I don't have to do this alone.
Teach me to rely on You when I'm weak.

―――――― **THINK ABOUT IT** ――――――

Do you understand that you never have to feel guilty
for being tempted? Can you even use temptation
as one more way to draw close to God?

The Grace of Friendship

*Let no corrupt communication proceed out of your
mouth, but that which is good to the use of edifying,
that it may minister grace unto the hearers.*

EPHESIANS 4:29 KJV

I know, Lord, that You reveal Yourself to me through my friendships. You have used these relationships to bless me and encourage me. But lately, God, I've begun to realize that this friendship I once treasured is no longer healthy. We no longer help each other to be our best selves; instead, we pull each other down. We're constantly giving each other little digs, smiling as we try to hurt. Instead of talking about You, we gossip and complain. Each time we're together, I come away feeling discouraged and hurt—and I'm afraid my friend is feeling the same, thanks to my negativity. Our friendship has become toxic, no longer a source of love and encouragement. Lord, I don't want this to go on any longer. Show me how to change. I pray that my friend's heart will also be open to Your reminders. May we together work to restore our friendship, sharing grace instead of poison with each other.

THINK ABOUT IT

Friendships often become toxic so gradually that we don't notice what is happening. Take a look at your friendships. Notice how they make you feel. What may need to change?

Comings and Goings

He will watch over your life; the LORD will watch over your coming and going both now and forevermore.

PSALM 121:7–8 NIV

The world is such a dangerous place, Lord. But it's not myself I worry about as much as all my friends and family. I'm scared every time a loved one is driving late at night. I'm filled with anxiety whenever a loved one is flying. I find myself imagining all the terrible things that might happen. News stories about freak accidents haunt me, and I picture them happening to someone I love. God, I ask that You take away my fear. Help me to trust my loved ones to You. I know You are watching over them. You are with them when they come and when they go. You love them far more than even I do, and You will hold them in Your love forever. No matter what happens, there are no accidents in Your perfect plan for our lives.

──────── **THINK ABOUT IT** ────────

Can you claim God's promises for your
loved ones (as well as for yourself)?

Confession and Prayer

Therefore confess your sins to each other and pray for each other so that you may be healed. The prayer of a righteous person is powerful and effective.

JAMES 5:16 NIV

God, there are certain things about me I keep secret because I feel so ashamed. I couldn't bear for them to know the truth. I'm certain I would lose their respect. I could never hold my head up again; I'd be too embarrassed. So when I read this verse, Lord, about confessing my sins, I just want to squirm. I don't *want* to let others see the imperfect, broken person I really am. But then, as I read this verse again, I notice something: James is telling people to confess their sins *so they can be healed.* By bringing my secret out into the air, I might finally find a way to be free from it. By allowing others to pray for me, I could be made whole. So, Lord, I ask You to show me the right person (or persons) to talk to. Make it clear to me whom I can trust with my secret—and then give me the courage to be vulnerable. I want to be healed.

THINK ABOUT IT

Has it ever occurred to you that you're not alone—because pretty much *everyone* has things they keep secret? When we trust each other enough to share our secrets, without fear of rejection, God can do surprising things.

Differently Abled

*I know that the Lord will maintain
the cause of the afflicted.*

PSALM 140:12 KJV

You know, Lord, that I live in a world that's not designed for people who are differently abled. Things that other people take for granted are daily challenges for me. And then there's the prejudice and discrimination I face; people assume that since there are some things I cannot do I must not be good at *anything*. They see my disability and overlook all my abilities. They're uncomfortable around me, as though my condition might be something contagious. Some days I think the rejection I experience from other people is harder to bear than my disability itself. Thank You, Lord, that even when other people seem to find it hard to accept me, You love me just the way I am. In Your eyes, I'm perfect and whole. You're working on my behalf to build a better world, a world where everyone is accepted and no one is excluded. Thank You that You're always on my side.

THINK ABOUT IT

Can you think of ways that you have experienced
the presence of God "maintaining your cause"?

Family Feud

*If possible, so far as it depends on
you, be at peace with all people.*

ROMANS 12:18 NASB

This feud within our family, Lord, is like a snowball, picking up size and momentum the farther it rolls. I thought I could stay out of it, but now I realize I'm starting to get sucked in. I'm beginning to take sides. I find a certain ugly pleasure, a sick fascination, in hearing the latest awful thing that someone has said or done. Forgive me, Jesus. I know this division in our family doesn't please You. Help me to resist the urge to gossip and bad-mouth. Give me the courage to refuse to be sucked into this fight. Show me ways to be a peacemaker.

___

THINK ABOUT IT

Why do you think it is so hard to stay neutral in a family argument? What steps can you take that will help you resist the urge to get involved?

Perfect Love

Such love has no fear, because perfect love expels all fear. If we are afraid, it is for fear of punishment, and this shows that we have not fully experienced his perfect love.

1 JOHN 4:18 NLT

I confess, God, that I'm still afraid of so many things in life. I'm afraid of sickness and disease. I'm afraid of what the future may hold. I'm afraid of getting old. I'm afraid of change. I'm afraid of death. My fear tells me, Lord, that I still don't completely believe in Your love. Part of me still thinks You're not strong enough to keep me safe; part of me wonders if You really care about my life. Thank You for being patient with my fears. Draw me closer to You. Teach me that Your love is real. Help me to rest in You, knowing that Your perfect love surrounds me and I have no need to fear.

THINK ABOUT IT

We usually don't trust people we don't know very well. How can you get to know God better so that you will trust Him more?

Peace-Loving

But the wisdom from above is first of all pure. It is also peace loving, gentle at all times, and willing to yield to others. It is full of mercy and the fruit of good deeds. It shows no favoritism and is always sincere.

JAMES 3:17 NLT

I know my family loves me, Lord—but lately the people who love me most are stressing me out! I'm so tired of trying to be a peacemaker. And I'm tired of feeling like I always have to defend myself. It's hard to hold on to my patience, when some days I just feel like screaming at them all! Give me Your wisdom, I pray, so that I can see ways to relieve the tension in my family. Teach me to be gentle. Remind me that I don't have to be right all the time. Give me mercy and sincerity in all my interactions. Show me opportunities to perform small acts of love. Remind me never to play favorites. Transform my heart so that I can be a vehicle of Your peace.

THINK ABOUT IT

When James said that "wisdom from above" is pure, he meant that it's not distorted or diluted by the selfishness that so often tinges our thoughts and actions. It's completely free of self-interest. How can you avail yourself of this heavenly wisdom today?

Love Your Body

After all, no one ever hated their own body, but they feed and care for their body, just as Christ does the church.

EPHESIANS 5:29 NIV

You want me to take care of my body, Lord. I know that. My body matters to You the same way my children's bodies matter to me. Because I love them, I want them whole and healthy—and because You love *me*, You want me whole and healthy too. You don't want me to ignore my body's needs, and You don't want me to engage in risky behaviors that could jeopardize my health. But despite what the apostle Paul says in this verse, sometimes I *do* hate my own body. I don't care what's good for it. I abuse drugs and I take risks with my body's safety. Forgive me, Jesus. Give me greater love for my own flesh so that I will no longer be tempted to do anything that might hurt it. Teach me to care for my body the same way You care for me.

THINK ABOUT IT

Did it ever occur to you that if you truly love yourself, you won't abuse drugs?

Trust Busters

Let all bitterness, and wrath, and anger, and clamour,
and evil speaking, be put away from you, with all malice.
EPHESIANS 4:31 KJV

Lately, Jesus, I'm finding it harder to trust other people. I suspect everyone around me of harboring evil in their hearts. I didn't used to be like this—so what changed? As I think about it, holy Friend, I realize that more and more my friends and I focus on negative things when we talk. We're bitter and angry, and the more we talk about our bitterness and anger, the worse we feel. Together we've created a mindset by which we look at the world and everyone in it with distrust. Instead of seeing goodness, we see only evil. So it's no wonder that I don't trust people anymore. I'm always expecting the worst of them. Cleanse my heart of this negativity, I ask You, Jesus. May I see once more with Your eyes, perceiving the goodness in people rather than the evil.

--- **THINK ABOUT IT** ---

How do your conversations affect the way you view others around you? Remember, distrust is contagious.

Self-Examination

"This is what the LORD says: Be fair-minded and just. Do what is right! Help those who have been robbed; rescue them from their oppressors. Quit your evil deeds! Do not mistreat foreigners, orphans, and widows. Stop murdering the innocent!"

JEREMIAH 22:3 NLT

Sometimes, God, we act as though You only care about people's souls, not their bodies. But again and again, Your Word tells us that's not the case. Scripture insists that we work to build a world where injustice no longer kills, oppression no longer robs, and prejudice no longer limits the lives of some people while other people are thriving. Lord, make me willing to see where I have contributed to injustice. Give me courage to speak out. Give me wisdom to take action. Use me to build a safer, more just world for all Your people.

--- **THINK ABOUT IT** ---

Injustice isn't something that only exists "out there"; it also exists in our own hearts. Are you willing for God to show you any areas where you harbor prejudice, any ways that you have allowed oppression to continue in our world?

Doubts for the World's Future

With God nothing shall be impossible.

LUKE 1:37 KJV

Oh God, I'm so filled with doubts about the future. I know that You've promised never to leave me, and I know You always seek to bless me. But when I look at the world today, I can't see how things are going to work out. Every time I read the news, I hear about another disaster, another threat to our safety and well-being. Will there still be a world for my children and grandchildren—or will we destroy our planet and ourselves along with it? Lord, take my fears and doubts. I know that You are still working in our world. I know that nothing is impossible for You. Please work miracles in our broken world. Restore us and make us whole.

——————— **THINK ABOUT IT** ———————

Have you tried praying each time you read bad news? Turn each new threat over to the One who loves you.

Courage!

Energize the limp hands, strengthen the rubbery knees. Tell fearful souls, "Courage! Take heart! GOD is here, right here, on his way to put things right and redress all wrongs. He's on his way! He'll save you!"

ISAIAH 35:3–4 MSG

Father, lately we are living in an atmosphere of fear. We're afraid of germs and disease; we're afraid of violence and war; we're afraid of natural disasters and climate change. We're even afraid of each other. Use me, I pray, to dispel this atmosphere of fear. May I speak words of courage and hope to everyone I encounter (whether in person or on social media). I don't want to spread complacency, Lord, but I do want to fight the apathy that comes from fear. Teach me to encourage others to take action rather than be paralyzed by fear. Remind me always to point to You, the One who is ever ready to work with us to put the world to rights. Thank You that You are here with us in the midst of our troubled world.

----- **THINK ABOUT IT** -----

Can you pray for an opportunity today to spread
active courage in place of paralyzed fear?

The Prison of Addiction

Remember them that are in bonds, as bound with them.

HEBREWS 13:3 KJV

God, may I never look down on those who suffer from addiction. Teach me to see with Your eyes of love, realizing that addiction is like a prison cell—it puts bars around a person's life, bars that can seem impossible to escape. May I feel the suffering of those who are trapped by addiction. Give me ways and opportunities to express Your love to them. Show me anything I can do to help open their prison doors so that they can go free. May I always hold them in my prayers.

THINK ABOUT IT

The author of this verse from the book of Hebrews was talking about literal bonds, but he makes clear that we are to identify with those who are not free, whatever those bonds may look like. Can you see that addiction is as much a prison cell as if it put actual bars around its victims?

Tears for a Lost Pet

God shall wipe away all tears from their eyes.
REVELATION 21:4 KJV

The loss of my pet has left such a big hole in my heart. Home just doesn't seem the same without her. I keep expecting to see her in her usual spots. The house is empty without her friendly presence. I miss her warmth, her unconditional love. I miss the way she always made me smile. Thank You, God, that You understand my sorrow. Not everyone knows how much a pet can mean, but You do. I thank You for this little life You entrusted into my care, and I thank You for all the ways she blessed me. May her memory continue to bless me. Wipe away my tears, Lord, and comfort my heart. Give me the assurance that You will never forget my pet.

THINK ABOUT IT

The Bible doesn't tell us what happens to animals
after death—but we do know that God cares for
animals and that He does all things well. Can
you entrust Him with your beloved pet?

Spiritual Eyes

We live by believing and not by seeing.
2 CORINTHIANS 5:7 NLT

Each day when I wake up, Lord, my illness is still with me. I hear it talking to me throughout the day, whispering, *You're too weak to do anything important. You're too sick to be of any use. Your life is over. Just give up.* Remind me, God, that those are lies. Even in my illness, You have a purpose for my life. You can still use me. And because of You, my life will never end, even when my body finally gives up the fight. Help me, Lord, not to listen to the lies my illness tells me. Teach me to look past this sickness and see the glory and blessing You have for me. Give me spiritual eyes so that I can see the reality of Your presence shining all around me. Help me to believe that You are stronger than my illness.

THINK ABOUT IT

A chronic illness can demand all your attention, but can you ask God to shift your attention to Him? Can you ask Him to help you see through the disease and catch a glimpse of His hand at work in your life?

Good Anger and Bad Anger

*Go ahead and be angry. You do well to be angry—
but don't use your anger as fuel for revenge. And
don't stay angry. Don't go to bed angry. Don't give
the Devil that kind of foothold in your life.*

EPHESIANS 4:26 MSG

Whenever I lose my temper, Lord, I feel guilty—but this verse reminds me that anger is not a sin. Psychology also tells me that anger can be a healthy emotion, one that pushes us to work for justice in the world. It can impel us to speak up when things aren't right. Even You got angry, Jesus! But I know that if I nurse my anger, clinging to it and refusing to let it go, it can turn sour inside me. When that happens, instead of inspiring acts of justice, it can lead to acts of violence. It can turn into hate. So, Lord, thank You for the gift of anger—but remind me always to release it into Your hands. I don't want to use anger as an excuse for sin.

────────── **THINK ABOUT IT** ──────────

When you look back at your life, can you see an
instance when your anger led to something good?
Can you also see a time when you held on to your
anger too long and it ended up hurting someone?

Truly Healed

O LORD, if you heal me, I will be truly healed; if you save me, I will be truly saved. My praises are for you alone!

JEREMIAH 17:14 NLT

Thank You, Lord, for Your healing love. Even now, as I lie in bed feeling sick, I know Your Spirit is with me. Not only are you healing my body, touching each of my cells and restoring them, but You are also healing my mind and spirit. You know exactly what I need. I pray that You would use this time of sickness when I've been forced to retreat from my busy life. Help me to hear Your voice speaking to me as I lie here. May this quiet time also be a time of inner healing. I ask that I be truly healed—body, mind, and spirit—so that I can return to life with greater energy. Make me whole, I pray, that I may serve You better.

THINK ABOUT IT

How might God speak to you during a time of sickness in ways you might otherwise be too busy to hear?

Relying on God

*We were crushed and overwhelmed beyond our ability
to endure, and we thought we would never live through
it.... But as a result, we stopped relying on ourselves
and learned to rely only on God.... We have placed our
confidence in him, and he will continue to rescue us.*

2 CORINTHIANS 1:8–10 NLT

God of mercy, I need Your help. Losing our home has crushed me. After all these months of financial stress and not having the shelter of a familiar place to come home to—well, that seems like just too much to bear. I feel like such a failure because I couldn't prevent this from happening. I know my family needs me to be strong, but I just don't have any strength left. Thank You, Lord, that You are my home and my resting place, even when my physical house is gone. Watch over my family, I pray. Give us a sense of security that comes from You. Teach us to rely on You now, and show us where to go from here. Rescue us from this situation and give us hope.

--- **THINK ABOUT IT** ---

What does it mean to stop relying
on yourself and rely only on God?

Our Forever Home

This world is not our permanent home;
we are looking forward to a home yet to come.

<small>HEBREWS 13:14 NLT</small>

I hate the thought of leaving this world, Lord. I don't want to lose all the familiar things I love: a cup of coffee in the morning, the pleasure of a good book, my children's smiles, the warmth of my husband's arms, the scent of freshly mown grass, fireflies on a summer evening, the wind in the trees—and so many other countless lovely things. But I have to believe, God, that if this world is full of beauty, heaven will be even more amazing. So dying won't mean leaving everything behind that I love—instead, it will mean finally having the fullness of everything, the complete shebang, with absolutely nothing missing. And best of all, it will mean that I finally come home to You, to live in Your presence forever.

THINK ABOUT IT

What scares you most about dying? Can you take comfort from verses like this that speak of heaven as *home*?

Sing!

"Sing, barren woman, you who never bore a child; burst into song, shout for joy, you who were never in labor. . . . Enlarge the place of your tent, stretch your tent curtains wide, do not hold back. . . . Do not be afraid; you will not be put to shame. Do not fear disgrace; you will not be humiliated. . . . For your Maker is your husband—the LORD Almighty is his name—the Holy One of Israel is your Redeemer; he is called the God of all the earth."

ISAIAH 54:1–2, 4–5 NIV

Oh Lord, I long for a child. My arms and heart feel empty, as though I will be forever incomplete until I can hold my baby in my arms. But each month I am disappointed yet again. My longing weighs me down, consumes me. But God, when I read the Old Testament, I see that again and again You blessed infertile women. This intimate womanly problem was one that concerned You then, and I believe You are concerned with my pain now. Teach me to praise Your name, even in my longing and emptiness. Give me Your joy, I pray. Expand my life. May I be fruitful.

——————— **THINK ABOUT IT** ———————

We often speak of God as Father or Friend—but what do you think it would mean to think of God as your Husband?

115

Aching Bones

Have compassion on me, LORD, for I am weak.
Heal me, LORD, for my bones are in agony.
PSALM 6:2 NLT

It's hard to have a good attitude when I'm sick, Lord. All I want to do is complain: my head hurts, my muscles hurt, my very bones ache. Thank You that You understand. Like my mother when I was little, You stay close when I am sick. Your Spirit is tenderly tending to me. You have compassion for my weakness. Help me to rest in You, dear Lord. Use this time to draw me closer to You. In Your timing, make me strong and healthy once again. Thank You that You love me just as much when I'm sick and weak, doing nothing but lying in bed, as You do when I am busy and active and full of energy.

THINK ABOUT IT

What spiritual lessons can you
learn during times of sickness?

Safe with God

Then shall the dust return to the earth as it was: and the spirit shall return unto God who gave it.

ECCLESIASTES 12:7 KJV

Dear Lord, I know I'm an adult—but I feel like a frightened orphan. I've never lived in a world that didn't hold my parent. I feel as though the foundation I took for granted all my life has suddenly disappeared. How can life go on without the love and support of my parent? Thank You, God, that I know my parent is not gone forever. Although the body has died, the spirit is still alive. I will have to learn to do without the warm smile, the loving hands, the familiar conversations, but my parent is safe with You. You will never lose the spirit I have loved so much all these years, and one day we will be together again with You.

--- **THINK ABOUT IT** ---

We're used to thinking of our parents as simply Mom or Dad. Now can you take comfort in knowing your parent is a spiritual being who will live for eternity with God?

Space to Heal

I'm hurt and in pain; give me space for healing.
PSALM 69:29 MSG

I'm hurting, God. As I lie in this hospital bed, my body feels as though it was put on a rack, all my muscles stretched to the breaking part. "That's just the anesthesia," the nurse tells me, and I'm trying to be brave, to be a grown-up—but I just want to curl up in a ball and cry. It hurts so badly, and what's almost worse, my body feels invaded, cut and stitched back together again. Lord, please come into my hospital room and be with me. May I feel Your soothing presence. Use this time when I've been forced to take a step back from life to teach me more about You. Heal my heart as well as my body. Thank You for loving me. Thank You for being here with me.

——————————— **THINK ABOUT IT** ———————————

In what ways might God want to heal your heart as well as your body? How might this time of physical recovery be a "space for healing" at the spiritual level as well?

Choosing Your Friends

Don't befriend angry people or
associate with hot-tempered people.

PROVERBS 22:24 NLT

The book of Proverbs is full of practical, no-nonsense relationship advice. It reminds me that I need to take an active role in choosing whom I spend time with. I know, Lord, that everyone deserves my love and respect—but that doesn't mean I need to spend so much time with certain people that I absorb their bad attitudes. Give me insight, I pray, when it comes to my friendships. May I choose wisely, opting for friends who encourage and uplift me rather than friends who discourage me and pull me down. Show me how to set loving boundaries that protect Your Spirit's presence in my heart.

THINK ABOUT IT

After spending time with a friend, do you feel a little happier, a little closer to God? Or do you find yourself feeling angry, discontented? What are you absorbing from the people with whom you spend time?

Your Bodyguard

Is anyone crying for help? GOD is listening, ready to rescue you.... If you're kicked in the gut, he'll help you catch your breath. Disciples so often get into trouble; still, GOD is there every time. He's your bodyguard.

PSALM 34:17–20 MSG

Lord God, Your Word tells me that You are always listening to me, ready to help. I pray today that You would wrap me in Your love. I ask for Your guidance and protection. Wherever I go today, guard me. So many things can go wrong during the day, but I know that no matter what happens, You'll be there. You'll hear me when I cry. You'll wrap Your arms around me if events take me by surprise. I don't know what this day may hold; I can't predict what accidents might befall me; but You, Lord, know the future. Your love is my bodyguard, going before me, sheltering me from harm.

THINK ABOUT IT

One of the worst things about unexpected crises is that they upset our plans; they make us realize we are not in control of our lives. Can you trust God's plan for your life, no matter what happens?

Ready to Let Go

We brought nothing into this world, and it is certain we can carry nothing out.

1 TIMOTHY 6:7 KJV

God, You have blessed me with so many wonderful things—a family, a career, a home, friends. I am grateful for all Your gifts, but I also ask that You remind me not to cling to them too tightly. May I love all You have given me while holding them in my heart lightly, ready to let them go so that I can move on into eternity with You. I possessed nothing when I was born, and I will possess nothing when I die—nothing except Your love, which has always been mine and always will be mine. Help me to face death without fear, knowing that even in death You will be with me. Make me ready to let go.

—————— **THINK ABOUT IT** ——————

When you think about your death, what frightens you most? Can you give this fear to the One who loves you?

Your God

For this God is our God for ever and ever;
he will be our guide even to the end.

PSALM 48:14 NIV

Lord, I find this legal situation so confusing. I'm not sure about the right course of action. I feel so anxious about all the proceedings. Thank You, Spirit, that You are with me, each step of the way. I am so glad that nothing—even this unfamiliar and frightening situation—can come between You and me. I pray that You would work through everyone involved—the lawyers, the judge, myself, and also my opponent—so that Your will would be done. Help me not to cling to my own way; keep me humble even while You give me the courage I need to stand firm. May I rest in Your guidance, trusting You to do what's best for everyone.

THINK ABOUT IT

In the midst of litigation, what does it mean
that God is *your* God, that He is guiding you?

Friendships Restored

*Don't think of them as enemies, but warn
them as you would a brother or sister.*

2 THESSALONIANS 3:15 NLT

Jesus, these people hurt me in the past, and now I'm always expecting them to do so again. Whether they know it or not, my distrust is always between us. I can't think of them the way I used to. Our friendship has been damaged. I feel as though I'm the innocent party in this situation—but, Jesus, is there some action I should take to restore our friendship? You know I'm far from perfect myself, and there have been times I've let people down too. With Your help, maybe I can reach past my distrust and talk to these people openly about my feelings. Show me, Lord, what to say. If at all possible, restore the friendship between us, I pray.

THINK ABOUT IT

When someone hurts us, it's easy to put up walls to protect ourselves from further hurt. What do you think God is asking you to do in situations like this?

Work Burdens

Cast your burden upon the LORD and He will sustain you.

PSALM 55:22 NASB

My job is wearing me down, Lord. I've reached the place where I dread going into work every day. The tension in my workplace is overwhelming. By the end of each day, I'm exhausted. I'm relieved to go home, but then I can't stop thinking about work for the rest of the day. My thoughts keep me awake at night, and then I'm that much more discouraged the next day when it's time to head off to work again. I don't know what the answer is, God. I can't quit, and I don't see any other way out of this situation. But I know You never want me to be miserable; You always want to give me joy and peace. So, Lord, I give You the heavy load that my job has become. Please help me carry it. Give me renewed strength and energy. Sharpen my mind so that I can find new ideas to get me through this. Sustain me, I pray.

THINK ABOUT IT

Is there a way you can step back from your job, even for an hour or two in the evening or on the weekend? You might be able to gain a new perspective that will help you see the situation more clearly.

Dead to Sin

He Himself brought our sins in His body up on the cross, so that we might die to sin and live for righteousness; by His wounds you were healed.

1 PETER 2:24 NASB

Oh Jesus, I'm so ashamed of this sin that I've kept hidden so long. Even when things are going good on the outside, on the inside I always know that I'm carrying this secret. It's been weighing me down for far too long, holding me back from the life You want me to live. Thank You, Lord, that even though this sin looks so huge and immovable to me, You are big enough to take it away. Show me how to die to the part of me that still clings to this sin. I want to live for You, completely, with all my heart and mind and body, with nothing held back. Heal me, I pray.

─────── **THINK ABOUT IT** ───────

Are you willing to surrender your sin to Jesus?

Fretting

Refrain from anger and turn from wrath;
do not fret—it leads only to evil.
PSALM 37:8 NIV

I'm realizing, Lord, that anger and fretting aren't the same thing. Healthy anger is a reaction to a wrong; it impels me to take action to put things right. But when I let my anger stew day after day deep inside my heart, it turns into fretting. It's destructive. It doesn't push me forward toward something better; instead, it's like quicksand, keeping me mired in the memory of past injuries. Any action that rises out of this kind of anger is likely to be hurtful, both to myself and others. So, Lord, I ask You to give me the strength to release my anger into Your hands. Help me not to cling to it, letting it fester inside me. Show me if I need to take action, but let me turn away from violence and hatred.

THINK ABOUT IT

The word *fret* comes from an Old English word
that meant "devour, feed upon, consume."
How might anger be devouring your soul?

Safe in the Father's Hands

It is not the will of your Father which is in heaven,
that one of these little ones should perish.

MATTHEW 18:14 KJV

Nothing in my entire life has hurt as bad as this, Father. I don't know how I can keep living when my child is dead. It was my job to keep my child safe; I was meant to die first, while my child lived to a ripe old age. Why did You let this happen? How could You have allowed my child to die? I can't find comfort anywhere—except in this: my child is safe with You. You were the One who brought my child into being, and You will hold that little life safe in Your hands for all eternity. Thank You that one day we will be together again. Until that day, please show me how to live now that my child is gone.

--- **THINK ABOUT IT** ---

Even in your grief, can you trust your child to the Father?

Quick to Hear, Slow to Speak

Be quick to hear, slow to speak, and slow to anger.

JAMES 1:19 NASB

Lord, I know we're meant to be the body of Christ—but lately, whenever our church gets together, all we seem to do is argue. We disagree about the smallest things, and yet it seems so important to each of us to have our own way. I've tried to justify my own behavior by telling myself that I just want things done the right way, but I have to confess that I'm so sure of my own position that I haven't really been listening to other points of view. Next time I'm together with church members, remind me, Lord, to listen before I speak. Teach me to hear what others have to say before I react. May I stop trying to get my own way and instead cooperate with Your body.

THINK ABOUT IT

Are you willing to listen to other points of view?
Can you open both your ears and your heart?

Cutting Corners

GOD hates cheating in the marketplace;
he loves it when business is aboveboard.
PROVERBS 11:1 MSG

It's so easy sometimes, Lord, to cut little corners. I don't mean to cheat anyone (not even the IRS), so I tell myself I'm just trying to get a good deal. . .or I'm getting the most for my money. . .or what I'm doing doesn't really count as cheating because everyone else does the same thing (or at least *almost* everyone else does). And then I read Bible verses like this one, and I hear Your Spirit gently chiding my heart, reminding me that honesty is important to You. It doesn't matter what "everyone else" is doing, and You care far more about what's right than You do about making a profit. Readjust my priorities, Lord, so that I value what You value. Forgive me for my dishonesty, and give me the strength to change my ways.

—————— **THINK ABOUT IT** ——————

When you find yourself being willing to be dishonest in small ways, where are you placing your priorities? What needs to change?

More Than You Think

All glory to God, who is able, through his mighty power at work within us, to accomplish infinitely more than we might ask or think.

EPHESIANS 3:20 NLT

Oh God, I'm so upset about the loss of my job. I feel angry and resentful that this happened—but I also feel ashamed and embarrassed. Maybe most of all, I feel scared. How are we going to pay our bills without my income? Will I be able to find another job? God, I don't know the answers to those questions, I really don't. But I know Your power is unlimited, and I believe You have a plan for my life. Please work in my life now. Show me what to do next. Give me a sense of peace, knowing that even now You are putting together amazing things for my future.

THINK ABOUT IT

What is the hardest thing about losing your job? Can you give whatever that is to God, believing that He will surprise you with all He will do next?

Good Medicine

A cheerful heart is good medicine, but a
broken spirit saps a person's strength.

PROVERBS 17:22 NLT

It's hard to have a cheerful heart, Lord, when I'm feeling so sick, but I know that my negative frame of mind won't help me heal. Give me joy even in small things: the pleasure of a good book, the comfort of my bed, the warmth of a cup of tea. Help me to stop fretting about all the things that aren't getting done while I'm sick, and instead, may I relax into the peace of Your presence. Meet me here, Lord, as I lie here sick, and shift my attention away from my discomfort. You are the great Healer, and I need the medicine of Your Spirit. Heal me—heart, spirit, and body—and renew my strength.

——————— **THINK ABOUT IT** ———————

What can you do while you are sick that will help
to cheer you up? Take time to be kind to yourself!

Spoiled Children

*You lust for what you don't have and are willing to kill
to get it. You want what isn't yours and will risk violence
to get your hands on it. You wouldn't think of just asking
God for it, would you? And why not? Because you
know you'd be asking for what you have no right to.
You're spoiled children, each wanting your own way.*

JAMES 4:2–3 MSG

It's easy for me, Lord, to think of violence as something that
happens "out there," committed by "bad people," while I am
innocent and removed from such behaviors. And yet, God,
I realize that I live in a society that privileges some people
while it oppresses others—and violence too often arises from
this. Before I put the blame on other people, help me to look
at my own heart. May I be willing to surrender my privilege
so that Your peace and justice may have room to spread
throughout our society.

—————— **THINK ABOUT IT** ——————

Sometimes when we read Bible verses, it's easy to apply
them to others rather than ourselves. What might God
be saying to *you* through these verses from James?

Blessing Even When It's Hard

Do not repay evil with evil or insult with insult. On the contrary, repay evil with blessing, because to this you were called so that you may inherit a blessing.

1 PETER 3:9 NIV

The end of my marriage has caused so many bad feelings, Lord. Not just in me and in my ex, but also in our family and in our friends. It's so tempting to vent my bitterness and outrage, hoping to pull others to my side, so easy to feel justified in sharing my anger and hurt with everyone. God, You know I need friends to support me during this time—but remind me to confide only in those who will help me see Your perspective. Cleanse from me the desire to hurt my ex the way he has hurt me. Despite the destruction of our marriage, I pray that You would continue to bless him.

THINK ABOUT IT

If you are willing to bless your ex, how might that be a blessing to you as well? Could it help you to heal and go on with your life?

God Is Working!

God is working in you, giving you the desire
and the power to do what pleases him.

PHILIPPIANS 2:13 NLT

Lord, I've struggled with this same hidden sin for so long that it seems impossible I'll ever be able to overcome it. I'm so grateful, though, that I don't have to be free from sin for You to love me. You love me just as I am. I don't have to earn Your love by being good. At the same time, I know that You want what's best for me—and this sin I've been hiding isn't what's best. It eats away at me from the inside. It keeps me from being all that You created me to be. Jesus, I want to please You. Give me the strength I need to change. I can't do this on my own, but with Your help, I know I can do anything, even overcome the hold this sin has on me. Thank You that You are working within me even now.

THINK ABOUT IT

Instead of trying to overcome your sin with sheer
self-discipline, have you tried simply giving it to
God in prayer every day and every night?

Asleep in Jesus

*For if we believe that Jesus died and rose again, even so
them also which sleep in Jesus will God bring with him.*

1 THESSALONIANS 4:14 KJV

My heart has broken into pieces, Lord. Now that my child
has died, I know I will never be the same. Time can never
take away the emptiness in my heart. Only eternity can do
that. Thank You, loving Christ, that You conquered death.
Thank You that my child is safe in Your arms right now. Hold
this small beloved person close. Don't let my child be afraid
or sad. Help me to rest in the confidence that all is well with
my child, for my child is with You. Now that a piece of my
heart is already in eternity, teach me to live even closer to
You while I am still in this world. Thank You that one day my
child and I will be reunited.

THINK ABOUT IT

Can you picture your child lying
peacefully asleep in the arms of Jesus?

Venting

Fools vent their anger, but the wise quietly hold it back.
PROVERBS 29:11 NLT

Lord, this relationship of ours is no longer functioning in a healthy way. All we do when we're together is vent our anger. We grouch and kvetch about everything, including our husbands, our children, our other friends, the national government, our church, and local politics. We're both equally to blame, for we feed off each other's anger so that it grows ever bigger and bitterer each time we're together. While we're talking, it seems like I'm having a good time—but I always come away feeling bummed out with the world. God, I ask for your help with this relationship that has grown sick. May I be willing to take the first step toward change. Show me what to say to my friend so that we can join forces and work together against this negativity we've allowed to consume us.

THINK ABOUT IT

We all need to vent our anger and frustration sometimes, and it's good to have a trusted friend who understands. Can you distinguish between the healthy conversations that allow you to leave your anger behind—and the ones that feed your anger and make it grow?

Putting Addiction to Death

*My old self has been crucified with Christ. It is
no longer I who live, but Christ lives in me. So I
live in this earthly body by trusting in the Son of
God, who loved me and gave himself for me.*

GALATIANS 2:20 NLT

Christ, I hate to admit that I have this addiction—but I do.
I can't hide from the truth any longer. So I'm facing it now,
and I'm bringing it to You. I know that You live inside me and
that You have the power to help me become the person I was
created to be. I ask You to help me now. Show me who to
talk to; tell me where to go for help. I know that Your power
is greater than the hold this addiction has on my life. I trust
You to heal me. You gave me Your life, and now You continue
to give Yourself to me. You hold nothing back, and so I want
to hold nothing back from You. Make me whole, I pray. Put
my addiction to death so that I can truly live.

THINK ABOUT IT

Addiction can make us feel embarrassed and ashamed
to ask for help. Do you grasp the reality that Christ does
not condemn you; He only longs to help and heal you?

In Everything

In every thing give thanks: for this is the will of God in Christ Jesus concerning you.

1 THESSALONIANS 5:18 KJV

If I'm honest, Lord, I've always kind of hated this verse. How do You expect me to give thanks in everything? And how can this be Your will for me now, when You know how badly I hurt all the time? I'm sorry, but I just can't thank You for the pain. Now, though, as I read this verse again, I notice something: it doesn't say to give thanks *for* everything but only *in* everything. So, Jesus, in the midst of my pain, show me the things I still have to be thankful for. Remind me of the blessings that are still mine. Teach me to focus on those things rather than the pain. Replace my constant complaints with gratitude for all You continue to give me. Show me ways I can still be of use to You and others. Do Your will through me.

——————— **THINK ABOUT IT** ———————

What does it mean to be thankful in the midst of pain— not *for* the pain but for the other things God has given you? How might this change in focus change your life?

Nothing Too Hard for God

Behold, I am the LORD, the God of all flesh:
is there any thing too hard for me?
JEREMIAH 32:27 KJV

I am helpless, God; there's nothing I can do to change this situation. I've tried everything, and nothing has worked. Now I'm giving up. I'm going to stop trying to figure this out on my own, and I'm giving it to You. I know that's what I should have done in the first place, but thank You that it's never too late to ask for Your help. You are the God of all that lives; Your Spirit sustains all creation, so I know You can handle my problems. Nothing is too hard for You. Teach me, Lord, to rely on Your strength and insight instead of my own. Do on my behalf what I am helpless to do for myself.

THINK ABOUT IT

Are you willing to accept your helplessness—
and wait to see what God will do?

Angels

*He shall give his angels charge over
thee, to keep thee in all thy ways.*

PSALM 91:11 KJV

Dear God, I am facing a surgery that makes me feel anxious and afraid. I ask for Your protection as I enter the operating room. May I sense Your angels' presence standing all around me. Calm my mind as I surrender to anesthesia; help me to put my trust in You. As the doctors work on my body, please guide their hands. When I wake up, remind me that You are still there with me. Go with me through the healing and recovery process, I pray. Keep my eyes fixed on You, and restore my strength so that I can serve You.

THINK ABOUT IT

What scares you most about this surgery? Can you imagine a troop of God's angels taking away your fear?

Refuge from Depression

*But rejoice, all who take refuge in You, sing for
joy forever! And may You shelter them, that those
who love Your name may rejoice in You.*

PSALM 5:11 NASB

My depression is keeping me from rejoicing, Lord. Please lead
me to the right source for help. Thank You for understanding
what I am going through, and thank you that Your Word tells
me that even Your Son went through hard times emotionally.
I pray You will use this difficult time to draw me closer to
You. Thank You that I am not defined by this weakness. Help
me to focus on what is true and not focus on how I feel. I
take refuge in You. Shelter me, I pray, and restore Your joy
to my heart.

--- **THINK ABOUT IT** ---

Depression clouds our understanding and perceptions.
How might you shift your focus so that you can see
Jesus more clearly? What action might you take?

The Impossible Is Possible

Jesus looked at them intently and said,
"Humanly speaking, it is impossible. But not
with God. Everything is possible with God."

MARK 10:27 NLT

Dear God, I don't know how to rise above this addiction. It's not that I want to depend on anything other than You—but You know the pain I feel and how easy it is to reach for the thing I know will ease that pain. Lord, I ask You to soothe my anguish with Your eternal love. Smooth the sharp edges of my life, showing me that You have the power I need to rise above my past and live for You in the present moment. Remind me that I can look forward to better times and that I can endure anything with You by my side. I know that anything is possible with You.

THINK ABOUT IT

What is it that keeps you tied to your addiction? Is it something you can bring to God as your first step toward healing?

Many Rooms

"Do not let your heart be troubled; believe in God, believe also in Me. In My Father's house are many rooms; if that were not so, I would have told you, because I am going there to prepare a place for you."

JOHN 14:1–2 NASB

Jesus, I thank You for the love that my husband and I have shared. Thank You that even death cannot destroy that love. I am so glad for Your promise of life that continues on into eternity, and I pray that my husband is filled with joy as he moves into his new home with You. You know how lonely and lost I feel without him, though. Keep my eyes fixed on You as I walk through this time of anguish. Make me ready to one day go home to You too.

——————— **THINK ABOUT IT** ———————

We sometimes imagine heaven as being a place of golden streets and fluffy clouds—but Jesus spoke of a "house" with "many rooms," implying that heaven is as filled with variety as this world is. Can you imagine the "home" where your husband dwells now? What does it look like? Can you take comfort knowing he is safe there with Jesus?

Make Things Right

"If you enter your place of worship and, about to make an offering, you suddenly remember a grudge a friend has against you, abandon your offering, leave immediately, go to this friend and make things right. Then and only then, come back and work things out with God."

MATTHEW 5:23–24 MSG

You are a God of relationships, Lord. Again and again throughout Your Word, I see how important our connections with other humans are to You. You even make it clear that we can't be right with You if we're not right with others. And so, Lord, I bring to You this relationship that I've been forced to realize is no longer healthy. Forgive me for my part in what went wrong. Show me how to make things right. Make our relationship pleasing to You once again.

——————————— **THINK ABOUT IT** ———————————

When you examine your life, do you see any relationships that need your attention? What steps can you take to restore them to health?

God to the Rescue

The righteous person faces many troubles,
but the LORD comes to the rescue each time.

PSALM 34:19 NLT

Give me the courage, Lord, to face these challenges that have come into my life. Help me to persevere and not give up, knowing that You will always come to my rescue when I need You. Instead of blaming You or looking elsewhere for the answers, remind me to look to You and trust completely in You. Help me surrender everything to You—the circumstances as well as my emotions, my thoughts, my actions, my control—knowing that You are already working to bring a resolution to this situation. Thank You, God, for hearing and answering my prayer.

THINK ABOUT IT

As you face this set of challenges, ask yourself:
Am I willing to turn my control over to God? Or
am I still trying to handle things on my own?

Encouragement for the Doubting

Be merciful to those who doubt.

JUDE 1:22 NIV

Lord, I know that all of us have times of doubt. Help me never to look down on anyone who is doubting. Instead, may I reach out in love and support, as others have so often supported me. I know, Jesus, that You are the Author of our faith. Faith isn't something we have to muster up out of sheer determination; it's something You give to us. Empower us to let go of the way we idolize the visible and the known in our lives so that You can replace our doubts with faith. Remind us not to sit and stew in our fear and doubt, but instead may our days overflow with prayer. Teach us to encourage one another and be patient with each other's doubts.

THINK ABOUT IT

Is there someone in your life today who may need your encouragement to rise above her doubt?

Job Stress

Moses said to the LORD, "Pardon your servant, Lord. I have never been eloquent, neither in the past nor since you have spoken to your servant. I am slow of speech and tongue." The LORD said to him, "Who gave human beings their mouths? Who makes them deaf or mute? Who gives them sight or makes them blind? Is it not I, the LORD? Now go; I will help you speak and will teach you what to say."

EXODUS 4:10–12 NIV

God, Moses didn't think he could do the job You'd given him to do; I understand the feeling. Like Moses, I'm all too aware of all the ways I'm not skilled enough, all the ways I don't know enough, and all the mistakes I've made in the past. Remind me, God, as You reminded Moses, that You are the one working through me as I do my job. Help me to rely on You rather than on my own abilities.

––––––––– **THINK ABOUT IT** –––––––––

Moses sounds like he's being humble, but it's clear that God has a bone to pick with him. Do you ever let false humility hold you back from the work God is calling you to do?

Honoring Your Parents

"Honor your father and mother. Then you will live a long, full life in the land the LORD your God is giving you."

EXODUS 20:12 NLT

Heavenly Father, my parents are a precious gift from You. Thank You for allowing me the joy of having them for many decades; thank You for all I have learned from them down through the years. I pray now, as they are growing older, that You would help them to continue to grow in grace and in their relationship with You until the very end of their time here on earth. Please grant me wisdom and strength to care for them in a way that honors them and honors You. Give me patience and love, and may I never give in to irritation or resentment.

--- **THINK ABOUT IT** ---

Your parents may need your care now in ways that they didn't when you were young—but are there things they could still teach you if you were open to learning?

Family Pain

*"Do not nurse hatred in your heart for any of
your relatives. Confront people directly so
you will not be held guilty for their sin."*

LEVITICUS 19:17 NLT

God, You know how painful it is when a family member breaks our trust. I ask for Your guardianship of my heart and mind. I know that anyone intending to harm me or treat me abusively is never someone with whom You want me to spend time. At the same time, though, I believe You long to heal our family. Remove the hate and hurt we feel. Show us how to get the help we need to heal. Empower me to seek help and counsel from You, as well as from those who are trained to help with situations like this. May we once more be able to talk openly with one another.

THINK ABOUT IT

Family issues can be some of the most confusing to solve. Who might God want to use to give you help and insight?

Safe with God

"Everyone who lives and believes in Me will never die. Do you believe this?"

JOHN 11:26 NASB

Oh Jesus, I am so lonely without my husband. I know that You love him even more than I do, though, and that he is safe with You. Grant me the strength I need to bear this sorrow, and help me to look for opportunities to seek out those less fortunate than me. Keep me from feeling sorry for myself; even in my grief, inspire me with love for You and for my neighbor so that I can help to carry on Your work of love in this world. Thank You that one day my husband and I will be reunited in eternity.

THINK ABOUT IT

As Christians, we claim to believe in eternal life, but when someone dies, our belief is put to the test. Do you *really* believe that your husband is safe with God? If not, ask God to comfort your doubts and give you hope.

The Unity of the Spirit

Be completely humble and gentle; be patient, bearing
with one another in love. Make every effort to keep
the unity of the Spirit through the bond of peace.

EPHESIANS 4:2-3 NIV

God, You made us in Your own image and redeemed us through Jesus, Your Son; and You call us to join together in love and service, that the world may see You through us. Take away the arrogance and impatience that have infected our church. Break down the walls that separate us; unite us in bonds of love; and work through our struggles and confusion to accomplish Your purposes. Remind me that I am far from perfect; make me patient with others' imperfections. Restore our bond of peace, I pray.

--- **THINK ABOUT IT** ---

When you look at the discord in your church, what is the biggest factor that has broken your unity in the Spirit?

Love Instead of Fear

*"Do not fear them, for the LORD your
God is the One fighting for you."*

DEUTERONOMY 3:22 NASB

Lord Jesus, I know that You told us to pray for our enemies, and so I'm doing that right now. I ask first that You would saturate my life with Your Spirit's power and might. Take away my fear and replace it with trust in Your love. Send that love flowing through me, and forgive me for holding on to any resentment, self-righteousness, or hatred. I release into Your hands all thoughts of revenge. May I have the strength I need to bless my enemies. Thank You that You will protect me. Free me from fear and hatred, and give me a spirit of love and power. Bless these individuals with Your grace.

THINK ABOUT IT

How does fear interfere with the love God wants
you to show to everyone, even your enemies?

Your Heavenly Nurse

Whenever we're sick and in bed, GOD becomes
our nurse, nurses us back to health.

PSALM 41:3 MSG

Almighty God, you are the source of all health and healing. In You I find wholeness and rest. You know that my illness is chronic, which means it stretches out indefinitely into the future. Give me hope in You and protect me from discouragement. Grant me an awareness of Your presence, and increase my confidence in You. In all this pain and weariness, Lord, teach me to yield myself to Your never-failing care, knowing that Your love and power surround me. Increase my trust in Your wisdom. Be my heavenly nurse, giving my heart, soul, and body exactly what they need.

THINK ABOUT IT

Today, as you face your illness once again, can you imagine that you have a heavenly nurse who is constantly at your side, caring for you in all the ways you need most?

The Peace of Jesus

*Peace I leave you, My peace I give you; not
as the world gives, do I give to you. Do not
let your hearts be troubled, nor fearful.*

JOHN 14:27 NASB

Dear Jesus, thank You for the calm and peace You promise to give me even when I'm at my most anxious, in the middle of life's chaos, when life is spinning out of control. Help me to remember that when I feel overwhelmed by what I can't predict or plan, You already know what will play out, and You'll be with me through the process. Help me, Lord, to trust You as I steady my mind and heart on Your promises. Remind me to care for my body in the ways it needs so that my thoughts can embrace Your peace more easily. Thank You, Jesus, for sharing Your own peace with me.

—————————— **THINK ABOUT IT** ——————————

How is the peace of Jesus different
from any peace the world can give?

A Time to Die

To every thing there is a season, and a
time to every purpose under the heaven:
a time to be born, and a time to die.

ECCLESIASTES 3:1-2 KJV

I am grateful to You, God, for creating my pet and for entrusting him to my care. I know that all lives must die, and I knew this day would come—and yet my heart is breaking at the loss of this small life. Lord, as I took care of my pet in life, I ask that You would watch over him in death. You entrusted him to my care; now I give him back to You. May his memory continue to bless my life with love. Thank You for showing me Your unconditional love through my pet's life.

--- **THINK ABOUT IT** ---

What are the permanent gifts that
your pet's life has left with you?

Saved from Destruction

He sent His word and healed them,
and saved them from their destruction.

PSALM 107:20 NASB

Jesus, during Your time on earth, You ministered to all who came to You; You never judged or withheld Your healing touch. Look with compassion now upon all who through addiction have lost their health and freedom. Restore them to wholeness, I pray. Remove from them the fears that beset them, and strengthen them in the work of their recovery. Give patient understanding and persevering love to those who care for them. Send out Your Word to heal and save.

--------- **THINK ABOUT IT** ---------

How might you reach out in love to
someone who suffers from addiction?

Sweet Sleep

When you lie down, you will not be afraid;
when you lie down, your sleep will be sweet.

PROVERBS 3:24 NASB

I'm having so much trouble sleeping, Lord, that I don't have the energy to function well during the day. Even worse, when I'm so tired, I can't experience the peace You want for me. As I prepare for sleep tonight, please relax my body. Send me thoughts that will quiet and calm my mind. Remind me when I can't sleep to pray about whatever is worrying me. Thank You for Your constant care and unconditional love. Take away all my fears so I can rest in You.

THINK ABOUT IT

Have you asked God to show you what is causing your insomnia? Is it something spiritual, something emotional, or something physical? Have you talked to your doctor about the problem?

Precious in God's Sight

*Precious in the sight of the LORD is
the death of his faithful servants.*

PSALM 116:15 NIV

God of all comfort, I am so sad as I face a life without my parent in it. I know that we will be reunited one day, but my heart longs to be together now. Even Jesus cried when he was at the tomb of his friend Lazarus, so I know You empathize with my grief. Even in my sorrow, I thank You for the sweetness of Your abiding presence. I am grateful for my parent's life. Thank You for being with them at the moment of their death and for keeping them safe for all eternity.

—— **THINK ABOUT IT** ——

What do you think the psalmist meant when he said
that death was "precious in the sight of the LORD"?

Perfect Peace

You will keep in perfect peace all who trust
in you, all whose thoughts are fixed on you!

ISAIAH 26:3 NLT

Lord, I admit that I often forget that You are with me. I forget to think about You throughout the day. So it's no wonder, I suppose, that worry so often consumes my thoughts. I need to get to know You better. I need to become more familiar with Your Word and Your promises. Help me to put You first in every area of my life. Remind me to live one day at a time. Teach me not to worry about tomorrow but instead focus on what You're doing in my life right now. I know that You will take care of each of my needs—spiritual, financial, relational, physical, and emotional. Help me to trust You more and worry less.

--- **THINK ABOUT IT** ---

How might fixing your thoughts on
God be a good antidote for worry?

Resting in Safety

No wonder my heart is glad, and I rejoice. My body rests in safety.

PSALM 16:9 NLT

Lord, as I prepare for surgery, I can't help but feel nervous—but I know that I can rest in Your safety, for You are in control. I pray for Your peace to fill my mind as I drop into the unconsciousness of anesthesia. I ask that while the surgeon works on my body, Your healing hand would be at work as well. May I be a conduit for Your love during my time in the hospital so that each nurse and orderly, each doctor and aide is blessed by Your Spirit through their contact with me. After the surgery is done, help me to deal with the pain, and restore me to health, I pray.

THINK ABOUT IT

As you prepare for surgery, you may not feel much like rejoicing—but can you rest in the knowledge that God will hold you safe?

God Reality

"Steep your life in God-reality, God-initiative, God-provisions. Don't worry about missing out. You'll find all your everyday human concerns will be met."

MATTHEW 6:33 MSG

This burden I'm carrying at work, Lord, feels too heavy, too cumbersome to pick up and carry day after day. Please give me freedom from this weight. Change the circumstances of this situation, I pray, and free my heart and mind from the anxiety it causes. Guide me with Your Spirit, so I can know how to resolve, manage, or walk away from this worry. Thank You that You are my Comforter and my Friend. You care about each detail of my life, and You are already working on my behalf to bring peace and restoration to this situation. Help me always to live in Your reality, trusting in Your initiative and provision.

THINK ABOUT IT

What does it mean to live in "God-reality"? How might this shift in perspective change how you feel about your job?

Betrayed by a Friend

*Even my close friend, someone I trusted, one who
shared my bread, has turned against me.*

PSALM 41:9 NIV

This betrayal, Jesus, has wounded my heart—but I pray that
it would not keep me from sharing Your love with others. As
I move forward with other relationships in my life, help me
not to punish those who are innocent by assuming they too
will betray me. Restore my ability to trust. Work in the heart
of the friend who betrayed me, God, and show me ways to
rebuild trust in this relationship if that is possible. Remind
me that You too were betrayed by a friend, and yet You never
stopped reaching out in love. May I follow Your example.

--- **THINK ABOUT IT** ---

Has betrayal changed the way you think
about other people in general? How might
God want to heal you from this hurt?

A Joyful Death

*"You will come to the grave in full vigor,
like sheaves gathered in season."*

JOB 5:26 NIV

God, thank You that death can be a time of joy as well as sorrow. As I face the death of this loved one, I give You thanks for shared meals, laughter, long talks, and all the other memories. This person will be forever sewn into the fabric of my being, and I am grateful. May I remember all that I have learned from this relationship, and may I have opportunities to pass that wisdom on to others. As my loved one straddles this world and the next, may we both sense that this is not the end. A great adventure awaits this person I love so much, another chapter in the book of eternity. I release this loved one into Your presence, Lord, knowing I can trust You with this precious life.

--- **THINK ABOUT IT** ---

What legacy has your loved one left you? What memories will you treasure and take with you?

The Loss of a Child

Jesus said, "Let the little children come to me...
for the kingdom of heaven belongs to such as these."

MATTHEW 19:14 NIV

Oh my Lord, my arms are empty, longing for my child. I see my child everywhere in my mind, and life feels empty when I realize I will never see this child again, not in this life. If I'm honest, Lord, I'm angry too. How could You take this child who had so much life ahead? Thank You that I can express my anger and anguish to You. Jesus, hold me as I live through this endless process of grieving. May I one day be able to cherish my memories without feeling overwhelmed with grief. I need You to redeem this loss that seems so senseless. Fill my empty, aching heart with Your love, I pray.

—————— **THINK ABOUT IT** ——————

Do you feel comfortable telling God all your feelings? You don't need to hold back; He is longing to hear and help.

Crying in the Night

Arise, cry out in the night, as the watches of the night begin; pour out your heart like water in the presence of the Lord. Lift up your hands to him for the lives of your children.

LAMENTATIONS 2:19 NIV

Things always seem worse in the dark, Lord, when I can't sleep. Wrap Your arms around me, I pray, as I lie here crying, beset with fears and sorrows. Remind me to use this sleepless time to talk to You. Thank You that You are listening as I pour out my heart. I ask that You be with my children and all the people I love. I put them in Your hands now—and I'll do so again tomorrow night and the night after. Take my anxiety and sadness from me, and replace it with Your peace. Even if sleep still evades me, may I rest in Your presence. Let me relax in the knowledge that You have everything under control.

THINK ABOUT IT

While you wait for sleep, can you take advantage of this time by praying?

Releasing Grudges

*"When you are praying, first forgive anyone
you are holding a grudge against, so that your
Father in heaven will forgive your sins, too."*

MARK 11:25 NLT

Jesus, thank You that You have forgiven all my brokenness, all my mistakes, all my pride and selfishness. I confess that I have not extended that same love and mercy toward others who have offended me. Instead, I have held anger, bitterness, and resentment in my heart. Now, though, I want to release this grudge that has held me in bondage. Set me free, I pray. Heal my wounded heart, and give me the courage to be vulnerable once again. I don't want anything to come between You and me.

--- **THINK ABOUT IT** ---

How might unforgiveness keep you
from a close relationship with God?

Right Paths

Direct your children onto the right path,
and when they are older, they will not leave it.

PROVERBS 22:6 NLT

God, I can't control the paths my children choose to take as they grow older—so I'll have to trust You to guide them now that I no longer can. Create in them pure hearts, I pray, and renew a steadfast spirit within them (Psalm 51:10). I wish they did not have to deal with the consequences of the mistakes they've made; I wish I could spare them any pain; but I know that You can work in all the pieces of their lives, even the painful ones. I put them in Your hands when they were little, and now I put them there again. Thank You that nothing can separate my children from Your love.

THINK ABOUT IT

Trusting God to take care of your children is one of
the hardest things to do—but He loves them even more
than you do. Imagine that you started your children
out on a path that leads to God. Can you picture
Jesus continuing to guide them along that path?

Never Forgotten

*"Are not five sparrows sold for two pennies?
Yet not one of them is forgotten by God."*

LUKE 12:6 NIV

God of love, in the book of Genesis, I read how You created the animals to be our companions on this earth. In Your love, You allow human beings to befriend other creatures, and You use them to show us Your love. By Your wise design, we share our lives with these creatures, becoming friends in a very real way. But their lives are so short compared to ours, Lord, and now it breaks my heart to let this animal go. Be with our family as we grieve this loss. Thank You for the assurance that You care for animals and will not forget our pet.

—————————— **THINK ABOUT IT** ——————————

What does it mean to be remembered by God?

Harmful Paths

Violent people mislead their companions,
leading them down a harmful path.

PROVERBS 16:29 NLT

I have come to realize, Lord, that this friendship is not healthy. In fact, it is poisoning my mind and heart. It has led to me taking paths away from You. And yet, God, I know You love imperfect people extravagantly—and I confess that I am far from perfect. May I not be blind to my own role in this toxic relationship. Help me see the truth about myself. Be my shield and defender, I pray, and show me how, when, and where to set boundaries in this relationship. Bless my friend. May we both be healed so that You can shine through us. Set our feet back on the right path, Lord, the path that leads to You.

—————————— **THINK ABOUT IT** ——————————

Do you have the courage and honesty to ask
God to show you where your own responsibility
lies in a friendship that has turned toxic?

Carried in God's Arms

"Even to your old age I will be the same, and even to your graying years I will carry you! I have done it, and I will bear you; and I will carry you and I will save you."

ISAIAH 46:4 NASB

I thank You, Father, for all the ways You used my parents to shape my life. Despite their faults, they have shown me Your love again and again down through the years. And now, as they grow older, our roles are being reversed. Now they need my care, as I needed theirs when I was small. Even more, they need me to show them Your love. Give me patience, wisdom, and an understanding heart. Help me continue to show respect and appreciation. Thank You that You are with my parents, and as their abilities diminish, You will hold them close. Carry them in Your arms, I pray.

THINK ABOUT IT

How can you demonstrate God's love to
your parents in some small way today?

Tears

He will swallow up death in victory; and the Lord
GOD will wipe away tears from off all faces.

ISAIAH 25:8 KJV

Jesus, I miss my parent. I know I took that familiar presence for granted; after all, I've never known a moment when my parent wasn't alive in the world. Now I miss the comfort of my parent's arms, the generous love, the smile of welcome. I feel small and lonely. Please cover me with Your love and surround me with Your arms. Fill my thoughts and dreams with the hope of heaven. Give me the vision to trust that my parent is safe now with You, and one day we will be together again. Soothe my aching heart and wipe the tears from my face with Your gentle hand. Thank You that death never has the final word.

--- **THINK ABOUT IT** ---

Although we don't know what heaven is like, we can use our imaginations to bring us comfort. Can you picture your parent happy and well with God?

Confession

If we claim we have no sin, we are only fooling ourselves and not living in the truth. But if we confess our sins to him, he is faithful and just to forgive us our sins and to cleanse us from all wickedness.

1 JOHN 1:8–9 NLT

God, I'm scared of people finding out who I really am. I'm scared of being seen as a fraud, a hypocrite. I'm scared that everyone will abandon me, and I'll be alone in my sin and shame. But, Lord, I'm also scared of my heart growing colder and colder toward You. I wish there was an easy way out of this situation, but I know the only way forward is to follow You. I'm done making excuses, done pretending. I need Your grace, Lord, to help me change. I come to You, confessing my sin, asking for cleansing, for forgiveness, and for redemption. I can't fix myself. Only You can make me clean again.

─────────── **THINK ABOUT IT** ───────────

How does keeping a sin hidden
allow it to grow even larger?

The Most Intimate Betrayal

*A crowd came, and the one called Judas, one of
the twelve, was leading the way for them; and he
approached Jesus to kiss Him. But Jesus said to him,
"Judas, are you betraying the Son of Man with a kiss?"*

LUKE 22:47-48 NASB

Lord, to my shame I have committed adultery. I have broken
my marriage vows. I have betrayed my husband. Like Judas
who betrayed you with a kiss, I have pretended to love my
husband, while all the time, behind his back, I was seeking
my own pleasures at the cost of our marriage. Thank You,
God, that there is no sin too big for You to forgive. Show
me how to go on from here. Work a miracle in my marriage;
give us both fresh love for each other. I know that the marriage we once had is utterly broken—but I believe You can
build something new, something even stronger in its place.
Remake our hearts, I pray, so that our marriage will again
shine with Your love.

―――――――――― **THINK ABOUT IT** ――――――――――

Are you willing to let go of the past (both the good parts
and the bad) so that God can create something new?

God Never Gives Up

Being confident of this very thing, that he
which hath begun a good work in you will
perform it until the day of Jesus Christ.

PHILIPPIANS 1:6 KJV

Jesus, the world seems to be spinning out of control. Everywhere I look, I see chaos—and I don't see a way to restore order to the mess. I long just to throw in the towel and say, "Enough. I'm done. I give up." Give me a new perspective, Lord, and blow away the clouds that dim my vision. Remind me, whenever life seems hopeless, to turn my eyes to You. As I look back at history and at my own life, I see that Your hand was always working, even when things seemed the worst. Give me new confidence in You now, I pray. Thank You that You are still working—and You never give up.

———— THINK ABOUT IT ————

Can you increase your hope for today by
looking at what God has done in the past?

Enough for Today

"Don't worry about tomorrow, for tomorrow will bring its own worries. Today's trouble is enough for today."

MATTHEW 6:34 NLT

Oh Lord, I am wound up inside. I feel I cannot continue to meet the demands placed upon me. I worry that I am burned out. I worry about being worried! I fear I may buckle under the weight of all this anxiety. God, I am so tired of carrying this stress around. I desperately need Your peace. So I come to You, to rest in Your presence. May I find shelter from my worries. Lead me to a new state of mind, a fresh perspective—one that's grounded in trust. Remind me to stop borrowing trouble. Restore my heart.

THINK ABOUT IT

When we worry, we fix our minds on the future instead of dealing with what is right in front of us. What might you have overlooked because of your worries?

Respect and Unconditional Love

*Do not provoke your children to
anger by the way you treat them.*

EPHESIANS 6:4 NLT

Father, thank You for the privilege of being a parent to my children. Thank You for the time I had with them as children. Today I release them as adults to Your care and guidance. Remind me to keep my opinions to myself unless they're asked for. May I not anger my children with my disapproval and nosiness. Help me to show them respect and unconditional love. I trust You to guide them into paths that will lead to the fullness of life. Watch over them, I pray. Help me to trust them to You.

—————— **THINK ABOUT IT** ——————

In what ways have you provoked your children to
anger? Do you need to ask their forgiveness?

Content with What You Have

Keep your lives free from the love of money and be
content with what you have, because God has said,
"Never will I leave you; never will I forsake you."

HEBREWS 13:5 NIV

Lord, I surrender my financial affairs and concerns about money to Your divine care and love. Take my worries about money and replace them with faith in Your care. I commit to being grateful for all You have already given me. Help me to learn to manage my finances wisely, seeking help where needed. Remind me to be content with what have instead of always wanting more. Thank You that You are always with me.

THINK ABOUT IT

We usually think that more money is the answer to financial strain—but are there ways you could simplify your life that might decrease your financial worries?

Resurrection Hope

Jesus told her, "I am the resurrection and the life.
Anyone who believes in me will live, even after dying."

JOHN 11:25 NLT

Jesus, since my husband's death, I feel such absence in my home and in my heart. Please fill the emptiness with Your presence. I feel loss—of my husband's companionship, his support, and even my own identity. Please make me whole. I feel sadness, as though my heart has broken. Please comfort me and be my sanctuary. I feel anger that he left me. Please give me peace. I feel hopelessness. Please give me hope in Your promises. My loss of my husband has consumed me. Please be my everything. Give me faith that my husband is still alive with You.

———————— **THINK ABOUT IT** ————————

If you believe in Jesus, you too can live, even
after your husband's death. Can you claim
the promise of John 11:25 as your own?

Awesomely and Wonderfully

For You created my innermost parts; You wove
me in my mother's womb. I will give thanks to You,
because I am awesomely and wonderfully made.

PSALM 139:13-14 NASB

Loving God, You make each person in Your image. Each individual is Your gift of love to the human race. I praise You, Lord, that each of us is unique and each is perfect in Your sight, "awesomely and wonderfully made." Remind me, Lord, to see You in all who live with different abilities. May I never reject them or create obstacles for them to overcome. May I work instead to facilitate access and welcome. I want to cooperate with You to create communities open to the gifts of each individual. May I never forget that Your body is incomplete whenever anyone is excluded or left behind.

―――――― **THINK ABOUT IT** ――――――

Have your words or actions ever excluded or failed
to welcome someone who is differently abled?

Lust for Money

Lust for money brings trouble and nothing but trouble.
Going down that path, some lose their footing in the
faith completely and live to regret it bitterly ever after.

1 TIMOTHY 6:10 MSG

You know, Lord, that I live in a society that is constantly encouraging me to be greedy for money and the things money can buy. I don't want to excuse my greed, though. Help me to be more aware. Remind me to consciously reject society's values and choose Yours. But I am also aware of being greedy for other "currencies" too. I get greedy for control; I get greedy for people to notice me and appreciate me. Sometimes that greed gets mixed up with my greed for money too, because there's a part of me that believes that if I have more money, then I'll have more control over my life and people will admire me more. I'm sorry, Jesus. Keep my eyes fixed on You, I pray, and may I grow less focused on money.

——— THINK ABOUT IT ———

What are the things you are greedy for?

The Generosity of God

Return to your rest, my soul, for the
LORD has dealt generously with you.

PSALM 116:7 NASB

Lord, I need Your peace to soothe my heart. Each time I find myself awake in the middle of the night, the pressing needs and worries I'm facing feel overwhelming. I ask for Your love to surround me. I lay my burdens before You, every single one, knowing they're much safer in Your hands than they are in mine. I surrender to You every anxious thought. Help me to trust You more. Thank You that through every weakness and difficulty I encounter, Your strength is displayed in my life. In the darkness of the night, when I'm at my lowest, I choose to hope in You. You have been very generous to me, Lord. Let me rest in You.

THINK ABOUT IT

Instead of focusing on worries when you can't sleep, can you count all the ways God has been generous to you?

Taught by the Lord

"All your children will be taught by the LORD, and great will be their peace."

ISAIAH 54:13 NIV

Father, I can no longer teach my children the way I could when they were little—but I know that You are teaching them. I pray that You will reassure them that You are love. Remind them when they are lonely or heartbroken or scared that not only do I love them but so do You. May they never feel unloved, no matter how many times the world hurts them. Supply them with friends and coworkers they can genuinely trust and grow with, people who will show them You. Remind me always to show them love in ways that make them secure in the knowledge that they are loved exactly where and how and for who they are. Teach their hearts, I pray, and give them Your peace.

THINK ABOUT IT

Can you trust that God is still teaching your children, even when they seem to have gone far away from God and you?

Still Fresh and Green

They will still bear fruit in old age,
they will stay fresh and green.

PSALM 92:14 NIV

Thank You, God, for my parents' lives. Please give me the wisdom and sense of timing to talk to them about what they want for their future care. Enable me to follow their plan, Lord. Help me to be flexible and have the ability to go with the flow as my parents age. I pray that I will not get angry when things don't go as I want, when my parents' unexpected needs arise. Help me to discover the humor in unusual situations; may my parents and I not lose the ability to laugh together. Most of all, Lord, I want my parents to know they are loved. May Your love flow through me to them and through them to me. Bear fruit in all our lives, I pray. Keep us growing and green, no matter how old we get or how life changes.

--- **THINK ABOUT IT** ---

What fruit might your parents be
bearing even now, in their old age?

One God

"You can't worship two gods at once. Loving one god, you'll end up hating the other. Adoration of one feeds contempt for the other. You can't worship God and Money both."

MATTHEW 6:24 MSG

Lord, please forgive me for my greed, my selfishness, my arrogance. Forgive me for putting anything ahead of You. I like to think that I don't really care about money—but You know, Lord, that I too have been infected by the world's materialism. Remind me to see with Your eyes, valuing the things You value. May I never make my bank account my god. Make me a good steward of the financial blessings You have given me. May I not to cling to money but instead use it as one more resource for Your kingdom.

THINK ABOUT IT

In what ways have you been infected
by the disease of materialism?

Subject Index

About the Author

Rae Simons is the pseudonym for the author of many spiritual and educational books. She has written and edited for Barbour Books for nearly thirty years. She and her husband (along with two dogs and a cat) live in New York State.

Find Strength in Talking to God in Difficult Times

199 Encouraging Prayers for Difficult Times

Here's a practical and encouraging book containing 199 short prayer starters that will help you pray confidently during difficult times.

Paperback / 978-1-63609-007-8 / $4.99

Bible Promises and Devotions for Difficult Times

This book provides encouraging scriptures and thoughtful readings that cover dozens of important life topics—from anxiety to death of a pet and job loss to prodigal children.

Flexible Casebound / 978-1-63609-200-3 / $19.99

All at once a soft breathless cry took me out of my dream. I sat bolt upright in bed *Whuzzat?*

Dead silence. Did I dream it?

Just as I was about to go back to dreamland, I noticed something very strange.

A faint corona of blue light gleamed beyond the window, somewhere out there in the yard. Blinking in confusion, I swept the blankets aside and tottered across the room.

Chilly night air helped to sharpen my mental focus. Peeling back the gauzy drape, I glanced through the frost-rimmed window.

A bright flickering sapphire light illuminated the horizon. The glow threw the shelterbelt treetops into sharp silhouette. Frowning in bewilderment I thought, What on earth is *that?*

Prairie fire? City lights? *UFO*

Then, with no warning at all, the flickering light winked out.

Yielding to a mammoth yawn, I released the drape and toddled back to bed.

CORONA BLUE

J.F. TRAINOR

ZEBRA BOOKS
KENSINGTON PUBLISHING CORP.

For "the computerheads"
Carolyn and David Rzepecki,
whose technical assistance
proved invaluable.

"Progress is man's ability to complicate simplicity."
THOR HEYERDAHL

ONE

He stood in the field off to my left. A gaunt, sinister figure in a fraying black trenchcoat, with a dark gray fedora concealing much of his face. The relentless Dakota wind plucked at his ragged sleeves. At first I gave him a wide berth. And then, as an afterthought, I leaned against the cab's right window and showed him my upraised thumb.

"Happy Halloween, Mr. Scarecrow!"

If he answered, I certainly didn't hear him. That's no surprise, really, considering the clamor raised by my Case International 1688 combine. Well, not *exactly* mine. The combine belonged to one Joshua M. Elderkin, the farmer I'd been working for since my return from Washington a week ago. The rumble of its two-hundred-and-sixty horsepower engine rattled my teeth. That sound, however, was a soothing whisper compared to the grinding shriek of the auger and the *bang-bang-bangetty-bang* of ripe corn ears tumbling into the steel bin.

The cab rocked slightly in the prairie wind. Shivering at the sudden chill, I zipped up my parka and wished for a woolen hat instead of my corduroy ball cap. Already it was down to forty-two degrees Fahrenheit, and KORN, 1490-AM on the radio dial, predicted a light snowfall.

The wind stirred up the chaff again. Despite the best efforts of the filters, a flurry of grit, dust, and cornsilk went swirling around the cab. I sneezed once, clapped my left hand over my nose, and steered one-handed as my combine went hurtling downfield at the hair-raising velocity of fourteen miles per hour.

Pursing my lips, I gingerly shifted position in the operator's chair. Sore gluteal muscles throbbed at the onset of returning circulation. My behind felt as if it had been riddled with novocaine. Obviously, Case International hadn't designed this big red harvesting machine with the female anatomy in mind. How did Trudy stand it?

Putting both hands on the wheel again, I watched six rows of brownish yellow cornstalks collapse beneath the combine's spike-toothed cutter bar. I imagined my parole officer, Paul Holbrook, going down the exact same way, disappearing into the snappers, getting munched and crunched and spit through the rotary, and eventually winding up on a supermarket shelf in Oacoma.

I glimpsed myself in the tilted windshield, then displayed a sour expression. My prison mom at Springfield, Becky Reardon, had dubbed it a *fussbudget face*. Obsidian eyes slitted in irritation. Two vertical ridges above the bridge of my nose. Tightly compressed lips.

I winced at my reflection. Farmer Angie! Long, raven-black hair spilling down from her corduroy seed cap. Petite, slender Anishinabe princess all decked out in her canvas work gloves, steel-shanked work boots, black jeans, and mountain parka of a shade we country people call *John Deere-green*.

This was my punishment for returning from a week of job-development leave with no job. Both Paul and his boss, Randolph T. Langston, really chewed my ass when I came trotting back to Pierre. Of course, they would have yelled a lot louder if they'd known I was out in Port Wyoochee, Washington, clearing a friend of a murder rap. I didn't bother to enlighten the gentlemen. Some things a lady keeps to herself, especially if she wants to avoid a return engagement at the Big Dollhouse.

Paul Holbrook felt I ought to sample a job a little more strenuous than my usual Work Experience occupation. Maybe then, he added, I might begin to appreciate waitressing. Hence my new career as a combine jockey.

I soon lost interest in combining Holbrook. Cornfield monotony tends to stifle imagination. Ahead of me stretched two hundred acres of tall, ripe corn, a lake of tawny vegetation streaming toward a grove of shelterbelt silver maple running alongside Enemy Creek.

Two hundred acres! I did a little mental math. Let's see now. If a man on foot walking one acre covers approximately ten miles, then two hundred acres is the pedestrian equivalent of two thousand miles. The Case combine clips six rows at a whack. So we divided that two thousand by six and . . . guess what, Angie? Today you'll be driving this combine three hundred and thirty-three miles. Which is the same as driving it from nearby Mitchell all the way to Deadwood, South Dakota!

While chugging across the prairie at the speed of an arthritic buffalo, I was almost tempted to tickle the toggle again. Send the dump auger swinging back and forth. Anything for entertainment! Then I noticed Brad's pocket-sized Walkman dangling from the rearview mirror. Smiling gratefully, I reached for it with both hands.

As the maples' ruddy leaves drew closer, Willie Nelson reminded me that there was nothing he could do about it now. Don't fret, Willie. You've done enough just dampening the earsplitting roar of that diesel engine.

When the earphones began spitting static, I popped out ol' Willie and rummaged in the oil-stained coffee caddy for a fresh cassette.

Oh, terrific! I thought, lifting the cassette with my fingertips. There was no mistaking the portly gentleman in the gray suit, black string tie, and white Stetson.

Oh, no! Not Country Bull Durham!

My uncle Walter is a great Country Bull fan. He once heard the Bull play backup guitar for the immortal Hank Williams in Hayward, Wisconsin, long, long before I was born. Me, I lean more toward Clint Black and Randy Travis. Still, anything's better than listening to corn ears careening into that holding bin.

As I reached for the Walkman, the combine's man-sized front tire dipped into a badger hole. The cab jostled from side to side. Leaping out of my fingers, the cassette clattered to the cab's steel floor.

"Shit!" Bowing at the waist, I reached for it. The cassette lay just beyond my straining fingers.

"More trouble than Paul Holbrook!" I muttered, leaving the driver's seat. Kneeling beneath the steering wheel, I reached for it once more.

Suddenly, the combine's side windows exploded like Waterford crystal dropped from a rooftop. A Plexiglas monsoon pelted my seed cap. My upraised left hand detected the rush of superheated air. *A bullet!*

Blam-blam! Twin gunshots overwhelmed the clamor of shattering Plexiglas. Deep-toned blasts that sent a frosty chill racing up my spine. *Somebody's shooting at me!*

The adrenaline rush turned me into a startled jackrabbit. Gripping the wheel with both hands, I spun it to the right. The combine startled me by turning to the left. Only then did I remember an important fact about combines. They steer with their smaller rear tires, meaning they turn in the opposite direction indicated by the steering wheel.

Determined to present the unknown gunman with a difficult target, I crouched beneath the wheel and rotated it to the left. My combine veered toward the shorn corn rows at the field's edge. Shaking all over, I stomped down on the accelerator.

Too late, I noticed the switchgrass coming up fast and remembered the drainage ditch running the length of the field. Without thinking, I spun the wheel to the left. Then panicked as the combine lurched straight toward the ditch.

All at once, the cab tilted sickeningly downward. I slid down the steel floor and slammed into the corner. The combine shuddered as if struck by a grenade. Shaking the Plexiglas slivers out of my hair, I switched off the engine.

Dead silence. Somewhere overhead, I heard the faint honk of migrating Canada geese. That sound soon faded, replaced by the soft mutter of the prairie wind through bare maple branches.

Move, princess! I thought, scrambling out onto the cab porch. Out of the goldfish bowl—now!

Taking one giant step, I launched myself into space. The ditch's muddy wall soared to greet me. I struck the spongy turf with a muted grunt, rolling with the impact. Two seconds later, I halted, taking care to stay beneath the rim, with my cheek firmly pressed against the cold, dank soil.

Who's doing the shooting? I wondered.

There was no shortage of enemies on my back trail. Well, that's one of the drawbacks of being Outlaw Angie.

Paranoia gave my memory banks a thorough ransacking.

Two shots. Maybe three if the sound of shattering windows drowned out the first boom. Pretty loud shots. A rifle, perhaps? So who's handy with a rifle? Linda Beckworth? That Cotter guy from the Adamite church? And if it's one of them, how on earth did they ever find me in *South Dakota?*

Continuing silence improved my self-confidence. I yanked my paranoia out of the driver's seat and stuffed it back in its upstairs closet. If it wasn't an old enemy of mine, then who . . . ?

Quick progression of thoughts. Josh's wife was supposed to

be combining today. But Trudy came down with a vicious migraine, and I volunteered to take her place.

Ridiculous! I thought. Who'd would want to kill Trudy Elderkin? That woman makes friends the way a bear eats cherries . . . frequently and in bunches.

So maybe it wasn't deliberate, I reflected. Maybe some Halloween joker decided to shake up the combine driver. Maybe he took aim at the combine's holding bin—and *missed!*

I glanced at the lopsided combine. The steel cutter bar and snouts on the right-hand side had carved a wavy rille into the ditch's muddy sidewall. The bullet had burst both side windows, passing right through the cab.

Sudden primordial shiver. Had I not been scrounging on the floor for Country Bull—had I been sitting upright—I would have been right in the bullet's flight path!

Pushing aside that chilling thought, I concentrated on the bullet's trajectory. The combine's right window had been facing Enemy Creek at the moment of impact. The bullet still had plenty of zip when it struck, so the shooter couldn't have been too far away.

Tilting my head upward, I could see the maples' barren upper branches. Forty yards? Yeah, that was just about right. The shot had been fired from those shelterbelt maples bordering the creek.

I decided to have a closer look at the shooter. A very careful look. I wasn't totally convinced that he was a teenaged practical joker or a frustrated nimrod getting an early start on whitetail season. So, brushing the remaining Plexiglas shards from my parka, I kept my head and shoulders below the ditch's horizon and catwalked briskly down the muck-lined trench.

Heart thumping, I flattened against the combine's steel bin. Then I crouched behind the small rear tire, risking a lengthy peek.

Dry cornstalks rustled in the prairie breeze. The maple

limbs, forty yards distant, resembled cracks in the ceramic of the dour overcast sky. I saw no movement in the trees, but I was taking no chances. Following a relaxing ten minutes spent crouched behind that tire, I padded farther down the ditch, peered over the rim, and made a wild-ass dash into the corn.

My vigilant gaze drifted through the maze of tall, tawny cornstalks, rustling leaves, and unshucked ears. Just in case my friend had the same idea, using the tall corn to mask his approach. I wanted no sudden, awkward tête-à-têtes with a sniper.

Gradually I zigzagged through the corn, taking care to avoid rustling the leaves, putting up with the foot-catching tangle of dead weeds, fallen stalks, and last year's root stubble.

As the corn thinned out, I dropped silently to all fours, scanning the terrain ahead. Tall switchgrass fronted the mature maples. Just beyond, the creek burbled down its narrow channel, making a guttural splashing noise.

Brushing the long strands of hair away from my forehead, I moved into the trees. Puzzled frown. No broken stems. No slender upturned leaves. No signs of human passage at all.

Reverting to girlhood, I played hopscotch on the stones in the creekbed. Made it all the way across without wetting my tan work boots. Back on dry ground, I darted behind the nearest burr oak. Took a deep breath and had another look around.

Just ahead stood a wilderness garden of hackberry and prairie thorn. Beyond that, reaching nearly half a mile across the flatland, was a recently harvested cornfield. A handful of surviving splintered cornstalks testified to the efficiency of the modern combine. A dirt road bordered the far side of the field. Running its length was another stand of burr oak, their thick branches heavy with dry brown leaves.

Who did the shooting? I wondered. And how did he get away so quickly?

All at once, the image of a toppled scarecrow captured my peripheral vision. I looked straight at it, then gasped out loud. That facedown form was a little too solid to be filled with straw. And no scarecrow of my acquaintance had ever worn a woolen suit in navy-blue pinstripe.

The man lay on his front side in the stubble about three feet shy of the thicket. I reached him in less than a minute. Kneeling at his side, I planted my palm on the back of his bald head. A faint warmth suffused the skin. My fingertips darted to his throat. No pulse. He was dead.

Gripping his shoulders, I noticed that his Kojak hairstyle was the result of heredity, not personal choice. No barbershop fuzz running from ear to ear. Narrow, crinkled ears. He had an expensive and well-cultivated tan. His cranium, face, and hands were the same shade of cinnamon. Two ugly, blood-stained craters sullied the spine of his suit jacket.

Check his feet, Angie. Well, he certainly didn't buy those dark brown hand-stitched oxford brogues at Kmart. Fresh buff-colored mud spattered the toes. The man had been running when he was shot. Trying to get away from the shooter, most likely.

Grunting, I wrestled the victim onto his back. The corpse made a soft sucking noise as I rolled it out of the blood pool. One look at his chest and I gagged. The bullets had shattered both lungs. Hydrostatic shock had killed him in microseconds, bursting his heart like a water-filled balloon.

My gaze avoided the bloodstained melange of torn cloth, splintered flesh and scattered lung tissue that had once been the victim's vest. Instead, I studied his face while my hands searched his pockets, committing his features to memory.

One of the new people, I mused. Known as Caucasian in cop language. Age somewhere around forty. Sightless chocolate brown eyes peered at the snow-laden overcast. Prominent wrinkles across the forehead. A blunt, tip-tilted nose. Sallow cheekbones and a square jaw. Frowning thoughtfully, I thumbed open the cooling lower lip. Hmm, still got his own teeth. Nicotine stains, too. My new acquaintance was—*had been* a smoker.

My pocket search came up empty. Sitting back on my heels, I did some rapid thinking. Not good, princess. A smoker wouldn't leave home without his crushed pack or matchbook or cigarette lighter. Meaning somebody beat me to the search—*the killer!*

I could pretty well reconstruct the sequence of events. Twenty minutes ago, Unsuspecting Angie had been driving her combine on the other side of Enemy Creek. Meanwhile, here in this deserted cornfield, Mr. Beach Tan suddenly broke away from his killer companion. The killer got off three shots. The first one passed through the woods and scored a direct hit on my combine. The second two—the shots I heard—dropped the victim before he could reach the relative safety of the burr oak.

Making a gruesome face, I rolled Mr. Beach Tan back into his original position. I had no idea how the local law was going to take this. I could just see the headline in the *Daily Republic*. EX-CONVICT FINDS MURDERED MAN IN CORNFIELD—SHERIFF HAS MANY QUESTIONS. There'd be hassles enough without additional flak for tampering with a crime scene.

So back you go, my friend. Pardon the inconvenience. I'll be back with the posse shortly. The professionals can take it from there.

My hand lingered on his navy-blue jacket. Playing a sudden hunch, I reached down and forcibly turned back its woolen collar. A small cloth-of-gold tag gleamed against dark satin. Craning my neck, I read the elegant script. *Birnbaum's*.

So now I had a clue, albeit a slim one. Like the shoes, Mr. Beach Tan's suit hadn't come from the bargain rack. Birnbaum's. My lush lips pursed thoughtfully. An exclusive clothing store, obviously. But not in South Dakota. And I should know. During my time here, I've become intimately familiar with every stylish clothing store from Sioux Falls to Rapid City.

One hunch just naturally led to another. I began wondering how Mr. Beach Tan made his living. My fingers gingerly palpated his lifeless sun-browned hands.

Firm and supple palms. No calluses. Whatever he was, that man was no farmer. His hands are much too smooth. Turning one over, I blinked in surprise at the pushed-in knuckles. A fighter? My follow-up glance negated that notion. His biceps didn't quite fill the jacket's upper sleeves. He had a firm grip, no doubt, but he seemed to be lacking in upper body strength. I'd say a white-collar worker. Only how does a file clerk or a CPA come by a boxer's misshapen knuckles?

Just then, I experienced an icy tremor at the nape of my neck. That sudden awareness of hostile intent. I hadn't felt a twinge that sharp since the time that crazy Elena Varo chased me with her razor-sharp homemade shank.

They say we all have a sixth sense, a precognitive intuition that kicks in during times of extreme danger. I'd developed mine in prison. Random, senseless acts of violence were an everyday occurrence at Springfield. A woman either heeded those warning impulses, or else she spent a lot of time getting patched up in the infirmary.

Acting on impulse, I cast a quick peripheral glance over my shoulder. Nope, nobody in the field. Extend the visual reach toward the shelterbelt oaks. Uh-oh! Did I just see a branch quiver out there?

I didn't wait for confirmation. Rising suddenly, I dashed into the underbrush. Hackberry twigs raked my jeans as I ran. I made a beeline to the creek, pushing droopy oak branches out of my face. Heavy footfalls pummeled the turf far behind me. Panic sent a fresh spurt of adrenaline surging through my legs. I took a running leap from the creek's bank.

Momentum carried me all the way across. Touching down, I

cut to the left and plunged into the maple grove. Find some cover, princess. No sense leading him straight to the combine.

Hopping a clump of dried pasqueflowers, I ducked behind the thick trunk of a mature maple. Pressing my shoulder blades to the gray fissured trunk, I drew in a long, slow breath and listened carefully.

The sound of weighty footfalls suddenly ended, giving way to a guttural gasp of disgust. Then the hushed noise faded into the sharp spattering of Enemy Creek.

Relief turned my knees into overcooked macaroni. Hushed feminine sigh. He'd stopped at the water, thank heavens.

Feeling a little bolder, I put my cheek to the maple bark and peered beneath the lowermost bough. A peaceful country scene met my inquisitive gaze. Silver maples and sleepy burr oaks and the narrow creek running between a pair of muddy banks. My unknown pursuer had fled.

I was of a mind to do exactly the same, but I made myself sit quietly at the foot of that maple for another five minutes. Just in case he had gone to ground, waiting for me to show. Then I returned to the Elderkin field by a long, roundabout route.

Avoiding the silent combine, I stayed hidden in the corn. The killer must have gotten a pretty good look at me while I was examining Mr. Beach Tan. Assuming he still had his gun—and that was a *very* reasonable assumption—he'd definitely start shooting if he came across a petite, indigenous woman with long black hair.

So I positioned myself near the farm's dirt road, sitting between two tall stalks, elbows at rest on my knees. Chin resting on one hand, I sighed and waited for one of the Elderkins to show.

About thirty minutes later, a big Ford tandem-axle truck came rumbling down the road. The dust cloud nearly eclipsed the empty grain cart hitched to its rear. As it turned into the field, I recognized the rawboned, sandy-haired man behind the wheel.

"Brad!" I hollered, hopping to my feet. My arms waved frantically. "Brad, wait! Hit the brakes!"

"*Angie!?*" Peering through the open passenger window, Brad Elderkin shot me a look of mild astonishment. He was thirty, a tall, lean, thick-wristed man with Trudy's fine sandy hair and his father's vulpine face. He wore his hair short, parted on the left, with the tiniest of pompadour peaks. Grecian nose, broad mouth, low, thin eyebrows and friendly gray-green eyes. Toting all those hundred-pound hay bales had put an extra-thick layer of muscle on his neck and shoulders. He stomped the brake pedal, and the grain truck screeched to a dusty halt.

Breaking into the clear, I ran to the truck. Eyes narrowing in concern, he pushed open the passenger door for me.

"What's wrong, Angie?"

"A man shot at me." Breathlessly I climbed into the cab. "Up by the creek. He hit the combine."

"Were you hurt?" he asked, his voice a warm baritone.

I shook my head. "The bullet broke the windows. Missed me." Sudden fearful shiver. "Not by much, though."

Swiveling the stickshift, he pumped the gas pedal. Bouncing from side to side, the truck rumbled downfield. Turning the wheel, Brad aimed us at the derelict combine. "Hunter?"

Vigorous shake of the head.

Brad's eyes narrowed. "He shot at you *deliberately?*"

"No, he wasn't aiming at me. It was a stray shot." Catching Brad's puzzled glance, I tried to make my story more coherent. "He shot somebody else. A man! On the other side of the creek." I pointed at the row of silver maples. "He did it on purpose, Brad. Murder! I saw the victim. He fired three shots. First one hit the combine."

As we drove across the field, I quickly explained about my impromptu search. I'll say one thing about Brad Elderkin. He was all business. He listened without comment to my breathless tale, parked the truck, told me to stay put, and had a look at the combine. No smirks of disbelief. No patronizing bull-shit. He took me at my word. Returning to the truck, he asked me to hand him the dash-mounted cellular phone.

He tapped out seven digits, put the receiver to his ear, frowned and waited.

"Howdy, Lorna. This here's Brad Elderkin . . . Yeah, yeah, I'm fine. So's Ronnie . . . Listen, Sheriff Fischer around? . . . Well, you'd better fetch him. Let him know we got some trouble out here . . . There's been a shooting . . . That's right, Lorna, a shooting . . . Somebody shot at Angie . . . No, she's okay. Just shaken up a mite." Grim smile. "Tell him he'd better send out a cruiser. We're off County Road 22, just north of Enemy Creek. Big red combine. Can't miss it." He made a humming sound of assent. "Don't worry. We ain't goin' any-where . . . Bye!"

I stepped down from the cab as Brad made his second call. "Dad? It's me . . . Come on down. We got trouble. Some ass-hole took a shot at Angie." He listened intently, then added, "No need. I just called it in. Right! We're up by the shelterbelt . . . Angie's all right. Want to talk to her? Okay, be seein' you!"

After that, Brad offered me a cup of hot coffee straight out of the thermos. He would have made a very thoughtful hus-band—were he not already married.

The story of my life—the good ones are always taken!

Less than ten minutes later, a rusting Dodge Dakota lum-bered off the road and hurtled through the stubble, its rear tires tossing up twin sprays of soupy mud. That must have been some trip with no shocks. The passengers didn't seem to mind, though. The moment the sagging Dodge groaned to a halt, they came pouring out of the cab.

First out was Brad's baby sister, Kristy. She was sixteen, a tall, leggy, coltish girl. She shared her father's gray-green eyes with Brad, but there all resemblance ended. Silky, honey-blond hair and exquisitely hewn features. A slim nose and a delicately tapered chin. Take her out of the denim jacket and jeans, put her in this year's most stylish swimsuit, snap a picture, splash it across a Norwegian travel poster, and you'd have legions of college boys booking a one-way flight to Oslo.

Coming up right behind Kristy was Brad's wife, Veronica. Known to the family and most of Davison County as Ronnie. She was my age and two inches over my five-foot-four. Slender, dark-haired lady with a heart-shaped face, deep-set eyes the color of polished oak, and a dainty, lush-lipped mouth. Her smile was wide, warm, gracious, and tinged with relief.

At Ronnie's heels sauntered my new Work Experience employer, Joshua Montgomery Elderkin. The fabric of his work-stained coveralls seemed barely able to contain his hard-muscled body. The family resemblance was glaringly obvious. It was as if somebody had taken a taut buffalo hide and stretched it over Brad's angular features. Broiling summer sunshine and autumn's prairie winds and winter frostbite had scoured Josh's face, seared it, hammered it, giving it the consistency of saddle leather. There was, I knew, a pale white band at the top of his wrinkled forehead, where his seed cap usually sat.

"You all right, girl?" he asked, his gimlet eyes narrowing in concern. Bass voice, heavy on the consonants.

I nodded. "Fine, Josh. I can't say the same about the combine. Sorry."

"Don't fret it none." Gnarled hands on his narrow hips, he surveyed the lopsided machine. "Weren't your fault."

"Angie! Somebody *shot* at you!?" Excitement obliterated Kristy's customary aura of teenaged cool. Gripping my sleeve, she asked, "What *happened?* Mama said—"

"Let her tell it, Kris," Brad interrupted, screwing the cap back onto the thermos.

One foot on the combine's rear drawbar, I told my story, beginning with my efforts to retrieve Country Bull. I didn't get very far. A Davison County police cruiser, topside light flashing, pulled off the road and rumbled across our trimmed field.

The deputy was about the same size as Josh and Brad, wearing a fur-trimmed brown leather bomber jacket over his khaki uniform. A golden badge gleamed against the leather. Sand-colored Stetson and surplus army paratrooper boots and a thick gun belt bristling with law-enforcement paraphenalia—black leather holster, matching handcuff case, speedloads and palm-sized walkie-talkie. A smooth black tonfa baton slapped his striped pants leg. I recognized the service revolver. Smith & Wesson Model 19. A deep-throated .357 Magnum with molded rubber grips.

He had something of a squared upper face, with a single wrinkle running across his forehead, sparse auburn eyebrows, deep-set predator's eyes in a dull shade of blue, a straight Scandinavian nose with a noticeable tip, and tension brackets on either side of his hard, thin-lipped mouth. Wiry auburn hair peeked out from beneath the rodeo flanges of his Stetson.

"On my way over to Ethan when I got the call." The deputy's voice was a droning off-key baritone. He didn't return our welcoming smiles. Maybe he was still pissed off about getting booted out of the church choir. His hard-eyed gaze picked me out of our quintet. "Don't believe I've seen you 'round here before, gal."

"Dan, this here's Angie Biwaban—" Kristy began.

But Deputy Dan cut her right off. Thin lips curled in a mirthless smile. "Sorta wandered off the reservation, eh?"

"Not even close, Deputy." Somehow I managed to hold onto my gracious smile.

"She's workin' for me, Kramer. Helpin' with the harvest." Standing behind me, Josh planted a paternal hand on my shoulder. "Some crazy son of a bitch took a shot at her."

"Okay, gal. Let's hear it." Kramer unzipped his jacket, reached inside and then withdrew a small tan notebook.

So I told him everything, right up to the moment Brad's big truck had entered the field. Deputy Kramer took copious notes, occasionally pausing to clear the gunk from the tip of his ballpoint pen. When I finished, he asked me for my name, age, and address. I complied.

". . . Elderkin Farm, RFD #3, Yorktown, South Dakota."

Scowling at me from beneath the Stetson brim, he snapped, "I *know* where they live, honey. I just want to know where you lived *before* you came out here."

Mild grimace. Telling him the truth wouldn't exactly improve that sunny disposition. But he had my whole name, and he could very easily find out by putting through a radio call. Bite the bullet, princess.

Flashing a tepid smile, I delicately folded my hands in front of me. "Uh, 2317 Prospect Avenue, Pierre, South Dakota."

Kramer's harsh eyes blinked wide. He recognized the address of the Dunning House, the state's halfway house for female parolees. Pocketing the notebook, he gave me an authoritative nod. "Let's have a look at that dead man, miss."

And off we went. Angie the trail guide and her talkative safari. Me in the lead, Deputy Dan right behind, then Josh, Brad, Kristy, and Ronnie. I headed straight for the maples, wandered among them for a few minutes, picked up my own trail, and followed it to the creek. As we hurried along, Kramer quizzed me about the dead man I'd seen. How tall? Heavyset or scrawny? What kind of clothes? Any distinguishing marks?

In no time at all, we reached the deserted cornfield on the other side of Enemy Creek. Weaving my way through the prairie thorn, I said, "I found him right over—"

My sidewinding gaze pinpointed the spot. The words died in my throat.

He was gone!

"No!" Bursting out of the undergrowth, I ran across the field. I couldn't believe my eyes.

Impossible! I thought. He couldn't have—!

Then my keen gaze detected an irregularity. One of the rows was oddly flattened, as if someone had been kicking loose dirt away from it. I looked closer. Stirred fresh soil and many splintered cornstalks.

Sure enough, someone had given that spot a thorough going-over, removing every handful of blood-soaked earth.

The safari gathered around me. Painfully conscious of the deputy's exasperated scowl, I turned to face him. Sudden wild sweep of feminine arms. Sheepish Angie smile.

"Honest! He was *right here!* I swear—"

The Elderkin men looked at each other. Kristy's pretty face crinkled in bewilderment.

Try again, princess. "He was shot dead. I saw him." I pointed at the ground. "Right here!"

Kramer pushed back his Stetson, exposing a widow's peak of wiry auburn hair. Long sigh of frustration. Turning his back on me, he walked a small circle. "All right. Where is it?"

"The body!?" Uncertain grimace. "I don't know—"

"The *booze!*" Kramer shouted, facing me. "What'd you do with that bottle, gal?"

"Bottle!?" My eyes flashed in indignation. "I-I wasn't drinking—!"

"Really?" The deputy made a snaking motion with his hand. "Then how come that combine was fishtailin' all through the corn?"

"I swerved to get out of the line of fire!"

"Don't give me that horseshit." Snort of contemptuous disbelief. "Tell me the truth, gal. You were hittin' the ol' firewater, weren't you? You ran Josh's combine right into that ditch!"

"Excuse me for confusing you with the *facts*, Deputy!"

Kramer tucked away his notebook. "I'll have all the facts I need when I find that bottle."

"What about the broken window!?" I challenged.

"You hit the side of the ditch, didn't you?"

"I hit on one side only. *Both* windows are broken!"

Logic fazed him but only for a moment. His visceral hatred of indigenous people quickly conjured up a plausible explanation.

"Impact must've shaken loose the dump auger," he said, features tensing with anger. "It swung down and broke the other one."

My, it's amazing how prejudice warps the processes of the human mind. Most frightening of all, Kramer was beginning to believe his own pipe dream. In desperation, I turned to the Elderkins. "Will you please talk sense to this man?"

Laconic frown from Josh. "Comin' down kind o' hard on the girl, ain't you? That auger looked okay to me."

Brad took a step forward. "Come on, Kramer. Hear her out."

Shaking his head, the deputy unsnapped his handcuff case. "Fellas your age ought to have more sense than to get hitched up with them liberal social programs. Work Experience!" Deep guffaw. "You let Injuns off the reservation, and the first thing they're doin' is shakin' hands with John Barleycorn." Turning to me, he tilted his chin toward the Dodge. "Hands on the hood, gal. You know the routine."

Grim smile. So that's what this was all about. I opened my mouth to protest, then thought the better of it. No sense bucking the inevitable. Head bowed, I stepped forward and planted my palms on the truck's pitted surface.

"That's right," Kramer crooned, clicking the steel ring shut. "You do that right fine, gal. Then again, this ain't exactly the Debutante's Ball for you, is it?"

No argument from Angie. For once in his misbegotten life, the deputy was right. *It wasn't!*

TWO

"How do you pronounce this?" the honey-haired deputy asked.

Sprawled in an aged oak chair, I let out a weary sigh. "Biwa-ban. *Bih-wah-bahn.*" I cast an anxious look at the wall-mounted Western Electric clock. Twelve minutes past six. I wondered what time they fed the prisoners here at the Davison County sheriff's office.

Carefully she looked over my intake forms. I'd spent the last eighty minutes filling them out. Detailed questionnaires about my personal and medical histories, my involvement with the criminal justice system, and my term of service at the South Dakota Correctional Facility for Women at Springfield.

The deputy was in her middle twenties, with the posture and queenly bearing of a high school gymnast. Pretty Slavic features, slightly cleft chin, stern and businesslike emerald-tinted eyes. A generous bosom disturbed the fabric of her khaki uniform shirt. She'd probably heard more than her share of tiresome jokes in the squad room. The mammary swell aimed her shirt pockets at the ceiling. Pinned above the left pocket was a nameplate reading *Lambanek*.

"This one here?" She tapped her pencil against the page. Her small lipsticked mouth tried to shape the word. "A-ah-ah-nih—"

"*Ah-nish-ih-nah-bay*," I said. "It means *original people*. It's what we call ourselves."

Her forehead wrinkled in confusion. "Is-is that some kind of Sioux?"

I grinned. Better not let my ancestor, Kichiwaubishashe, hear that. He led the Noka, the Bear clan, against the Lakotas three hundred years ago, during the war for control of the Oshkebuge-zibi. The River of the New Leaves. These days, Rand McNally calls it the Minnesota River.

"Not quite," I replied. I hated to use the C-word, but I had no choice. "It's Chippewa."

Putting down the form, she said, "Well, why didn't you just write *Chippewa?*"

Somber Angie glance. "Tell me, what kind of name is Lambanek?"

She flashed me a guarded look. "It's Czech."

"Would you like it if I called you a *hunkie?*"

"Of course not!"

"Right. Because it's insulting," I replied, crossing my legs. "Like calling Italian people wops. That's how *we* feel about the word *Chippewa.*"

Unwilling to further discuss the issue, the deputy returned to her paperwork. Judging from the highly annoyed look on her face, this wasn't the moment to ask about supper. So I laced my fingers together, settled back in the roomy chair and looked around the sheriff's office.

It was about the size of a ranch house kitchen. Oaken furniture dating from the McKinley administration. Ten-year-old desktop computers. Plastered walls painted a sallow light green. Someone had put up a pair of colorful posters touting the Corn Palace. One youthful deputy manned the dispatch console. Across the room, my nemesis, Deputy Kramer, tentatively tapped out his arrest report with two uncertain index fingers.

I had already been through one round of indignities—booking, fingerprinting, strip-search, and breathalyzer test. There were two charges against me, malicious mischief and operating a farm vehicle under the influence of alcohol.

It would be interesting to see the results of that Breathalyzer test.

"Sign here." Deputy Lambanek rolled a pen across her surprisingly tidy desktop. She followed up with a thick pile of intake documents. "One signature on each form." Lacquered red fingernails tap-tapped her telephone. "Soon as you're done, you can make your phone call."

So I began signing, pondering the greatest of all mysteries. Namely, how did the new people ever get *Chippewa* out of *Anishinabe?*

One case of writer's cramp later, I dropped the pen and reached for the telephone receiver. My first impulse was to call my grandfather in Minnesota. Then I hesitated. My anxious gaze flitted toward the deputy's desk calendar.

Damn! I would have to get arrested this week. Right now Chief's closing up our cabin at Tettegouche. He might still be there. Then again, he might've already moved back to the Fond du Lac reservation. Fifty-fifty shot either way. If I guess wrong, there goes my one and only phone call.

If it was up to Chief, he'd live at Tettegouche all year round. But the family gets a little nervous about a seventy-five-year-old man living out there all by himself. One good Lake Superior blizzard, and he'd be snowbound for days.

Briefly I considered my parole officer. However, it was too late in the day to reach Paul. The Department of Corrections office closed at five.

That left me with one other option.

Disarming Angie smile. "Can I make a long-distance call?"

The deputy lifted her chin. "Where to?"

"Pine Ridge."

"Go ahead. But make it short."

My fingers tapped out the number. The speech center of my brain changed gears, shifting from English to Lakotiya. I had plenty to say, and I didn't want Kramer or Lambanek listening in.

Two rings, and a vaguely familiar female voice came on line. "Hello?"

"Hau, Ina Echam'namapeya!" I said, *"Jill tokiyaya he?"*

"Angie!" Mrs. Stormcloud's voice was a blend of surprise and regret. "You just missed her. Her date picked her up fifteen minutes ago. Where are you calling from?"

"Mitchell. The sheriff's office. I'm in trouble, Mother Stormcloud. Real trouble!"

"What's wrong, *winchinyona?*"

"There's this deputy. He's a real *oonzeh odoka.*" I sneaked a glance at Kramer. Oblivious to the insult, he kept right on typing. "I think he's related to Custer. He pulled me in on some bullshit charge. It's a roust, Mother Stormcloud, pure and simple. Grab a pencil and pad, would you?"

Paper rustled at the other end of the line. "Go ahead, Angie."

"Have Jill get in touch with my grandfather. If he's not at Tettegouche, try the Fond du Lac reservation in Minnesota." I rattled off the area code and number. "And get me a lawyer! I'm due to appear in District Court first thing tomorrow morning. If I don't have counsel, that deputy's going to ship my ass straight back to Springfield."

"Understood, *hokshayopa.* Do you want Jill to get in touch with your parole officer?"

"Don't bother, Mother Stormcloud. He'll get the word."

Doleful frown. No doubt there'd be a teletype from the Sheriff's Department sitting on Paul's blotter first thing in the morning.

"I'm calling Jill at the Cineplex right now. Don't you worry,

Angie. We'll get you out of there." I could feel the concern in her voice. "Take care of yourself."

Grinning, I replied, *"Lila pilamaya, Ina Echam'-namapeya. Wakan Tanka nici un."*

After I hung up, Deputy Lambanek ordered me out of the chair, seized my upper arm, and conducted me downstairs to the Depression-era cell block. Stale odors buffeted my face as we marched down the corridor. The stiff scent of ammonia predominated, but I could still detect traces of dried urine and alcoholic vomit.

"Here we are." Deputy Lambanek introduced me to my accommodations. The cell was five by five, with steel bars on three sides and a peeling cinderblock wall at the rear. Two fold-down steel-frame beds were chained to either side. Rolled-up mattress pads were tucked between the chain and the frame. There was a distinct lack of blankets. Even less inviting was the leaking porcelain toilet bowl in the right-rear corner.

Jangling of keys. Creaking of tired hinges. Tart feminine command of "Inside!" And the door clanged shut with a dreadful finality. The cell was slightly roomier than my old *personal space* at Springfield but nowhere near as pleasant as the Thunderbird Lodge.

Turning, I eyed the grim-faced deputy through the intervening bars. "Any chance of supper?"

Deep frown. The kind deputies reserve for people with prison records. "We don't offer room service, Miss Biwaban."

I was hungry enough, so I swallowed my pride. "I haven't had a bite to eat since five this morning."

Sympathy softened her features. Rehanging the keys on her belt, she murmured, "I'll see what I can do."

"Thank you." I wasn't being sarcastic. I already had one enemy in that sheriff's office. I didn't need to lock horns with the entire department. One thing I learned in the Big Dollhouse—you don't survive without friends among the guards.

I unrolled the mattress, patted it down, and then stretched out, using my forearm as a pillow. Long sigh of dismay. No telling how long I'd be a houseguest of Sheriff Fischer's, I thought, so I might as well get comfortable.

Staring at the ceiling, I thought about my good friend and former cellmate, Jill Stormcloud. Back at Springfield, we'd spent many an evening in hushed conversation. Discussing what women in prison usually talk about—their men and their mothers. When we finally exhausted those topics, we made a game of teaching each other our respective languages. Thanks to Jill, I could speak Lakotiya as fluently as anyone at Pine Ridge.

Sorry to ruin your evening, *amiga*. But I'm going to need your help if I'm to avoid a return engagement at the prison laundry.

Then I thought of Deputy Kramer. Sudden warpath scowl. Son of a bitch! I wonder how many ex-cons that bastard's put behind bars. Kind of a sloppy job at the crime scene, too. He didn't even try to search the area. He made a snap judgment and slapped the handcuffs on. Bet he's a political appointee. Probably has a relative on the county board.

Well, I was grateful to the deputy for one thing. My arrest had whisked me out of the danger zone. For the time being, I was safely out of the killer's gunsights. He wouldn't be able to reach me. Not in here.

Wry Angie smile. You've really done it this time, princess. You're the only witness to a murder in which the corpse has disappeared. The killer saw you at the scene. He knows that you know. Worse than that, he knows what you look like! And you didn't even get a glimpse of him.

Frosty paranoid shiver. Mister Beach Tan's killer could conceivably be anyone in Mitchell. Male, female . . .

Hmm, maybe we can scratch *female*. Mister Beach Tan tipped the scales at close to two hundred. I didn't know very many women who could lift that much weight on their own. Unless the killer was Rachel McLish. Which I doubted!

My forehead tensed in bewilderment. How did he do it? I wondered. How did he pull that vanishing act with the corpse?

Forcefully I redirected my thoughts. Pondering that would keep me awake all night. Crossing my legs at the ankle, I gazed at the peeling ceiling and wondered what Paul Holbrook would have to say about all this.

Good old Holbrook. If anybody could get Sheriff Fischer to take me seriously, my stalwart parole officer could.

Just then, I heard a clamor in the outer hallway. Swinging my legs off the bunk, I sat up straight. Into the cell block came a parade of civilians, men and women in rain gear and heavyweight jackets. Puzzled frown. Surely the sheriff didn't permit guided tours of the county jail!

Then I noticed the trio of somber deputies moving the column along. The lawmen segregated the group by gender and marched the men further down the hall. Into my cell block streamed the ladies—some of them alarmed, some of them angry, most of them highly excited—chattering at one another. The lead deputy had to holler to make himself heard. "Awright! Pair off! Two to a cell. Let's not take all night, ladies."

A couple of minutes later, the stern-featured deputy led one of the women to my cell. She was in her middle twenties, two or three inches taller than me, with short, ash-blond hair that looked as if it had been styled by Mr. Christophe, a pert nose, a slight overbite, elegantly trimmed eyelashes, and maybe a shade too much mascara. Silvery loop earrings dangled from her small delicate ears. Navy peacoat, snug indigo jeans, and a cream knit turtleneck that tickled her chin like a surgical neck brace.

"Hey, Biwaban!" The deputy's key rattled in the lock. "Got a roommate for you. Fresh fish!" The barred door swung open. "Better listen good, Sievert. She'll tell you what to expect when you get to Springfield."

As the woman stepped over the threshold, I heard a faint sharp smack. My roommate's mouth dropped open. Bluish gray eyes sparkled in rage. "Owww! Son of a—!"

Clang! The lock snapped shut. Gingerly touching the seat of her jeans, Ms. Sievert glared at the chuckling deputy.

"Friend of yours?" I asked, rising from my bunk.

She gave me a look. "Hardly!" Turning away from the door, she added, "His name's Linton. He comes into the bank all the time. Until tonight, he's been content to stare." Uncertain smile. Tentative extension of her long-fingered hand. "Uh, hi! I'm Julie Sievert."

Flashing a warm reassuring smile, I gave her hand a gentle shake. "You're a banker?"

"Teller, actually. At the Commercial Bank over on North Lawler." Rueful grimace. "That may change, though. Especially if Mr. Dillard sees the eleven o'clock news. And you?"

"Angie Biwaban. Apprentice farmer."

"Excuse me?"

"It's a long story." I was mightily intrigued by the campaign button on Julie's peacoat. Big white button with the letters SPSD. I tilted my head toward the other prisoners. "What's all this about?"

"We were holding a protest rally over in Mount Vernon," Julie explained, folding her arms. "Protesting that new transmission line Sam Covington wants to run through the county. About fifty of us showed up."

"You were arrested for trespassing?"

Julie nodded. "The sheriff busted us right after we put our group's stickers on the tower. He said that was vandalism."

"What was on the sticker?"

"Here, I'll show you."

Julie reached into her coat pocket and withdrew a bright orange plastic sticker. The face showed a transmission tower and the legend WARNING! THIS TOWER IS HAZARDOUS TO YOUR HEALTH.

"What does SPSD stand for?" I asked.

"Safe Power for South Dakota," she replied. "My boyfriend Scott started the group. He's a physics professor at Dakota Wesleyan." Curious look. "I don't think I've seen you around town. Where are you from?"

"Duluth, Minnesota. I was living in Pierre. I moved to Yorktown just last week."

The women in the adjoining cell came over to the bars. One of them gave me a long, searching look. She was a farm wife, aged thirty-five or thereabouts, with a round, sun-weathered face, curly dark brown hair and a slightly protruding lower lip. Recognition gleamed in her acorn brown eyes. "Hey, ain't you Josh Elderkin's hired girl?"

"That's right." Winsome Angie smile.

Julie formally introduced us. "Angie, this here's Brenda Traudt. Brenda, Angie Biwaban."

I recognized the last name. The Traudts owned a dairy farm a couple of miles north of the Elderkin place. Brenda was delighted to encounter a neighbor in these dismal surroundings. She fired a flurry of questions at me, inquiring about the health of Josh and Trudy and the kids and old Miss Edna, Trudy's widowed aunt.

". . . course, that pacemaker sure slowed Miss Edna down some," Brenda said. Reminiscence softened her blunt features. "She's had it ten years now, and she's still complainin'. She told me it was a damned inconvenience, havin' to change the setting every time she wanted to climb the stairs. Poor Miss Edna. She don't get around half as much as she used to. Sure is a damned shame. Well, at least she's got Trudy to look after her now." Sudden look of intense curiosity. "What are you doin' in here, Angie?"

"I'm sort of wondering the same thing myself, Mrs. Traudt."

"What's the charge?"

"Operating a combine under the influence of alcohol."

Brown-eyed look of keen appraisal. "Don't look drunk to me. And I know drunk. My daddy came home often enough smellin' of White Mule. Made it hisself. Had him a still in the cottonwoods down along the Jim."

"Who made the arrest?" asked Julie.

"Dan Kramer," I replied.

Brenda nodded as if that explained everything. "He's snake-mean, that Danny. Couple years behind me in school. Picked a fight one time with Joe Spotted Horse. Joe whipped his ass good. Hated Indians ever since. That's one ol' boy you'd better stay away from, Angie."

"Will do!" Still curious, I led us back to the original topic of conversation. "Why were you guys planting stickers on transmission towers?"

Julie exhaled deeply. "You're new around here. So I guess you haven't heard about the project."

"Project?" I echoed.

"The Southeast Hydroelectric Initiative Project. Otherwise known as SHIP."

Sour smile from Brenda. "Ought to stick a *T* on the end instead!"

"It's the brainchild of Owechahay Power," Julie added. "You've heard of them."

I had. Owechahay Power, OP for short, touted in numerous television commercials as "your energy friend," was one of the three largest electric companies in South Dakota. If ever you're in Sioux Falls, look for their lofty glassine skyscraper on Sixth Street. Can't miss it—there's a great big OP on the penthouse.

"Five years ago, the Corps of Engineers finished that new dam on the Missouri River. The Charles H. Burke Dam. OP won the contract for the hydroelectric station." Julie seated herself on the corner of my bunk. "Originally, the station was supposed to serve the Chamberlain/Oacoma area. There was supposed to be a lot of new development down there. An Indian casino, two new malls, large housing developments. Then the recession came along and . . . well, that was that. OP was stuck with plenty of leftover kilowatts, so they came up with SHIP." She made a long sweeping motion with her right hand. "They want to run a brand-new transmission line due east through Brule and Aurora counties, cut through the southwest corner of Davison County, and link up with the main line in Bridgewater."

"What for?" I asked. "There can't be more than eight hundred people in Bridgewater."

"Actually, there are less. Six hundred and fifty-three, according to the last census." Julie's mouth formed a distasteful moue. "It's the usual power company scam. They promise all kinds of pie-in-the-sky benefits. Give us right-of-way, and we'll run distribution lines off the main. Industry will be knocking on your door. There'll be hundreds of new construction jobs. Best of all, your rates will be coming down."

"Bullshit!" Derisive snort from Brenda. "Hens'll be layin' six-sided eggs the day electric rates come down!"

"If OP really wanted to lower their rates, they could do it in Oacoma. There's already a power surplus." Thoroughly agitated, Julie rose from the bunk. "But no . . . to maintain their all-important fee structure, they've petitioned the Department of Public Utilities to let them ship the surplus power across three counties!"

"Gonna run that damned high-power line across some of the most productive farmland in America!" Brenda's soft chin quivered in indignation.

"How far has the project gone?" I asked.

"Brule and Aurora approved the project last year. Owechahay Power's going all out to lay that transmission line. They've already reached the northern end of Yorktown." Frowning, Julie paced our cell. "Our county board hasn't voted yet. But we hear Sam Covington's been doing a lot of politicking behind the scenes."

"Who's Covington?"

"He's chairman of the Industrial Development Commission," Julie replied. "Owns the Middle Border Savings Bank right here in town."

Brenda grinned. "No shit on that man's shoes."

One hand on a vertical bar, Julie added, "Not only is the project unnecessary, Angie, it's a direct threat to Yorktown and every township in the south county."

I thought immediately of the Elderkins. "How so?"

Features tense with concern, Julie outlined an imaginary tower with her hands. "The project is building a 900-kilovolt transmission line. That's almost double the voltage carried by most power lines." She bit a corner of her lower lip. "Oh, I wish Scott were here to explain it. He's the physicist. You see, Angie, every power line generates an electromagnetic field. What we call an EMF. The hotter the power line, the larger the EMF field. The plain fact is, any electrical device you plug in and use creates an EMF force field. Low-frequency fields are considered harmless. But high-frequency EMF's, such as microwaves, can severely damage animal cells."

"What's the safety limit, Julie?"

"The EMF fields occurring in nature are a very weak 0.5 milligauss. The safety limit set by the EPA is 2 milligauss."

I leaned against the doorframe. "And beneath a high-voltage power line?"

Julie gave me a sickish look. "That's where the real hazard lies. Standing directly beneath a 500-kilovolt line, you're exposed to 100 to 600 milligauss. The field weakens the farther away from the line you move. That's why those high-tension towers all have a right-of-way measuring 100 yards. Beyond that point, EMF exposure falls to 20 milligauss." Tart look. "Which, by the way, is *still* ten times greater than the national safety limit. But OP won't talk about that!"

Just then, the matronly woman sharing Brenda's cell stepped up to the bars. "Don't you believe a word that company says, girl. Ben and I farmed twenty-five years up in Esmond. Had us a prize herd of black Angus." Her head tilted to the left. "There was one of them big high-voltage lines back of the north forty. Year after year, our calf losses were double our neighbors. Cows kept miscarryin'. We had a man come out from Pierre to test the water. Said it was just fine. Then we sent a letter to them Owechahay folks. They sent us this glossy color magazine tellin' how great they were!"

Unquenchable hurt filled the woman's face. Gripping the bars, she murmured, "B-Ben talked about goin' to see a lawyer. Never quite got around to it, though. Too much to do on a farm, I guess." Muffled sniffle. "Then one day he was carryin' a sack of feed into the barn, and he keeled right over. Just like that. He was dead by the time I reached him. He was five months shy of fifty. Doctor said he had a growth inside his brain. Little thing 'bout the size of a crabapple. Cancer. No tellin' how long it'd been in there." Her dark eyes turned savage. "I don't believe a word they say—that damned lyin' power company! I don't, girl, and neither should you!"

Bursting into tears, she turned away suddenly. Brenda put a comforting arm around her, steering the distraught woman toward a quiet corner of their cell. "Gonna be all right, Esther . . ."

I sensed Julie's gaze on me. Faced the younger woman once more. Her face was somber. "She lost him only last summer."

"And their farm?"

"Sold at auction. There was no way she could run it by herself. She's living here in town with her daughter now." Julie's voice lowered to a whisper. "There are a lot of scientists who'd agree with her. I know Scott would. He says health effects have been documented in EMF exposures greater than 5 milligauss. High-frequency fields hamper the body's immune system, allowing cancers to flourish. Swedish researchers have found a direct link between high-frequency EMF fields and leukemia in children." Her knuckles whitened as she clutched the bars. "There are 350,000 miles of transmission lines in this country, Angie. Too damned many of them run right past schools!"

As I opened my mouth to comment, Deputy Lambanek stepped up to our cell door. "Biwaban? I'm going off duty in a few minutes. I can pick you up something at Burger King."

"And something for Ms. Sievert, too?" I caught the leery expression in the deputy's eyes. Flashed my brightest Angie smile. "I'll pay you back first thing tomorrow morning."

She thought it over momentarily. "All right." Out came her back-pocket notebook. "What are you ladies having?"

As things turned out, I had the whole cell block to myself that night. Shortly after Julie and I consumed our Whoppers and medium Cokes, her boyfriend, Scott Hasner, arrived with the bail bondsman and freed all fifty-three jailed members of Safe Power for South Dakota. My new acquaintances trooped out in single file, squeezing my hands, wishing me luck, and promising to see me at our arraignments in the morning.

Promptly at ten, the overhead lights dimmed. I unzipped my parka, unbuttoned my blouse and, facing away from the door, dipped my fingers into the left cup of my brassiere. Retrieved the fifty-dollar bill I always keep hidden there. Emergency money. One President Grant in each cup. And, no, I didn't learn that trick at Springfield. I learned it from Aunt Della!

When the trustee made his rounds, I flashed the fifty and traded it for a pair of cream-colored Navy blankets. Then, removing my parka, I folded it twice, pressed it into a reasonably puffy pillow, and went to bed.

Snug and warm beneath my woolen Navy blankets, I stared at the darkened ceiling and wondered what kind of EMF force field a 900-kilovolt power line threw out.

Rough night! I remember only fragments of the night-mares. Miss Carlotta raising her meaty arm to slap. Elena's lascivious grin as she lifts her razor-sharp shank. Lunatic whistling of the insane pilot, mingled with the muted *chuff-sigh* of shoveled sand.

The final nightmare stayed vivid in my memory. Angie frantically climbing an impossibly tall transmission tower. Down there, in the darkness, the killer's feet pounded steel crossties in grim pursuit. *Tank-tank-tank!* And then, from above, the rush of displaced air. Looking up, I saw a man's limp body plunging toward me. I hugged the beams as he plummeted past, catching a fleeting glimpse of his placid face. It was Mister Beach Tan.

I awoke with a shudder, my mouth hot and dry. The sight of those jailhouse bars triggered a panic-stricken reaction. *Elena!* I looked every which way, ready to ward off that woman's assault. And then I realized this wasn't the Discipli-nary Unit in Billsburg. Shaking all over, I sat upright in bed. Shudder of relief. *County jail!*

Ten minutes later, a woman deputy came to fetch me. She let me wash up in the ladies' room, lent me a plastic hair-brush, and then marched me into the squad room. Breakfast was on the county. Scrambled eggs, two overdone sausages, a slice of rye toast, and a glass of tepid orange juice. Then, flanked by a husky male deputy, I was marched upstairs to the courtroom.

The corridor was rapidly filling with SPSD defendants. I spied Kramer, with his Stetson tucked under his arm, talking to a wire-haired man in a dark gray suit. All at once, I heard a familiar alto shout. "Angie!"

I turned, and there was Julie Sievert, dressed to the nines, weaving her way through the crowd. Just behind her was a tall, ruddy, sandy-haired man with brittle eyebrows the same shade as his thick hair, sky-blue eyes, a blunt nose, and a broad, friendly smile with just a hint of overbite. Tweed sportcoat with leather patches at the elbows, dress slacks, button-down shirt with light blue stripes and a navy-blue tie. At first glance, he reminded me of a coach in Pop Warner football. Then I noticed the SPSD button on his lapel.

"Angie, I want you to meet Scott." One look at the love-light in Julie's eyes, and I really didn't need the introduction. "Scott, this is the woman I was telling you about. Angie Biwa-ban."

"Hi!" He had a firm masculine handshake. "Julie tells me we might be able to interest you in a membership."

"You can skip the sales pitch, Scott." Oooooh, love that sexy smile! "I'm a longtime member of the Sierra Club."

"So how long will you be in the area?" Scott asked. "We can always use another environmentally aware volunteer—"

"Mr. Hasner?" A heavyset fortyish man, armed with a pen and a bent notebook, barged into our conversational circle. "My name's Tate. *Sioux Falls Argus-Leader.* How do your people intend to plead during this morning's proceedings?"

Facing the reporter, Scott said, "Innocent, of course."

"Are you still pursuing an injunction against Owechahay Power?"

"We have our court date, Mr. Tate. January eighth."

Scribbling away, Tate tossed his journalistic bomb. "Mr. Hasner, how do you justify taking construction jobs away from a rural county mired in recession?"

"For one thing, Mr. Tate, those are *temporary* jobs. They won't survive the construction of the power line." Scott's bari-tone voice tingled with suppressed anger. "Let's get some-thing straight right now. Our group is not opposed to economic development. Our name says it all—Safe Power for South Dakota. If OP wants to run that transmission line through Yorktown, let them put it underground. Burying power lines eliminates the danger of EMF exposure."

Other reporters joined us. I spotted a TV crew setting up on the fringes of the crowd and quietly slipped away. When you're wanted in three states, you tend to become extremely camera shy.

Leaning against the bulletin board, I watched the impromptu press conference. Scott made a very articulate spokesman. All at once, I heard a woman clear her throat behind me.

I turned. The newcomer was an elegant and slender lady whose age I pegged at thirty. She was a queenly five-feet-six, with a pert nose, a delicate chin, eyes sparkling like emeralds, and firm, full lips. Her hair glistened like cornsilk, curling inward at the collar. Styled sheepdog bangs, parted in the center, concealed her high intelligent forehead.

What really impressed me, though, was her outfit. I don't know where that woman did her clothes shopping, but it certainly wasn't South Dakota. She wore a tailored woolen suit in a smart shade of raspberry. Trim one-button blazer and hip-hugging slim skirt. Lace-trimmed white blouse with a big soft satin wing-tie. Taupe panty hose and Dutch chocolate high-heeled *peau de soie* pumps.

"Excuse me, young lady . . ." Smoky contralto voice. "Have you seen another Native woman here? She's a few years older than you. Her name's Angela Biwaban."

Crooked Angie smile. No makeup and my farmer togs made me look more adolescent than usual. Believe me, it's a mixed blessing. You don't know how many times I've been carded in Pierre.

"Look no further. Jill sent you?"

Emerald eyes widened in mild surprise. "Yes. I'm Sarah Sutton." Quick presentation of her business card. "From Jill's description, I expected someone . . . er, a little older."

"Don't worry—I am." Glancing at the card, I let out a hushed whistle. Hipple, Tanner, Page, and Sutton. Whoa! That is one high-powered law firm. They ought to have their own show. *Pierre Law.* And the lady was a full partner, too. I sure had plenty of questions for my friend Jill.

Snapping open her briefcase, Sarah shot me a no-nonsense look. "All right. Let's have it, Angela. What are you doing here?"

So I told Sarah Sutton all about the combine and the stray shot and finding Mister Beach Tan in that neighboring field, concluding with my arrest at the hands of Deputy Kramer. Sarah kept interrupting me with questions. She had many, many questions.

"The body was gone when you returned to the field?"

Curt nod from Angie.

"Are you certain he was dead? Did you actually touch the body?"

I clammed up at once. After all, I'd only met this woman five minutes ago. I didn't really trust her yet. Meaning that I wasn't about to admit to having tampered with a crime scene.

That could put a quick, decisive end to my parole!

"Welllll . . . he *looked* dead."

Sarah's mouth tensed in an arch smile. "I think the locals were having a little Halloween fun with you, Angela." Shuffling some legal-size papers, she added, "Did that deputy share the results of the Breathalyzer test with you?"

"No, ma'am."

"Hmm, interesting . . ."

While she studied the papers, a balding, heavyset man with a face like a fussy baby ambled through the crowd. Pudgy features lit up as he spotted my companion. "Sarah!"

Sarah flashed a truly dazzling smile. "Hello, Gabe."

"What brings you all the way down here?" he asked, tenderly squeezing her proffered hand. "This time of day, I'd figure you to be at the statehouse."

"Oh, just a favor for a former client." She tucked away the legal papers. "When are you and Emma coming up to Pierre? We've missed you at the club."

"Well, we've had the grandchildren at the farm every weekend. You know how it is."

She let out a muted chuckle. "Not quite." Looping her arm around Gabe's, she walked him into the vacant courtroom. "Listen, could I see you in your chambers for a moment? A situation has come up, and I really think we ought to talk about it."

And away they went, leaving me stranded in that crowded corridor. I shook my head slowly. That settles it, Jill Stormcloud. You and I definitely have to talk!

The courtroom was a spacious chamber with an arched ceiling, a pair of sunburst windows behind the gallery, and a high tooled oak judge's bench. Flanking it on either side were upright-aluminum poles displaying Old Glory and the South Dakota state flag. A paneled door on the right led to the judge's chambers.

I picked out a seat in the packed gallery. As I was making myself comfortable, the wire-haired man I'd seen earlier appeared at the judge's doorway. Pointing at me, he said something. His words melted into the gallery's conversational hubbub. Frowning, he made an impatient gesture of invitation with his hand.

Entering the cozy oak-trimmed judge's chamber, I saw Gabe behind the desk, resplendent in judicial black, with a shaken, white-faced Deputy Kramer at his side. Standing demurely in front of the desk, holding her briefcase like an oversized purse, was Sarah Sutton.

"Angela, you'll be pleased to know that Deputy Kramer has offered to drop both charges." Dimples enhanced her smile. "We just had a little chat about proper police procedure, and everything's been settled."

Judging from the snarl on Kramer's face, I sincerely doubted that. He stood at attention, still holding the Stetson at his side, tight-lipped and fuming. I watched the ruddy color rise from his khaki shirt collar.

Just then, the wire-haired man appeared at the doorway. "Mrs. Sutton? You have a phone call. Your office in Pierre."

"Thanks, Oscar." Turning to me, she smiled. "Don't go away, kiddo. I want to talk to you." Ladylike smile at the judge. "Back in a minute, Gabe."

The moment the door closed, Kramer let out a gasp of fury, slamming his hat on the desk. "Goddamn it all to hell, Judge! Are you gonna sit there and let that fancy-assed blonde wipe her shoes on me!?"

"Sure looks that way, Danny." Leaning back in his swivel chair, the judge shook his head ruefully. "I've seen trips to the woodshed before, but yours was surely a classic."

Kramer's face turned the color of the Elderkin combine. "You're gonna let that gal come into *my* county and—!"

"Danny," Judge Carlson interrupted, "I'm going to explain this so even a dumb shitkicker like you can understand it. That there is Mrs. Sarah Sutton. When she isn't shaking hands at the statehouse, she represents Fairmont Foods. Name ring a bell? It should. That name's on an awful lot of grain elevators between here and Aberdeen. Company owns supermarkets from Columbus, Ohio to Casper, Wyoming. Plus a whole bunch of corporate farms here in South Dakota. Why, if you set those Fairmont farms side by side, you'd have a spread as big as New Jersey. And that big ranch out in the West River—the Bar-F-Bar—that's a Fairmont operation, too. Makes the old Diamond A look like a feed pen." His grin broadened. "So if Mrs. Sutton comes down here and says she's of a mind to tear the hide off one of my deputies, I'm going to let her. I'm too damned old to hunt up a new job."

"I don't have to take her shit!"

"No, you don't. Fact is, you can put that badge on my desk right now, go on home and start packing a suitcase. See if they're hiring in Nebraska." He cast a solemn-eyed glance at the deputy. "Come on, Dan. You were in the wrong, and you know it. You had no call to go slapping the cuffs on this well-mannered young Indian lady. Cal's warned you about that sort of thing, boy." He leaned forward, leveling a blunt forefinger. "I'm going to give you some free advice. You'd better hope Sarah walks out of here today and forgets all about you. Next time you lock horns with that lady, you'd better start reading bus schedules. Because you're all through working in South Dakota!"

Kramer's gritted teeth barely contained his inarticulate rage. Grabbing his Stetson, he tore out of the office. I winced at the door slam. Judge Carlson rose majestically from his chair, then aimed a meaningful scowl at me.

"You going to behave yourself in my county, young lady?"

Solemn Angie smile. "Absolutely, Your Honor."

"See that you do." He shepherded me to the door. "And you'd better get that smirk off your face. Your turn in the woodshed's coming right up. Sarah wasn't exactly impressed with your record."

My smile wilted. "Well, you see, Your Honor, since my release, I've been having these adjustment problems—"

"You picked the right lawyer then, Miss Angie. Believe me, Sarah thrives on attitude adjustment."

There's just one problem, Judge, I thought, leaving the crowded courtroom. I didn't pick her! Oh, Jill, what have you gotten me into?

The last thing I needed right now was representation by some pushy lady lawyer. La Sutton was one of those take-charge women. She wouldn't rest until she'd poked her pert nose into every intimate corner of my life. And that could be extremely hazardous to my continued freedom. Under assumed names, I was wanted for sundry felonies in three states. How could I be sure Sarah wouldn't turn me in?

The lady in question strolled out of the Clerk of Courts office, leather briefcase in the crook of her arm. Mild tilt of her soft chin. "Let's take a walk, Angela."

Ambling away from the courtroom, we halted beside the water cooler. Sarah set her briefcase on the old-time wooden bench, then confronted me, planting her hand on my shoulder.

"Jill didn't tell me you were a *Bobbi Jo*."

I blinked. The lady was awfully familiar with Springfield slang. A *Bobbi Jo* is an inmate of the Disciplinary Unit in Billsburg. Which is where you go when you misbehave at Springfield. The slang comes from one of our nicknames for the place—*Petticoat Junction*. Me, I always called it *Miss Carlotta's School for Girls*.

"Judge Carlson told me." Sarah's features tensed in annoyance. "That was a surprise. I don't like surprises when I represent a client. How long were you in Mrs. Calder's custody?"

Fussbudget face. "Too long!"

"Angela!"

"Sixteen months."

"You had a very unsatisfactory record at Springfield."

Smiling, I raised my forefinger. "But excellent S.A.T.s!"

Her eyelids closed in frustration. "Now, look! I don't take many criminal clients. But those I do take I expect a lot from. Ask Jill. When a girl signs on with me, the first thing she does is straighten up and fly right. And if she thinks she can waltz *me* around the ballroom floor . . . well, she'll find herself back in the Springfield laundry so fast, her foolish little head will spin!" Lips turning upward in a superior smile, she added, "Now that we understand each other, Miss Biwaban, let's hear your story, eh? The embezzlement—did you do it?"

"Hold on, lady! I haven't signed on for anything." I pushed her hand off my shoulder. "Thanks for springing me. I'll mail you the fee. In the meantime, why don't you go chase an ambulance back to Pierre?"

Sarah's lips parted in indignation. But before she could properly vent her feelings, I heard a familiar baritone voice.

"So there you are!"

I whirled at once. *"Kemo Sabe!"*

Standing at the edge of the stairs was my parole officer and part-time hemorrhoid—Paul Holbrook.

As parole officers go, Paul's not that bad looking. He's quite tall, well over the six-foot mark, with curly, wheat-colored hair, low, thick eyebrows and a pair of warm, friendly chestnut-colored eyes. His face is a tad on the lengthy side, with a strong jawline—the kind associated with the RCMP. Sergeant Preston, that is, not Yukon King.

"Hi, Angie . . ." All at once, Paul's gaze drifted past me, and those humorous brown eyes gleamed suddenly. "Sarah!"

"Hello, Paul."

Gone was Take-Charge Sutton. In her place stood this soft-voiced blonde flashing a butter-wouldn't-melt-in-my-mouth expression. She spread her arms in invitation. Rooted to the spot, I watched my parole officer scoot right past and gather that woman into a sedate bear hug. Clenched my teeth as she playfully kissed the corner of Paul's mouth.

Holding her at arm's length, Paul said, "Been awhile, hasn't it? I didn't know you were back in criminal practice."

"I'm not. I took this case at the behest of a former client." Her arms remained draped around Paul's neck. "Tell me, are you still with the Department?"

He nodded. "Uh-huh. Langston took over for old man Robb."

Tightening the knot of his tie, she smiled coyly. "You should've gotten that job, Paul."

"You know me, Sarah. I'm no administrator. I'm a field man. Always have been, always will be."

"Same old Paul. You're looking remarkably fit."

His grin found me. "Angie keeps me hopping."

Emerald eyes zeroed in on me. Her subtle smile hinted at retribution for past Angie impertinence. "Your client, eh?" Feminine fingertips smoothed the lapel of his herringbone blazer. "You know, Paul, we really ought to get together sometime. Why don't you call me when you get back to Pierre?" Catlike glance at me. "Now that we're both working with young Angela, we really ought to sit down and think through a positive program of rehabilitation."

Young Angela!? Obsidian eyes glittered furiously.

"That's not a bad idea, Sarah."

She knew just when to release her grip. "Then call. You can leave a message with our receptionist."

With that, she stalked off, briefcase wedged beneath her arm, tall heels rapping the oakwood floor. Paul's trailing gaze never wavered. Male lips pursed in thoughtful reminiscence.

Coming up beside him, I gave Paul's hip a vigorous nudge. Instantly he glanced my way.

"Hanes," I muttered.

"What!?"

"Silk Reflections." Innocent Angie look. "The way you were staring at her panty hose, I just figured you wanted to know."

Pink colored the tips of his ears. "I was *not* staring."

"Yes, you were, Holbrook. Don't deny it." Frosty glower. "Let's face it . . . she's an attractive woman. For her *age!* Those Swiss plastic surgeons did a marvelous job on her face-lift, don't you think? To say nothing of the liposuction on her rear end—"

"An-ge-la!"

"Of course, she still needs that girdle—"

"Enough, princess."

"More than enough!" I snapped. "You ought to see yourself, *Kemo Sabe*, standing there with steam coming out of your ears! Dis-grace-ful!"

He tried hard not to smile. "You said it yourself. She's a very attractive woman."

"Well, don't get too hot and bothered, Holbrook. I hear there's a *Mister* Sutton."

"Past tense, Angie. There used to be."

My head swiveled instantly. "You know quite a bit about that woman, don't you?"

Ignoring the jibe, Paul gently grabbed my upper arm and led me down the hallway. "Don't you have a court appearance this morning, Miss Biwaban?"

"Not anymore, Holbrook."

Curious gaze. "What do you mean?"

"Slinky-dink La Sutton got the charges dropped." Seeing his look of unbelief, I added, "Don't believe me? Well, ask Judge Carlson. You can't miss him." Reaching up, I tweaked Paul's chin. "He's got a lipstick smudge just like yours!"

Paul's ears turned redder. His thumb scoured the point of impact. "All right. We'll try the clerk's office."

"No wonder she's such a successful lawyer. So long as she keeps her lipstick loaded—!"

"Angieeeee!" Stopping short, he fired an exasperated glance at me. "Are we going to listen to this all the way back to the farm?"

"No. Just until you tell me where you know that peroxide blonde from!"

Exhaling in exasperation, Paul counted off on his long, sinewy fingers. "One, that is none of your business. Two, Sarah is *not* a peroxide blonde."

Outraged gasp. "How do *you* know?"

THREE

The spat petered out on our way back to the farm. Try as I might, I couldn't goad Paul into telling me about his past relationship with Sarah Sutton. Oh, I knew a lot about him. That he was born in Huron and grew up on a farm outside of Iroquois. That he'd gone into the Marine Corps just after high school. A Panamanian hand grenade had ended Sergeant Holbrook's military career, sending him home with veteran's disability benefits and turning him into a Department of Corrections parole officer.

However, when it came to the topic of La Sutton—Paul's firm masculine lips sealed right up.

Paul proved to be a far better listener. I told him all about the shooting, and he wasn't quite as ready as Sarah to dismiss it as a Halloween prank. He promised to speak to Sheriff Fischer personally and advised me to remain on the farm.

"You'll be safer there than in town, Angie," he told me. "Stay out of sight and keep out of trouble. I'll ask the Highway Patrol to search that field. In the meantime, if anything happens—*anything at all*—give me a call in Pierre, and I'll have you placed in protective custody. Okay?"

I nodded. But I wasn't so sure I liked that last part. Protective custody. That could mean being confined to quarters in the Dunning House. Or even worse—the minimum-security wing at Springfield. Distasteful frown. I'd had quite enough of cold steel bars the previous night in Mitchell.

As I entered the barn, I saw Josh, Brad, and Kristy guiding Herefords into their milking stalls. All three Elderkins looked up in surprise.

"Angie!" Kristy slammed her gate shut. "How did it go at the courthouse?"

Brad cracked a smile. "The Prodigal Farmhand returns."

"If you're expectin' a fatted calf, gal, you'd better lend a hand at the feed bin." Even Josh's normally dour expression reflected an air of amusement.

I relaxed. After all, I hadn't known how the family would react. They'd only known me for seven days. At least they were willing to hear my side of it.

Kristy hurried right over. "What happened, Angie? Did you have a trial? Did Judge Carlson—?"

Josh cut right in. "Kris, you'd better get the rest o' them cows in here."

Teenaged disappointment. "Daddy!"

"You can hear it all at supper, gal. Go on now." Josh made a shooing motion with his hand. Then he glanced my way. "You got somethin' you want to say, Angie?"

I cleared my throat. "Uh, Josh, about the combine . . ."

"Funny you should bring that up." He hung an empty aluminum pail on a wall peg. "Brad and me—we must've tromped all over that field yesterday afternoon." Ironic sidelong smile. "You know, we never did find that whiskey bottle Kramer was yellin' about."

"Me, I don't think it exists outside of that Danny Kramer's imagination." Brad dumped a pailful of grain into the feed trough. "Dad and I just want you to know, Angie. When you go to trial, we'll be in your corner. We're willing to testify that you weren't drunk."

"Thanks, fellas." How nice to know that Kramer's roust hadn't altered the way they looked at me. "But it won't be necessary. Kramer offered to drop the charges."

"He what!?" Josh squinted in disbelief. "You'd better run that one by us again, Angie gal."

So I gave the Elderkin men a *Reader's Digest* version of the deputy's encounter with Slinky-dink. When I finished, Brad let out a chuckle. "I guess Danny got his fingers burned that time." His handsome face turned serious. "My fault, Angie. I should have warned you about him. Kramer really has it in for Indians. Thinks that badge of his gives him the right to shove them around."

Of course, I'd heard the exact same thing from Mrs. Traudt. It sounded as if Deputy Kramer didn't have too many fans here in Yorktown. "I'm surprised he's still packing a badge."

"Don't be." Josh scowled, lifting a feed sack. "His uncle's on the sewer commission. Real tight with the sheriff."

"Is Kramer a local boy?" I asked.

Nodding, Josh replied, "Mitchell born and raised. Had a good record in the Army, I hear. No taste for farmin', though. When he came back, he wanted one o' them NHL jobs."

"NHL?" I echoed.

Brad grinned. "No Heavy Lifting."

Supper was waiting by the time we returned to the house. Trudy put out quite a feast. Sort of a welcome-home banquet for the Prodigal Farmhand. Ribs, rice pilaf, corn bread muffins, and simmering potato soup. Believe me, it was quite a change from the bill of fare at the Davison County jail.

Afterward, Josh and Brad huddled around the home computer to see if their current cash balance would cover the costs of on-site combine repair. Jer got on the phone and dickered with the parts supplier in Sioux Falls. I followed the Eld-erkin women into the parlor.

The TV was on, but other than Jer's wife, Carol, no one was paying any attention to it. Not even Kristy, who lay prone on the floor, scanning her algebra book, periodically tossing anxious glances at the telephone. Judging from her expression, Jeremy was inadvertently impeding an important Friday night phone call. While Trudy and Ronnie worked on their needlepoint, I lounged in the La-Z-Boy and read the *Daily Republic*.

All at once, a blaring police siren captured my attention. Carol's compulsive channel-clicking had picked up *America's Most Wanted*. Ignoring the proceedings on-screen, I turned the page and studied the clothing ads for Geyerman's. Mmm-nice selection of slit skirts. Suddenly, John Walsh's mellow voice cut into my consciousness.

"Working alone and on his own time, Deputy T.P. Braddock solved both murder cases. It was Braddock's greatest triumph, and it was also his last. The heroic deputy was killed by the murderer during their final confrontation at Dynamite Pass."

Hands shaking, I lowered the newspaper. The TV showed an oil portrait of my one-time acquaintance, Ty Braddock, hanging in what looked like the Utah statehouse. Spotlights gave Ty's face a saintly aura he had never had in life.

"This week, in Salt Lake City, the governor proudly unveiled Braddock's portrait, the latest addition to the Roll of Honor, the roster of all Utah lawmen killed in the line of duty."

Tayaa! I gaped at the screen. Braddock in the Roll of Honor!? Give me a break!

Of course, I had only myself to blame. I was the one who had originally given Ty credit for catching my cousin's killer—a falsehood necessary to facilitate my escape from the Beehive State. I could have taken credit, sure. And then the whole story would have come out, and right now I'd be sorting laundry at the Utah state women's prison.

The necessity for falsehood didn't make it any easier to accept. Frown of amused indignation. Ty Braddock winds up on the Roll of Honor, and I end up on the dodge. There's just *no* justice!

Indignation gave way to alarm as I suddenly realized what was coming next.

"The FBI is still looking for the woman who called herself *Sara Soyazhe.*" Mr. Walsh reappeared in the bustling hot line studio. "Her real name is unknown, but she is believed to be an American Indian in her twenties. The Bureau has given her the code name *Pocahontas . . .*"

I tasted potato soup at the back of my throat. On-screen, to the left of Mr. Walsh, appeared a disturbingly accurate, full-blown sketch of Chief's favorite granddaughter.

"Pocahontas was sighted last month in the state of Washington. If you've seen this woman, please—" *Click!*

All at once, I found myself being roared at by the MGM lion. Quickly my gaze shifted to Carol. "Why'd you switch?"

"I *hate* those cop shows," Carol said, nestling into the plush cushions of the couch. "Besides, it's Romance Week on AMC."

"Yeah?" Ronnie looked up from her sewing, peering at her sister-in-law over the rims of her glasses. "What's on?"

"*Gigi.* My all-time favorite."

Bless you, Leslie Caron! I thought.

Shaky-kneed, I rose from the easy chair. The damp blouse clung to my shoulder blades. As I headed for the kitchen, Trudy shot me an inquisitive glance.

"Angie! Aren't you going to watch it?"

Pausing at the doorway, I shook my head. "I thought I'd get an early start on those dishes."

"Need some help?" Trudy asked, putting her quilt aside.

"Unh-uh." Pert Angie smile. "Relax and enjoy your movie. I can handle it."

Washing and towel-drying the Elderkin dinnerware gave my badly jangled nerves a chance to settle. That artist's sketch had really given me a turn. I wondered how many people back home in Duluth had been amazed by the remarkable resemblance to Angie Biwaban. Wondered, too, if my grandfather had seen it. Perhaps I ought to try again to get in touch with Chief.

Just then, I became aware of another presence in the kitchen. Glancing over my shoulder, I saw Miss Edna clutching her trusty walker. She wore a belted terry robe over her nightgown. Stray tendrils of fine white hair nestled against her deep-wrinkled forehead.

Tilting her small head toward the parlor, she asked, "You know him?"

Shaking hands folded the dampened dish towel. "Know who?"

"That Utah deputy." Miss Edna flashed a canny smile. "Nothing wrong with my eyes, girl. Just my ears that are wearing out." Aged blue eyes gleamed with curiosity. "I was watching from in here. You tensed right up when you saw his picture."

Somehow I forced myself to remain nonchalant. "I remember the case. My Aunt Della told me about it. She lives in Utah."

Edna seemed to accept my explanation. She asked me for a glass of water, and I ran one under the tap for her.

As I handed it over, she thanked me, then inquired, "How long were you in that prison, Angie?"

I stared in surprise. Oh, well, Trudy had warned me about her aunt's outspokenness. Finishing her sip, Miss Edna shot me a crisp look. "When you reach my age, young lady, you'll find there ain't much time left for beating around the bush." She put the glass on the Formica counter. "So what were you in for?"

"Embezzlement." Sighing, I leaned against the kitchen table. "I used to work for the Tax Assessor's office in a little town out in the Black Hills. I needed some money to pay for my mother's cancer operation. So I, uh, sort of yielded to temptation."

Her small hand touched my forearm. "You had no other choice?"

Memories brought a sorrowful tickle to my throat. I shook my head, adding, "It was a very tricky operation. The only man who could do it was this bright Belgian neurosurgeon, and he wanted his money up front. Mother had no health insurance. It was all up to me." Brittle smile. "So I took money from the accounts and crunched numbers to cover the losses, figuring to pay them back over time. Then I got caught, and the judge sentenced me to five years in Springfield."

"And your mama?"

"She died." Tears teetered at the brink of my lashes. "It-It happened just before I made parole."

Miss Edna's hands brushed my face. They felt like velvety mittens filled with sticks. Aged features softened in sympathy. "You put it behind you, you hear? You did your time, and it's over. Don't you let it weigh you down. Hold up your head, girl. You finish this here parole and find yourself a good man and get on with your life. Twenty years from now, no one's even going to *remember* you were in the pen, much less give a damn."

My smile turned arch. "The state of South Dakota has a long memory, Mrs. Mutchler."

"Fiddlesticks!" Blue eyes flashed fire. "Who gives a damn what's in some file drawer somewhere? Folks have short memories, Angie. You're not the only girl who ever made a foolish choice when she was young. Believe me, there's no shortage of respectable East River ladies now collecting the Social Security who'd surely like to forget a certain lively Saturday night forty or fifty years ago. Five years and they'll forget all about it. And don't you give me that look, young lady. I know what I'm talking about."

She said it with such firm conviction that I was almost tempted to ask how she came by such knowledge. But before I could do so, she lifted her small cleft chin and nodded in the direction of her first-floor bedroom.

"Now that you've had most of the day off, young Angie, do you think I could prevail on you to do my hair? Normally, I'd ask the boys' wives. But Ronnie's all thumbs, and that Carol stands around afterward, acting as if I'm supposed to put cash money in her palm." Her smile widened. "Mostly, though, I like the way you do it. You've got good hands, girl."

"Mrs. Mutchler," I said, gesturing at the bathroom doorway. "It would be a pleasure."

So I got out the Prell and gave the lady's baby-fine white hair a gentle shampoo. Following a quick session with the blow dryer, I escorted her into her bedroom, got out the carton of plastic curlers, seated her on the bed, and set to work.

Floral-patterned wallpaper covered the bedroom walls. A stained oak baseboard circled the room. There was a bit too much furniture for the room, all of it from Miss Edna's old farmhouse. Trudy had told me that her aunt had brought it with her when she'd moved in with the Elderkins. Queen-size polished oak bed with a panel headboard. A matching nightstand with two bronze drawer handles. Chateau-style grandfather clock in bright cherry wood. And a very valuable antique three-piece chest of drawers with a tall, slim, middle mirror.

Four black-and-white photographs stood on display atop the nightstand. I recognized a much-younger Edna as the farm wife in one of them. Another showed a well-to-do couple in front of the Corn Palace a generation earlier. So I gave voice to my curiosity.

"My parents," she told me. "Frank and Jane Enright. My mother was a McCabe."

Carefully I twisted a lock of hair around the spool. I gathered that *McCabe* was a great name in Mitchell.

"It was the railroad that finally decided the location of the town. That was in 1879," she told me. "The Chicago, Milwaukee, and Saint Paul sent a party to survey the area. Grandfather McCabe was with them. You see, Angie, the original settlement, Firesteel, was much closer to the river. While they were surveying that site, Grandfather McCabe found a piece of driftwood. 'This site will never do,' he said, 'If the river flooded it once, it will do so again.' So they moved the town a couple of miles west and renamed it Mitchell. In honor of Mr. Alexander Mitchell, the president of the railroad. Now, the Enrights—they arrived in the spring of 1880. Very late in the spring! There was a terrible blizzard that year. The town was snowbound for sixteen weeks."

"Are you shitting me!? Sixteen weeks . . . whoops!"

The plastic curler popped out of my grasp like a runaway bar of soap. It bounced once on the quilted coverlet, then plummeted to the floor.

"I'll get it." I rounded the foot of the bed, then knelt on the dark shag rug. Reaching for the curler, I spied a modern addition to the lady's Edwardian bedroom—a cable TV outlet set right into the baseboard. A shiny coppery metal plug filled the coaxial cable's circular aperture.

Rising from my knees, I asked, "What happened to your TV, Mrs. Mutchler?"

Her veined hand waved impatiently. "Oh, I told Josh to get rid of it. There's nothing on, anyway. The only show I ever liked was *Our Miss Brooks*." Fond smile. "Reminded me of my days at Mitchell High during the war. Mr. Graham got drafted, and the school committee asked me to fill in for him." She raised her chin slightly, allowing me to continue. "Besides, I don't mind watching television in the parlor. It does me good to be up and about. I have no desire to spend my life in bed, dear. Not at my age." Wry sidelong smile. "I'll be flat on my back soon enough."

Unable to resist temptation, I teased, "Got a new boyfriend?"

Her reverberant laughter spilled into the kitchen. For a moment, I panicked, remembering Miss Edna's pacemaker. Fortunately, she weathered the mirthful outburst without going into cardiac arrest. And she was still wearing her broad, silly grin when Trudy showed up to say good night.

Saturday dawned cold, crisp and clear, heralded by a persistent wind. The temperature had dropped overnight, turning the drizzle into a mild snowfall. Patches of damp snow littered the shorn cornfield when we arrived.

No trouble spotting the big Case combine. Just follow Angie's panicky zigzag trail through the ripe corn. The huge red machine stood several yards east of the shelterbelt, tilting nose-down in the runoff ditch.

Following a very bumpy ride across the stalk-strewn field, Josh parked beside the ditch, and the three of us continued on foot. The wind plastered my evergreen mountain parka against my front side. The chill ate right through those flannel-lined khaki twill trousers Trudy had given me.

Clad alike in bulky coveralls, corduroy seed caps, and heavy-duty work gloves, Josh and Brad seemed oblivious to the wind. As for me, however, I was mightily glad to be wearing my worsted-woolen ski cap and my black leather gloves. To say nothing of my Anishinabe knee-high moosehide moccasin boots. I'd made them myself, using Grandma Blackbear's patterns, during a snowbound college break at Tettegouche. They're as impervious to water as the Rocky Mountain dipper. Good thing, too. After two days of drizzle and an overnight snow, the cornfield was about as firm as tapioca pudding.

Plodding through the mire, Josh voiced similar thoughts. "Guess we got us some time to get the combine fixed."

"That's for sure," Brad said, studying the yellowish brown cornstalks. "Gonna need at least four days for the fields to dry."

"You'd better hope them snows stay in Wyoming, boy."

"Don't sweat it, Dad. There's plenty of November left."

The combine's picker head pitched downward, with the mammoth front tire down in the ditch. Josh crouched and examined the steel snouts and chain-driven snappers for collision damage. Meanwhile, I climbed the stepladder, past the sporty black-and-white *Case International* racing stripe, and knelt on the cab porch. Scowled at the jagged remnants of windowpane. Shattered glass from both windows littered the interior. Country Bull's cassette lay on the floor, right where I'd dropped it. A chill that had nothing to do with the prairie wind rippled through me. A close call, indeed!

Brad's work-roughened hands touched my shoulders. "Sorry, gal. I know you want to help, but there's only one seat in that cab."

So I rejoined Josh on the ground, and together we watched as Brad fired up the 260-horsepower engine. First there was an ear-throbbing roar, then a puff of light gray smoke. Then the picker head rose with a sharp hydraulic hiss, the engine thundered, and the giant Goodyear farm tires began to turn.

Brad rocked the combine back and forth. Drive wheels kicked up a shower of snow and mud. And then, nimble as a mountain goat, the combine lurched out of the ditch and rolled backward through the corn stubble. Sudden twinge of Angie jealousy. Brad made it look so easy.

Just then, Josh and I heard the crescendoing growl of an approaching pickup. My peripheral vision picked up a dull red

Jeep Cherokee bouncing through the ruts. Broken cornstalks vanished beneath its black bumper. It pulled up a short distance away. The door's stylized legend read,

DOUG'S FIX-IT
MITCHELL, SD

The driver was a heavyset Caucasian in his early sixties. He reminded me of a potato—solid, durable, and slowly turning brown. He wore a rugged denim work jacket with a corduroy collar, matching bib overalls, and a charcoal chamois work shirt. Sun-wrinkled features and broad, knuckly hands clearly identified him as a farmer. But his hairstyle was more suited to an aging Hollywood star. His hair was a lush silvery-gray. A neatly combed widow's peak tended to exaggerate the receding hairline above his large, flat ears. He had kind of a rugged, square face, with a Churchillian nose, high cheekbones, thin lips, and a noticeable shelf of jaw. Warm country smile. "Howdy, Josh."

" 'Lo, Doug." My employer brushed the mud from his knees, then stood erect. "What brings you out so early in the morning?"

"Oh, I stopped by Darla's an hour back. Heard you boys was havin' combine troubles." He shook hands with Josh, then had a closer look at the mud-caked snouts. A pained expression crossed his weathered face. "Ouch! Who did that?"

Chuckling, Brad hopped down from the stepladder and ruffled my woolen cap. "Angie's just getting her learner's permit."

Doug laughed. "Gal, you ain't supposed to go plowin' in a combine."

I took no umbrage at their good-natured teasing. "I guess that was Lesson Number One, Mister—?"

"Krause. Doug Krause." And he offered me his hand.

"Doug, this here's Angie Biwaban," Josh said, flashing a

rarely seen smile. "She's staying up at the house with us for a spell."

"Pleasure, miss." Doug's hand was surprisingly gentle. Knicks and scabs around the knuckles hinted at a career repairing farm machinery. "Where are you from? Fort Thompson?"

It was a natural mistake. Fort Thompson was the closest Lakota reservation. Smiling, I shook my head. "Duluth, Minnesota."

Gesturing at the silent combine, Josh said, "If you're hankerin' for some mornin' work, Doug, grab your toolbox. I'd like a quick look at the rotary and the auger."

"You got it, Josh."

The handyman flipped open the Cherokee's rear hatch, then extracted a toolbox the size of a tabletop refrigerator. Brad took one end, and together they hauled it over to the combine, faces reddening in exertion. After Doug set it on the ground, the reason for their strain became apparent. As the lid came up, seven gadget-strewn drawers slid forward. There must have been *three hundred* tools in there—sockets, pliers, ratchets, wire strippers, wrenches, spinner handles, and extension bars. The weight equivalent of five Angies.

Returning to the cab, Brad fired up the engine again, then carefully lowered the picker head to the ground. Twin metallic clangs, and the locking bolts disengaged. Slowly the combine backed away from its derelict head, exposing the rotary—the whirling steel tube that carries the corn into the machine's innards.

As soon as Brad shut down, Josh and Doug approached the rotary, pliers in hand, and began the examination. I managed to remain an interested observer for about ten minutes. Then my gaze began drifting toward Enemy Creek and the murder scene. Pleading Mother Nature, I moseyed into the upright corn, then angled off toward the creek.

Keeping my head down, I padded through the switchgrass

at the edge of the field, zigzagged between the brittle branches of the prairie thorn and hackberry shrubs, and slipped into the silver-maple grove.

Thanks to the recent rain, Enemy Creek was up, but I managed to span it with a running leap. Dessicated pasque-flower stalks and black Samson snatched at my moccasin boots. I halted in the shadows of the burr oak, carefully scanning the harvested field.

Keen Anishinabe eyes sought the telltale traces of yesterday's passage. Oh, the mob scene was easy to spot. And Kramer's paratrooper boots had left footprints that filled with meltwater like miniature ponds. But I found only one or two of my own dainty work-boot tracks. If not for those splintered stems of milkweed, I might have spent *days* trying to locate the actual spot.

Squatting on my haunches, I scanned the muddy ground. Damp snow littered the field like a plague of freckles. I yielded to a pronounced fussbudget face. Not good, princess! By now, the melting snow must have washed away any remaining traces of Mister Beach Tan's blood.

Lifting a milkweed twig, I gave it an impatient snap. Almost wished it was Deputy Kramer's neck.

Congratulations, deputy! I fumed. Thanks to your monumental incompetence, someone in this county just might have gotten away with murder.

Uttering a mild sigh, I stood erect. Might as well hop to it. One point in my favor, though. If the killer had moved Mister Beach Tan, then he couldn't have carried him very far. Nobody—not even Arnold Schwarzenegger!—is going to lug one hundred and ninety pounds of deadweight for any length of time. The body had to have been stashed nearby.

I found the spot where our impromptu posse had burst through. Patiently my gaze surveyed the autumn vegetation, seeking telltale clues. Nothing!

So I doubled back to the murder scene and headed north. My gaze flitted from the brown switchgrass to the wind-stirred blazing star to the serviceberry branches, already picked clean by the raccoons and the porcupines. I've been reading trail sign since I crawled out of my cradleboard. Truthfully, though, I really ought to give credit to my superlative teachers—Daddy and Chief. My grandfather is something of a legend on Superior's north shore. They say he could track a blackfly from Duluth to the Pigeon River!

Strolling about seventy feet downrange, I spotted a large serviceberry bush off to my right. The sight gave me pause. Interesting! They look mighty feeble for such mature plants. Time for a closer inspection, princess.

Wading through the tall switchgrass, I noticed that their top-tier twigs were missing most of their leaves. And no wonder! Their main stems had been snapped. When a plant dies, uppermost leaves are the first to fall.

Tossing the crude camouflage aside, I smiled grimly at the sight of the matted-down grass. A thread fluttered from a serviceberry twig like a miniature pennant. I plucked it free, rolled it between my fingertips, and then held it up to the sunlight.

Navy woolen thread, its color identical to Mister Beach Tan's suit jacket. It had caught on the stem when the killer dumped the body in there.

Crouching Anishinabe-style, I rested my chin on my upraised knees and scrutinized the sodden ground. And there it was—a man's footprint. Size ten or eleven, maybe. Looked like some kind of work boot. Very vague tread marks. The recent heavy rains had rendered them unidentifiable. Deep toe impression. Hardly any imprint of a boot heel. The man was running.

Graceful as a whitetail, I stood and moved slowly across the field. Melting snow veiled the nearest tracks, but I picked up a matching pair just beyond. Skirt the great big mud puddle. And, yes, here he is again, still running, heading straight for that burr oak shelterbelt on the other side of the field.

Now I had enough to reconstruct the killer's movements. He had a car concealed in the grove, and he returned there right after the shooting. Maybe he had to make an important phone call or something. Boy, he sure must have *jumped* when he looked back and saw me crouched beside Mister Beach Tan's body!

So he waited for me to enter the woods and then came tearing after me, very much intent upon silencing the sole eyewitness to the crime. But I eluded him in there, and that made him panicky. So he returned to the body, picked it up and toted it a dozen yards up the field. Dump it, conceal it with some hastily snapped bushes, and run like hell for the car.

I made a fussbudget face. The killer's actions just didn't make sense. Why go to all that trouble to conceal the body? He must have known I'd be returning with the sheriff. It didn't really matter how well he'd hidden it. A detailed police search would have turned it up.

Why didn't the killer simply run for it?

And why the need for *temporary* concealment? Obviously, the killer had never intended for that to be Mr. Beach Tan's final resting place. He'd planned to return for it later. The camouflage shrubbery was merely designed to shield the body from our posse's prying eyes.

Thanks to that lunkhead Kramer, the killer had had ample time to find a more secure hiding place for the victim. Hmm, now there's an interesting question. Did the killer return for Mister Beach Tan's remains? Or did he send an accomplice while he was busy firming up an alibi?

Listening to the rustle of leafless branches, I slipped into the narrow shelterbelt grove. The trail of running footsteps came to an abrupt end at a muddy country road.

Suddenly, my heart leaped. Etched into the shoulder's moist clay was the tread of a four-ply tire!

Instantly I dropped to my knees. Well, now! If I could identify that tread mark, I just might be able to learn the make and model of the killer's car.

Dismay smothered my chuckle of delight. There was no mistaking those checkerboard indentations. A Goodyear Wrangler, I mused, a favorite truck tire of off-road drivers. The killer had driven some kind of 4 by 4 pickup.

Boy, that's a big help. Pickups must be the favorite form of transportation here in the East River!

Scowling in frustration, I hiked back to the creek.

Ten minutes later, I found the Elderkins and Doug Krause sliding the rotary back onto its steel housing. As he turned the spinner wrench, Josh grumbled, "Girl, if you were lookin' for an outhouse, I could've told you." He tilted his head southward. "Nearest privy's three miles yonder."

"Sorry." Sheepish Angie smile. "I had to hunt a bit for some adequate cover."

Brad smiled. "Won't find much this time of year."

The machinery settled into its housing with a grinding thump. Doug snapped the retaining bolts shut. "Okay, that ought to do it." He wiped his greasy hands on a tattered cloth. "When we get her back, you'd better let me grind those chain sprockets. File down the auger teeth, too."

Arching his back, the patriarch grimaced. "Doug, my last name ain't Rockefeller."

"Hell, Josh, you know I'd never pad a repair bill." The handyman assumed an air of wounded friendship. "One job, one price. That's the way I've always done business."

"I think we're more concerned with how long this job is going to take," Brad said, handing the older man his wrench.

"Four days."

"Cut it down to three, and you've got a deal," Josh said,

shaking hands. "We've got to be ready to cut soon's that field dries."

My wandering gaze traveled from the combine to Doug's Jeep Cherokee. Hastily I scanned the white lettering on his right tires. Michelin RoadHandlers. One pickup down. Another fifty thousand to go!

Josh's friendly nudge brought me out of my reverie. Nodding at our truck, he added, "Let's head home, Angie."

After lunch, the men returned to the fields, and I helped Trudy clear the dishes. Edna sat at the lengthy dining-room table, a cable-knit wrap about her thin shoulders, drinking coffee with Trudy's older brother, Clement Mutchler. He'd stopped by for some hot food on his way to town.

Every time I encountered Clem, I had to smile. Trudy's brother bore an uncanny resemblance to the late, unlamented Ayatollah Khomeini. Take the Ayatollah and shave off the mustache and the flowing beard ... change the eyes from dark brown to pale blue ... paste on a pair of jug-handle ears ... ditch the turban and caftan and plunk him into a seed cap and soiled denim overalls, and you'd have a dead ringer for Trudy's brother. Bristling eyebrows and prominent nose and a narrow chin. Tall and cadaverous, with lanky, loose-jointed arms and legs. The cuffs rode high, exposing his skinny ankles and woolen tube socks. He looked as if a strong wind would knock him over. But I'd seen that man shoulder a hundred-pound hay bale as effortlessly as I lift my purse.

As Trudy and I were putting down a fresh checkerboard tablecloth, Miss Edna flashed us a curious look. "I thought Carol was stopping by today."

Smoothing the linen, Trudy smiled. "She phoned the first thing this morning, Aunt Edna. They changed the day for her aerobics class."

"Aerobics!" With a snort of distaste, Edna put her cup and

saucer on the table. "If she's looking for exercise, why doesn't she clean that house?"

Wincing, Trudy replaced the slim glass centerpiece. Her rueful gaze found mine.

Adjusting her glasses, Miss Edna remarked, "You're too forgiving, dear. Some folks ain't ever going to change. You ought to know that."

"Good Book says we shouldn't ought to judge anyone," Trudy replied, showing a fond smile.

"Could be." Edna looked up sharply. "But that don't mean I'm going to let Sam Covington pass the plate in church."

Putting down his empty cup, Clem chuckled. "It'd sure be a damned sight lighter by the time it got to the vestry."

My ears perked at once. I remembered what Julie Sievert had told me about Mr. Covington.

Lifting the coffeepot, I sidled into their conversation. "Done much business with him, Mrs. Mutchler?"

"Not if I can help it." She gave me an imperious nod. Quickly I refilled her cup.

"I'm not sure I understand." I put the pot back on its ceramic baseboard.

Clem grunted. "Covington could slide down a wood screw like a banister. No trouble at all."

"He's been after me to sell that land Daddy left me along the Jim." Miss Edna paused for a brief sip. "Close to four thousand acres in all. Couple of working farms down near Ethan." She flashed a wry smile. "No way a woman my age could farm it, so I've been renting to a young couple just married and starting out."

Clem's eyes brightened in reminiscence. "Aunt Edna, you remember the time Sam's daddy ran that silo?"

"I surely do!" Vehement ladylike nod. "That's who he gets it from—old Phil!"

Seeing my perplexed expression, Clem explained, "I'm tellin' you, Angie. Phil Covington was as crooked as a dog's hind leg. Used to keep a great big Frigidaire right next to the silo." Sly country wink. "Bet you can't guess why."

Anishinabe shrug. "You've got me, Clem. Why?"

" 'Cause that's where he kept the *rats!*" He chortled so violently the straight-backed chair creaked aloud. "Big ol' barnyard rats! That bastard had a freezer *full* of 'em. He'd see a farmer comin'. And then, once the weighin' bin was full—soon as the farmer's back was turned—he'd reach in and grab a dead rat and toss it in with the grain!" Sudden gritty smile. " 'Course, soon's his rake turned up that rat, he'd pull this sorrowful face and tell the farmer, 'Got to come down some on the price, hoss. Rats been at it.' Sure enough, he'd cut ten percent right off the wholesale. I *never* knowed that son of a bitch to play square with a farmer!"

"Clem!" Trudy's plump face showed irritation. "You watch your mouth!"

"Dammit, Trudy, I heard that story from Lars Hansen's own lips. He ain't told a lie all his life, and what is he? Pushin' on ninety?" Knowing glance. "Don't think old Lars wasn't surprised when he found that frozen-stiff rat in his corn right smack dab in the middle of August!" Eyebrows bristling, he glanced at the antique cuckoo clock. "Well, I guess I'd better hit the road, Sis." His gaze drifted toward the parlor. "You finished that afghan for Bonnie yet?"

Trudy's fingers flew to her lips. "Lord, I've had that hanging around since Sunday. Things have been so hectic . . ." Embarrassed smile. "I don't know when I'm going to get it over there."

"I'd take it, but I'm headed in the wrong direction." Reaching the coatrack with several long-legged strides, Clem grabbed his sheepskin jacket. "Want me to give her a call?"

"I'll do it," I offered, smoothing my corduroy jeans.

"Bless you." Trudy cast me a warm thankful smile. "And you won't even need your car. Bonnie's farm is over yonder."

Her hand drifted toward the northeast. "Touches ours kitty-corner. You can ride Chatelaine."

"Are you sure Kristy won't mind?" I asked.

"Positive." Arch smile from Miss Edna. "Mainly 'cause *you'll* be leadin' the cows in on your way back."

Rueful Angie grimace. Ahhh, life on the farm! Where the chores just keep on coming!

Chatelaine was a four-year-old buckskin mare with high, delicate ears, lean thoroughbred legs, and a night-dark mane and tail. She seemed a little skittish when I first put the saddle on her. So I took the trailing rein and walked her out into the back forty, letting her get used to the unfamiliar scent of Angie. Some carrots, a gentle nose rub, and some whispered endearments completed the process of fraternization. She stood perfectly still as I swung into the saddle. And then, with a low-pitched whinny of impatience, she set off at a brisk canter.

We reached the Elderkins' back fence fifteen minutes later. Judging from the way Chatelaine strained at the bit, I had a sneaking suspicion Kristy had been training for the horse show out here. Three times I nudged the buckskin into a spirited gallop, and, at the end of each run, Chatelaine pawed the pasture turf, eager for more. She cast speculative glances at that tall wire fence. That was one whim, however, I refused to indulge. So we trotted the length of it and at last came to the aluminum-bar gate linking our homestead with Bonnie's farm.

From conversations around the dinner table, I knew that Bonnie Dietz was the baby of the Mutchler clan. She'd made her first appearance in the maternity room when Clem and Trudy were in high school. She was in her late thirties, had been divorced for a few years, and worked as an R.N. at the Methodist Hospital in Mitchell.

Tall bluestem brushed the stirrups as I prodded Chatelaine across the field. Scandinavian-style circular haystacks predominated. I heard the sharp flutter of wings, turned quickly and saw a ring-necked pheasant taking to the air. Ahead stood the Dietz farmhouse, a white two-story bungalow with dark green shutters and a large Queen Anne back porch. Stark, aging willows flanked either side of the house. Off to the right loomed a century-old red barn and a modern aluminum-capped silo.

Chatelaine whickered as I tugged on the reins. Swinging one leg over the pommel, I slid off the saddle and looped the long rein around the handle of a rusty water pump. Took one step in the direction of the house. And then the harsh sound of shattering ceramics stung my ears.

Of course, it could have been a case of butterfingers on Bonnie's part, but I didn't think so. Trudy had told me that her baby sister lived alone on the farm. And there were two cars parked beside the house. One of them had Iowa plates.

I had a feeling the lady's visitor might not appreciate a total stranger knocking on her back door, so I decided to make my visit a tad more formal. As I headed for the front porch, however, I heard a muffled sound through the window. A sound that raised the fine hairs on my neck. A woman's desperate weeping.

Concerned frown. What was going on in there?

Yielding to curiosity, I eased up against the shingled farmhouse wall, put one moccasin boot on the cellar windowsill, and gave myself a boost. Nose to the glass, I peered into a small empty sitting room. The inside doorway showed me a narrow view of the kitchen. A short, slender woman in farm clothes sat at the round table, sobbing and sniffling. She wore her brownish blond hair in a utilitarian wedge. Dabbing at the tear trails, she glanced anxiously toward the front porch.

Now, there's a clue I should have heeded. But I was too busy wondering what the trouble was. And why that poor woman looked so frightened.

I didn't really catch on until I heard the harsh triumphant

laugh to my left. My head instantly swiveled, and I caught a fleeting glimpse of a sneering, light-haired, horse-faced man gleefully swinging an automatic pistol.

Whonk! I ducked at the last second, but the steel barrel tagged me upside the occipital bone. Fireworks turned my field of vision into a Lucasfilm special-effects extravaganza. Down I went in truly absurd slow motion, my consciousness sinking into a dreamlike mist.

Next thing I knew, I found myself facedown on the cold, damp grass, blinking and moaning, my nose a few inches from a man's Fieldmaster work boot. Somewhere, far above my head, a demented tenor voice shrieked, "Bitch! Caught you, didn't I? Caught you snoopin' around! She sent for you, didn't she? Admit it!"

Still too stunned to move, I let him rant and rave.

"How long you been snoopin' around, Injun gal, eh? How long? Answer me!"

Uttering a snarl of displeasure, he gripped my parka shoulder and threw me onto my back. The sudden violent motion intensified my raging headache. Another soft Anishinabe groan.

"You better start talkin', gal!"

My vision swam back into full focus. The chuckling looney-tune loomed over me, his pistol poised and ready. His tongue furtively caressed his chapped lower lip. Hickory brown eyes radiated a gleam of sheer insanity.

"Talk sweet to ol' Delbert, sugar." His sick, merciless chuckle turned my bloodstream to ice. "Or forever hold your peace!"

FOUR

One glance at that Taurus automatic pistol turned me into a chatterbox.

"I-I wasn't snooping. Honest!" Timid Angie smile. "I came to return Mrs. Dietz's afghan. I heard the crash, and I thought somebody was hurt."

The nine-millimeter Brazilian pistol hovered an inch from my nose. Horse Face glowered at me. "How'd she get word to you?"

"Beg pardon?"

"How'd she tell her kin I was here?" he demanded. "You lyin' Injun! Doc Semple sent you, didn't he!?"

Puzzled glance. *"Who?"*

"Get up, you little—!"

Grabbing a fistful of parka, Horse Face hauled me to my wobbly feet, then slammed me against the house. The Taurus's cold steel barrel nuzzled the back of my ear. His dreadful tenor voice rasped, *"Move!"*

With his bony hand on my collar, and the Taurus prodding my skull, I stumbled into the front yard. Horse Face marched me up the porch stairs, panting like a hound dog on a raccoon hunt. With his free hand, he opened the front door, then shoved me across the threshold.

The parlor's decor was unmistakably feminine. Lace antimacassars on the upholstered furniture. Tasteful watercolor landscape paintings. Handmade hooked throw rugs. I heard a drumroll of soft footsteps, followed by a frightened gasp.

Standing in the dining-room doorway was the distraught blond woman I'd been earlier. She was a slender five-foot-five, with Trudy's soft chin and pale blue eyes. Long-sleeved velour blouse and snug blue jeans. Expression of sudden alarm.

"Delbert, no!"

Unzipping his jacket, Horse Face chuckled. "Didn't work out the way you figured, did it, bitch?"

"Delbert . . . you don't want to hurt her." Hands lifted in supplication, she padded forward. "She-She's no threat to you. Please let her go."

"First you tell me how you did it, Bon." Giving me another shove, Delbert leveled the gun at her. "How'd you get word over to your sister's place?"

"But I didn't—!"

"And who is this squaw, anyway?" His palm swatted the back of my head.

Bonnie Dietz gave me a long, hapless look. "I . . . I . . . I don't *know*."

"She told me your sister sent her." He poked my collarbone with the gun muzzle.

"With the afghan." Accommodating smile. "Remember?"

Bonnie's face registered confusion. Well, I could hardly blame her. With this lunatic rampaging through the house, it was awfully difficult to keep your mind on embroidery.

"She doesn't know you!" Delbert spat, raising the pistol high. "You lyin' little squaw!"

One love tap with the Taurus's barrel was quite enough. So I backpedaled away from him, bumping my calves against the cherry wood coffee table. "Look! Check the saddlebag if you don't believe me—"

"That son of a bitch Semple sent you here, didn't he?" Insane anger darkened his narrow features. "You *followed* me here from Iowa!"

I raised my hands like a good little hostage. "Uhhhm—I'm afraid you have it all wrong, mister."

"Son of a bitch sent you to *spy* on me!" he roared. "You followed me from the hospital. You're that nurse on the night shift . . . what's her name!?"

"Delbert," I said, my voice low and nonthreatening. "Look, I'm not a nurse. I hate bedpans. The afghan is in my saddlebag. Bonnie gave it to Trudy awhile ago. *Capisce?*"

Distrust filled his expression. I could make no dent in the twisted logic of the insane. Bonnie didn't know me—ergo, I was automatically a hospital spy. Nervously I eyed the Taurus. His index finger rested lightly on the trigger.

"Sure, I seen you around. Handin' out all them pills. You got all them poor crazies buffaloed. Not me, though. I ain't lettin' Doc Semple mess with my head." Spittle flecked the corners of his mouth. "No fuckin' way!"

Sitting on the couch, Bonnie murmured, "Delbert, you're supposed to be taking your prescription."

"That's how Doc Semple's erasin' my memory!"

Bonnie's blue eyes filled with tears. "You know how you get when you don't take your medication."

"Medication time! Medication time!" His insane bellow sent a fearful chill through my bloodstream. "You like them damn pills so much, Bonnie, you take 'em!"

"I only want what's best for you—"

"Yeah!?" he thundered. "Then why'd you stick me in that mental hospital? Ain't nothing wrong with my head. Why'd you sign them damned papers?" Crossing the parlor with bold quick strides, he seized a fistful of Bonnie's hair. "I thought I could *trust* you! You're my *wife!* But you're just like all the rest. You were plottin' with *them* all along! Who'd you sell me out to? Who?"

Bonnie buried her face in her hands and wept. I had the queasy feeling this wasn't the first such argument in the Dietz household.

"It's that son of a bitch Fischer, ain't it?" Pistol at the ready, Delbert hurried to the window. "He's been after me since I was a kid. Blamin' me for Holly Larsen! Fischer and all them damn cops! Raggin' on me. Just itchin' for me to make the wrong move. And they think I don't know who's behind 'em." Uttering a shaky laugh, he took a paranoid look around. "I know! I had nothin' to do with that little girl. Dammit, Bonnie, you know that. How could you sell me out to that son of a bitch?" The Taurus quivered in his hyperactive grip. "I'll bet you know who it is, don't you, Bon? Yes, you do! And now you're gonna tell me . . ."

Bonnie sobbed in despair. I shuddered at the maniacal expression on his narrow face. I had a pretty good idea what he intended to do, and I couldn't let it happen. So . . .

"Leave her alone, shitbird!" Penitentiary Angela.

Delbert stopped short, reacting instinctively to my prison voice. He must have heard the same tone many times from those hospital attendants. Hickory eyes flickered in fury, and he turned the pistol in my direction.

"What did you call me!?"

"You've got ears, you demented asshole." Sitting stock-still, I fixed my gaze on the knuckles of his pistol hand. My moccasin soles pressed the floor. Calf muscles tightened, ready to spring the instant his trigger finger twitched.

Well, at least I'd diverted his attention away from Bonnie. Now, if I could just live through the next two minutes . . .

Scowling, Delbert took an ominous step forward.

Jutting my chin toward the window, I inquired, "Are you expecting company, Dietz?"

Instantly Delbert's gaze flitted to the window. Thin lips tightened anxiously. "Maybe." He jabbed the pistol at me. "What do you know about that?"

Boy, talk about paranoia. I lifted both shoulders in an insouciant shrug. "Not a thing."

"You're lyin'!" His scowl deepened. "I saw him! I saw that man who was followin' me. It ain't the first time I've been followed by enemies, y'know. I know when I'm bein' tailed." Sidelong frown. "Who is he?"

Major dilemma! How do I play *Twenty Questions* with a lunatic? No matter how I replied, he'd probably disbelieve me. Even worse, he might express his displeasure with a gunshot.

I needed to buy time. Time enough for the family to get worried and call the sheriff. And what better currency to make that purchase than the paranoid's own strange fantasies?

Nervous Angie glance. Very easy to concoct, given the circumstances. Awkward stammer. "I-I-I don't know what you're talking about."

Delbert's eyes flashed in sudden comprehension. "He's the one who sent you here, isn't he?"

I fired a quick glance at the door, as if I expected someone's imminent arrival. "Look, you're crazy. I never—"

Rushing across the room, Dietz seized my shoulder and slammed me against the couch. The pistol muzzle grated my cheek.

Grabbing his arm, Bonnie cried, "No! Delbert, no!"

"Talk!" Shouldering his ex-wife aside, he pushed me deeper into the cushion. "Who is he? Why'd he send you here?"

Now that I had Delbert's full attention, I fed him my impromptu tale. Grimacing at the pistol's painful prod, I stammered, "I-I don't know! H-Honest! Guy came up to me in . . ." *Tayaa!* Quick, princess, think of an Iowa city. ". . . Fort Dodge! Big guy! Blond hair. Looked kind of like that guy on TV—John Goodman. Gave me four hundred bucks. Told me to keep an eye on Delbert Dietz." Panicky blink. "I-I've got nothing against you, man. The suit offered me a scan job. Half up front, half when I see him again."

"What about the other one!?" he yelled.

Other one? My imagination kicked into overdrive. "I-I didn't talk to him. He s-stayed in the car. Out of sight, you know? He didn't want to be seen. I only dealt with Mr. Sutton."

He shot Bonnie a feral grin. "Afghan, huh? I *knew* she was a spy!"

It was a strange experience to see the fervid belief in those mad, hickory-colored eyes. I had just confirmed his deepest fears.

"How?" he asked breathlessly. "How'd they find me?"

"Easy!" Another step into Delbert's World. "Your teeth have metal fillings, don't they?"

Jackpot! A weird understanding glimmered in Delbert's eyes. I kept right on feeding his paranoia.

"Sutton said something about a beam. Bouncing it off the the satellite. It's a weak signal, but . . ." My gaze shifted to the window. "Well, they must have a transmitter in the silo. With a whip antenna, I'll bet they could reach—"

Muttering incomprehensible curses, Delbert released me and galloped to the front door. "Don't you move, Bonnie!"

The crashing door punctuated the threat. Four gunshots resounded in quick succession, and I knew he was firing at the lightning rod atop the silo.

"Come on!" Rising from the couch, I grabbed Bonnie's wrist and hauled her along. Perfect diversion! But we had to move fast. Even a lunatic won't stay conned for very long. "Where's the telephone?"

"I-In the k-kitchen!" Bonnie sobbed.

Within ten seconds, we zipped over the threshold. Dutch doors—great! I slammed both halves, turned the lockbolts, and, for good measure, rolled the heavy Amish milk jug against the paneled bottom door. Bonnie made a beeline to the wall-mounted telephone. As she frantically tapped out 911, I grabbed one of the straight-backed chairs and jammed it beneath the antique sycamore doorknob.

"Lorna? . . . Bonnie Dietz." Wracked by terrified sobbing, she managed to gasp. "Send help! D-Delbert's h-here, and he-he-he's got a gun!"

My desperate gaze circled the kitchen. Four-piece walnut dinette set. Tall green refrigerator. Twenty-year-old gas stove. Formica-topped counter and lacquered knotty pine cupboards. Not much in the way of cover, especially if Delbert decided to shoot through the tall windows on either side of the refrigerator.

Think like a lunatic, princess!

Hmm, Delbert's going to be royally honked when he realizes I've tricked him. Meaning he'll be much too furious to play it cute. He'll try the direct approach. Kick in the door.

My gaze raked the countertop, seeking a weapon. Then I spied the large Mason jar Bonnie used as a flour bin.

Grabbing the jar, I ducked beneath the horizon of countertop. Crouched with my shoulder to the wood. Heart hammering like a tickertape, I loosened the jar's brass cap and waited.

Bumff! Delbert's first kick rocked the bottom door on its hinges. The milk jug toppled. "Come out of there, you two!"

Hefting the weighty jar, I swallowed hard. And wondered if Delbert had ever had to defend his *personal space* against inmate marauders. He might know this trick.

The second kick warped the wood. Chair legs shrieked as they scraped the floor. Another frenzied kick. The lockbolt bent sharply. *BUMFF!* The bottom door sprang open, knocking the chair aside, littering the floor with wood splinters.

"Goddamned little squaw! I'm gonna—!"

I heaved the jar with a short, sharp motion. Just like bailing out a leaky canoe. Ten pounds of fine white flour splashed his face, caking the eyes and nostrils, turning him the color of Bonnie's stove. Gasping and coughing, he shot upright ... and thumped his spine on the upper Dutch door.

With his pain-filled roar ringing in my ears, I threw myself on his gun hand. He had forearm muscles like telephone cables. Grabbing his wrist, I slammed it repeatedly against the stove. The Taurus slipped from his numb fingers, clattering to the floor. Rage deepened his pained bellow. With a single fluid sweep of his bruised arm, he hurled me away.

Airborne Angie! Twisting in midflight, I let myself go limp and came down hard on Bonnie's dinette table. It shuddered under the weight of my hundred and five pounds. My flailing legs dislodged the lazy Susan. Delbert came charging across the kitchen, features warped with fury, a white-faced refugee from Monstervision. Knuckly hands gripped the front of my parka, yanking me off the table.

Lifting both arms, I slithered downward—right out of my bulky parka. Dropped into a crouch, planted both moccasin soles firmly on the floor, then launched myself like a human torpedo. The top of my head scored a direct hit on Delbert's lower abdomen. Groaning in agony, he did a Humpty Dumpty backflop.

My knees struck linoleum. Scrabbling to the left, I spotted Delbert's pistol and dove for it. My clawing hand fell short. Male fingers clutched my corduroy-clad legs, and then I was sliding backward—away from the gun!

Shrill dismayed gasp. Panicky glance over my shoulder. Delbert's flour-caked face promised no mercy. Gripping my belt, he muttered, "Come here, you!"

Survival instincts rushed to the fore. Planting both palms on the floor, I did a quickie gymnast routine. Bend at the waist, draw my knees to my chest, kick like a Missouri mule! My soles left matching footprints on Delbert's flour-covered face. He plunged backward again, both hands flapping. We both reached our knees at the same instant. I was too far away from the pistol, so I grabbed the next best thing—the Mason jar.

Fingers clutching the rim, I let fly with a roundhouse right. Flour particles left a faint white contrail.

Whonk! I expected the jar to shatter when it collided with his skull. It didn't! Instead, it ricocheted, throwing me way off balance. I wound up flat on my back beside the counter. My arm tingled from the impact.

By then, however, Delbert Dietz was no longer a threat. He lay in a circle of flour dust, mouth open, limp and lifeless. For a split second, I thought I'd killed him. And then I heard the still sound of his comatose breathing. A shiny goose egg sprouted two inches above his ear, slowly turning crimson.

Exhaling in relief, I glanced at the Mason jar. A flour starburst marked the point of impact. The glass wasn't even cracked. Sour smile. Another television myth disposed of!

First to reach the scene was a cruiser from the South Dakota Highway Patrol. It came racing up Bonnie's long, dirt road, dust streaming from all four tires, the proud vanguard of the law-enforcement parade, which included three county cruisers, a Black Mariah, and a hummer manned by the Mitchell P.D. SWAT team.

And so, I spent the next two hours on the front porch, huddled in my parka, answering questions for a pair of tall, brawny, earnest troopers. Trudy Elderkin arrived with the sheriff midway through my Q & A session. She threaded her way through the throng, then gathered her sobbing sister into a comforting embrace.

No sooner had I finished with the troopers than the sheriff's men appeared with Delbert in tow. They'd let him clean up a bit at the sink. Flour still caked his clothing, though. Holding a damp facecloth against his lump, he shot me a vengeful look. A grim-faced deputy grabbed his collar and gave him a rude shove. "Pick up the pace, perp!"

All at once, I felt the weight of a hostile glance. Turning to the right, I spotted Deputy Dan Kramer glaring at me. As he slammed the cruiser's rear door behind Dietz, I hoped he'd forego the comments and cart Delbert off to the slammer.

Of course, that was just too much to hope for.

"Might have known I'd find *you* here." Kramer's eyes were hard and baleful beneath the Stetson brim. His tongue made a clucking sound of disapproval. "You just can't seem to stay out of trouble, Indian."

Ladylike Angie smile. "And I try so hard, too."

"What were you doing here?"

"Returning Mrs. Dietz's afghan." I tilted my head toward the barn. "I rode over from the Elderkin place."

Scowling, Kramer backed me right up against the porch railing. He was so close I could count the shaving nicks on his chin. His icy smile looked as if it had been set in concrete.

"Maybe you ought to get that fancy-ass lawyer down here again." Kramer's voice was a vile whisper. "Let's see that blonde get you off this time."

Warpath scowl. "You charging me, Kramer?"

"I'm considering it." Once again, his hand came to rest on the Smith & Wesson's butt. "That's some dent you put on that ol' boy's head."

"Friend of yours?"

"Everybody in the department knows about Delbert." Fond memories warmed his chilly smile. "Old lady must've dropped him on his noggin one time too many. Always was kind of a fruitcake." Making a fist, he gently touched me beneath the chin. "Ought to be more concerned 'bout yourself, Angie gal. An A and B charge'll put you right back in Pussy-land."

"Assuming the case ever gets to court."

Dull blue eyes gleamed hatefully. "You know, it'd almost be worth bustin' your ass just to get that shyster gal back here. No fancy-ass blonde's gonna come sashayin' into *my* county and tear strips offa me! And no goddamn little Indian squaw's gonna stand there and smirk about it, either!" Squaring his shoulders, he took a step back. "That blonde is nice and safe up in Pierre. *But you ain't!*" His index finger stabbed at my nose. "Before you leave this here county, Miss Angie, you're gonna be awful damned sorry you made that phone call!"

Kramer descended the porch steps, handcuffs jingling on his gun belt. I watched him climb into the cruiser. Rueful grimace. Thank you, Mrs. Sutton! That take-charge approach of yours may have kept me out of the slam, but it's left me with a bad enemy. The deputy was a small-minded man with a big, fragile ego. *And* a .357 Magnum! Definitely a bad combination!

As I descended the porch steps, a gravelly male voice called out, "Rein up, gal."

Turning, I spied a heavyset, sixtyish man in a heather-gray woolen suit ambling across the lawn. He was just under six feet tall, with a weathered Teutonic face, crisp blue eyes, a small thin-lipped mouth, and a noticeable double chin. His ample tummy nearly split the seams of his leather vest. Definitely an aficionado of the Old West. Bandanna print tie, elaborate concho clip, Texas-sized belt buckle, saddle tan Tony Lama boots, and a brushed white Stetson with a cattleman's crease. A leather wallet dangled from the breast pocket of his suit jacket. Pinned to the leather was a polished gold shield.

"Miss Biwaban?" He had a voice like an echo in a deep well. "My name's Fischer. Sheriff Cal Fischer." Without a hint of self-consciousness, he tipped his immaculate Stetson. Then, taking my arm, he led me away from the milling lawmen. "Let's you and me take a walk, young lady."

Our stroll ended at the farmhouse corner. Oblivious to the hum of the OP electric meter, Sheriff Fischer doffed his hat. A breeze stirred his sparse gray hair. "Now what's all this about Delbert Dietz assaultin' you?"

I repeated the same tale I'd told the troopers. Sheriff

Fischer listened intently, occasionally making humming sounds of understanding, and scribbled away diligently in a pocket notebook. When I finished, he asked to have a look at my head.

"Yeah, that's some bump." He thumbed my long, raven-black tresses aside, carefully studying the bruise. "He come at you without warning?"

I nodded. "Uh-huh. I turned, and there he was—Delbert Dumb Butt, swinging that pistol at me."

Sheriff Fischer smiled. I think he liked the nickname. "Any idea where he got the gun?"

"Sheriff, I couldn't *begin* to guess."

Pocketing his notebook, he added, "Had a nice chat on the radio with the Iowa State Patrol. Delbert busted out of the state looney bin two weeks ago. Didn't bother to notify us. Whatever happened to professional courtesy, eh?" Sudden shrewd glance. "What's he got against you, Miss Biwaban?"

"I think he mistook me for one of the nurses."

"Ever see him before today?"

I shook my head. "And never again, I hope!"

Gravelly chuckle. "I thought you promised Judge Carlson you were going to stay out of trouble, Miss Angie."

Sheepish grin. "Sometimes it's unavoidable, Sheriff."

His blue eyes riveted me to the spot. "Like the other day?"

My shoulders turned tense all at once. "Look, I wasn't trying to bullshit Kramer. I saw a dead man in that field—"

His palm rose quickly. "No need, gal. I read the report." He put his Stetson back on. "Had a talk with your parole officer, too. Thought that boy looked familiar. Quarterbacked for Iroquois. Saw his team play the Huron Tigers . . . oh, some years back. Paul said we ought to take a closer look at that field. And we did. Fact is, I was just getting cleaned up when this call came in." Unreadable expression. "One of my men found a trickle of blood on the bottom side of a prairie thorn. Dried blood. Portable lab kit identified it as human. Going to have to wait a few days for the full report from Pierre, though."

Excitement quickened my heartbeat. The sheriff's stern gaze never let up, not even for a second. "Now, it could be a blood splash from a close-up gunshot. Or maybe some farmer forgot to wear his gloves and got himself a little scratch. Until I know for certain, I'd surely appreciate it if you'd stay handy for questionin', Miss Angie. You will do me that favor, won't you?"

"Question, Sheriff—do I have a choice?"

"I'd say it breaks out three ways, gal." Sheriff Fischer ticked them off on his fingers. "One, cooperate with us and you'll continue to enjoy the Elderkins' company. Two, refuse to cooperate, in which case you can have your old cell back. Three, give me a real hard time, and I charge you with obstructin' justice. You know Department of Corrections rules better'n I do. A parolee doesn't have to get convicted to finish her term. One itty-bitty arrest, and she's back on the laundry." He hitched up his belt buckle. "Paul tells me you still got a year or two left to serve."

My initial impulse was to break off a cornhusk and stuff it up Holbrook's nose. But I was grown up enough to bow to the inevitable. Masking my true feelings with a pleasant smile, I answered, "Always willing to cooperate with the law, Sheriff."

"Good girl." He gave my shoulder a proprietary pat, then ambled off to join the troopers.

So I stood beside Bonnie's farmhouse, mulling over my new social status. Somewhere between *material witness* and *suspect.* Pondered my next move.

One thing for certain, I couldn't afford these repeated contacts with the local law. Three states had warrants out for me, and, after that failed manhunt in Washington, the FBI was really hot to toss a loop around *Pocahontas.* If Sheriff Fischer came across one of the Bureau's wanted posters . . . well, I could forget all about Mister Beach Tan's killer. I'd have enough to do, adjusting to life at the federal women's prison in Alderson, West Virginia.

Like it or not, I'd just been drafted into the hunt for Mister Beach Tan's killer. Somehow I had to find the man who'd fired those shots—find him *before* he fixed my lovely face in his gunsights—and arrange for him to tumble quickly into the arms of the law.

No trouble, right? I mean, a gunman whose face and form I never saw, whose victim has now disappeared without trace, leaving just enough evidence to implicate me!

No doubt about it, princess. It's *nandobani* time!

Four o'clock found me in the corral, mounted on a dun gelding named Smoke, trying to run a surly Hereford and her frisky calf up the ramp into the barn. As cow ponies go, Smoke was one of the better ones. He never reacted to the prima donna's head-tossing feints, and he kept a respectful distance from her hind hooves. I let him do most of the work, slapping my coiled lasso against the saddle and emitting occasional Anishinabe war cries.

Tiring of the game, Flossie plodded up the ramp with matronly dignity, her bawling offspring right behind. Kristy rode over on Chatelaine, leaned out of the saddle, gripped the gate, and swung it shut. Then we wheeled about and headed for the stable.

Questions came spilling out of Kristy the minute we removed the horses' saddles. She'd heard about Bonnie's ordeal from her mother, and she wanted the whole story firsthand.

Running an oval brush down Chatelaine's winter coat, she exclaimed, "You knocked him *out!?*"

I nodded. "Self-defense, Your Honor." Tenderly I eased the bit out of Smoke's mouth.

"You sure are lucky, Angie." Her pretty face turned somber. "Delbert could have really hurt you."

Removing the saddle blanket, I prodded, "Like he did your aunt Bonnie?"

Nodding, Kristy swept the brush through her mount's tail. Sadness softened her adolescent features. "She-she never said *anything*, Angie. We had no idea h-he was—" Unpleasant memories stilled her voice. Brushing more vigorously, she flashed me a bewildered glance. "I-I don't understand it. I just don't! Aunt Bonnie didn't have to put up with him. She had *us*. Why didn't she come to us?"

Smoothing the currycomb over Smoke's sleek mane, I replied, "I don't know, Kristy. For some women, it's a shameful thing." Pausing, I wondered how best to describe it. It's not the easiest task in the world, trying to describe domestic abuse to a sixteen-year-old girl. "Marriage is very important to a woman. She puts everything she has into it. Then she wakes up one fine morning to find that he's taken off his Prince Charming mask. That the man she loves is a sicko who enjoys hurting her. Maybe it . . . well, maybe it's a little hard to give up the dream, Kristy. So she tells herself that it's her fault, that she's the one to blame, that she's done something to provoke him." I glanced at her over Smoke's bare back. "And it never is, believe me! If she weren't there, he'd probably be kicking the family dog. Or the kids! Some guys are like that." Bright Angie smile. "Fortunately for us . . . not all of them."

"Maybe you're right." Her cornflower-blue eyes turned thoughtful. "Gram says Bonnie married him 'cause people kept teasing her 'bout being an old maid." Stern glance of disagreement. "People can be so *stupid!*"

"No argument here." I put down the currycomb. "How long have they been married?"

"Little over three years. Actually, it's more like two years, I guess, 'cause Delbert took off for Iowa just before last

Christmas." Despondent look. "That's when we found out about Aunt Bonnie." Affectionately stroking Chatelaine's neck, she added, "I just wish he'd go away for good and leave us all alone."

Smoke let out a hungry whicker. Eager to drop the subject, Kristy shoveled some grain into his feed pail. Smiling my thanks, I secured the stall door and inquired, "Need any help with the milking?"

"Thanks, Angie, but Daddy and I can handle it." Her hand lifted in a cheery wave. "See you inside."

I watched her leave. She walked with light, carefree stride of the very young. Or the very innocent. Tall, slender girl in her farm denims, blond ponytail carelessly sweeping her collar. I watched her and hoped that the world would never turn her into a victim . . . like her aunt.

Pausing at the stable door, I switched off the lights and reflected on the day's events. You know, maybe Bonnie Dietz was a little bit luckier than the average abuse victim.

She had a family who cared.

"Don't you move, Miss Angie Biwaban!"

I flinched as the metal bar spanned my derriere. Shooting a glance over my shoulder, I spied a determined Miss Edna right behind me. Her walker trapped me in the corner of Trudy's L-shaped kitchen counter.

Putting down a can of green beans, I remarked, "Mrs. Mutchler! I thought you were watching Phil."

"Oh, I can watch that smooth-talkin', white-haired galoot any time." Sapphire-colored eyes glimmered in annoyance. "Nobody ever tells me *anything!* Sheriff calls. Josh 'n' Trudy go tearin' out of here like the barn's afire. I never seen the like. You 'n' Kristy 'n' everybody else rush right by like I'm the couch or somethin'. I want to know what's going on! And you're going to tell me, Miss Angie Biwaban!"

And so, while I got a start on supper, I gave Trudy's aunt a detailed description of the battle at the Dietz farm. She interrupted only once, telling me to melt the butter in a small saucepan *first* and then mix in the saltines. That's the right way to whip up a tasty vegetable casserole.

When I finished, Miss Edna gave her small head a weary shake. "I've been a Presbyterian woman all my life, and I have never spoken an evil word against kin. But I've got to say it. That Delbert's as crazy as a jackass on locoweed."

I tried to cheer her up. "He's only kin by marriage."

"That's bad enough." She smoothed the fringe of her knit navy shawl. "He always was a mean one. I remember when he was a kid. Always threatenin' to get back at folks."

"Did he ever follow through on it?"

"You bet!" Decisive nod from the elderly lady. "There was a Fourth of July, oh, way, way back. Van Torkildsen yelled at him 'cause Delbert's firecrackers were scarin' his geese. Few days later, Van found some of his prize Angus cows dead at the pond. Natural pond, fed by an artesian spring. The water had turned alkali." Her lips tightened at the memory. "Van never could prove he did it. But I tell you this, Angie . . . I saw Delbert that day as I was driving back from Mitchell. He was slappin' white dust off himself and grinnin' like he was awful pleased about something."

Turning the knob on the gas stove, I observed, "Good thing he lives here. If he ever pulled that shit in Texas, he'd get his ass shot off."

"He came damn close to it around here, girl!"

Tongue in cheek, I said, "You know, Delbert seems to feel he's been unfairly blamed."

"Did he tell you that?"

"Yeah." I picked up a wooden spoon and stirred the browning saltines. "He said he gets blamed for everything that goes wrong around here. Said it all started with somebody named Holly Larsen."

Had I glanced away a millisecond earlier, I never would

have seen it. But no, I had just finished stirring, and I wanted to ask her about the Parmesan cheese. And that's when it happened.

The name *Holly Larsen* had a galvanizing effect. Miss Edna sat bolt upright. A strange tension bunched her thin shoulders. Her chin rose warily. She seemed to be avoiding direct eye contact with me.

I remarked, "Mrs. Mutchler?"

Then she looked straight at me, her features bland.

"Are you all right?" I asked.

"Fine." Wan smile. "Today's excitement must be getting to me, Angie. I think I'll lie down for a while."

I offered to help her, but she waved me off with an energy that belied her claim of fatigue. "I can manage just fine, young lady." Her dainty forefinger picked out the baking dish. "And don't forget to grease that before you add the vegetables."

"Yes, ma'am."

I watched Miss Edna hobble into her bedroom. The door closed quickly. Shrugging, I grabbed a stick of butter and proceeded to smear the inside of the baking dish.

You've piqued my interest, Edna, I thought. Who is this Holly Larsen, anyway? And why did that name upset you so?

Trudy came into the kitchen a few minutes later. Dabbing at a smudge on her cheekbone, she exhibited a weary smile. "How's the casserole coming, Angie?"

Lifting the glass lid, I offered it for inspection. "All set to go in."

Following a brief survey, Trudy pronounced herself satisfied, and together we put it in the stove. As she closed the enameled door, she asked, "Where's Aunt Edna?"

"Lying down." I jutted my chin toward the bedroom. "Been kind of a hectic day for all of us, I guess."

"You can say that again."

Concerned look. "How's Bonnie?"

"Not too good." Trudy's lips quivered, but somehow she

managed to contain her tears. "Doc Macpherson's keeping her overnight at the hospital. He's given her something to help her sleep." Forcing herself to remain chipper, she opened the refrigerator. "You people are probably starved. How about some rolls to go along with that casserole?"

"Sounds great! Where's the aluminum pan?"

Ten minutes later, we had supper thoroughly underway. Trudy stood at the sink, filling the kettle from the faucet. Leaning against the counter, I tried to think of a clever way to soothe my itching curiosity. Unable to come up with one, I opted for the direct approach.

"Trudy ... do you mind if I ask you a question?"

She recapped the kettle. " 'Course not."

Watchful for any reaction, I murmured, "Who's Holly Larsen?"

Trudy stood erect suddenly. Her knuckles whitened as she gripped the kettle's handle. No doubt about it—that name was definitely a showstopper here in Yorktown.

Frowning, Trudy glanced my way. "Where did you hear that name, Angela?"

"Sheriff Fischer." Plausible untruth. Both she and Josh had seen the sheriff talking to me.

"Oh, Lord!" Her face had a sickish look. "He still thinks Delbert was responsible?"

"Was he?"

"I don't know." Plainly agitated, Trudy carried the kettle to the stove. "Sheriff Fischer arrested him. That was the first time Delbert got *sent away*." Fingers trembled as she lit the gas. "Cal Fischer was a deputy back then. A long time ago. Delbert was only thirteen or fourteen, I-I think. Oh, Angie, whenever I think of that poor little girl ..." Swallowing hard, she forced herself to continue. "They were neighbors of ours. Sam and Alice Larsen. Like I said, a long time ago—thirty years, I reckon. Brad was just a baby. I prayed for them to find her, but they never did. It-it's every mother's nightmare.

Someone stealing your child. And when it happened here—right here in Yorktown!" A hellish shiver ran through her. "I tell you, Angie, I was a nervous wreck. Brad must've been three years old before I'd even let him out of my sight."

"How old was Holly?"

"Eight." Trudy smoothed her apron. "Alice had two kids, both girls. Holly and Laurel. Holly was the oldest. It-It happened in March, I think." She nodded to herself. "That's right. Thirty years ago last March. Holly always got home around three-thirty. You could set your watch by it." Her head shook sadly. "Alice always blamed herself for what happened. She felt that if she'd been home . . . It was just one of those things, Angie. Sam had taken a load of hay up to Wessington Springs. While he was gone, little Laurel gashed her hand on the fence. Alice drove her to Doc Macpherson's office in Mitchell, and by the time they got back, it was gettin' on to quarter of four. Holly was old enough to know where the key was. So when Alice got home, she called Holly's name, but there was no answer. That's when she phoned the sheriff."

"And what did he find?"

"He talked to the driver and all the kids on the school bus. They all had the same story. Holly boarded the bus with her classmates. She was carryin' her notebook, her arithmetic book and a Flintstones lunch box. The driver let her off at the usual spot—right at the end of the Larsens' driveway. It was a long driveway. Quarter mile, I'd say. Sam built a plywood shelter beside their mailbox. That's where she'd wait for the bus in the bad weather."

"What time did he let her off?"

"Same time as always. Three-fifteen." Trudy's features saddened. "And that was the last anyone ever saw of her. That poor little girl . . ."

Three-fifteen, I thought. Alice Larsen returned at quarter

of four. Leaving the perpetrator with thirty minutes to grab
Holly. If he'd had the farm under surveillance, and if he'd seen
both the Larsen truck and family car gone . . .

You realize, Miss Biwaban, that your theory suggests a
premeditated snatch.

"Did they ever find any trace of her?" I asked.

Solemn nod. "They found her lunch box."

"When?"

"A few days later. The kidnapper must have tossed it in the
brush."

"Where was it found?"

"That's the awful part, Angie." Trudy's tearful gaze traveled southward. "They found it near Enemy Creek, maybe
fifty yards from the road." A solitary teardrop meandered
down her cheek. "All these years I've asked myself—is that
where it happened? Is that where she got killed?" Sudden soft
sniffle. "Poor Alice! Losing Holly just about cut the heart
right out of her. We-We told her it wasn't her fault . . . said
maybe it was God's way of callin' Holly home . . . but-but she
didn't listen. She died about six years later. Sam put the farm
up for sale. Took Laurel down to Texas."

No comment from Angie. An eerie chill trickled up my backbone. Two phrases reverberated in my mind. *Enemy Creek.*
Fifty yards from the road. The spot where Holly Larsen's
lunch box had been found thirty years ago.

The exact same spot where I'd found the gunshot corpse of
Mister Beach Tan on Halloween day!

I turned in early. It had been a grim supper. Kristy tried
hard to lighten the tone, chitchatting about the upcoming harvest, but I was the only one who responded. Josh and Trudy,
plainly worried about Bonnie, frowned and picked at their cas-
seroles. Miss Edna seemed unusually standoffish. Oh, she was
polite enough. Young ladies of her generation had politeness

drummed into them. Still, it was plain that she didn't really want to join our conversation.

Okay, I admit it—that bothered me. A lot! I was growing mighty fond of Miss Edna. She reminded me so much of Grandma Biwaban. I was almost half tempted to push the issue, but I didn't. After all, I was hired help, not family.

Following supper, I caught up on my correspondence. Penned a chatty missive to my own no-nonsense aunt. Dear Aunt Della—How's everything in good old Heber City? Yes, I am the picture of health. No, I'm not married yet. Yes, I realize I am twenty-eight years old, and what of it?

Following a shampoo, a shower, a session with the blow dryer and the customary one hundred strokes, I put on my blue satin camisole and perused the many paperback novels on the handmade bookshelf. The bedroom belonged to Kristy's older sister, Tara, recently married and now living up in Huron.

Quite a selection of romance authors, Tara. Mary Kingsley, Jo Ann Ferguson, Emma Goldrick, and Dee Holmes. I plucked one of Kingsley's books, *An Intriguing Affair*, off the shelf. Scampered barefoot across the carpeted floor. Gratefully crawled beneath the covers of Tara's canopied bed. Flicked on the overhead lamp and nestled against those big soft pillows.

The day's cumulative strain finally caught up with me. My eyes refused to stay open. Leaving Regency England, I put the book aside, switched off the lamp, rolled over and went to sleep.

A familiar dream—Tettegouche. A recurring dream during my stay at the Big Dollhouse. My father, dead these past fifteen years, and I. A sunrise hike down to the mouth of the Baptism River. Tendrils of mist billowing upward. Chatter of birds. Faint rumble of the nearby falls. Out from under the elms and aspens, down into the rock-walled basin. Curling breakers battering rhyolite cliffs. Loose stones spilling out from under my moccasin soles. And, suddenly, there it is—

Kitchi Gammi, the great sea of the Anishinabe. Whitecaps flashing on the dark blue waters. Low-hanging overcast partially veiling the bronze summer sun . . .

All at once, a soft breathless cry annihilated my dream. The sound pursued me into wakefulness. I sat bolt upright in bed, my sleepy eyes blinking, looking about in a dull stupor. *Whuzzat?*

Dead silence. Tara's furniture assumed monstrous shapes in the gloom. Brushing the hair away from my face, I licked dry lips and exhaled wearily. Let my hearing probe the far corners of the room. Nothing. No sound. Did I dream it?

That mattress looked very inviting. Just as I was about to yield to its temptation, I noticed something very strange.

A faint corona of blue light gleamed at the sharp edge of Tara's chest of drawers. Blinking in confusion, I stared again.

Corona blue? My sleep-fogged mind fumbled for an answer to this phenomenon.

The blue aura began to dim. I realized that its source was beyond the window, somewhere out there in the yard. Sweeping the blankets aside, I left the bed, wiggled my feet into a pair of fleecy slippers, and tottered across the room.

Chilly night air helped to sharpen my mental focus. Peeling back the gauzy drape, I glanced through the frost-rimmed window.

A bright flickering sapphire light illuminated the horizon. The glow threw the shelterbelt treetops into sharp silhouette. Frowning in bewilderment, I thought, What on earth is *that?*

Prairie fire? Not very likely. It isn't moving, and there's no smoke.

City lights? Nope! Mitchell's the only city around here, and it's on the other side of the house.

UFO? Fussbudget face. Oh, come on! Don't be ridiculous, princess!

On the other hand, if Travis Walton shows up, I'm heading for Duluth!

Forehead crinkling, I studied that weird blue corona on the horizon. Then, with no warning at all, the flickering light winked out.

Motionless I stood, staring out the window. I knew this was no dream. My knuckles could feel the cold radiating right through the glass. I watched and watched, but there was no further disturbance on the horizon.

Yielding to a mammoth yawn, I released the drape and toddled back to bed.

FIVE

When I awoke the next morning, gray daylight lit up Tara's bedroom. I heard a whispery skittering noise, turned in bed, and saw frozen raindrops spattering the windowpane. Sitting up, I blinked and ran a clumsy grooming hand through my tangled mane.

Poor Josh! I thought. More inclement weather. Those fields will take forever to dry.

I went straight to the window. Wanted to see if I could spot any evidence of last night's mysterious corona. No such luck. The frozen rain had coated the glass with a thin layer of rime ice. Peering through it, the barnyard view resembled the distorted image in a funhouse mirror.

So I showered and dressed and spent twenty minutes in front of the vanity mirror, choosing a properly balanced mix of mascara and lipstick. And then it was downstairs to greet the Elderkins.

I found a full complement at the table. Everyone but Miss Edna. Trudy put out quite a spread. Sausage links, fried eggs, ham and cheese on English muffins, orange juice and coffee. Josh, Brad, and Jeremy ate with gusto. Kristy, wearing an orange sweater with a ribbed roll crewneck and form-fitting pepper-wash jeans, confined herself to toast and orange juice.

I glanced at the black-cat clock on the kitchen wall. The hands read six-fifteen.

Jeremy smiled at me as he reached for a muffin. He was Josh's second son, a year younger than me, as tall as Brad but a bit thicker in the neck and shoulders. Short sandy blond hair, with a slight curl at the forehead. Low eyebrows, Grecian nose, and his father's vulpine chin. His mackinaw shirt fit snugly. That physique would have won him instant admission to the Mister America contest. The first time I ever laid eyes on that man, my heart went into overdrive. And then, my lips pursing in dismay, I noticed the golden ring on his left hand.

You know what's *really* wrong with this country? Farm boys get married too darned early . . . before I get to meet them!

Jeremy had a pleasant baritone voice. "Slept right through the rooster, Angie."

Josh cracked a rare smile. "Gettin' to be a regular lady of leisure."

"Leave her alone, you two." Trudy put a platter of fresh breakfast rolls on the lazy Susan. "Ignore them, Angie. This family's got too many would-be comedians." And she ruffled her son's hair.

Laughing, Jeremy split open his muffin. "I'll bet it makes more money than farming."

"Yeah, and you can eat all the tomatoes the audience throws at you, too," said Brad, lifting his coffee mug.

The old man chuckled. "Be the biggest harvest you ever had, boy!" His smile faded abruptly. "Everything makes more money than farming."

Determined to hold onto my schoolgirl figure, I put in an order for *Breakfast a la Kristy* and joined the family chitchat.

Kristy told us about her school project—a brief but comprehensive history of the Elderkin family. Apparently, the family had been living here on *Michimackinakong* since the seventeenth century.

"... so, after leaving Plymouth, the Elderkins moved to Attleboro—"

"*Attleboro!?*" I echoed, grimacing in disbelief. "Are you shitting me?" I laughed. "What kind of a name is that?"

"That's the name, Angie. I looked it up. Attleboro's a city in southern Massachusetts. Lot of jewelry factories there. In fact, they're having their tricentennial this year."

Grinning, I shook my head. *Attleboro!* That's almost as silly as *Chippewa.* Honestly, where do the new people come up with these names?

"Our family lived in Attleboro for half a century," Kristy continued. "Then they moved to Killingly, Connecticut. A lawyer named Johnathan Elderkin was town councilman there in 1758. After the Revolutionary War, our family bought land in Ohio. Near Millersburg. We've still got kin there. My great-great-grandfather, John Randall Elderkin, came to South Dakota in 1870. He's the one who homesteaded the farm."

Brad then asked about my family, and I demurred, explaining that any such recital could take all day. Both the Biwabans and my mother's family could trace their lineage back to Mudjeekawis, founder of the Noka, who was hunting woolly mammoths on the shores of Lake Nipigon when the Greeks laid siege to Troy.

"Kristy," her mother called, as we rose from the table. "You'd better go wake Aunt Edna. I don't want her breakfast getting cold."

"Sure, Mom."

Turning to the girl's father, I asked, "What's on tap for today, Josh?"

"We're gettin' that combine up and runnin'," he said, lifting his navy-blue parka from the coat hook. "Why don't you give Trudy a hand with . . . ?"

The question dwindled into silence. Josh stared past me, his features tensing in puzzlement. Turning, I spotted an ashen-faced Kristy in the bedroom doorway.

"Daddy?" Eyes wide with alarm, she blurted, "Some-Something's wrong with G-Gram—"

Trudy rushed into the bedroom, followed by her husband and sons. I was right on Brad's heels. Frightened Angie gasp. Miss Edna lay motionless in bed, small mouth agape, chin lifted slightly, staring at the white ceiling. Thin arms lay rigid on the coverlet.

"Aunt Edna!" Trudy cried, shaking the old woman's frail shoulders. "Aunt Edna, wake up! Please!"

I grabbed Miss Edna's left wrist. Her tendons were rigid, the skin as clammy as moist parchment. All except for what looked like a small sunburnt patch near the bone. No pulse! My fingertips flew to her larynx. No vibration in the carotid artery. Instantly I planted my left hand on the old woman's sternum, covered both the hand and the sternum with my right, leaned forward and pushed down hard.

Josh bellowed, "Angie!"

Repeating the compression stroke, I gasped, "Her heart's stopped! I know what I'm doing!" Again and again the same downward stroke. "The Park Service taught me CPR."

No lie! When I was nineteen, I joined the Student Conservation Association, working as a coed rangerette at Canyonlands National Park.

Give that Park Service training an *A* plus, people. Even after nine years, I knew instinctively what to do. Keep the shoulders positioned directly above the victim's chest. Depress the lady's sternum two inches. Relax pressure and let the breastbone rise. Fifteen chest compressions, breathe deeply and blow fresh air down her throat.

Rising after the second exhalation, I gasped, "Call 911! Tell them to bring a respirator!"

Nodding, Kristy darted into the kitchen.

I was still at it when the ambulance arrived. Gasping and puffing, perspiration streaming down my face, I locked both arms and repeatedly pressured Edna's chest, determined not to lose her. A thin film of perspiration soaked the old woman's nightgown. Her fixed stare never wavered.

The rescue crew slipped a plastic mask over Edna's parted lips. The doctor replaced Trudy at the bedside. His name was Brenning. Heavyset man in his late forties. Dark brown hair going white at the temples. He put his stethoscope on Miss Edna's breastbone, then aimed a bright penlight at her eyes.

Sad shake of the head. "You can stop now, miss."

Defiant Angie glare. "Why?"

"She's dead," he replied, calmly removing his stethoscope. "Rigor's just setting in. I'd say she's been dead at least four or five hours."

Covered with perspiration, I took a deep breath and stood erect. Behind me, I heard the Elderkin women burst into tears.

Twenty-four hours later, Sheriff Fischer called Josh and presented the coroner's verdict. In medical school they call it *myocardial infarction*. Also known as cardiopulmonary arrest. Sometime during the night, Miss Edna's heart had ceased its steady drumbeat.

The way Josh told it, the sheriff didn't sound all that surprised. After all, Miss Edna was over eighty years old, and it was the third heart attack of her life. Her second one, twelve years ago, had resulted in the installation of the pacemaker.

Miss Edna's funeral took place on the morning of Wednesday, November sixth. The weather matched my despondent mood. An impenetrable rampart of gray overcast covered the prairie sky, throwing into stark relief the nearby rooftops and the slim spire of the First Presbyterian Church.

Stepping out of the black limo, I was astonished at the size

of the crowd. Half of Mitchell must have been there. Then I
remembered Miss Edna telling me about her background. The
Enrights had been one of the town's leading families.

Waiting for us on the church steps were Clem Mutchler,
looking very self-conscious in his ill-fitting dark suit, and Bonnie Deitz, clad in black like Trudy, Kristy, and me. Her face
looked pallid and haggard, as if she had just been through a
lengthy illness.

So there I stood in the Elderkin family pew. Tearful Anishinabe princess dressed for mourning. Black blazer, with
slim skirt to match, and a white lace-trimmed, ruffle-front
blouse. Standing with the Elderkin women, shedding a few
tears of my own, listening to the minister's thoughtful sermon
and Trudy's unabashed weeping. They were closer than some
mothers and daughters, those two.

The drive to Graceland Cemetery took us down East Fifth
Avenue, then slowly up North Main Street. We passed right
through the tourists' mecca, but I gave it no notice. I was too
busy thinking about Trudy's aunt, that feisty old lady with the
aluminum walker, who'd gone out of her way to make me feel
welcome in her home. The memory of her tart advice kindled a
bittersweet Angie smile. Sure going to miss you, Miss Edna.

We buried Trudy's aunt beside the long-dead husband, on a
low grassy knoll overlooking the cove at the southern end of
Lake Mitchell. Across the narrow asphalt lane stood the mar-
bled gravestones of Edna's parents. Bare elm branches rustled in the breeze as we took our places on the lawn-colored
carpeting beside the grave. Her mahogany coffin, surrounded
by floral displays, lay on a bright brass bier.

The eulogy concluded with a quote from scripture—John
chapter ten, verse twenty-eight.

Afterward, a half-dozen women encircled Trudy and Bonnie, offering hugs and words of comfort. A moist-eyed Clem
shook hands with the minister. I heard a muffled sniffle off to

my right, turned and saw Kristy hastily snapping open her purse. Fortunately, I had a package of tissues in hand.

"Th-Thank you, Angie." Mouth trembling, she dabbed at the tears on her cheeks. "You're a good friend. Know that?"

My throat tightened with emotion. "I try to be." Looking around, I remarked, "I didn't see Carol with Jeremy."

"She couldn't make it." The angry sparkle in Kristy's eyes warned me against further discussion of the topic. Apparently, there'd been some friction between Miss Edna and the daughter-in-law. Handing back my tissues, she added, "We haven't really thanked you for trying to save Gram. You did so much, and we—"

All at once, Kristy's mouth twisted in sorrow, and her words melted into an anguished sob. I opened my arms; then we clung together for a long moment, embracing and seeking the right words to comfort each other. And, in the end, realizing that words weren't really that necessary.

Afterward, Kristy rejoined her mother. Dabbing at my eyes, I accepted the condolences of a Mitchell couple and drifted back to the limo, flanked by a stream of grim-faced mourners.

Along the way, something bit into my small toe. Judging from the pressure on my toenail, I'd picked up a bit of gravel crossing the lawn. Sudden grimace. Believe me, high-heeled pumps are painful enough without pebbly intruders.

Unwilling to put on a graveside balancing act, I hobbled over to the nearest elm. Once out of sight, I planted my derriere against the trunk, balanced myself on one three-inch heel, lifted my left leg. Off with the ouch shoe. Ohhh, heaven! Upending the pump, I gave it a hearty shake. A dime-size pebble plummeted earthward.

Slipping my shoe back on, I heard a familiar masculine voice rising angrily nearby. Josh's voice.

". . . not too sure I like your sense of timing, mister!"

Another voice intruded—a calm, evenly modulated baritone. "Now, Josh, there's no need to get riled."

Curious, I peered around the elm. There was Josh, gimlet-eyed old farmer in his dark serge suit, facing another man, a man in his early forties, wearing a crisp navy-blue suit with a banker's white pinstripes. The stranger was a couple of inches under the six-foot mark, with a broad, earnest face and noticeable jowls. Twin creases ran across his high forehead. Sparse brown eyebrows and impeccably styled hair. Crisp Saxon nose, alert bluish-gray eyes, and a hefty upper lip sporting a Tom Selleck mustache. He had the annoying habit of continually tweaking the knot of his silken club tie.

Josh was not mollified. "There's a time to talk business, Sam, and Miss Edna's funeral sure ain't it."

"You're a busy man, Josh." Ingratiating smile from the newcomer. "At least think it over, eh?"

"I already gave you my answer."

"Use your head, Josh. Agriculture's been losing money for years. You're fifty-four years old. You may not live long enough to see it pick up again." The businessman frowned. "This is your chance to get out and get out clean. Most people leave their farms up to their ears in debt. Not you. If you play your cards right, you could walk away with, oh, a quarter to a half million in your pocket."

Josh's eyes narrowed. "My land's worth a whole lot more than that."

Tilting his head, Sam replied, "Not with that loan you're carrying."

"I'm good for it. You know that."

Sam's gaze lifted. Eyeing the thick overcast, he shook his head sadly. "Time's running out, Josh. It may be another week before you can harvest that corn. And we're getting mighty close to the middle of November. The weather could turn at any time. What happens then?"

Josh kept his poker face, but those clenched fists and whitening knuckles testified to his anxiety. Through gritted teeth, he snapped, "We'll survive. We always have."

Exasperation flitted across Sam's face. "Damn you, Josh Elderkin, you got too much backbone, and that's all there is to it. This isn't about survival. It's about you retirin' with a nice big pot of money. A half million in cash, invested in the right mutual funds, could provide you and Trudy with a mighty nice retirement down there in Florida."

Josh's tone turned even frostier. "What about my boys? Brad's sort of had his heart set on carryin' on after me."

"He's young. He and Ronnie can always start over."

"Up to their ears in debt?" Josh challenged.

I didn't like the glittering smile Sam put on. He reminded me of a Colombian drug dealer offering a discount. The nine-millimeter kind!

"You show me a South Dakota farmer who's not in debt, and I will gladly shake that man's hand." Giving Josh's shoulder a jovial slap, he added, "Just think on it some. That's all I'm askin'. Come on. I want to pay my respects to Trudy and Bonnie."

I kept out of sight as they passed by. Sam the Banker intrigued me. Surely his purchase bid could have waited until after Miss Edna's burial. Why the unholy haste to make a pitch to my Work Experience employer?

Fussbudget frown. And did I detect a mildly threatening undertone in Sam's remark about farm debt?

Before I could mull it over, my ears detected a quiet footfall behind me. A familiar male voice whispered in my people's language. "What have I told you about eavesdropping?"

Sporting a wry grin, I peeked over my shoulder. There stood my grandfather, Charlie Blackbear. He's a heavyset guy, four inches over my petite height, with a broad, square head and thin white hair meticulously combed back. With those deepset obsidian eyes and prominent crows' feet, he looks like old Rain-in-the-Face. Which is why I gave him the teasing nickname of *Chief.*

Of course, I only call him Chief when we're speaking English. When we converse in Anishinabemowin, it's always *Nimishoo* and *Noozis.* Grandfather and Granddaughter.

"Watchiya, Nimishoo." I nodded in greeting. "When did you get here?"

"Early this morning." Stepping forward, Chief aimed his thumb southward. "Stopped at the Economart and asked for directions to the Elderkin place. Cashier told me they were burying their aunt today. I followed your procession from the church." Motioning for me to follow, he added, *"Ambe, Noozis. Da naa, ani-waabamaadaa Bronconinaan."*

So we went looking for my grandfather's trusty Bronco pickup truck and found it parked beside a sizable box-elder maple. He opened the passenger door for me.

"Did you get Jill's message?" Lifting the hem of my narrow skirt, I clambered into the cab.

"Not until the day before yesterday," he replied, rounding the Bronco's hood. "Message was waiting for me when I got back to the reservation."

"Did I catch you in midmove?"

"Gawiin, Noozis." He shook his head. "I'm already moved in. I was up on the Gunflint Trail."

"Hunting guide?"

Quick decisive nod. "Bob and Genn Stonepipe are booked solid this year. Busy season up and down the trail, Justine tells me. Ran into Sam Cook up on Saganaga Lake, too." He cast a sharp look my way. "You'll get all the details at eleven, missy. Right now, though, you just tell me what kind of a mess you've gotten yourself into."

"I didn't get *myself* into anything, *Nimishoo!* I was minding my own business, running this combine, when—"

"Combine!?" he echoed. "When did *you* learn to drive a

combine?" I started to reply, and he lifted his blunt brown hand. "Whoa-whoa-whoa . . . let's start at the beginning, eh?"

And so, as we drove back to Mitchell, I brought my grandfather up to date.

Chief steered the Bronco down North Main Street, past the Super City Mall. Plenty of glass-fronted stores in there. Randall Foods and ShopKo and Mexican Express and Thunes True Value ("We learned long ago that if we worked on your friendship, our business would take care of itself").

Midwestern Mitchell came to an abrupt end at the corner of East Seventh Avenue. Beyond that point, for approximately four blocks, North Main turned into the Yellow Brick Road. Dorothy, Toto, and the entire Munchkin Marching Band could have gone skipping down the centerline, and no one ever would have noticed. Not with that Art Deco police station and the medieval crenellated battlements of the Enchanted Doll Museum. Right next door was Uncle Zeke's, a gift shop that resembled an Old West trading post. And across the street loomed the most startling edifice of all, that refugee from Baghdad of the Caliphs, the one and only Corn Palace!

There it stood, a solid manifestation of Scheherezade's wildest imaginings. A Moorish palace straight out of the Disney movie *Aladdin*. Five onion-shaped towers, four minarets, and at least half a dozen flagpoles. Forty tons of grain had been glued to its exterior to create those grandiose murals. Ears of dessicated corn, strands of flax and millet, bushels of dried oats. The towers were painted an enchanting sky-blue, with broad golden bands depicting cavorting buffalo.

As always, a crowd surrounded the Corn Palace. Farmers, truckers, housewives, students from Dakota Wesleyan. Chief parked his Bronco in Uncle Zeke's lot. With all those faces upturned to admire the cereal bas-reliefs on either side of the front entrance, no one paid much attention to the Anishinabe couple headed for the Dairy Queen.

Chief and I selected a small table beside the wall. A bright-smiling teenager in a pale green short-sleeved uniform came to take our order. Pinned above her left breast was a nametag reading STACEY. She returned in a remarkably short time, bearing the steaming coffee beaker, and told us to signal when we were ready for lunch.

Lifting his paper cup, Chief switched to English. "I'd say you've got your share of troubles, young lady."

"Tell me about it!" Glum expression. "I was kind of hoping to keep a low profile around here, you know?"

"Your friend Mister Beach Tan sorta put the kibosh on that, didn't he?"

"Chief, when I found that man, I never, ever expected him to get up and go for a stroll!"

"I wouldn't joke about it, Angie. You said yourself that sheriff half believes a shooting took place. You're the only person who claims to have seen this guy. What happens if Fischer takes your helpful advice for a confession?"

"You really think he'd charge *me!?*"

Chief ran his thumb along the paper rim. "Why not? You admitted to being at the scene. And you've done time for a major felony."

"Embezzlement isn't murder, Chief."

"If he can't come up with anyone else, you're going to start looking mighty good to him, girl." Frowning, he paused for a hasty sip. " 'Course, it could get a lot worse."

Resting my chin on the heel of my hand, I muttered, "Really? How!?"

"Fischer just might call on the FBI. They'll backtrack everybody involved in the case. And that includes *you,* miss." His warpath scowl deepened. "What happens when they double check your whereabouts last month and find out that Miss Angie Biwaban was nowhere near Belle Fourche, South Dakota!?"

I winced. The Bureau was probably still steaming about *Pocahontas's* Houdini-style vanishing act out there in Port

Wyoochee. The last thing I wanted to do was attract their official attention. Those boys don't enjoy having their noses tweaked.

"That's right." Grim nod from my grandfather. "And if they make the connection between Angie Biwaban and *Pocahontas*—"

"Chief, you don't have to go into the gory details." I definitely needed another jolt of hot coffee. "Suggestions?"

"We have to find out more about Mister Beach Tan."

"We?" Angie the Echo.

"You don't think I'm going to stand by and let some *gitghimookoman* take potshots at my granddaughter, do you?"

Giving his hand an affectionate squeeze, I murmured, *"Miigwetch, Nimishoo!* But you don't know what you're getting into." My gaze took in the growing cluster of lunch patrons. Making the switch to our language was the best defense against passing eavesdroppers. "We're looking for a man whose name I don't know. Whose face I never saw before. And I was with him less than five minutes before he vanished—"

"And that was long enough for you to secure a detailed description, right down to the brand name on his suit jacket," my grandfather interrupted. "You know, that name rings a bell."

"Birnbaum's?"

Quick nod. "I know I've seen it somewhere before. Months ago. Some newspaper back home."

Arch smile. "He didn't get that tan in Saint Paul, *Nimishoo.* Not at this time of year."

"Yeah? Well, judging from your description, he sure didn't belong in that cornfield." Seeing my smile fade, he leaned forward in his seat. "What is it, *Noozis?*"

"Holly Larsen." I peeled a paper napkin from the tabletop dispenser. "She was eight years old when she disappeared. That field. That's where her lunch box was found thirty years ago. Not far from where Mister Beach Tan was shot."

"Think there's a connection?"

Purse the lips. "I'm not sure, *Nimishoo*. It could all be coincidence."

"Pretty strange coincidence. Two disappearances thirty years apart. And from the *same* cornfield."

Nodding, I voiced partial agreement. "*Eyan, Nimishoo*. But our friend's too young. He must have been nine or ten when the Larsen girl vanished."

Chief shrugged. "Maybe he saw something back then."

Skeptical look. "And kept silent for thirty years!?"

"Maybe he didn't realize the significance of what he saw," my grandfather said thoughtfully. "Maybe it nagged at him—drew him back here. Or maybe he simply made an offhanded remark—and the wrong pair of ears were listening."

"So there is a connection."

"Perhaps." Chief can be irritatingly enigmatic at times. "I read it four ways, *Noozis*. One, the shooting had nothing to do with Holly Larsen. Two, your victim was innocently poking around. Somebody got nervous about his presence at the scene and blew him away. Three, your victim was investigating the girl's disappearance. Holly's abductor get very antsy about that. And—blam!—same result as Number Two."

"And the fourth?"

Chief's visage looked as stern and as craggy as a rhyolite bluff. "An offshoot of Number Three, *Noozis*. Mister Beach Tan was investigating the Larsen girl's disappearance. Her killer knew about the inquiry and lured him into the field. In other words . . . deliberate cold-blooded murder for the purpose of ending the investigation. The killer intended for Mister Beach Tan to disappear all along."

Slumping in my chair, I let out a soft moan. "Isn't this where I came in?"

"Not exactly." His expression grew sterner. "Now you know something you didn't know before."

"Like what?"

"The odds." Chief reached for his deerhide wallet. "Of the four possibilities, two are directly linked to the little girl. Meaning there's a fifty-fifty shot your murder victim went down because of Holly Larsen. And that tells you something about the killer."

"Such as?"

"Noozis!" Removing a ten from the billfold, he flashed me a look of mild annoyance. "I'd have thought you would've figured it out by now." Small victorious smile. "The killer lived here thirty years ago!"

Twenty minutes later, Chief's Bronco was tooling down West Havens Street. Glancing at the rearview mirror, I watched the Corn Palace's bright towers slip behind the distinctive red roof of Colonel Sanders's establishment. Ahead the discount motels and Twenties bungalows thinned out considerably, giving way to fields of ripe corn, aluminum silos, and an occasional red gambrel-roofed barn.

We picked up South Dakota 754 about eight miles west of Mitchell, turned left, and zoomed due south to Yorktown.

As we approached the township, I caught sight of the huge roadside billboard put up by the Farmers and Merchants Association. Our area mascot, Cornelius Cobb, a bright yellow corn ear with the dazzling orthodontia of a Disney cartoon, welcomed us with upraised arms. Beside Cornelius, a blaring legend proclaimed

WELCOME TO YORKTOWN!
The Sweet Corn Capital of South Dakota
Population—47

Our arrival had boosted that total by about five percent. Instant population explosion! Chief slowed the truck as we approached the intersection of Route 754 and County Road 19. And I had a look at the throbbing heart of the metropolis.

Four buildings in all. A Depression-era red brick post office. Weber's General Store with its built-in cafe. A modern John Deer dealership. And, last but certainly not least, lively York-town's one and only industry—Mom's Auto Body. The sound of sledgehammers carried over the Bronco's idling engines. White welding sparks glimmered in the darkness beyond those three open garage doors.

Chief hung a left at the intersection and ferried me out to Elderkin Farm. Josh, Trudy, and the boys were unlocking the barn when we arrived.

Once the car was parked, I introduced them to my grandfa-ther. Handshakes all around. Noting the Bronco's Minnesota plates, Josh remarked, "You passin' through, Charlie?"

Chief nodded. "I was out in Utah visiting my daughter—Angie's aunt. Heading back to the Northland." His palm squeezed my shoulder. "Thought I'd see if this one's behaving herself."

Brad smiled. "She's doing just fine, Mr. Blackbear."

Trudy's expression turned thoughtful. "Where are you staying, Charlie?"

Chief tilted his head northward. "Ain't sure yet. I thought I'd give the Thunderbird a try."

"No need for that." Smiling at her husband, Trudy added, "We've got plenty of room right here."

Josh looked receptive to the idea. "You could stay in Nick's room, I reckon."

Lifting one hand, Chief demurred. "Now I don't want to put you folks out—"

"Why, it's no trouble at all. 'Sides, it'll give you more time to spend with Angie." Grief dampened Trudy's welcoming smile just a little. "We've got a reputation for hospitality to uphold."

"Whenever Mom hears that knock on the door, she sets an extra plate at the table," Brad remarked.

My grandfather grinned. "Well, you can set it if you like, Miz Elderkin, but just make sure Angie *washes* it."

Pained grimace. "Thanks a lot, Chief!"

"Knowing you . . . you need the practice."

Well, there was no shortage of dishes to practice on. We had eight for dinner, including Bonnie Dietz. I thought perhaps she and Trudy would want a little time alone. But no, they turned up in the kitchen less than a half hour after Kristy and I started, turning my plans for a simple soup-and-sandwich combo into a full-scale hot supper featuring ham loaf, mashed potatoes, corn on the cob, and Bonnie's famous sweet-and-sour gravy.

Afterward, those good sports, the brothers Elderkin, reached for linen towels and offered to dry. I took them at their word, and we had the dishware sparkling in just under twenty minutes. No sooner had I doffed my apron than the telephone jangled.

Kristy rocketed out of the kitchen. "I'll get it!"

Believe me, there is nothing speedier on the planet than a sixteen-year-old girl answering the phone.

"Angie!" she called. "It's for you."

Striding briskly into the den, I smiled my thanks and accepted the receiver. Leaning against Josh's oak desk, I said, "Hello?"

A feminine giggle tickled my ear. *"Hau, Pahaton wetonsh-nahoon!"*

I brightened instantly. "Jill!"

"You've pissed off Mrs. Sutton, you naughty girl. I just got an earful in person. How could you, Biwaban?"

"Very easily, Stormcloud, and with pleasure. What a bitch! How'd you get hooked up with La Sutton, anyway?"

"Long story, Angie."

"How about the *Reader's Digest* version then?"

"Okay. When I was having my, ah, troubles, I dropped in at New Horizons, you know, that little storefront legal office in Pierre. The director introduced me to Sarah, and she agreed to take my case. No charge."

Visualizing the lady's impeccable wardrobe, I remarked, "That must have been a new experience for our Sarah."

"Wrong! She helped founded the place, Angie. Has a seat on the board, too. And you know that program for teenaged single mothers?"

"The one across the river in Fort Pierre?"

"You've got it. That's Sarah's, too. She's really into community affairs."

Well, that explains how she met Paul. Mild warpath scowl. I was far more comfortable with the concept of Sarah Sutton as the high-powered rich-bitch lawyer. Community affairs, eh? One of Paul Holbrook's interests. Not good, princess!

Frosty tone. "Well, the next time I meet Lady Bountiful, I'll be sure to curtsy."

"Ooooooh! She read you the riot act, too, eh?"

"She did. For a minute there I thought she was going to *ground* me. I'm a little too old for a stepmom, Jill."

I heard a gleeful chuckle at the other end. "Sarah always reminds me of my candy-striper days. There was this senior R.N. at Rapid City Regional. A real dragon lady." Soft sigh of reminiscence. "Funny thing, Mother gets along just fine with Sarah."

"I'm sure Aunt Della would, too." Shifted the receiver to my other ear. "I don't want to sound ungrateful or anything, Jillian, but . . . uh, couldn't you have sent somebody else?"

Moment of awkward silence. "I goofed?"

"Big time, *amiga*."

"Maybe you'd better tell me everything, Angie."

So I did. I covered it all, from the first bullet strike on the combine to Chief's arrival in Mitchell. My tone chilled as I described Sarah's encounter with Paul.

"Oh, dear." Jill sounded both embarrassed and contrite. "I had no idea they knew each other." Slight gossipy tone. "So what does this mean for you and Paul?"

"Absolutely nothing! Why should I care if some slinky-dink blonde drapes herself all over Holbrook!?"

"If you don't care, woman dear, then why are you so upset?"

"*Upset!?*" Instantly I lowered the decibel level. "Jill, I am *not* in the least upset." Deep ragged breath. "Better change the subject, *amiga.*"

"All right." I heard paper tearing at Jill's end. "Why don't you give me the farm's address. I'd like to send a sympathy card to Miss Edna's family."

"Sure! Send it to Elderkin Farm, RFD #3, Yorktown, South Dakota 57395."

Curious, my Lakota friend asked, "What was the cause of death, Angie?"

"Heart attack, according to Doc Brenning."

"What kind, dear?"

I responded, "There's more than one kind!?"

"You bet," said Jill, the former L.P.N. "Coronary occlusion. Cardiac arrythmia. Ventricular fibrillation—"

"That's the one he mentioned," I interrupted. "Ventricular whatzit."

"Fibrillation," Jill replied. "That means very rapid irregular contractions of the heart's muscle fibers. A normal heart does 60 to 80 beats per minute. Rigorous exercise boosts the beat up to 200. In a fibrillation seizure, the heart convulses at 300 to 500 beats per minute. It literally shakes itself apart." Sympathetic tone. "How old was Miss Edna?"

"Couple of years over eighty," I replied.

Mild sigh. "Well, at least she didn't suffer."

The certainty in Jill's voice piqued my interest. "Why do you say that?"

"They go quickly in a fibrillation attack. Twenty seconds, at most. It's like a charley horse in your chest."

Thinking back, I remembered the vague breathless cry that

had roused me from slumber. At first I thought I'd dreamed it. Now I wondered if I'd heard Miss Edna crying out.

"Jill . . ." I asked, my voice thoughtful. "Could a fibrillation heart attack shock the victim awake?"

"Highly unlikely, Angie."

"Would they cry out?"

"Not if they were asleep." Jill's voice wavered slightly. "I've seen it happen, here at Pine Ridge. The old people—they rarely make a sound. The body sort of leaps in bed. Facial muscles contort in agony. And then it's all over."

"You're sure of that?"

"I'd bet my striped cap on it. Why do you ask?"

Dodging Jill's question, I answered with one of my own. "What does a heart attack victim look like?"

"Usually we find them with the mouth open, as if they were trying to catch their breath. Their skin is clammy—"

"How clammy?" I prodded.

"Not much. Just a touch of dampness."

All at once, I stood erect. Obsidian eyes narrowed in deep thought. "The victim doesn't sweat much?"

"Angie, she doesn't have *time*. It's all over in twenty seconds." Nervous laugh. "This is really a very morbid subject, Biwaban. Can't we talk about something more pleasant?"

"Okay." I tried to sound upbeat. "Tell me about the guy who took you to the movies."

And, as Jill cheerfully described her date, I thought back to that night. Ransacked my memory for that faint breathless cry I'd heard downstairs.

A cry, if Jill was correct, Miss Edna could not have possibly made.

Could Doc Brenning be wrong about the cause of death?

I had more than a few questions for that man.

Thoughtful frown. What had happened in Miss Edna's first-floor bedroom that night?

Questions, questions.

SIX

"Birth announcement?" The head librarian blinked in mild surprise. She was a slender lady in her late thirties, with frosted light brown hair and inquisitive hazel eyes. A cable-knit cardigan covered her shoulders like a cape.

"Yes, ma'am." Amiable Angie smile. "You see, I was born here in Mitchell. We moved to Minnesota when I was six months old. I hoped to get a photocopy of that day's newspaper. Do you have the *Daily Republic* on microfilm?"

"Of course." Lifting the gatepost, she stepped out of the central kiosk. "Thirty years ago, you said?"

"Uh-huh. March the twenty-fourth." Moving at a brisk step, I followed her into the reference section.

"We store two months on each tape," she said, halting before a tall gray filing cabinet. Sidelong smile. "You'll find your birthday toward the middle of the reel."

She rolled open a middle drawer, then extracted a small aged cardboard box. A lacquered thumbnail opened the top flap. Pulling out the tape, she led me over to a microfilm reader.

"Do you know how to run one of these things?" she asked.

Vigorous nod. "I had plenty of experience in college."

Handing over the tape, she wished me luck and left.

Now then, princess, let's have a look at the original news stories dealing with Holly's disappearance.

According to Trudy, the girl had vanished sometime in March. I began with the first day of that fateful month, poring through the *Daily Republic* page by page.

Behind me, I heard the shuffling of feet, punctuated by an old man's cough. It was nine-fifteen. Early morning for the librarian, but to me, it felt like midday.

My grandfather, the Elderkins, and I had been up since five. After the morning chores, I'd volunteered to do the day's shopping. Josh had suggested I take Chief along and show him the sights. We left the farm at seven-thirty, heading east in my car—a dark green vintage 1969 Mercury Montego affectionately known as Clunky.

Why Clunky and not Chief's Bronco? Simple! Clunky's South Dakota plates were a lot less likely to attract the attention of the local law.

On the way into Mitchell, Chief offered to check the local motels, to see if anyone resembling Mister Beach Tan had checked in recently. I offered him the use of Clunky, but he preferred to walk. So I dropped him off at the Coach Light Motel on West Havens and told him I'd pick him up later at the truck stop just off the interstate.

Slowly I rolled the plastic tape, serenaded by the reader's electronic hum. A stream of articles and ads crossed the viewscreen. And then, quite suddenly, a bold black headline jumped out at me.

POLICE SEEK MISSING CHILD

YORKTOWN—Police and volunteer searchers combed Davison County last night looking for little Holly Larsen.

Eight-year-old Holly was reported missing by her mother, Mrs. Alice Larsen, at 4 P.M. yesterday.

Holly, a third-grade student at Rosedale School, was last seen shortly after three o'clock when the school bus left her at the front gate of her family farm.

According to Sheriff Benjamin Wirtz, the Larsen girl has light blond hair styled in a pageboy and was wearing a navy-blue winter jacket, a matching pleated skirt, and a knit hat with a white pompom.

When she left the bus, she was carrying her notebook, an arithmetic book, and a Flintstones lunch box.

"If anyone has any information regarding this girl, we would appreciate it if they would come forward," Sheriff Wirtz said.

Hitting the fast-forward button, I jumped into the next day. The continuing mystery resulted in a larger headline.

WHERE IS HOLLY LARSEN?

YORKTOWN—That is the question on everyone's lips as police widen their search for the little Yorktown girl, missing since Tuesday.

The Highway Patrol and lawmen from Anson and Aurora counties have joined the search for Holly, age 8, a third-grade student at Rosedale School. The girl vanished shortly after getting off the school bus near her home on County Road 19 in Yorktown.

Bus driver Hugo Beckers, 67, of Union township, was questioned at length by Sheriff Wirtz yesterday.

According to Beckers, young Holly got off the bus "same as always" at the front gate of the family farm.

"She waved to us as I pulled away. She was always a cheerful little thing," Beckers said. "Last I saw of her, she was heading up the driveway."

When asked if he saw anything out of the ordinary, Beckers replied, "I'm telling you the same thing I told Ben Wirtz. The only thing I saw was a two-toned '55 Chevy. Passed me on County 19 about five minutes after I let Holly off, heading back toward Mitchell. I saw it whiz by as I was turning on my windshield wipers."

There were rumors of a suspect brought in for questioning by Deputy C.D. Fischer this morning. Sheriff Wirtz declined to comment.

"No one has been charged yet. The investigation is continuing," Sheriff Wirtz said.

Delicate eyebrows lifted. Deputy C.D. Fischer, eh? That had to be my friend Cal. Apparently, he'd inherited the sheriff's chair from old Ben Wirtz.

Hugo Becker's offhand testimony also intrigued me. Playing a hunch, I turned the knob and brought the paper's Page One masthead into view. My gaze zeroed in on the weather forecast. *More rain; snow flurries possible.*

Warpath scowl. Now I understand why old Hugo had turned on those windshield wipers.

I was beginning to get a feel for the circumstances of Holly's disappearance. But I needed more names if I was ever to retrace that thirty-year-old trail. And so, on to the next issue. . . .

HOLLY'S LUNCH BOX FOUND!

YORKTOWN—The Highway Patrol's K-9 unit discovered the lunch box belonging to Holly Larsen in a farm field near Enemy Creek early this morning.

The missing girl's parents, Mr. and Mrs. Samuel Larsen of Yorktown, identified the lunch box as their daughter's.

According to Deputy Jake Norton, the Flintstones lunch box was found at 7 A.M. this morning by Trooper Don Ziegler and his German shepherd.

"Rex gets the credit for this one," Ziegler said. "He sniffed it out from fifty yards away. We found it under a hackberry bush."

Deputy Norton said the dog followed a scent trail from that spot to Enemy Creek. The trail faded at the water's edge.

Norton added that the lunch box itself bore many dents and dirt marks.

"My guess is it was battered during the scuffle," Norton said. "The perpetrator then tossed it in the bushes. There's no question in my mind that this is a case of foul play."

The field's owner, Mrs. Birgitta Ostlund of Mitchell, was questioned by Sheriff Wirtz and Deputy C.D. Fischer at 10 this morning.

Mrs. Ostlund, 72, told police that the field hadn't been farmed since she and her late husband, Ragnar, moved to Mitchell back in 1959.

"Mostly I let my neighbor raise bluestem on it for hay," she explained. "I don't know who's been out there lately."

Tears came quickly as reporters asked Mrs. Ostlund about her reaction to the disappearance.

"Taking that little girl away from her mama—who could do such a terrible thing?" Mrs. Ostlund said. "Eight years old. That poor dear little lamb! Oh, I hope the sheriff finds her."

As things turned out, Mrs. Ostlund's hope was in vain. The *Daily Republic* carried the Larsen story for many weeks thereafter. Usually as INVESTIGATION CONTINUES. The follow-up stories became shorter and shorter. And then, by the middle of April . . . silence.

It was just after noontime when I left the library. A cluster of pink note sheets filled my fist. The names were few—Wirtz, Beckers, Norton, and Ostlund—but at least it was a start.

I backed Clunky out of the small library lot, crept up Sanborn, and turned right onto West Fourth. Two more blocks put me back on bustling North Main. I shoehorned Clunky into a parking space in front of the vacant Woolworth's, put a quarter in the meter, and strolled down the street to Saterlie Drug, exchanging friendly smiles with passersby. Anishinabe princess in her khaki safari jacket and white twill slacks, silken raven hair sweeping her shoulders. Midwestern Angie.

The drugstore had a little bit of everything. Cheery, well-lit interior. Candy and cosmetics and magazine racks. My nose detected the persistent scent of rosewater and perfume.

After closing the phone booth's accordion door, I put Northwestern Bell's directory on the podium and opened it to the B's. Might as well start at the beginning of the alphabet.

No Beckers. Bus driver Hugo must've been the only one. Since he was 67 at the time of Holly's disappearance, most likely he'd made that permanent move to Graceland Cemetery.

There were two names under Norton, J.H. and J.S. Popping a quarter into the slot, I tried J.H. first. The phone at the other end rang and rang. No answer. Jiggling the receiver cradle, I retrieved my quarter and tried the other one.

Four rings later, a feminine alto answered. "Hello?"

"Afternoon!" Upbeat Angela. "Is this the J.S. Norton residence?"

She sounded cautious. "Yes, it is."

Wild guess. "Hi, my name is Cecilia Hartford, and I'm with Northwest Guaranty Insurance. Could I speak to your husband?"

Her tone cooled rapidly. "Jim and I have enough insurance, thank you."

"Wait, Mrs. Norton! My company's offering special low-cost coverage to law-enforcement officers and their families—"

"Law enforcement!?" Puzzled echo, followed by an amused chuckle. "You've got the wrong Norton, honey. You're looking for Jim's uncle."

I glanced at a pink note sheet. "Uncle Jake?"

"That's him. You can reach him at nine-nine-six—"

The number, of course, was identical to J.H. Norton's. Well, I could always try him later. After thanking the nice lady for her time, I depressed the cradle, listened to the dial tone, and thumbed through the phone book again.

I found one listing for Ostlund. After reinserting my quarter, I tapped out the seven digits. A woman's voice answered. I gave my insurance scam another try.

". . . so you see, my boss wanted me to get in touch with Birgitta. The money's been sitting in that account for nearly forty years, and the company's hoping she'd be willing to redirect it into our new mutual fund."

"Oh, Lord! You're about twenty-five years too late, Miss Hartford." The lady sounded apologetic. "Birgitta was Jeff's *grandmother!* She passed on *decades* ago. I-I don't know what to tell you."

"Then Birgitta's estate has already been probated?"

"Twenty-five years ago, yes."

"Did she leave any children?" I asked.

"Two. A daughter and a son—Jeff's dad," Mrs. Ostlund replied. "But they're both dead. Karin passed away . . . oh, better than ten years ago. And Bart—why, he died last year. It was the leukemia what killed him. Wasted him right down to nothing. I think he weighed a little over a hundred when he died."

Murmur of sympathy. "Sorry to hear it, ma'am."

"I-I think maybe you'd best be speaking to my husband."

Feeling a guilty twinge, I made my disengagement. "Better yet, Mrs. Ostlund, why don't I have Finance draw up a detailed statement for that account? I'll send it to your husband along with a letter of explanation." Reassuring tone. "Now, this may take a while, so don't be surprised if you don't hear from the company right away."

Thanking her for her time, I hung up.

One last peek at the phone book. There were no listings for Wirtz.

So I tried Jake Norton's number again, letting it ring and ring. No response. Frowning, I replaced the receiver in its cradle, then jotted down Jake's address on the pink sheet—1026 West Second Avenue. Perhaps a personal visit might change my luck.

Jake Norton lived in a rundown two-story apartment house, white with splintered green shutters, less than a block from the Chicago, Milwaukee, St. Paul, and Pacific Railroad tracks. The heart of Mitchell's industrial district. Bracketing the apartment house on either side were fly-by-night sheet-metal foundries. Cardboard patched many upstairs windows. Like the CMSP&P tracks, the steel fire escapes were caked with rust.

As I stepped onto the porch, a skinny, sour-faced French-Canadian woman appeared in the doorway. Jake's landlady. She told me she wasn't buying anything. Showing a broad Angie smile, I asked if Mr. Norton was home.

"'Course he ain't!" Knuckles whitened as she gripped her broomstick. "Damn lazy, good-for-nothin' drunk! He only comes here to sleep. He's gone by ten every mornin'." Gimlet eyes narrowed suddenly. "If you were really a friend of his, you'd know that!"

"I never said I was a friend." I kept a wary eye on that broom. She looked manic enough to use it. Striking my Mary, Queen of Scots pose, I displayed a serene smile. "My name is Janet Hillary Guinier, and I'm a counselor with the state Department of Substance Abuse. I'm here to see how Mr. Norton's coming along with his retirement."

The mere mention of a state agency seemed to have a calming effect. "You the folks that got him that night watchman job at the plant?"

Brisk nod. "How's he making out?"

"Well, he's working the second shift, but damned if I see any cash money." She had a very low boiling point. "Son of a bitch still owes me for October! You see him, you tell him he'd better have some foldin' green in his hand. Or the next time he lights out for the Silo, I'm changin' the lock and dumpin' his junk all over the sidewalk!"

"The Silo?" I echoed, arching an eyebrow.

"That's where you'll usually find Jake Norton this time of day." Her pointed chin swiveled southward. "Just across the tracks, over yonder on Ash."

Taking the lady's advice, I crossed the railroad tracks and entered a neighborhood of aging Victorian homes with high porches and pitted brick chimneys.

The Silo sat on the corner of Ash and Edmunds, the last of a dying breed. No sparkling cocktail lounge, this, but a walk-in neighborhood bar with its name spelled out in golden letters on the big front window. Bright brass horizontal rod and neatly pressed green curtains. Checkerboard tiled flooring and a large mahogany bar. Small circular tables and wall-length mirror and polished oak trimming. The color TV sat on a corner shelf, permanently tuned in to the Sports Channel. I didn't know they still had places like this in America. Take away the TV, slap some bat-wing doors on the entryway, and Wyatt Earp would have been right at home.

The bartender showed some mild interest when I walked in. He was a broad, durable, middle-aged Italianate man with slicked-back hair and an Errol Flynn mustache, wearing a surprisingly neat white apron. I asked for a cold Lowenbrau. He dug a short-necked bottle out of the ice chest, then opened it with a deft twist of the wrist. Dark eyes inquisitive, he put a clean glass beside the sweating bottle.

"Jake Norton?" I asked, slipping him a fiver.

"By the window."

Ex-Deputy Norton resembled a halfback on the fortieth anniversary of his college playoffs. Stevedore shoulders, broad biceps, and a tummy like one of the Black Hills. A Marine D.I.'s crewcut had turned his white hair into a fine array of bristles. He had a blunt, square Scandinavian face hammered by all the cares of his cop years. His mouth looked as if a geologist had split a boulder with a pickax. He wore a faded mackinaw shirt with the cuffs rolled back slightly. I caught a glimpse of a Korean dragon tattoo on one thick, hairy wrist. Standing beside his tattooed wrist were a shot glass and a fifth of Jack Daniel's, both of them half full.

Putting my change away, I heard a stealthy wolf whistle emanating from the far corner. Oh, well, Mother warned me about places like these. Suppressing an arch smile, I headed for Jake's rickety table.

I had my cover story all prepared. Budding journalist doing a syndicated feature story on the Holly Larsen case. As I made my approach, however, Jake obliterated it with four muttered words. "Well, well . . . *Angela Biwaban.*"

I masked my sudden alarm behind a bright, puzzled smile. "Oh, have we met, Mr. Norton?"

"No, but I read about you the other day." Blunt fingertips swatted whiskey-stained sports page. "Hey! Did you really flatten that dipstick Dietz?"

"I cannot tell a lie, Deputy Norton—"

"No need to be so formal, honey." Chuckling again, he gestured at an empty chair. "Make it Jake, eh? Been a long time since I wore the badge."

I seated myself and took a dainty sip of Lowenbrau. One elbow on the table, Jake gave me a shrewd sidelong look. "Kinda nice to step into a quiet bar, eh? After all them months inside."

Putting down my glass, I intercepted his questioning gaze. "You've done some checking, Jake."

"Not me. Cal Fischer. But I've still got some friends in the department." Wry grin. "Cops like to talk, Angie, 'specially to other cops." Pouring himself a generous slug of bourbon, he turned serious. "Come lookin' for me, eh?"

I nodded slowly.

"Then it's got to be about Dietz, right?" With a mildly trembling hand, he upended the shot glass. Whiskey cough. "You meet any biker girls in Springfield?"

"A few," I replied, wondering where he was going with this.

"Piece of advice, gal. Get in touch with 'em. Invite 'em out here for a visit. Tell 'em to bring their boyfriends." Raspy chuckle. "One big happy family! Fischer'll shit a brick—sideways!"

"What do I do when they get here, Jake?"

The ex-deputy's expression turned deadly serious. "Have four of the boyfriends pay a call on Delbert. Give him a message. Short and sweet. He messes with Angie, and he gets his face shoved up a Harley's tailpipe." Refilling the glass, he muttered, "That's the only way you're ever going to keep that fruit loop off your ass."

Brave little smile. "Now that I'm a solid citizen again, I was kind of hoping the sheriff's department would protect me."

Rueful bass chuckle. "That kind of reasoning can get a little gal killed."

"Isn't Delbert going to be enjoying the county's hospitality for a while?"

"Don't bet the rent on that, Angie gal. I heard the mental-health people are tryin' to get him sprung. They sent a lawyer from Sioux Falls." He knocked down another slug. "It's what them shrinks call *mainstreaming into the community.*"

"You're shitting me!"

"I never shit people I'm drinkin' with." Lifting the glass, Jake studied the light flashes in the whiskey. "Delbert sort of falls through the holes in the mental-health net. Too crazy for the joint. Ain't crazy enough for the zombie ward."

"How well do you know him?"

"Well enough." Shake of the grizzled head. "Lord knows I've busted his ass often enough. Delbert's a local boy. Grew up over there in Beulah township. 'Bout forty-six years old, I guess. Wasn't much of a farmer. He's sure a fine hand at carvin' stuff, though. Y'know, like statues and stuff."

"Sculpture?" I prompted.

"Yeah." Pleasant memories softened those hard, blunt features. "When he was sixteen, he carved a merganser duck out of a block of pine. I swear, you'd have thought it was goin' to rear up and flap its wings."

"I'm surprised he didn't develop the talent."

"I'm not." Brawny shoulders shrugged. "Delbert never got much encouragement at home. He never could please that old man of his. You know, my older brother worked for Wolfgang Dietz one summer. Son of a bitch never had a good word to say 'bout anythin'. He'd hurt his face if he ever tried to smile. He must've been fifty-five when Delbert was born. Ahhh, the old fuck never shoulda married."

It didn't sound like a nurturing environment for anyone, least of all a fledgling artist. Jake seemed to read my thoughts. Lifting his glass again, he shook his head sadly.

"Seen people treat their dogs better'n ol' Wolfgang treated that boy." His face closed like a fist. "Answered a lot of calls out there over thirty years back. Nowadays they call 'em *domestic disturbances.* For them, though, it was like one long intermittent brawl. I'd get there and find the old fuck swingin' a rake and Delbert hidin' behind his momma. If I was lucky, I'd get 'em split up before the hittin' started." Another toss of the whiskey. "That ol' son of a bitch took a swing at me once." His forefinger shot upward. *"Once!* Good thing I saw it comin'. Got my billy unhitched and let him have it. Kneecap sounded like a walnut crackin'. He hit that ground like a hay bale comin' out of the loft. Man, if them Lutherans had heard him cussin', they'd have drummed him right out of the church." He tried to smile but didn't quite make it. "That old fuck died the year Delbert turned fourteen. 'Course, Delbert was gone by then."

Seeing a sudden opening, I remarked, "He got picked up when the little Larsen girl disappeared."

The whiskey haze faded from Jake's eyes, banished by sudden surprise. "You've done some talkin' 'round town."

Folding my arms, I smiled. "Since the incident, everybody seems to have a Delbert story for me."

Slouching in his chair, he murmured, "That wasn't exactly his debut at the courthouse."

"How long was he gone, Jake?"

"Judge committed him for six months."

"A fourteen-year-old boy?"

"Even then Delbert made one hell of a first impression."

"I hear he wasn't charged."

"No evidence." Another alcoholic shrug. "All that boy did was get himself committed." Amber whiskey splashed the tabletop as he refilled his glass. "They took him away from that farm . . . 'bout ten years too late, I reckon."

"Who made the arrest?" I asked.

He frowned. "There was no arrest, Angie. Delbert got pulled in for questioning."

"Whose idea was that?"

"Deputy C.D. Fischer. Mister Hotshot himself. 'Bout one week into the investigation, he told ol' Ben Wirtz he had himself a hot lead. Next thing you know, there's the Dietz boy answerin' questions in ol' Ben's office."

"Why did Cal Fischer pull him in?"

Jake scowled at his reflection in the glass. "Mister Hotshot had what the FBI calls a *confidential source*. Claimed they saw a teenaged boy in that field off County Road 19 that Tuesday—the day Holly Larsen disappeared."

"Pretty thin, Jake."

Fingering the shot glass, he scowled, "That was my opinion at the time, Miss Angie."

"What made Fischer think it might have been Delbert?"

"Emma Dietz's maiden name was Berg. Same name as Birgitta Ostlund before she married." His raspy voice turned derisive. "And Delbert had no alibi. He claimed he came straight home, but the neighbors disputed that. Fischer turned up two who saw Delbert pedaling home after five-thirty on his bike."

"Did he admit to killing the Larsen girl?"

Sour smile. "Ten months after the Q & A session, Miss Angie, followin' intensive therapy by the best child psychiatrists in the state, Delbert looked Ben Wirtz right in the eye and, in all honesty, claimed his name was Marvin. Ten minutes later, he was calling himself Oscar. Spookiest thing he ever saw, ol' Ben said." Sad shake of the head. "I don't know if Delbert even remembers what happened. Took too many hits with that rake, I guess."

"So the Larsen case is still open?"

"Officially." Holding up the bottle, Jake gave the label a dull stare. "'Course, ol' Ben was satisfied."

"But you weren't." Staring at him, I made a steeple of my fingers. "Did you ever pursue it?"

His whiskered chin rose sharply. An ancient resentment blazed in the depths of those watery-blue eyes. He was silent for a long moment; then he leaned forward, as if trying to protect the near-empty bottle.

"You got any idea of where Ben Wirtz is buried, Miss Angie?"

"No." Ladylike shake of the head.

"Key Biscayne, Florida." Ghost of a drunken smile. "He moved down there when he retired . . . oh, eighteen years ago." Bitterness laced his inebriated chuckle. "Did pretty damn good for a farm country sheriff, eh? Yeah, that's the way it goes. You can be a good cop . . . tough, professional, you know. Or you can be a gladhander like old Ben Wirtz."

"Or Cal Fischer?"

Morose scowl. "Yeah, he's another one. Called himself C.D. Fischer when he was on patrol. Which wasn't often. He was hankerin' after a cushy desk job his first year on the force. Spent all his free time down at the party headquarters, shakin' hands, stuffin' flyers in envelopes. Used to take his vacation in early November so he could help with the election." One last hasty swallow. "Sure paid off for him, though. When ol' Ben lit out for Florida, Cal Fischer moved right into that big swivel chair." Lifting his head, he looked around dully, as if seeing the place for the very first time. "Me . . . well, here's where I ended up."

Alcohol had brought him to the brink of a talking jag. Lounging in my chair, I let him talk.

"Yeah, yeah . . . tough, professional. No time for brown-nosing. Don't take shit from anybody." Jake's boozy stare found the window's golden lettering. He seemed fascinated by it. "Best damned deputy in the East River. Five commendations from the Sheriff's Association. And what do I got to show for it, eh? A pissant pension and a permanent seat in here." All at once, his gaze swiveled my way. "Lost my wife 'cause o' this place, did you know that?"

"No, Jake." Solemn-eyed Angie.

"Years ago." His unfocused gaze drifted back to the bottle. "Hell of a broad, that Inga. But she just didn't understand. No one does. Got to be a cop to understand."

"Understand what, Jake?"

"Why I spent my off-duty time in here." Desperation softened his gravelly voice. "You see so much of it, you know? So much of the shit. You can't take it home with you." Red-rimmed eyes fluttered shut. "I-I needed to be with other cops. City, county, it didn't matter. I had to talk to *somebody*, and they're the only people who understand." Sudden accusatory glance. "Inga didn't and neither do you. Nobody's ever shot at you."

I could have corrected him on that, but I let it pass.

"Inga wouldn't listen. She thought it was 'cause I didn't want to come home. I-I I—loved that woman, but goddammit she just didn't *understand!*"

Long moments of silence. Jake seemed to have forgotten my presence there. He sat with his arms folded on the table, glaring at the bar's name as if it were somehow responsible for all the misfortunes of his life. Leaning forward, I struck the empty bottle with my fingernail. The glass made a hollow clinking sound.

"Would you like me to get you anything?"

His shoulders lifted in a negative shrug. I took that as my cue to depart. Rising from my chair, I murmured, "Take care of yourself, Jake."

His only response was an incoherent mumble.

Returning to the bar, I handed over my empty bottle and glass. The Italian bartender nodded his thanks. With a sad smile, I added, "I don't think Jake's going to make it to work tonight."

"They know better than to expect him, miss." Peering over my shoulder, he shot the ex-deputy a pitying glance. "It ain't like a real job, you know. They just give him a few hours here and there." Catching my look of curiosity, he added, "Plant management's mighty grateful to Jake. He broke up a heist at their payroll office back in the Sixties. Tackled the gang singlehanded, he did. No time to call for backup. They opened fire on him the minute his cruiser rolled into the lot."

Reciting from memory, I murmured, "Best damn deputy in the East River."

He dropped my empty bottle in the trash bin. "Lot of folks around here feel that way."

"Add me to the roster." I opened my purse, dug out my wallet and withdrew a twenty. "Make sure he gets home all right, will you?"

Nodding, he slid the bill under the counter.

And then I strolled out of there, my features grim, leather

purse dangling from my shoulder, mulling over my chat with Deputy Jake.

You did it all wrong, Mr. Norton. Instead of busting holdup men and racking up commendations, you should have put your time in down at county headquarters, shaking hands with the politicians. Who knows? You might have retired a sergeant.

Dry wheatgrass sprouted near the wooden railroad ties. The November breeze chilled my face as I hurried along.

I could see how Cal Fischer had become the sheriff's fair-haired boy. After many productive years of feeding at the public trough, Ben Wirtz had been confronted with a high-profile case that was rapidly going nowhere. An eight-year-old girl, vanished without a trace, and the whole state screaming for an arrest. That was excellent timing, Cal, turning up a new lead just as the Larsen case was about to fizzle.

I wondered who Fischer's *confidential source* was. Or if his source even existed.

As a deputy, Fischer must have been aware of Delbert Deitz's many cruel and erratic escapades. Even then, the odds against finding the slayers of missing children were depressingly high. Casting Delbert in the perpetrator's role would have served three purposes. One, defused the public outcry in the Larsen case by showing that the department could indeed achieve results. Two, hastened the hospitalization of the increasingly irrational Dietz boy. And three, made one Deputy C.D. Fischer look very, very good, a fitting successor to good ol' Sheriff Ben.

Rein up, princess. You're assuming that there is no source. That Fischer grabbed Delbert and used him to plug the hole in the Larsen case. But you could be wrong. Perhaps Delbert really did kill that poor little girl.

I thought of those mad eyes behind the Taurus pistol. Sudden icy shudder. Had Dietz always been this way? Or had thirty years of repeated incarcerations in mental hospitals turned him into a full-blown psychopath?

Thoughtful frown. No, I think I'll skip on an interview with Delbert Dietz. At least for now.

I was far more worried about Sheriff Fischer. If he had taken the easy way out in the Larsen case, that was extremely bad news for Chief's favorite granddaughter.

Just how hard would the sheriff search for the missing Mister Beach Tan? And, if he truly believed it was homicide, would he even bother to seek the real killer?

Especially when he had a ready-made suspect like me at hand!

As I drove into the truck stop, I spotted Chief waiting patiently beside an idling Peterbilt. Gray smoke drifted away from its vertical stacks. My long green Mercury rolled to a stop. Compared to the truck's diesel rumble, Clunky's eight-cylinder, 351-cubic-inch engine sounded like the trilling of a songbird.

As my grandfather got in, I offered a curious sidelong look. "How'd you make out?"

Fatigued sigh. "Did you know, Angie, that there are eleven motels in this town?"

My hopes began to fade. "Our friend must have stayed at one of them."

Chief shook his head. "If he stayed at a motel, it sure wasn't here in Mitchell. I talked to every single manager. No luck!"

"How did they react when you described him?" I asked, steering Clunky out of the asphalt lot.

"They all looked mighty surprised." Aged Anishinabe smile. "No one's seen a suntan around here since Labor Day. No question about it, child. If that man was here in town, he sure would've been memorable." His smile widened. "Folks hereabouts take a keen interest in strangers."

Putting slight pressure on the gas pedal, I sent Clunky tooling north on Burr. "How did you explain *your* presence here?"

"Ohh . . . I asked a lot of questions about duck season."

Turning serious, he added, "Only two ways to read it, missy. Either he was stayin' with friends here in town. Or he was holed up elsewhere. Huron, maybe."

"Friends would have reported him missing," I observed.

"Unless they're the ones who shot him."

I shot my grandfather an exasperated look. "You're a big help, Chief."

"I try." He let out a teasing chuckle. "Seriously, though, I think it's Number Two."

"He was staying out of town," I murmured, my gaze fixed on the light afternoon traffic just ahead. "Why?"

Mild look of disappointment. "And you're the girl with the Master's in business? Think, Angie!"

My obsidian eyes blossomed in sudden comprehension. "He didn't want someone to know he was in town."

Nodding, Chief made coaxing motions with both hands.

"Because he came to town looking for that person," I added, my voice vibrant with excitement. "Sure! But the quarry found out he was here and lured him into Mrs. Ostlund's field."

"Ostlund?" Chief echoed.

"I'll explain on the way to the market." Stepping lightly on the brake, I flipped the blinker lever. "Chief, can you do me a favor?"

"Take a run up to Huron? You bet."

"Mister Beach Tan must've been staying there. He sure wasn't commuting from Sioux Falls every day!"

As we drove to the Super City Mall, I gave my grandfather a detailed report on my day, discussing in detail my trip to the library and Jake Norton's veiled hints that Sheriff Wirtz might have blown the Larsen case decades ago. Like me, Chief was very much interested in Cal Fischer's mysterious source. But neither of us could come up with a safe way to approach the current sheriff. So we let the matter drop. After all, I still had the food shopping to do.

Randall's was a large, brightly illuminated, low-ceilinged

supermarket. Tall front windows and long rows of fluorescent lights. Diamond-shaped display ads suspended from the ceiling. Glass-walled manager's office fronted by a skid piled high with sacks of road salt. While Chief perused the notices on the bulletin board, I maneuvered a shopping cart out of the line and headed down the produce aisle. I had to keep both hands on the pushbar. Having shattered its ball bearings, the left front wheel vibrated like a cement mixer. Trudy's grocery list nestled between the fingers of my right hand.

As I rounded the aisle, I spied a familiar face at the immaculate meat counter. When I saw the plastic-wrapped steak in his hand, I knew it was him. Only doctors can afford sirloin these days.

Bright-eyed Angie smile. "Hello, Doctor Brenning."

"Angela!" Dropping the steak in his cart, he turned and gently shook my hand. "What brings you into town?"

"Three grown men with farm-size appetites."

His laughter was subdued and polite. Then, his face turning serious, he asked, "How are the Elderkins making out?"

"Adjusting," I replied, grateful to him for leading into Miss Edna's death. There were questions I wanted to ask. "It's been hardest for Trudy, I think. She and Miss Edna were very, very close." Sudden intake of breath. "You know, we haven't thanked you for everything you did the other day."

"Thanks, Angela, but there really wasn't that much I could have done." Sincere regret. "Miss Edna had passed on long before I got there."

Quick sidestep into interrogation. "You know, I've been meaning to ask you about that, Doctor. Are you sure rigor had set in by morning?"

"Absolutely." Brisk nod. "Rigor was well advanced. By the time Kristy found her, she'd been dead at least four hours."

"Did you do the autopsy?" I asked.

Shaking his head, he replied, "The county pathologist."

"I've been wondering . . ." Purse the lips. "Did he find anything wrong with Mrs. Mutchler's pacemaker?"

"Of course not." He gave me a surprised look. "Her pacemaker was operating just fine."

"But it didn't prevent her heart attack—"

"That's a common misconception, Angela," he interrupted, showing a mild frown. "A pacemaker does *not* detect and prevent a cardiac episode. It merely runs an AC current through the heart's muscle fibers. The current is supposed to steady a fluctuating heartbeat. Sometimes it reestablishes a rhythm halted by cardiac arrest. But not always. I'd say Mrs. Mutchler sustained a massive ventricular fibrillation. No pacemaker could have possibly saved her."

My memory dredged up last night's telephone chat with Jill Stormcloud.

"Then she died very quickly?" I prodded.

"Within seconds."

"Twenty seconds?"

"More like fifteen."

A curious shadow crossed his distinguished features, and I knew he was wondering why I was asking these questions. Flashing a doleful look, I reiterated Jill's response. "Oh, well, at least she didn't suffer."

"She didn't, young lady. You can be certain of that."

And then I steered the conversation away from Miss Edna's deathbed, asking how long she'd been his patient. After a few physician reminiscences, we said our goodbyes, and he trundled his cart toward the checkout counter.

As I set off in search of my grandfather, I mulled over Doctor Brenning's assertions. Anishinabe eyebrows knotted in deep thought.

First Jill, the one-time L.P.N. and now you, Doc. Both of you came up with the same estimate—fifteen to twenty seconds. The verdict is unanimous. That's how long it takes a ventricular fibrillation heart attack to kill a human being.

But how could so much perspiration have soaked Miss Edna's nightgown in only *twenty seconds?*

I shook my head. It didn't seem possible, unless . . .

She took longer than that to die!

And if she did, then she certainly didn't die of a sudden ventricular fibrillation.

A icy tremor chilled my skin. Perhaps I hadn't been imagining things that night. Maybe I really did hear Miss Edna cry out as . . . *something* . . . killed her.

But what!?

Sudden warpath scowl. Perhaps I ought to ask a couple of other questions first. Such as *who* . . . and *why?*

SEVEN

"What makes you think Miss Edna was murdered?" my grandfather asked.

"None of it adds up, Chief," I replied, backing Clunky out of the parking space. "When I began CPR on Miss Edna, the front of her nightgown was damp with perspiration."

He glanced at me from the passenger side. Between us, on the long padded seat, huddled the grocery bags. "So?"

"So Doctor Brenning said she'd been dead four hours. The perspiration should have evaporated by then. *It didn't.*"

Playing the devil's advocate, my grandfather remarked, "She was under the blankets, Angie."

I watched the southbound traffic zoom past the mall entrance. "True enough, but her arms were *on top of* the comforter when we found her. Meaning her arms had been exposed to room-temperature air for at least four hours." I fired a knowing glance at Chief. "When I checked her pulse, I noticed that her wrist was just as damp as her chest."

Anishinabe scowl. "So she was sweating all over. Must have been damned painful." Uncertain glance. "Do people sweat that much in a heart attack?"

"Not in twenty seconds." Spotting a gap, I eased Clunky into the flow of traffic. "Both Doctor Brenning and Jill stated that a ventricular fibrillation attack would have killed her in fifteen to twenty seconds." Quick sidelong glance. "Chief, it's *impossible* for a human being to perspire so much in that length of time."

"What are you saying, Angie?"

"I'm saying she took longer than twenty seconds to die. I think Miss Edna took several minutes to die. She cried out during that time, and that's what jolted me awake."

The castlelike Enchanted Doll Museum whizzed past on our right. Compressing his lips thoughtfully, Chief said, "Whatever it was, it left Miss Edna with heart damage convincing enough to fool the doctor. Poison?"

"Could be." I nodded, keeping both hands on the steering wheel. "Let's backtrack a bit, okay? She perspired heavily. Why?"

"That's Mother Nature's cooling system," Chief pointed out. "When your core temperature gets too high, the body forces moisture out through the pores of the skin. Air flows over the sweat, cooling you off."

"Which tells us what?" I challenged.

"Miss Edna's temperature had to be over one hundred degrees Fahrenheit. The poison made her feverish—"

"And induced heart failure," I finished for him. "Well, there's a start."

"Not much of one, though. Think it through just a little bit more, missy."

"I'm not sure I follow you, Chief."

"How did Miss Edna swallow the poison?" he said, showing a troubled look. "You said yourself she never leaves the farm."

My mouth dropped in indignation. "Come *on!* Surely you don't think the Elderkins—!?"

"Who else had the opportunity, Angie?"

"They-They *loved* Miss Edna! You saw Trudy and Bonnie at the funeral. No way would they ever—!"

Scratching his nose, my grandfather let out an irritable grunt. "No need to jump down my throat, Angie. I'm just raising possibilities, that's all. Think back. Was Miss Edna ever alone at the farm?"

"No! Trudy was always there ..." A sudden memory stilled my reply. "No, no ... I'm *wrong!* Miss Edna was all by herself that afternoon."

Chief gave me an inquisitive look. "What afternoon?"

"Twelve hours before she died." Touching Clunky's brake pedal, I slowed at the corner of West Second Avenue. "The afternoon Delbert held me and Bonnie hostage. Josh and Trudy left for Bonnie's the minute the sheriff called."

"What time was that?"

"A little after three," I murmured, frowning at my reflection in Clunky's mirror. "And Kristy didn't get home until nearly five. Meaning Miss Edna was alone for two hours."

"Plenty of time for someone to drop by the farm and offer to make tea." Chief let out a quiet sigh. "All we need now is a motive."

Sudden fussbudget face. "Maybe we have one, Chief."

"Don't keep it to yourself, girl. I'd love to hear it."

"The night before Delbert turned up at Bonnie's, Miss Edna and I got to talking. She told me I ought to put the past behind me—get on with my life."

Chief cocked his blunt head. "Smart lady—good advice."

"Then she said something very strange." I extracted the quote from my recent memory. " *'You're not the only girl who ever made a foolish choice when she was young . . . I know what I'm talking about.'* "

Chief made a sour face. "You're reaching, Angie. Been a long time since Miss Edna was a young girl. She's lived in Davison County all her life. Never been in trouble before. Why should it suddenly develop now?"

Quizzical glance in my grandfather's direction. "Because Mister Beach Tan has come to town?"

Chief was silent for a long moment. As we started down West Second, he murmured, "You really think the two are connected?"

"It's possible. There are connections out there, Chief. Some vague and some not so vague. Mister Beach Tan was shot in Mrs. Ostlund's field near Enemy Creek. The field is where Holly Larsen's lunch box was found. The local law thinks Delbert Dietz was responsible for Holly's disappearance. Following a long and unexplained absence, Delbert shows up in town and terrorizes Miss Edna's niece. Then Miss Edna dies under very unusual circumstances." Slow shake of the head. "I'd say we've gone way beyond the realm of circumstance."

"Yeah, but what's the motive?"

"That's what we have to find out." Just then, the broad sign of the Commercial Bank caught my eye. Slowing down, I steered Clunky into the parking lot. "And I think I know just where to start."

Three-thirty found me standing on the lot's asphalt, my fanny at rest against Clunky's rectangular fender. There were almost as many cars in the lot as rain puddles. Cerulean gaps had appeared in the November overcast, and the clouds nearest the western horizon gleamed like polished brass. Arms folded, I watched patiently as the bank's employees came streaming out the rear door.

And there she was—Julie Sievert, lovely bank teller and part-time environmental activist. Ash-blond bangs and impeccably arched eyelashes. She was wearing a smartly tailored suit, mustard with brick-red piping, double-breasted jacket and pleated-front slim skirt. High heels rapped the pavement as she strolled toward a year-old Pontiac Grand Prix.

"There she is," I murmured.

Seated behind the wheel, my grandfather peered out the passenger window. "You want me to wait here for you?"

I nodded. "You know what Arnold says—*I'll be back!*" Striding away from my car, I shouted, "Julie!"

Halting at once, she turned my way. Pretty features brightened. "Hi, Angie! How goes it?"

"Ohhhh . . . can't complain." I nodded at the bank. "Just getting out of work?"

"Uh-huh!" Weary nod. "It's Thursday. Payday! They can be quite grueling."

"Tell me about it." Touching her elbow, I steered her toward North Lawler Street. "Come on, I'll buy you a coffee." She looked as if she was about to decline, so I added, "You can fill me in on what's been happening with SPSD."

On our way to the Town House Cafe, Julie exuberantly described the recent confrontation in civil court. Safe Power for South Dakota had persuaded the judge to order a new safety hearing before the Industrial Development Commission.

". . . so we're all set for tomorrow night," Julie said, sliding her chair away from the linen-covered table. "I hope you'll come, Angie. Believe me, we need all the help we can get."

"I'll be there," I promised, signaling the waitress. "Where are they holding the meeting?"

"The Corn Palace!" Triumphant grin. "Sam Covington is fit to be tied. He wanted the meeting held at the courthouse so he could keep our people out. But the judge let Scott pick the site."

Just then, the waitress appeared at our table, notepad in hand. Chubby woman in her early thirties, with a tight-fitting uniform and a broad, friendly Dakota smile. "Are you ladies ready to order?"

"Coffee—cream, no sugar." Julie sneaked a covetous glance at the pastry under glass. "And maybe one of those oatmeal cookies. Angie?"

"No munchies for me, thanks." I held up my hand. "I get enough calories on the farm. Make it black coffee, okay?"

While the waitress poured our coffee, Julie asked about the Elderkins. Miss Edna had many friends in Mitchell, Julie's grandparents among them. So I steered the conversation toward pioneer family history.

"Miss Edna told me her maiden name was Enright," I remarked, lifting my steaming porcelain mug.

Julie nodded. "Her daddy was Frank Enright. Lord, that family goes way, way back."

"Prominent?"

"You bet!" She blew on her coffee. "Right up there with the Fairmonts! They say Frank Enright used to go to Pierre, and the governor would come running out of the statehouse just to shake his hand." Her smile turned rueful. "He must be the only man in Davison County who ever got rich farming."

"How'd he manage that?" I asked.

"Timing, I guess." Julie's pretty face became pensive. "My people used to be farmers. They got wiped out in the Depression. Grandad moved into town and opened a paint store. The Enrights got hurt, too. Everybody did! But then, in 1939, old Mr. Enright bought or leased every acre of farmland he could lay hands on. People thought he'd gone plumb crazy. Nobody saw the war coming, but he did. He made a fortune supplying food to that Lend-Lease program."

"What did he do with the money?"

"He bought acres and acres of sage prairie out there in the West River. Grandad said he was *sure* Frank Enright had lost his mind." Bittersweet smile. "He was crazy, old Mr. Enright. Crazy like a fox! When ag prices started coming down again, he leased his land to Uncle Sam, first to the Defense Department for SAC bombing sites, later to the Department of Agriculture for demonstration cattle-grazing programs." She shook her head in reluctant admiration. "Before he died, Mr.

Enright put a lot of money into the Middle Border Savings Bank."

That name had a familiar ring. "Here in Mitchell?"

Julie's smile turned impish. "I'm not supposed to talk about them. MBSB is one of our distinguished competitors."

"Old money?" I inquired.

She shook her head. "Phil Covington chartered it forty years ago. They're heavily involved in loans to farmers . . . as are we all!"

Remembering my chat with Clem Mutchler, I remarked, "Sam Covington's dad?"

"Uh-huh! Sam took over as Middle Border CEO twelve years ago."

Following a sip of coffee, I murmured, "So Miss Edna's family money was invested in Covington's bank?"

Julie's hand waggled energetically. "No, no, no . . . Mr. Enright's involvement in MBSB ended long ago."

"How long ago, Julie?"

"Oh, years before I was born. Thirty years, I guess."

About the time that Holly Larsen disappeared, I thought.

Another brief sip. "Did Mr. Enright pull his money out?"

"Oh, no! Mr. Enright's will stipulated that the Middle Border shares be sold and his proceeds put into trust for Miss Edna. The sale took place after his will was probated. A bank in Sioux Falls administers the Enright Trust."

Memo to myself—find out the name of that bank and how much money remains in the trust.

Hoping to keep the conversation going, I said, "I hear she inherited a couple of farms, too."

"That's right. There's the original Enright farm, of course, on the Jim. Just north of it is the old McCabe place. That belonged to her mother's family. Her maternal grandfather was Big Tim McCabe."

All at once, in my mind, I was back in Miss Edna's bedroom,

doing her hair, listening to her talk about those farms. Together they encompassed around 4,000 acres.

"Julie . . ." I set down my coffee mug. "What's the going price for Davison County farmland these days?"

"The price per acre?" Bluish-gray eyes narrowed thoughtfully. "Oh, I'd say about $450."

While Julie daintily nibbled her oatmeal cookie, I did some rapid mental calculation. Interesting! On the open market, Miss Edna's two farms had an aggregate sales value of one-point-eight million. And that's *on top of* whatever's in the Enright Trust!

Julie cast me a curious look. "Why do you ask?"

I became Schoolgirl Angie. Innocent smile. "Sam Covington made Josh an offer for our farm."

Her eyes blossomed in sudden alarm. "He did!? *When?*"

"Right after Miss Edna's funeral."

Her expression turned sickish. "Is Josh taking him up on it?"

"Unh-uh! Turned him down flat."

Sudden relief. "Thank goodness!" Anger sparkled in those dark blue eyes. "You know why he wants the farm, don't you?"

No . . . but I'm hoping you'll tell me, Julie. I need as much background information on Covington as I can get.

"OP wants to run the proposed right-of-way straight across the Elderkin property. So far we've been able to keep the proposed transmission line outside the county." Woeful look. "If Sam Covington buys that property, he'll *invite* them in!"

Frown of concern. "How close to the Elderkin place is that 900-kilovolt line?"

"The northwest corner of Josh's property is on the county line. An OP transmission tower stands just beyond the trees."

Curiosity generated fresh questions. "How did Covington get hooked up with OP?"

Julie's hands fluttered in hapless indignation. "Oh, he's been in their corporate back pocket for years. Four years back, he picked up a farm at a bankruptcy sale over in Union township. Turned right around and sold it to OP. They put up one of those transformer substations." Scowl of disapproval. "As if we needed *another* one!"

I could guess the rest of it. "So how much did Owechahay Power contribute to Sam's campaign for the Industrial Development Commission?"

"Officially . . . zero!" Tart smile. "But there were an awful lot of little political action committees out there raising funds for him. By some strange coincidence, the PAC chairpeople were all from Sioux Falls."

"And all had upper-level management positions at OP?"

"Uh-huh! An amazing coincidence, eh?"

Relaxing in my straight-back chair, I remarked, "Kind of strange, isn't it? A banker actively seeking farm property. I thought they didn't like to get stuck owning real estate."

"Normally we don't. It's much better to have productive real-estate loans on the books generating income for the bank. Defaulted property tends to be an albatross." Julie's lips formed a thoughtful smile. "But the bank isn't Covington's only concern. He owns half a dozen local businesses."

"Including a real-estate firm?"

Pert nod. "Palace Realty, that's his. Biggest firm between Sioux Falls and Huron."

No mistaking the antipathy in her voice. "I take it you don't approve of Mr. Covington wearing two hats."

"No, I don't." She looked around hastily, as if fearful that we might be overheard. Her alto voice dwindled to a murmur. "He's a vulture, Angie. He puts the squeeze on farmers at the bank. There's no such thing as a loan extension at MBSB. The average farmer has to borrow $300,000—up front!—just to operate for one year. Those finance terms are ironclad. If the farmer makes just one mistake, he can lose it all! Sooner or later, he'll make that mistake. Or maybe the weather will make it for him. And then it's all gone."

"What does Covington do with all that land?"

Her mouth hardened. "He has it rezoned *rural/residential.* Then he hands off to Palace Realty. It's a scam, Angie, but it's generated a ton of cash for him."

I finished my coffee. "How?"

"Well, with his pull on the Planning Board, it's no problem getting his subdivision plans approved. Then Palace Realty sells off individual lots at a discount. Ten percent off the current market price. Buyers rush right in and snap them up. All kinds of buyers. Other realtors. Urban couples hoping to move to the countryside. All kinds."

I nodded in understanding. Anishinabe frown. Pretty slick, Mr. Covington! You pick up the farm for nothing, subdivide into planned neighborhoods, and offer choice lots at discount prices, ensuring a quick sale. And leaving your buyers with the problem of turning farmland into suburb. A difficult problem, indeed, for the second realtor trying to line up financing for a contractor. Or for the guileless young couple hoping to build their bucolic single-family home.

Hmm—could be Palace Realty cash is finding its way into the Middle Border Savings Bank. That's something else to check out when I get to Sioux Falls.

Julie said nothing. Lacquered fingernails tapped the rim of her coffee mug. She stared past me out the window, her brooding gaze fixed on the distant fiery Dakota sunset.

Flagging the waitress, I murmured, "Julie?"

Sudden wan smile. "Sorry. I was just thinking. About them." Her soft chin pointed toward the flaming horizon. "Farm people. Neighbors." Emotion thickened her voice. "They think we're all like him, you know. You stand behind the counter at the bank, and they give you that look. As if you're the enemy." Slender fingers gripped her cup. "It goes on and on and . . . and then you don't see them anymore. You hear about the foreclosure—the auction." A tearful tone crept into Julie's voice. "They're people I grew up with—people I've known all my life. Good people! Then they end up in Billings or Minneapolis or Omaha, living on Food Stamps, getting their kids' clothes out of dumpsters. It isn't fair! N-None of it!" Blue eyes filled with tears. "Oh, Angie, there are times when I just *hate* this job!"

While I paid the tab, Julie spent some time alone in the ladies' room, getting her composure back. When she emerged, most of her mascara was gone, but she was feeling much, much better. We stood on the sidewalk for a few minutes, chatting about the upcoming meeting. After again securing my promise to attend, she waved goodbye and stalked off in the direction of the Commercial Bank. I gave her a fifteen-minute head start, then returned to the parking lot.

On the way back to Yorktown, I told my grandfather what I'd learned about the Enright Trust and Covington's real-estate scam, concluding with Julie's feelings about the current farm crisis. Chief agreed that a visit to Sioux Falls was in order.

The last glimmer of sunset had faded by the time we turned off Route 38. Clunky's high beams illuminated the farm fields on either side of the highway. Thousands and thousands of tawny cornstalks went streaming past. Irony brought a grim smile to my lips. The world's most productive agricultural land, I thought, and very few people could make a comfortable living from it.

No, Julie, it's not very fair. Not very fair at all.

We found a "farm crisis" of our very own when we finally arrived at the Elderkin place. An irascible cow had given the generator a good solid kick on her way out of the barn that morning. And now Josh, Brad, Jeremy, and Kristy were crouched around the generator, serenaded by two-dozen impatient Herefords, trying to restore power to the milking machines. When I breezed into the house, my arms full of groceries, Trudy tap-tapped her wristwatch and gave me the exact same smoldering look I used to get from the assistant principal at Central High School.

Uh-oh! Better grab that apron, princess. Otherwise, we'll all be eating at nine o'clock.

Two hours later, Trudy's mood was much improved by the sight of her family wolfing down their hamburgers and potato salad. Following dessert, my grandfather offered to have a look at the generator. He's always been a handyman, and life at Tettegouche has only served to sharpen his skills.

Between us, Trudy and I finished the dishes in under fifteen minutes. Hanging up my damp towel, I offered an apologetic smile. "Sorry I was late, Mrs. Elderkin. I ran into Julie Sievert in town."

"No need to apologize, Angie." She pressed the back of her wrist against her wrinkled forehead. "It's been hectic for us all. I don't think I got to *half* the things I wanted to do today." She cast a regretful glance at Miss Edna's bedroom. "I really planned on cleaning in there."

Inquisitive glance. "I thought Carol was supposed to help you with that."

Trudy made no reply. As she turned away, however, I caught her veiled expression of disappointment. "It'll have to wait, I suppose."

"Not if I give it a start." Touching the woman's shoulders, I steered her into the parlor. "Go put your feet up. Relax. You've earned it."

"Angie! It's too much work. Let me help—"

"No way. You're taking it easy tonight," I interrupted. Domestic Angie. "Don't worry. I'm not going to do it all. I'll box your aunt's clothes. At least we can get that done."

"Well . . . all right."

Heading down cellar, I located the cardboard box the

Elderkin computer had arrived in, emptied it of old magazines and wrestled it up the dust-covered stairs. Soon I was hard at work in Miss Edna's bedroom, taking armloads of clothing out of her walk-in closet, laying them across the back of her vanity chair. One by one, I stripped each garment from its hanger. Strong feeling of déjà vu. I'd spent many an hour doing the same sort of work at Springfield.

When I finished, I replaced the wire hangers in the closet, quietly closed the bedroom door, and began my examination of the bed. Turning back the blankets, I saw the faint imprint of Miss Edna's frail body on the bottom sheet.

Hands on my knees, I leaned over and scrutinized the linen more closely.

Something's wrong here, Angie. I shouldn't even be able to see that impression. Had Miss Edna been poisoned, she would have been kicking and thrashing in bed. The sheet should be all wrinkled. And it isn't!

Standing up straight, I yielded to a fussbudget face. Could it be that she really did die of a heart attack?

Playing a hunch, I bent over again. Like a safecracker, I sensitized my fingertips by rubbing them briskly against the stiff denim fabric of my jeans. Slowly my fingertips glided over the bed linen.

How about that! Fresh linen has a smooth satiny feel. The fabric within her bodily impression feels flat, coarse, almost like sailcloth, as if it had been drenched and then dried over a period of hours.

No, I hadn't imagined it. Miss Edna had done some heavy sweating during her last few moments of life.

Yet the bottom sheet clearly showed that she had died almost instantly. How was that possible?

Pronounced fussbudget face. Terrific! If she didn't suffer a heart attack, and if she wasn't poisoned, then how did she die?

Intense cogitation produced no immediate answers.

With a snarl of frustration, I stripped the comforter from

the bed. I'd taken my murder-scene survey as far as I possibly could. Might as well get the housework done.

As I folded the coverlet, however, I noticed a dark lozenge-shaped smudge. Lifting the quilt one-handed, I prodded the stain with my thumb. It had an odd rubbery feel. At first I thought it was Kristy's chewing gum. Then I frowned.

Since when does bubble gum come in battleship-gray?

Hurriedly I stripped the bed to the bottom sheet. I stared at the impression Miss Edna's body had made, fixing its precise location in my mind. Then, my hands trembling with excitement, I spread the quilt over the bed.

A tuck here, a pull there, and I soon had the comforter restored to its original position. My gaze zeroed in on the oblong smudge, matching its location with my memory of the impression.

Thoughtful Anishinabe frown. The smudge occupied the same location as Miss Edna's left wrist. My frown deepened. I distinctly recalled touching that wrist on Monday morning, desperately seeking a feeble pulse. I remembered the damp-parchment feel of her skin. And that curiously dry suntanned spot near Miss Edna's wrist bone.

My eyes narrowed. No, you're not imagining things, princess. That's a perfect match!

Leading to another intriguing question. If Miss Edna had been sweating at the moment of her death, i.e. exuding enough perspiration to dampen the sheets, then why was that *one spot* as dry as desert sand?

Quickly I rounded the foot of the bed. Damn! If only I'd paid more attention when we rushed in here!

Kneeling beside Miss Edna's bed, I rested my aquiline nose on the horizon of bedspread and looked down the smudge's longitudinal axis. Panoramic vista of her rocking chair and a tall oaken chest of drawers.

Reaching the opposite side of the bed, I made a hasty genu-flection. Angela the Pious. Again I looked down the length of the smudge. Floral wallpaper loomed beyond the quilt horizon. Frustration extinguished my smile. Nothing!

But then, as I began to stand, I noticed something that filled my stomach with an ice-cold surge. That dark smudge pointed *directly* at the baseboard's cable TV outlet!

Within seconds, I was on all fours, peering into the coaxial cable's circular aperture. Fine hairs prickled on the back of my neck.

You remember the first time I was in here. Don't you, Miss Edna? You asked me to do your hair. I was putting in the curlers, remember? I dropped one, and it fell down here. I had a quick glance at this cable outlet, and I distinctly remember a coppery plug filling this hole.

The plug was gone!

In its place was a circular opening about one inch in diameter, with a smidgen of metallic slag pooled at the bottom. A frozen droplet teetered at the brink like hardened maple syrup.

So who's been in here, Miss Edna? And why have they been playing around with your cable TV outlet?

I had many more questions, but only a technician could properly answer them. So I rose swiftly, brushing off my knees, and headed for Miss Edna's vanity table. I could do the job better with a Swiss Army knife, but I was willing to settle for a steel fingernail file.

Luck was with me. Miss Edna's manicure kit occupied a front corner of the table's center drawer. I extracted a sharp-tipped file and returned to the oyster-colored outlet.

Changing my mind at the last moment, I sat on the edge of the bed and carefully scraped away the dark smudge. Angie smile of satisfaction. The file's edge sported a coating of rubbery material.

I wrapped the evidence in a tissue and tucked it in my jeans pocket. Then, kneeling on the floor, I chipped away at the frozen slag. The droplet clung tenaciously to the outlet. With an impatient grimace, I winkled the file's tip beneath the residue. An upward thrust flipped it skyward. I watched it clatter on the floor, then snatched it with my thumb and forefinger.

Holding it up to the light, I pursed my lips in puzzlement. Some kind of alloy. Alternating gleams of copper and silver. Or maybe it was zinc. Don't ask me. A metallurgist I'm not!

With a mild shrug, I stuffed the slag fragment into my jeans pocket along with the rubbery goop.

Suddenly, a female voice rang out. "What are you doing in here?"

Instant glance. I spotted Jeremy's wife, Carol, in the bedroom doorway. Brunette lady in a lime-colored turtleneck blouse and stylish Dutch chocolate slacks. Oh, terrific! *Now* you show up, Carol!

Delicate features tensed in suspicion. "I asked you a question, Angela."

Splaying the fingers of my free hand, I flashed an insouciant smile. "My nails."

Carol wasn't buying it. "On the *floor!?*"

"I dropped the file."

Moving forward, she sent her critical gaze around the bedroom. "Trudy said you were cleaning up in here."

"I was." Standing erect, I leisurely ran the file blade up and down my thumbnail. "I caught my cuticle on a sleeve."

"How unfortunate for you." She seemed to resent my presence there. "You really didn't have to do this, you know."

"Well, Trudy did want to get it done today."

Instantly she detected my veiled sarcasm. A very thin-skinned lady, indeed. "And what is *that* supposed to mean?"

"Maybe you shouldn't make promises you can't keep, Carol."

Emitting an indignant gasp, she marched right up to me. "Listen, honey, I was *busy*—"

"Doing leg lifts at the figure salon?" My scowl was easily a match for hers. "Trudy was counting on you to clean this bedroom."

"Really?" Carol's voice crept upward in volume. "Well, perhaps you'd be kind enough to inform my mother-in-law that I'm not the *hired help!*"

"You could tell her yourself," I snapped, dark eyes flashing. "But I guess it's too much trouble hauling that fat ass out of the easy chair."

"You impertinent little—!"

At that moment, Jeremy strolled through the doorway, his handsome face showing sudden anxiety. Broad work-roughened hands lifted in supplication. "Hey, now! Easy, you two. What seems to be the trouble here?"

I hooked my thumb toward Carol. "Got a lady here who's allergic to housework."

Sudden mirth nearly split Jeremy's face. Then Carol turned his way, and he stifled his burgeoning smile. The young wife leveled an accusatory finger at me.

"Jeremy! I want an apology from that—that *woman!*"

Weary conciliatory smile. "Carol . . . look, why don't we all count ten, go in the kitchen and have some coffee. Okay?"

"Sounds good to me." Schoolgirl Angie.

"I'm not budging from this spot until *she* apologizes!"

"Stick out your arms then," I said. "This room could use another coatrack."

Jeremy shot me a glance of annoyance. "Angela!" His hands started toward her shoulders, faltered, then dropped. "Come on, Carol. Don't make a big production out of it. Let's just drop the whole thing, okay?"

Outraged tone. "Did you hear what she said to me!?"

"Carol . . ."

"Why are *you* taking her side?"

"I'm not taking anybody's side. I'm trying to—"

Realizing that she couldn't intimidate me, Carol turned on

her husband. "It's bad enough I have to put up with this sort of thing from that spoiled-brat sister of yours. I'll be damned if I'm going to put up with insults from the *hired help!*"

"Carol . . ." He sounded as if he'd been through this same argument a hundred times before. "I'm sure Angie was just kidding around."

"I know an insult when I hear one." Aggrieved look. "I don't know why I even bother coming here. I've never been welcome in this house."

He flinched angrily. "That's not true, and you know it."

"And *you!*" Deftly she avoided his touch. "You have a home of your own, Jeremy Elderkin! Or have you forgotten that?" She took a quick angry breath. "What are you still doing here at this time of night?"

"I happen to work here, Carol." His temper was fraying. "Or have you forgotten *that?*"

"It's not supposed to be a twenty-four-hour job!"

"Well, I'm sorry, but we don't have time clocks on the farm." He gestured angrily at the barn. "Damned milking machines broke down. Why, if it wasn't for Angie's grandad, we'd still be out there—"

Carol didn't want to hear it. "You don't *have* to do this kind of work, you know!"

"Drop it, Carol."

"I will *not* drop it! You're spending your whole damned life here. And for what? A chance to break your back for three dollars an hour?" Misery contorted her pretty face. "Jeremy, we could—"

Only then did he raise his voice. *"Not now!"*

Carol stiffened instantly. Brown eyes gleaming with fury, she gave him a curt nod. "All right! If that's the way you want it." All at once, her voice turned shrill. "If you like this fucking farm so much, then why don't you *stay the night!?*"

Carol stormed out of the room, the door booming shut in her

wake. Jeremy's powerful shoulders sagged. He walked over to the window, stood there and listened as her car engine fired up.

Delicately I cleared my throat. "I, uh, guess I really put my foot in it, eh?"

Grim shake of the head. "It wasn't your fault."

Touching his sleeve, I showed him a sympathetic smile. "Cup of coffee still sounds pretty good."

As we entered the kitchen, I spied Trudy sitting in the parlor, hard at work on her knitting. From her troubled expression, I could tell that she'd heard every word. Still, she made no effort to join us.

Trudy Elderkin was one of those rare women who knew better than to meddle in their children's marriages.

The quarrel had really rattled Jeremy. I had the feeling it was just another skirmish in a long-running marital battle. Sitting on the edge of his chair, he held the coffee mug in both hands. Many pensive glances at the back door.

My spoon clinked as I stirred. "So why don't you give her a call?"

"Wouldn't help."

"Why do you say that?"

"Carol needs time to cool off." Frowning, he took a hefty swig of hot coffee. "She didn't mean to snap at you, Angie. Honest! She can be a very charming woman at times." He tried to sound convincing, but the words tumbled out in a lifeless monotone. "She's just worried about the harvest. Hell, we all are! I don't ever remember it going this late before."

Tucking my legs beneath the kitchen chair, I gave him a solemn glance. "Think we've got a chance to bring it in?"

"Sure! If the snow holds off."

Silence. Jeremy's fingers nervously drummed the tabletop. He looked everywhere but at me.

Ladylike sip. Better take the initiative, Angela.

"Carol doesn't seem to like farming."

"I guess not." Mirthless chuckle. "Well, I can't say I wasn't warned."

"Is she from around here?"

He nodded. "Mitchell. Her daddy owns a shop in town."

"So who told you not to marry a city girl?"

"Just about everybody in Yorktown." Rueful smile. "They said farm girls take to the life a whole lot easier. But me . . . I didn't listen."

Sublime Angie smile. "You were in love."

"Still am." But he said it without conviction.

"Where would Carol like to live?"

"Sioux Falls." Jeremy's mouth tightened. "Says I could get a job in the Falls real easy."

"Doing what?" I asked.

"Engine repair." He tilted his head leftward. "I work weekends at Mom Bechen's place."

I remembered the amusing sign. "Mom's Auto Body?"

"Yeah, but we do more than body work. Drop trannies. Install brake shoes. Grind valves. You name it." With a grimace of distaste, he set down his cup. "Hell, I know I could get a job. I could work *anywhere*. But I like it just fine right here. I like working with Dad and Brad. Can't she *see* that?"

She probably could, I thought. And that was the reason their marriage was beginning to unravel.

Reaching across the tablecloth, Jeremy gave my forearm a gentle squeeze. "Thanks for helping Mom with Gran's things."

"My pleasure." A recent memory turned my smile poignant. "It wouldn't have been easy for her. She was like a daughter to Miss Edna."

"You sound as if you've done this before, Angie."

"I have!" Then I told him about my cousin Billy. How I'd gone to Logan in Aunt Della's place to bring his things home.

When I finished, Jeremy ran his thumb around the empty cup's rim. Mournful sigh. "I still can't believe she's dead,

Angie. Gran was always so-so *alive*. She-She had more drive than a woman half her age. I-I keep expecting her to walk through that bedroom door."

"I know what you mean." I saw a possible opening, sidled my way toward it, and experienced a pinch of self-reproach for this tawdry manipulation of Jeremy's grief. "Her heart condition didn't slow her down at all, did it?"

"Not much! Gran had a rough time after that first attack. But the pacemaker really helped."

"Then she was always pretty active?"

"You bet, Angie." Reminiscent smile. "I don't think Gran ever had a sick day in her life, except maybe when she was sixteen."

"What happened when she was sixteen?"

Light chuckle. "She came down with mono."

I blinked. "Mononucleosis?"

Brisk nod. "Mono . . . kissing disease . . . whatever it is they call it. Put Gran flat on her back for six months. I don't think she ever would've admitted it if I hadn't—" And he cut loose with a burst of laughter.

Putting down my cup, I echoed, "If you hadn't *what*—?"

"Long story, Angie, but here's the gist of it." Telling the tale did a lot to restore his good spirits. "Gran's seventy-eighth birthday was coming up, and I was wracking my brains, trying to come up with a present for her. Then I decided to dig up her old high school yearbook photo. You know, take it to one of them custom photo places, get it reproduced on a card. So I went to the Mitchell library and asked to see the MHS *Warbler* from sixty years back." His eyebrows rose in mock surprise. "Guess what? There was no listing for Edna Enright. So I bought her a Sony Walkman instead." Muted laughter. "I sure teased the hell out of her that day. 'Why, Gran!' I says, 'I never knew you were a high school dropout.' And she got all red in the face and gave me a swat. That's when she told me about the mono. She was pretty sick, she

said. Her parents sent her to Sioux Falls to stay with her
McCabe cousins." Leaning back in his chair, he added, "Gran
told me she lived in the Falls for a couple of years. That's
where she finished high school."

Impish smile. "And did you ask how she contracted the
dreaded kissing disease?"

"Nope! I'm not that brave, Angie." He laughed again.
"Even at her age, she could still make a cane whistle."

Delighted laughter from the princess. My mind conjured up
a vision of the teenaged Edna in a horse-drawn sleigh, snuggled beneath a bearskin at her boyfriend's side.

Showing a fond smile, I murmured, "Sixty-five years
ago . . ."

Jeremy nodded and sighed. "County's sure changed since
then, Angie."

I thought of one such change and bounced it off Edna's troubled great-nephew. "Did she know a family named Ostlund?"

"Ragnar and Birgitta Ostlund? Sure."

"Any of the family still around?" I asked.

Jeremy's brow wrinkled thoughtfully. "No direct descend-
ants. Mrs. Ostlund had a younger sister, though, and she had a
daughter." He bit his lower lip. "Mrs. Gunderson. Damn, what
was her maiden name? Winnie Something." Finger snap.
"Stromm, that's it! Winifred Stromm. Mrs. Ostlund's younger
sister Erika married Nels Stromm."

Impressed by his knowledge of Davison County genealogy,
I asked, "Where does Mrs. Gunderson live?"

"Over yonder." He tilted his head to the northwest. "The
Gunderson place borders ours over by the power line."

I sat there very quietly. Jeremy's nod had selected the
kitchen wall directly beneath my bedroom window.

I'd been looking in the very same direction myself a few
nights ago. The night Miss Edna died. Beyond the horizon's
maple shelterbelt lay the source of my strange blue corona—
Winnie Gunderson's farm.

EIGHT

Friday morning, November eighth, found me in *Watpaipak-shan*. That's what Jill Stormcloud's relatives call the south-eastern corner of this state. The new people refer to it as "Siouxland." Not because of its Lakota population, mind you, but because it's home to that Little Metropolis on the Prairie, the one and only *Sioux Falls!*

I'd lived in the Falls for a while following my release from the Big Dollhouse, so I knew how to get downtown without getting stuck in that early-morning bumper-to-bumper parade on Twelfth Street. I dropped off Chief in front of the Federal Building, promising to meet him at the library at three. I found a niche for Clunky in a lot behind the Coliseum, gave the elderly attendant a five-dollar bill, and then strolled uptown.

As I reached West Sixth, I glanced to my right, taking in the awesome quartzite Old Courthouse Museum. Built in 1889, the same year as the Johnstown Flood, the former county courthouse boasted Romanesque arched windows, Teutonic gables, Gothic chimneys, and a lofty bell tower that lets you see all the way to the Minnesota line. First time I saw it, I thought the courthouse was having an erection. But that's no surprise, considering that it was the brainchild of Wallace L. Dow, the famed Prairie Architect. Yes, that's the same Wally who put a nose on the Dunning House, my former home in Pierre.

Compared to its neighbor across the street, however, the Old Courthouse Museum seemed as refined and as tasteful as the Tuileries. The Owechahay Power Building was a fifteen-story monolith in chalk white, with rounded rooftop corners and a band of Polaroid windows running down each side like black racing stripes. Emblazoned on the penthouse were two gargantuan letters—OP. Truly a definitive statement of ownership.

Into their well-lit atrium strolled Reservation Angie. Wide-eyed Anishinabe princess in her denim jacket and skintight jeans, concho earrings, and leather headband. A couple of suits steered me toward the personnel office. There my broad, countrified smile—and my clever infiltration plan—abruptly vanished.

Originally, I'd planned on slipping from Personnel into the main building. No such luck! OP had this place sewn up tight. Personnel had its own separate office at the front end of the atrium. To reach the elevators, you had to pass through a heavily guarded checkpoint.

I would have had better luck traipsing into the vault at the Federal Reserve Bank. Security plus! Wall-mounted TV cameras. Airport-style metal detector. X-ray scanner for brief-cases and handbags. Manning the security equipment were grim-faced members of OP's private police force. Men and women in their thirties, mostly, smartly turned out in crisp company uniforms—slate-blue shirts and navy slacks.

Performing a sharp left turn, I merged with the visitor stream drifting into the personnel office. A line of hopeful job seekers slowly made its way to the front desk. Trying to look employable, I took my place at the end.

When I reached the desk, a frosted blonde with impeccable lipstick gave me a world-weary look and handed me an employment application. The nameplate on her desk read MS. COATES. Her burnished fingernail pointed out an empty desk in the third row.

I fired a quick glance at my fellow applicants. The recession had provided a full house. All around me, earnest-looking adults hunched over their paperwork and scribbled with a desperate diligence. Leather-faced farmers and sad-eyed former yuppies and worrisome single mothers. Pencils danced erratically across the forms. Many crossouts and erasures. No room for error here. Not when a single misspelling could keep them out of that all-important job.

Filling out my form, I watched the OP cops detain every visitor at the metal detector. Regular employees flashed plastic badges and were passed through. All others were held momentarily while one of the security people phoned upstairs.

Glancing forward again, I noticed that Ms. Coates kept her ID tag pinned to the strap of her leather shoulder bag.

Then I noticed the Canon copier on the tabletop behind her desk. Sudden Angie smile of inspiration.

The lady looked up as I made my approach. Flawless eyebrows lifted in silent inquiry.

"Excuse me." Smiling sheepishly, I thrust the application form in her face. "Did I fill this out all right?"

Her view momentarily blocked, I plucked the ID badge from the leather strap.

"Let me see." Frowning in mild irritation, Ms. Coates snatched my application. Hastily I palmed her ID tag into my jacket pocket.

"You forgot to put your last name in the upper corner, dear." Her forehead crinkled in disapproval. Carelessness will not be tolerated in the OP steno pool, young lady!

"Sorry." Apologetic Angie. "Say, do you mind if I use your

copier?" Casual coed smile. "I've got to add my list of references to the application."

Anxious to be rid of me, she muttered, "Oh, go ahead."

"Thanks!"

Putting my back to Ms. Coates, I lifted the copier's lid, slipped the badge from my pocket, and plunked it facedown on the glass. The unit hummed as I punched the button. Sudden light flash. A flawless black-and-white copy slid into the exit tray.

After placing my copy on top of the lid, I glanced at her badge and penciled in the appropriate colors. Then, opening my fingers, I let the badge fall. It made no sound on the lush carpet. My moccasin pushed it back toward her chair.

With any luck, she'd probably think it had slipped off her purse.

After correcting my application form, I handed it over. She looked at me as if she expected a curtsy. I'm afraid I disappointed her.

"I'm sorry, dear, but there simply aren't any openings in the secretarial pool this week." She tucked my form into a manila folder. "However, we will keep your application on file. And you will be considered for any openings that may occur within the next six months."

I thanked the lady and departed, wondering how her canned response sounded to a recently evicted farmer's wife deeply in need of a full-time job.

Promptly at nine-thirty I walked into a rundown photo store on lower Minnesota Avenue, plunked a pair of fifties on the counter, and related my tale of woe.

Look, mister, I'm in a real bind. I left my OP badge in my sister Irene's car, and she's gone off to the Black Hills for the weekend. Sure, I could get a replacement at the office. But this is the third time I've lost it, and if I open my mouth I'll get canned. So could you please print me up a replacement? The color scheme's right here on this photocopy. See? That's my best friend, Elizabeth Coates. A hundred bucks for a replacement badge . . . deal?

The Grant twins swiftly convinced him. Entering the backroom studio, I doffed my Lakota headband, vigorously brushed my hair, and smiled winningly for the Nikon. He told me the badge would be ready in one hour.

So I spent the intervening sixty minutes at my favorite address in the Falls—4001 West Forty-first Street. Better known to East River residents as the Empire Mall.

When I emerged from the mall, my reservation denim had given way to a tailored wool-blend suit, taupe with a white pinstripe, complete with a double-breasted, padded-shoulder jacket and a straight, slim skirt. Taupe dress pumps with two-and-a-half-inch heels. And a white satin drape-neck blouse with loose, cuffed sleeves.

Returning to the photo store, I picked up my ersatz ID badge and gave it a critical scan. Bright yellow badge with the OP corporate symbol in the upper-right corner. Beneath the color photo of smiling Angie was my phony name in computerized print.

RENEE STANDING BEAR
OP PUBLIC RELATIONS

Stopping at the Old Courthouse Museum, I ducked into the ladies' room and fished my brand-new Topsy Tail out of my shoulder bag. Bought it from an aisle vendor at the Empire. Artful handiwork soon transformed my windblown hair into a stylish French braid.

At approximately ten-forty-five, I strolled back into the OP's corporate headquarters, my ID badge clipped to the strap of my shoulder bag. I joined a covey of secretaries returning from their midmorning break, showed the guards a megawatt smile, displayed my badge, and obediently passed beneath the metal detector.

Pausing at the elevators, I studied the building directory. Ah-ha! Administration . . . twelfth floor, natch. Finance . . . look at that! Two whole floors! They must be billing people out in Montana. Customer Service . . . Installation . . . ah, here we are. Project Development—sixth floor.

Elevator doors opened into a cream-colored corridor bustling with activity. Private offices lined either side of the hall. In front of them were many, many secretarial cubicles. Ringing telephones and clacking printers. Serious-faced women staring earnestly at computer monitors. A balding man whizzed by me, carrying a bulky folder, straining to reach the elevator before the doors closed.

Strolling past an empty desk, I snatched a manila folder out of the In-tray. Try to look busy, Angela. Thumb through the purloined folder. Stern fussbudget face. Ooooooh, these shoes hurt. Boy, that'll teach me to wear them straight out of the box. Quick glance around. Where is the main man, anyway?

My journey ended at the corner office. A gold-embossed sign proclaimed STEVEN F. PERRY—DIRECTOR. I found a bearded, middle-aged man in a Western-style gray suede sport coat and black dress slacks chatting with a most attentive secretary.

I cleared my throat. "Mr. Perry?" The honcho immediately turned my way, and I showed him a scintillating Angie smile. "Hi! Renee Standing Bear. Company P.R. Mr. Johnson sent me upstairs to talk to you. Got a minute?"

We shook hands. Perry's left eyebrow arched inquisitively. He had clear, forthright hazel eyes with just a trace of pouch beneath them. "I think so." He gestured at his office door. "This way, young lady."

Perry was a tall, slender man in his early fifties. Put him in a black frock coat and a black velvet cravat, and you would have thought he was President Garfield. Same clear, forthright dark eyes and aquiline nose and neatly trimmed Van Dyke beard. Sallow cheekbones and a very high hairline spoiled the presidential impression, however.

Once inside Steve's office, I marveled at the multiplicity of tinted windows. They offered panoramic views of downtown Sioux Falls, from the Old Courthouse tower to the Citicorp Building. I had no need of those wall diplomas to tell me Steven F. Perry was an engineer. All it took was one long, wandering glance at the cluttered desktop, top-of-the-line IBM computer, and the large draftsman's table strewn with blueprints.

Reclining in his swivel chair, Perry flashed me another curious look. "Now then, what can I do for our friends in P.R.?"

"There's a public hearing in Mitchell tonight," I said matter-of-factly, holding the folder on my lap. "Opponents of the power line will be there in force. I've got till two o'clock to come up with a release for the media."

He scowled. "Organized opposition?"

Brisk nod. "Safe Power for South Dakota. They're lining up experts to testify before the local Industrial Development Commission." Opening my folder, I added, "I need some background information on that project. Nothing too technical. Jobs, benefits, stuff I can use to put a positive spin on this thing."

Leaving the chair, Steve summoned me over to his drafting table. He pulled a blueprint off the shelf, slipped off its rubber band, and spread it out. As far as I was concerned, those chalk-white notations could have been written in Sanskrit. I did recognize the drawing, though. A steel transmission tower that looked like a customized capital *T*.

"Well, this is it, basically." Standing at my side, Steve thoughtfully fingered his beard. "We'll be using the standard steel suspension self-supporting tower design, but we've upgraded ours to a 900-kilovolt hot load."

"Hot load?" I echoed.

Proud smile. "There's a shitload of voltage running through those lines, Renee. Don't worry, though. We've made it as safe as a baby carriage." He pointed out the pod on the tower's crossarm. "A five-conductor bundle, see? Each conductor comes with 55 insulator units. And we've got two ground wires running at a fifteen-degree shielding angle. Top-quality wires, too. Seven-strand No. 8 Alumoweld." His voice was a strange blend of awe and triumph. "That line will stand up to anything. Blizzards, lightning bolts, you name it."

Glancing his way, I asked, "What about the EMF danger?"

All at once, he turned defensive. "What danger? No one in their right mind is going to build a house *directly beneath* that power line."

Persistent Angie. "How many milligauss are we talking about, Steve?"

"Uhm . . . 750 milligauss, max!" Showing a nervous smile, he spread his hands apart. "Look, there's absolutely no danger to the public. We're planning on a 150-yard right-of-way across Davison County."

I took quick advantage of the opening. "You have the right-of-way already planned, then?"

"Oh, sure." Stepping up to the table again, he spread a U.S. Geologic Survey map across the blueprint. Parallel red lines rocketed east from the county line, bisecting the Elderkin farm, then headed southeast toward Mitchell. His forefinger tapped Josh's farmhouse. "As soon as we get the deed to this place, Phase One goes into operation."

"Phase One?"

"Construction of the first towers. We signed the contract with Giambone Construction two weeks ago." Steve's gaze showed mild curiosity. "The *Argus-Leader* ran a story on that. Did you write the release?"

I shook my head. "Mr. Johnson did." Somehow I managed to mask my anger. "Tell me, how close are we to construction?"

"Very close, Renee. Foreclosure is imminent. But that's not for publication, of course."

"Of course." I veiled my furious reaction behind a bland publicist's smile. And asked the key question. "Have you had any dealings with Mr. Covington?"

"Not me." His thumb jabbed ceilingward. "That is strictly twelfth floor, honey."

Purse the lips. "Then I'd better not contact Mr. Covington when I get to Mitchell."

"You'd better clear *that* with Mr. Rasmussen first," he advised, then walked me back to the door. "Look, I've got some primary school handouts lying around here somewhere. Electricity for Idiots. You can use some of that in your story. I'll have Barbara dig 'em out." As he reached for his intercom, he glanced at the desktop digital clock. "Twelve o'clock." Backward over-the-shoulder glance. "Join me for lunch, Renee?"

Tucking the folder under my arm, I radiated a flirtatious smile. "Thank you, Steve. That'd be lovely."

With the OP design honcho at my side, I rode the elevator back downstairs to the lobby. My smile began to turn brittle. My suspicions about Sam Covington had been right on target. He was planning to foreclose on the Elderkins, grab the title to the farm, and then hand off to Owechahay Power. That pitch at Miss Edna's funeral must have been the opening gambit in his campaign to evict Josh and family.

As Steve and I stepped out of the elevator, a troubled engineer-type accosted us. He was almost young enough to be Steve's son, a nerdy-looking guy with rimless glasses and wiry red hair. Alert as a terrier. "Steverino! Just the man I've got to see."

Irritation flooded Steve's face. "What is it, Darren?"

"Lombardi again. He wants to see those preliminary design specs for the Oacoma substation. Chop-chop!"

"Right now!?"

"The Chase people are here." Darren sang, punching the silvery button. Elevator doors slid open. "Chop-chop!"

"Jesus H. Christ! Why don't they just *move in!?*" Features full of regret, Steve suggested, "Look, why don't you go on to the cafeteria, Renee? I'll join you in a bit."

"Sure, Steve."

As the doors slid shut, I caught a final glimpse of Darren's smiling face. Judging from the way his fond gaze slid from my hips to my ankles, I'm sure he wanted to join us, too. Sorry ... no such luck, fella!

The doors rolled open. Tugging at my shoulder strap, I strolled briskly toward the guard station.

Nearing the lobby corner, however, my ears detected a familiar womanly voice.

"I really don't see any other way out of it, Kyle. If you're truly serious about purchasing White River Electric, you're going to have to file for a new rate request with the Department of Public Utilities."

Deep rich male baritone. "Is that your considered legal opinion, Sarah?"

Sarah!? I froze in midstep, my heart pounding. Sidling up against the marble wall, I peered around the corner.

Oh, shit! I thought, ducking out of sight. Of all the people to show up in the OP lobby today, it just had to be *Sarah Sutton!*

My nemesis stood on *this* side of the guard station, blond hair exquisitely coiffed, chatting with a tall man of Scandinavian ancestry. Her stylish Niveau emerald suit, with its long cutaway-shaped jacket and slim skirt, clung to that whistle-bait figure. Lizard-skin slingback pumps and imported handbag to match. Well, with OP as a client, she could certainly afford it.

Her companion was at least as tall as Garrison Keillor. An imposing fellow in his early forties. Blunt, tanned face with bright blue eyes, a stubby nose, and a noticeable jut of chin. Low eyebrows and mild crow's feet. Another one with a hairline that started at the peak of his skull. What little hair he had was rapidly changing color from ash-blond to white. Judging from that tailored suit, he was definitely in OP's top management echelon.

"White River's a co-op." Sarah tossed her hair lightly. "The association's customers are paying a consumption rate five percent higher than your OP rate. It's against the law for the company to charge differential rates. And you can't just *promise* to equalize rates, Kyle, you have to do it."

Frowning, Kyle steered her across the lobby—*toward me!* "Look, what if we promise to seek rate parity within three years?"

Seeing them approach, I pivoted and darted back up the corridor. My hasty stride carried me out of earshot. Apprehension stiffened my shoulders. Any second now, I expected to hear Sarah's sudden gasp of recognition. *"Angela! What are you doing here?"*

Luck stayed with me. Slinky-dink was too engrossed in their conversation to notice the frantic brunette twenty feet ahead of her. However, the two of them were herding me deeper and deeper into the OP building. And I was rapidly running out of side corridors to duck into.

Ahead of me, the hall opened into OP's swank employee cafeteria. Veering to the right, I followed a trio of office workers down the side corridor. Spirits soaring, I quickened my step, intent on making my getaway.

And then the elevator opened at the corridor's far end, disgorging a crowd of lunchtime employees. My gaze zeroed in on two familiar faces. *Steve and Darren!*

About-face, Biwaban! No way are you lunching with those two! They'll want to walk you back to the P.R. office. And that could get very embarrassing, especially when *Renee* walks in and nobody recognizes her!

I reached the main corridor again in seconds, fired a glance to my left, and shivered like a wet canine. Sarah and Kyle, still discussing electric rates, had halved the distance between us. Pretending to smooth my hair, I veiled my profile and swept into the cafeteria.

I couldn't believe my eyes. OP's cafeteria was half again larger than the Central High School gym back home in Duluth. At least two hundred tables, draped in white linen, congregated beneath a cathedral ceiling. Much emphasis on natural wood in the decor. Polished elm and red pine. Bronze bas-relief panels and legions of bright green plants. Culinary sounds enveloped me as I strolled through the theater-size doorway. Chair legs grinding against tiled flooring. Rattling of plates and cutlery.

Halting at the cashier station, I displayed my OP badge, then flinched as I heard Sarah's voice *right behind me.*

"All right. Why don't we schedule a meeting for next Wednesday? Our firm would be delighted to represent OP during the acquisition process."

"Just a minute, Sarah." I heard Kyle's footsteps retreat into the hall. Sudden baritone shout. "Schumacher!"

Taking immediate advantage of the diversion, I scampered behind the nearest potted rubber plant. Peering through the greenery, I saw Sarah waiting patiently in the doorway while her companion, hands on his hips, faced Darren and Steve.

Managerial scowl. "Schumacher, what's this I hear about those ecology freaks meeting in Mitchell tonight?"

Darren's mouth made feeble fishlike motions.

But Steve jumped right in. "We're right on top of it, Mr. Rasmussen." What a brown nose! "Uh, that new girl down in P.R., uh, Renee . . . she's working up a media presentation right now."

"Well . . ." Genuine pleasure lightened the big man's tone. "I'm glad to see someone's on the ball around here." Poke of the forefinger. "Find this Renee and get her ass down here. I want to know what P.R.'s planning to tell the press."

They answered in unison. "Yes, sir!" And back they went, jogging toward the main elevators.

Head down, I made a beeline across the dining area, my knees as shaky as a newborn colt's. Oh, you've really done it this time, princess. Trapped in the OP cafeteria! Even if I managed to elude Sarah, I still had Steve Perry and Darren Schumacher to contend with. No way could I avoid them both. Yet, if I let those two bring me before Rasmussen with La Sutton sitting there . . . !

Dreadful tremor. I didn't have to be Nostradamus to predict my future. Angie in the Springfield prison laundry, watching an avalanche of dirty clothes come tumbling down the chute!

I took refuge in a small telephone alcove several feet to the right of the gleaming aluminum salad bar. Lifting the receiver, I concocted an imaginary conversation. "Yes, Mother . . . Yes, Mother . . . Of course he isn't married . . ."

Leaning against the wall, I watched Sarah and the CEO study empty tables. I have a better idea, you two. Why don't you go eat at Burgundy's? Are you tight with a buck or something, Rasmussen? *Tayaa!* Don't sit *there!* Oh, terrific! Right in front of the doorway!

As I hung up, a slim, dark-haired waitress arrived at Sarah's table and took their order. Averting my face, I made my way to the bar. Rasmussen didn't know me from Sitting Bull. No problem getting past him. But *Sarah!* Any move toward the door and she was certain to spot me.

Their waitress came straight to the bar. She had a lean but pretty Mediterranean face, with dark brown eyes and a lush mouth. A hairnet confined her luxurious brunette mane. The tart line of her mouth told me she didn't much enjoy waitressing as a career choice. And that gave me an idea!

She flagged the bartender. "Mr. Rasmussen will have the usual, Bob. The lady wants a Sweet Manhattan."

I showed the waitress an amiable smile. Tilted my head toward the couple. "Big tippers?"

"Tips!? In *this* place!?" Snort of disbelief. "No way, honey. OP is strictly straight salary."

"A bonus is always a possibility." I put my shoulder bag on the bar and zipped it open. "How would you like to make a quick hundred?"

Dark eyes showed skepticism. "Who do I have to kill?"

Taking a fifty out of my wallet, I murmured, "No one. Just make sure the cocktail lands in the lady's lap."

Avarice gleamed in her eyes, then yielded to cautious curiosity. "What's the angle?"

"The bitch walked off with my boyfriend." Funny how truthful that sounded. I slipped the fifty onto her tray. "Half now, half when you come back to the bar."

"My pleasure." Smiling with malice, the waitress folded the bill and tucked it into an apron pocket.

Bob the Bartender put the drinks on her tray. As she stalked off, I dropped the wallet back in my leather bag. Taking a deep breath, I listened carefully.

"Ohhhh! You *clumsy*—!" Sarah's outraged shout momentarily eclipsed the background cafeteria hubbub. Swiftly moving chairs scraped the tiles.

Unable to resist the impulse, I sneaked a quick glance. Sarah stood beside the table, her face livid, frantically dabbing at the stain with a linen napkin. Rasmussen looked on, aghast.

Feigning a look of contrition, the waitress mumbled, "Sorry, ma'am."

"Don't worry, Sarah. I'll have it sent right out to the dry cleaner." Blunt face reddening, Kyle turned on the waitress. "And it's coming out of *your* salary!"

"Yes, sir." The waitress didn't mind. After all, she was still sixty-five dollars ahead.

Rasmussen buttonholed another female employee and

asked her to escort Sarah to the lavatory. One highly annoyed Pierre lawyer marched out of there, high heels chastising the tiles.

As the smiling waitress drifted my way, she artfully extended her left hand, and I caressed her palm with the second fifty. A mild tug, and it was gone. Her grin widened as she passed me by.

Shouldering my bag, I left the bar and strolled swiftly to the exit. Rasmussen sipped his highball, oblivious to my passage. Reaching the corridor, I spotted the escort ushering Mrs. Sutton into the ladies' room.

Moments later, the escort emerged with Sarah's emerald skirt neatly folded over her arm. I watched as the woman walked straight to the receptionist's cubicle. Clutching my bag's strap, I made a slow and cautious approach.

The woman spoke briefly with the redheaded receptionist, then handed over Sarah's stained skirt. We passed each other as she headed back to the cafeteria. Thoroughly occupied with the switchboard, the receptionist draped the skirt over the cubicle gate.

Mischievous Angie smile. Should I? I hastened my step, grinning like a demon. Oh, hell! Why not?

Showing the harried receptionist a bright and eager smile, I trilled, "Hi! Renee Standing Bear, public relations."

"Uh . . . hi." Holding her headset, the redhead frantically tapped keyboard tabs. "That extension is busy right now. Would you like to hold?"

"One of our VIP guests had a little accident in the cafeteria. Mr. Rasmussen said to get right over to the dry cleaner's." I feigned a curious expression. "Oh, is this Mrs. Sutton's skirt?"

Nodding, the receptionist replied, "Sandy just brought it down."

"Okay. I'm out of here." Tongue in cheek, I grabbed the expensive Niveau skirt. "When Sandy gets back, tell her Mrs.

Sutton decided to wait in the executive meeting room. And I shall be back in . . ." Striking a pose, I glanced at my wristwatch. ". . . *two* hours! Take care!"

"You, too . . . uh, Renee, bye!"

Leaving the receptionist's cubby behind, I let out a juvenile chuckle and examined the fabric. Not too bad a stain. Once laundered, it would make a fine donation to the Salvation Army.

Quick peek at the satin-lined interior. Burst of merry laughter. *Size Ten!?* Too many rich desserts, Mrs. Sutton!

Just then, I noticed a small cloth-of-gold tag near the back seam. Recognition erased my gleeful smile.

Birnbaum's . . .

All at once, I was back at Enemy Creek, kneeling beside the corpse of Mister Beach Tan, turning back the suit-jacket collar.

Interesting, I thought. If Sarah Sutton does her clothes shopping there, it must be an expensive place. Which means the missing victim must have had a hefty bank account.

But I still couldn't quite reconcile the victim's posh wardrobe with his knockabout features and pushed-in knuckles. Was he some kind of mobster?

And where is this *Birnbaum's*, anyway? I've never heard of it. Fussbudget face. Or have I?

Chief's right. The name does ring a vague bell.

Of course, I could always go back to the ladies' room and ask Sarah. Yeah, right! And get turned in for parole violation. No way, gang! I'm waiting until that woman cools off.

And that just might be awhile, I thought, deftly folding the garment. Sarah is going to be steamed, standing around in her underwear for the next few hours.

Well, you brought it on yourself, dear. Maybe next time you'll think twice before vamping Paul Holbrook!

"Thanks for seeing me on such short notice, Mr. Kolquist."

"My pleasure, Renee." He gave my business card one final look, then handed it back. Earnest, businesslike look. "What can we do for our friends at Owechahay Power?"

Gordon Kolquist seemed impressed by my recently printed card. And no wonder. Neatly printed on the face of the small beige card was the legend,

> *Renee Standing Bear*
> *Financial Research Assistant*
> *Owechahay Power*

I'd run off a batch at a hole-in-the-wall print shop on West Fourth Avenue right after leaving the OP building. I'd needed a clean, crisp, no-nonsense card, with just enough corporate simplicity to con the head of our local Office of Thrift Supervision.

At first glance, Gordon Kolquist resembled the bankers he often worked with. Tall, forthright, good-looking man in his middle thirties, with an accountant's squint, a Scandinavian nose, a lantern jaw, and a small, tight smile. Dark curly brown hair draped across his upper-right forehead. He had the slim, flat waistline of a cross-country skier. His heather-gray suit was distinctly Western with its peaked yokes and suede elbow patches. Two things gave him away, however, his bright Brazilian silk tie and that schoolboy smile. Bankers never smile like that. They're too busy worrying about cash flow.

Kolquist escorted me into his private office. The decor was what they call "GSA Modern." Four-piece computer stations in mock oak, black leather office chairs, and battleship-gray filing cabinets. The seal of the U.S. Treasury Department dominated one pastel-green wall. Directly across from it hung a portrait of the First Couple.

After I seated myself, he sent out for coffee, and we spent a good ten minutes on idle chitchat. As I put my business card away, I gave him a fleeting glimpse of my phony OP badge. Milk-chocolate eyes twinkled in instant recognition.

"So what brings you over here, Renee?"

Crossing my legs, I took a dainty sip. "It's something of a bird-dog expedition, Gordon."

Puzzled blink. "What do you mean?"

"Well, to put it delicately, the end of the calendar year is coming up, and we have to reinvest a good portion of our annual earnings. OP has an opportunity to pick up some long-term bonds." Polite professional smile. "Bonds issued by a financial institution. Mr. Rasmussen asked me to look into it."

Mere mention of the great man's name had Gordon sitting upright in his swivel chair. Touching his floral tie, he showed me an expression of friendly efficiency. "You work *directly* for Mr. Rasmussen?"

"Coming up on my first anniversary." True enough. I had strolled past the CEO's table just one hour ago. Taking a small notebook out of my shoulder bag, I asked, "How's the banking picture in Mitchell these days?"

"Improving significantly." He welcomed this opportunity to show off his expertise. "It's been a rough fifteen years for that area. They lost three big employers in the Eighties—Hormel, Herder's, and Owatonna. And you know where farm prices have gone—straight down the shitter. I think it's bottomed out, though. Retail's done pretty good up there the past couple of years." Tilting his head to one side, he added, "I gather you're interested in the banks."

"Just one bank, Gordon. Middle Border Savings Bank."

Brown eyes blossomed wide. "Sam Covington's thinking about a bond issue!?"

"So far it's just talk." Scratching my nyloned knee, I added, "You seem a little surprised."

"Quite frankly, I am." He leaned back in the comfortable

black swivel chair, toying with a pencil. "A bond issue seems a bit premature."

"Why is that, Gordon?"

A sliver of tongue flicked over his lower lip. He looked around apprehensively, as if fearful that he might be overheard.

"I want this understood right now, Renee." Nervous fingers beat a tattoo on the blotter. "What I'm about to tell you . . . it goes no further than Mr. Rasmussen's office. Understand?"

"It'll remain a secret between me and Mr. Rasmussen," I promised. Girl Scout Angie.

"I know Covington. Good man. Comes from a respected family up there." Gordon's hand gesture moved northward. "When it comes to banking, though, he takes chances. He's a gambler, and he's been known to play sucker's odds. Up until a couple of years ago, it always paid off for him."

"What happened a couple of years ago?" I asked.

Gordon's hands outlined an invisible rectangle. "Let me explain, okay? MBSB had a very good cash flow. A real-estate firm was putting plenty of money into their vaults. Then Covington sank the money into a commercial development project in the east county. It was a savvy move. The Mitchell area is gradually turning into a regional retail center. But the timing was all wrong. No sooner had his contractors put in the field stakes than the recession hit."

"How much did he lose?"

Dead silence. I thought he wasn't going to answer, and then he let out a sympathetic sigh. "About ninety percent of it. He should have cut and run. Sold the commercial land at a discount and used the proceeds to soften the blow." Mild grimace. "He didn't!"

"A lot of people thought it would be a short recession," I remarked, tugging at my skirt.

"A Chernobyl for realtors was more like it!" Gordon paused

for a sip of coffee. "The S and L mess brought down the real-estate market in Texas. Then it was California. And then New England. By the time the domino crashed here in the East River, you couldn't sell that land for cow pasture."

"And that put an end to the real-estate firm pumping money into MBSB's vault," I added, thinking aloud.

Slow nod. "Covington tried to get the local real-estate market going by writing new loans for two hundred K homes. Wrong move at the wrong time. Most of the homes that money built are still empty."

"Which means that MBSB's portfolio consists mostly of nonperforming real-estate loans."

He nodded again. "I'd say it's a thirty-seventy split. Thirty percent tied up in that proposed mall. Seventy percent home-building loans."

"Doesn't leave much for reserves, does it?"

Embarrassed look. My questions were hitting a little too close to home. "You'd have to take that up with the Fed, Renee."

"Is MBSB on the watch list, Gordon?"

He tried to smile, but his mouth looked as if it had been sculpted from cement. "I'm afraid I can't answer *that* question, Miss Standing Bear. Confidentiality, you know."

I wasn't at all disappointed. In his roundabout way, Gordon Kolquist had already told me everything I needed to know.

Puckish Angie smile. "But, as you mentioned before, it's a bit premature for MBSB to be considering a bond issue."

"*Extremely* premature!"

Closing my notebook, I asked, "When should OP reconsider Mr. Covington's offer?"

Stroking his chin, Gordon leaned against the chair's armrest. He looked more than ever like an underpaid accountant.

"Give it a year, preferably two." He stood up the second after I did. "But let me give you my personal opinion, Renee.

If Sam Covington's still on his feet when the smoke clears, he's a damned miracle man!"

Promptly at four o'clock, I breezed into the lobby of the Sioux Falls Public Library. Windblown elm leaves trailed me through the doorway. A tone chimed as my moccasined foot landed on the rubber mat. My brand-new Glacee pumps were safely tucked away in my shoulder bag—right next to Sarah's skirt. No way was I walking all the way from the Federal Building in heels.

"Over here, Angie."

Turning, I spied my grandfather sitting beside the Easy-Eye section. His gnarled brown hand patted the cushion at his side.

"Did I keep you waiting long?" I asked, seating myself on the vinyl settee.

"Not more than an hour." Sharp sidelong look. "I don't remember that outfit."

"That's 'cause I just bought it." Smile of genuine pleasure. "I needed some camouflage for my scout."

He chuckled. "Any old excuse to hit the mall."

Giving him a playful nudge, I said, "So what have you been doing with your time, Mr. Blackbear, sir?"

"Found out something interesting." Reaching to his right, Chief produced an aged leatherbound volume. "Your friend Jeremy is mistaken about his Gran."

Opening it in midbook, he displayed a montage of black-and-white photos from long ago. Documentary photos straight out of *The Great Gatsby*. Pretty teenaged girls in cloche hats. Grinning rugged boys in lettered sweatshirts posing on the running board of an ancient Ford.

"What's this?" I asked.

"The 1929 yearbook from Sioux Falls High. That's the year Miss Edna's supposed to have graduated." His fingers ruffled through the pages, halting at a large group photo. "See for yourself. There's no mention of her."

"Jeremy could've gotten the year wrong."

Chief shook his head. "I checked other yearbooks, too. Including East Sioux Falls. Every yearbook from 1925 to 1935. If Edna Enright graduated from high school, it sure wasn't around here."

Folding my arms, I scowled. "I don't understand. Why did she lie?"

Shrugging, he closed the yearbook. "Your guess is as good as mine, missy." Obsidian eyes sparkled with curiosity. "Say, how'd you make out at OP?"

So I gave him a detailed rundown of my adventures in Corporate America, taking care to delete any mention of Sarah Sutton. You see, my grandfather disapproves of these occasional sophomoric pranks.

I finished up with a description of Covington's scheme to evict the Elderkins.

". . . makes perfect sense to me, Chief. The minute Covington called in Josh Elderkin's loan, I bet Miss Edna would have rushed right over to Mitchell. Remember, she was good for it. As the sole legatee of the Enright Trust, she would have had no problem borrowing from another bank. She would have given the money to the family, and they would have paid off Covington."

"Are you certain about that, Angie? Seems to me Josh is a mighty proud man."

"Well, if it came down to losing the family farm, I think he would have accepted Miss Edna's help."

Chief nodded slowly. "You're probably right. You know, if you look at it from Covington's point of view, Miss Edna's sudden death was real fortunate."

"Or *convenient*," I added tartly.

My grandfather gave me a long look. "Meaning?"

"Without Miss Edna's help, the Elderkins can't possibly

stave off foreclosure. Covington has them right where he wants them."

Still a bit leery, my grandfather said, "I don't buy it, Angie. Miss Edna must have had a will. Wouldn't Trudy and her kin be in line to inherit this Enright Trust?"

"Oh, sure! But by the time Miss Edna's will was probated, and Trudy inherited her share, it'd be too late." The library's automatic door slid open for us. "Covington forecloses on the farm, then hands off to OP."

Together we started down Dakota Avenue. A wintry gust chilled my face. Chief stuck his hands in his pockets.

"Is Covington really in that much trouble?"

Determined nod. "He's one step away from Chapter Eleven, Chief. The federal Office of Thrift Supervision is keeping a close watch on MBSB."

Pausing at the corner, my grandfather waited for the light to change. "So how does Covington benefit if he delivers that farm?"

The light winked orange, and I stepped off the sidewalk. Delicate shrug. "They must be paying him off."

"Angie . . ." My grandfather sighed. "How many acres do the Elderkins own?"

"All three fields? Oh, about a thousand, I guess."

"And if your friend Julie Sievert has her cost estimates right, that means the Elderkin property is worth $450,000, top dollar." Hunching his shoulders against the wind, he muttered, "I still don't buy it. If the Middle Border Savings Bank is in that kind of trouble, a chickenshit half-million ain't going to save it."

Fussbudget frown. Chief has the most annoying habit of torpedoing my favorite theories. Still, he'd given me something to think about. What exactly was the relationship between Mr. Covington and our friends at OP? And why was he so eager to create that right-of-way for the power company?

As we reached Clunky's parking lot, I unslung my shoulder

bag and remarked, "Say, how'd you make out with that slag I gave you?"

Masculine chuckle. "Been wondering when you were going to ask about that." Reaching into his jacket pocket, he produced a small cellophane envelope. "Took it to that TV repair shop on South Phillips. Fella name of Hollenhorst runs it."

"Could he identify it?"

Chief nodded. "Said it was heavy-duty industrial wire. Number Six ACSR."

"ACSR?" I echoed.

"Aluminum conductors, steel-reinforced." Slag rustled as he jiggled the envelope. "Ever heard the expression *three-wire service?*"

I shook my head.

"That's how the power company hooks your house up to the grid," he explained, as we walked along. "That cable running from the telephone pole to the service entrance head—it's three wires braided together. Two of 'em are *hot* wires. One hundred and twenty volts each. Third wire is the *ground*—carries no voltage at all."

"You got quite the education today, Chief." My forefinger touched the envelope. "Any idea what happened to this wire?"

Pocketing the slag, my grandfather sighed. "Hollenhorst isn't sure. Said something must have melted it. Lightning strike. Power surge. Could be anything, he told me."

"Question, Chief . . ." Opening my shoulder bag, I looked for my parking ticket. "Does this wire have anything to do with cable television?"

"Absolutely nothing."

Taking out my car keys, I asked, "Then what was it doing in Miss Edna's cable TV outlet?"

I found my own suspicions reflected in Chief's obsidian eyes.

"That's what we have to find out, missy."

NINE

Snow flurries caressed my face as I followed Josh and Kristy down West Fourth Street. They drifted out of the darkness, materializing suddenly in the streetlights' soft glow. Through the curtain of flurries, the Corn Palace looked like a mosque in wintry Samarkand.

There was nothing exotic, however, about the traffic choking North Main and the side streets. Cars and pickups lined either side, bumper to bumper. Quite a few had lime-green SPSD flyers tucked beneath their windshield wipers. Passing beneath the corncob-decorated marquee was the biggest crowd since the last appearance of Patsy Cline.

"Oh, Angie, we'll never find a seat," Kristy complained.

"Well . . . maybe not together." I turned to Josh. "What do you think?"

"I reckon the three of us could meet under the hoop when it's all over," he said, holding open the door for us.

"Good idea, Daddy." Kristy led us into the throng.

Conversation rebounded off the vast-arched ceiling. Unzipping my parka, I had a look around. To my right, the distinguished members of the Industrial Development Commission manned a banquet table onstage. Sam Covington stood at one corner, arms folded thoughtfully, chatting with a pair of portly, middle-aged men. Across the room, beyond the rows and rows of foldout chairs, Scott Hasner and Julie Sievert talked strategy with their colleagues. Protest placards sprouted like dandelions in April.

Just then, a heavyset, curly-haired farm wife came bustling our way, her arms laden with lime-colored flyers. "Howdy, Elderkins!" Bray of deep-toned laughter. "Glad you could make it."

Nodding, Josh accepted a flyer. "Evenin', Brenda."

Recognition eluded me momentarily. Then I remembered my recent night in jail. Neighborly smile. "Hi, Mrs. Traudt."

"How do, Angie." As she handed me a flyer, her expression turned sympathetic. "Josh, I sure was sorry to hear about Miss Edna."

"Thanks, Brenda."

Kristy looked around, thoroughly impressed. "How many people are here, Mrs. Traudt?"

Burly female shoulders shrugged. "Fire chief ain't closed the doors yet, so there can't be seven hundred. Got to be almighty close, though."

Leaving Josh to chat with Brenda Traudt, Kristy and I threaded our way through the crowd. I pointed out a pair of empty seats in the fourth row. All at once, a pair of fingers tapped my shoulder. I whirled like a startled raccoon.

"Hello there . . . Angie, isn't it?" He was a potato-shaped man, aged sixty or thereabouts, with sun-wrinkled features, large flat ears, and silvery-gray hair. The oval patch on the front of his brown jacket read DOUG.

Bingo! The man who helped us repair the combine. Two seconds' rumination produced a last name. "How goes it, Mr. Krause?"

Flexing one shoulder, Doug Krause showed me an amiable smile. "Ahhhhh, I can't complain." He looked about in seeming amazement. "Sure are a lot o' folks riled about that power line."

"Where do you stand on the issue, Mr. Krause?"

His smile showed embarrassment. "Well, to tell the truth, Angie, I really haven't given it much thought."

Kristy spoke up. "You know where Gram would have stood."

Thoughtful Angie frown. Did I detect a note of disapproval in the girl's voice?

If Doug took note of it, he gave no sign. "Miss Edna was a fine woman, Kristy. We're all going to miss her."

Kristy was not appeased. "Didn't see you at the funeral, Mr. Krause."

Apologetic shrug. "Sorry. Tractor repair over in Wessington Springs. Afraid I couldn't get out of it." His smile became anxious. "I put some flowers on Miss Edna's grave. Roses. You know how she loved them roses."

Kristy's eyes began to fill, and I quickly changed the subject. "So what do you think, Mr. Krause? Is the power line project going to help small contractors like yourself?"

Doug made a harsh sound of derision. "Never happen! They'll bring in their own contractors—as usual!" Genuine rancor colored his tone. "OP never did a damned thing for the little guy. Never has and never will."

"Come on, Angie." Kristy's fingers tugged at my long, loose sleeve. "We're going to lose those seats if we don't get moving."

We said our goodbyes to Doug the Fixit Man, then sauntered down the center aisle. As soon as we were out of earshot, I remarked, "That wasn't very polite, Kris."

"I know." Faint grimace of apology. "I'm sorry. Maybe I'm in the minority around here, but I just don't like him, Angie."

"He seems harmless enough to me."

"I-I don't know." She rubbed her sleeves as if warding off a sudden chill. "I've just never liked him, I guess, even when I was a little kid." Fond smile. "He gets along okay with everyone else in the family. Especially Gram."

"That was nice of him to visit her grave."

Kristy smiled in reminiscence. "Mr. Krause used to visit her a lot. I'd be coming home from school and see them on the front porch, drinking coffee and laughing together. He could really make Gram laugh. He used to drop by any old time. Gram never did mind, though. She loved having him come and visit."

"How long was he friends with Miss Edna?"

Adolescent hands fluttered haplessly. "Oh, God, I have no idea! Mom said he worked on Gram's farm for a spell. That must be where she met him."

"Mr. Krause used to be a farmhand?" I prodded, lugging my parka over my arm.

"Farmhand, machinist, little bit of everything," she replied. "Daddy says Mr. Krause is a drifter. Says he could've had his own store if he'd been willing to put down roots. Not him, though. Kind of like a tumbleweed, I guess. Every so often, he gets the urge, packs up that old pickup of his, and that's the last we see of him for a spell."

"Is he from around here?"

"I'm not sure, Angie. Daddy would know, though."

Just then, one of Kristy's classmates dashed up the aisle. He looked like a young Ricky Van Shelton. Tall, lean-featured, broad-shouldered, and square-jawed, wearing a blue denim jacket, black ranch jeans, and a big black Stetson. That country-boy smile enveloped us both, but he had eyes only for Kristy.

"*Kris!*"

"Hi, Pete!" One look at the lovelight in Kristy's gray-green eyes told me who this was. Only the most wonderful boy in the whole senior class! "I don't think you two have met yet." Impish sidelong smile. "Pete, this is Angie Biwaban."

"Hi, Angie!" Polite smile, and then his interest rebounded

onto Kristy. "We've got some seats up back. Me, Sonny, and Allison. Join us?"

Apologetic yet hopeful teenaged glance. Far be it from Angie to stand in the way of true love. "Go on! Remember, we're meeting your dad under the basketball hoop."

"See you, Angie!"

Up the center aisle they went, hand in hand, Josh's blond daughter and the boy in the black Stetson. Love in the country!

I wondered if Pete had any single older brothers stashed away back there on the farm.

Really, Angela! Where is your mind this evening?

The answer, of course, is that it was still digesting the information Chief had given me a few hours ago. Number Six ACSR electrical wire. What I'd seen in Miss Edna's cable TV outlet. What was it doing in there? Who had removed it? When and why?

Originally, I hadn't planned on attending this IDC meeting. But now I had two compelling reasons for doing so. Persuading Josh and Kristy to accompany me had given my grandfather an opportunity to study that cable TV outlet. Eluding one person, Trudy, was a whole lot easier than trying to dodge three randomly wandering Elderkins.

Also, studying Mr. Covington's performance would hopefully give me some kind of handle on him. I needed to find some ruse that would give me access to the man himself. I had to learn the precise nature of his dealings with Owechahay Power.

Risky? You bet! This time I was operating without a solid cover, in a city of just over fourteen thousand people. A place where most people already knew me as Angie Biwaban, recently released ex-convict. My approach had to be perfect. One wrong move, and Covington would be dialing Sheriff Fischer.

The IDC meeting got off to a slow start. Chairman's report, committee reports, old business—the usual parliamentary bullshit. I heard impatient mutterings all around. Feeling my derriere grow numb, I shifted position in the foldout chair. I was heartily thankful to be out of the Corporate Angie suit. Tonight's outfit was equally stylish but far more comfortable. Lengthy denim wrap skirt, black cobra-print Zodiac boots, and an open-necked classic white woven shirt with a flared collar and long blousy sleeves.

Just then, Sam Covington strolled up to the lectern. He had the good sense *not* to wear his three-piece banker's suit. His creased forehead perspired heavily beneath the bright stage lights.

"Mr. Chairman, on behalf of the Owechahay Power Company—"

Mere mention of the name drew a chorus of boos from the SPSD crowd. From their seats in the front row, Scott Hasner and Julie Sievert motioned for quiet.

Shuffling his papers, Sam tried again. "I am submitting for your approval this request for a demonstration project to be undertaken during the next calendar year. The LWA would run—"

A farmer hollered, "What the hell is an LWA?"

"Order!" The chairman rapped his gavel. "Let's have order here."

"It's a Limited Work Authorization, to be issued by the commission, permitting OP to do preparatory site work within the county limits." Impatience strained Sam's voice. "The company has petitioned us to allow them to erect a demonstration transmission tower pending full approval of the Southeast Hydroelectric Initiative Project by the county board."

A fleshy hand shot up. The owner was stout, female, and as dour as a Puritan. She reminded me of my second-grade teacher at Park Point Elementary. *Don't slouch, Angela!*

Definitely not the afternoon-tea type. Probably spent her evenings watching public television. Or writing letters to Congress.

"Mr. Covington?" Sharp clarion voice.

"Yes, Mrs. Fahnestock." Sam's smile didn't quite reach his eyes. No doubt she sent a lot of letters to the IDC, too.

Thumbing through a well-worn paperback, the lady said, "Mr. Covington, according to the charter, only the County Board has the authority to issue a Construction Permit."

Producing a handkerchief, Sam wiped his brow. "We're well aware of that, ma'am. An LWA is *not* a Construction Permit. It's a preliminary document. When it is time to build . . ." He caught himself just in time. ". . . *after* preliminary approval, Owechahay Power will file its permit request with the board."

Again the farmer's voice erupted from the audience. "Don't give us this lawyer doubletalk, Sam!" I fired a glance in his direction. I swear, he looked like Ross Perot's older brother! "If you're building' somethin', and this LWA lets you build it, then it's a goddam *permit.*"

Murmurs of approval from the crowd. The chairman's gavel beat out a brisk rumba. Folding her meaty arms, Mrs. Fahnestock looked at Sam as if he were a tardy schoolboy. "Why haven't you petitioned the board on this matter, Mr. Covington?"

Excellent question, Mrs. F! From my own experience in town government, I could easily guess why. Sam hadn't filed with the County Board because he wasn't quite sure the vote would go his way. Local opposition to the project was too strong. So he was resorting to half measures, trying to get LWA approval from a commission whose votes were already in his back pocket.

"My dear Mrs. Fahnestock . . ." Striking a pose of wounded dignity, Sam fiddled with the microphone. "Owechahay Power merely wishes to test the *feasibility* of its new transmission tower design. This is a demonstration project only. That is why they've requested a Limited Work Authorization." Accent on the word *Limited*. "Mr. Chairman, OP has sent several experts from Sioux Falls to testify this evening. I move that all questions be postponed until these gentlemen have concluded their presentation."

Covington's motion was quickly seconded, and the approval vote was unanimous. More shouts and mutters from Julie's people. And then it was time for the OP dog-and-pony show. CPAs talking about cost-plus benefits. Nerdy graduate students droning on and on about *overhead T&D, peak loads, topping cycles,* and *detuners.* Good thing Deputy Kramer wasn't there. He'd probably bust all those suits for talking dirty.

When Sam took the podium again, he became the High Priest of HVDC. That's "high-voltage direct current" to those of you who don't know how to read a meter. The new route to the Promised Land, or so Mr. Covington claimed.

"Now, I'm a reasonable man. I can understand the concerns of our friends and neighbors." A polite nod to the SPSD crowd. "But we've got to wake up and smell the coffee. This country is on the move. The economy is *growing*—"

"Can't tell that from ag prices!" came a male voice.

Of course, the whole audience roared at that, the IDC members included. Even Sam cracked a smile. But it was a very brittle, lopsided smile. It looked as if it might slip off his face and shatter on the stage.

"Well, maybe the Chicago Board of Trade ain't got the message yet, but the growth is there." Farm neighbor Sam. "The average is two percent per year. The demand for energy is growing right along with it. In 1990, this country was using eighty-eight quads of electricity per year. Now, I want you folks to think on that a minute. You know what a *quad* is? That's the electricity equivalent of 172 million barrels of oil. Or 40 million tons of coal. Or maybe enough electricity to light up all of South Dakota for the next twenty years. And we used eighty-eight of 'em nationwide. By the year 2000, we're going to be up to 100 quads per year."

I saw his hand tremble as he reached for the glass. A hasty sip removed the burr from his throat.

"My friends, that is a great opportunity. Industry's moving out of New England and the Great Lakes—coming out West—right here to South Dakota. And do you know why? Because we've got the energy, that's why. Electricity and plenty of it. Those Missouri River dams are cranking it out by the megawatt." Bluish-gray eyes burned with fanaticism. "Electricity means *jobs!* Good-paying industrial jobs for any county with access to a transmission line. Cheap power, new industry, hundreds of new jobs! Brighter lights, cleaner skies, better lives!" The way he recited his mantra, I wondered if he was trying to convince himself. "That's the kind of future I want for this county. Power *and* prosperity—that's my motto. I don't know about you, but I want a better life for my children. Welcoming that OP line will have our local economy turning handsprings in just six months. Bet on it!"

Cries of approval from around the auditorium. A baritone voice shouted, "Give 'em hell, Sam!"

"You've heard what these gentlemen had to say tonight," he added, clutching the podium. "There's not one iota of scientific proof the OP transmission line is a threat to your children's health." Trace of contempt. "With the possible exception of some Mickey Mouse survey by some lady doctor over there in Sweden. And I'll be frank with you, ladies and gentlemen, I'm not willing to sacrifice our economic future because some Nervous Nellie's hair stands up every time she walks under a power line—"

Scott Hasner burst out of his seat. "Mr. Chairman—!"

"Calm down, Mr. Hasner," he replied. "You'll get your turn to speak."

After taking a second to calm himself, Scott said, "The survey Mr. Covington is referring to studied 500,000 people born between 1965 and 1980. The study concluded that the incidence of leukemia among children living in close proximity to power lines was *four times greater* than the leukemia rate within the general population."

"That's Sweden!" yelped Sam. "A *socialist* country! A country thoroughly biased against private enterprise! The United States government has *never* endorsed the results of this survey!"

"Maybe they haven't endorsed it, but the EPA's Office of Health Research has called for further scientific study." Taking a flyer from Julie, the professor flourished it aloft. "You'll find a copy of the *Washington Post* article on page three of the flyer, folks."

Thumping the podium, Sam glared down at the interloper. "Perhaps we ought to wait until the EPA survey is completed, Mr. Hasner!"

"Fine idea, Mr. Covington. You could always table your request for an LWA." He winked at his followers. *"We're* willing to wait."

Crimson flooded the banker's face. In a tense, high-pitched voice, he shouted, "Mr. Chairman, I have the floor—!"

"Let him speak, Covington!" cried the collegian seated next to Julie.

Quivering in fury, Sam screamed, "Mr. Chairman!"

With the outcry from the audience, I could barely hear the pounding gavel. Scott headed for the stage steps, protected by a phalanx of supporters. Mingled boos and cheers. Covington protectively grabbed the lectern's mike. In the row behind Julie, a dozen coeds stood up, clapped their hands in unison, and began a lively contralto chant. "Safe Power!" *Clap-clap!* "Safe Power!" *Clap-clap!* "Safe Power for South Da-ko-ta!"

Suddenly, city patrolmen appeared in the wings. Competent young officers in dark blue jackets and peaked caps, their round silvery badges gleaming under the spotlights. One escorted Scott Hasner off the stage, oblivious to the shouts and catcalls. A middle-aged sergeant hastily conferred with Mr. Chairman.

I was more interested in Covington's reaction. Pulling out the hankie again, he mopped his sweaty face and glowered at Scott Hasner with unbridled hatred.

You're awfully eager to secure that power line for OP, Good Neighbor Sam, I mused. Why is that?

Mr. Chairman left me no opportunity to consider that question. Rapping the gavel once more, he replaced Sam at the podium.

"Ladies and gentlemen . . ." He looked about self-consciously. "We've been informed that the number of people present exceeds the Fire Code limit. This meeting will have to be adjourned." Deliberately he avoided Covington's exasperated gaze. "I will entertain a motion to defer the question until our next regularly scheduled meeting."

Howl of protest from the SPSD contingent. The bulk of the audience, however, realizing that no action would be taken tonight, rose from their seats and inched their way toward the aisles.

All at once, fine hairs prickled on the nape of my neck. That old prison awareness of a hostile gaze. Rising from my seat, I fired a hasty glance over my shoulder.

Standing in the center aisle twenty feet away was one of my latest acquaintances. Nerdy guy with rimless eyeglasses and wiry red hair. He stared right at me, features tense with confusion, thin lips shaping a soundless *"Renee?"*

Obsidian eyes goggled in recognition. *Oh, shit! Darren Schumacher!*

I sidestepped madly through the row, heading for the side aisle. Anishinabe ballerina doing *Tales from the Vienna Woods.* Didn't have to be a MENSA candidate to figure out what had happened. When Darren had failed to return with yours truly, Kyle Rasmussen had sent him to Mitchell in my place.

Reaching the aisle, I hung a sharp left and ran toward the empty stage. A quick sidelong glance showed Darren in the center aisle, struggling against the outgoing tide. His sharp cry sliced through the audience hubbub. "Renee! Where are you going? Wait!"

Damn, damn, damn! I thought, quickening my stride. He must have recognized my French braid. Now he's undoubtedly wondering why *Renee Standing Bear* showed up, after all. And he'll stay right on my tail until he gets some answers.

I hung a right at the stage steps, trailing a large farm family toward the side exit. *Got to lose him, princess—and fast!*

I spied Jeremy and Carol on the sidewalk outside. Maybe they could run interference . . . ? Nope! Forget it! Bad idea. Darren'd be on top of us before I could explain. And I didn't *dare* let him hear them call me Angie!

Just then, I spotted a small alcove on my left. The janitor's locker filled eighty percent of it, leaving a narrow space between the locker and the plastered wall. More than enough space for a nimble princess with a twenty-three-inch waistline. A cat-footed leap carried me into the opening. Flattening against the locker, I sucked in my middle, held my breath, and . . .

Darren galloped right past, pushing open the side door. "Renee!" Mischievous grin on the princess. His running footsteps rapidly faded. "Hey! Renee!"

Darting out the crawlway, I rushed back into the main auditorium. My hectic gaze zigzagged through the departing crowd, seeking the Elderkins.

All at once, a sinewy male hand clamped around my forearm.

"Hey!" I snapped. "What do you think you're—!?"

My lips parted in wordless shock. There was no mistaking that horsey face and those too-bright hickory eyes.

Delbert Dietz!

"Surprised to see me, squaw?" His demented chuckle hurled a gust of spinach-flavored halitosis into my face. "You know, I was kind of hoping to run into Bonnie tonight."

"Be glad you didn't. The family is out in force."

I gave my arm a sharp push, hard enough to smash a windowpane. Delbert's grip never wavered. *Uh-oh!*

"What are you doing on the outside, Delbert?" I did my best imitation of a Springfield guard. Anything but let him know how truly frightened I was. "What happened? Booby hatch run out of paper dolls?"

Jagged teeth ground in suppressed fury. Tightening male fingers poked craters in my sleeve.

"I know." Wincing, I held onto my fading Angie smile. "Your plastic scissors broke. Right?"

"Go ahead. Crack wise. You don't fool anybody. I can see how shit-scared you are."

"Actually, the expression is one of curiosity, Dietz." My hasty gaze circled the rapidly emptying hall. No sign of Mitchell cops. They must be outside with the protesters. "After your little *faux pas* at the farm, I would've thought you'd be down in Sioux Falls, busting boulders with a sledgehammer."

"Yeah? Well, you bet wrong, An-ge-la." He tasted every syllable. "No way that fuckin' Fischer could hold me. My case-file's still open at the Department."

"Department?" I echoed.

"Department of Mental Health." Delbert's cackle stung like a sandpaper massage. "They sent an outreach worker to Mitchell the minute they got word. Said I'm not responsible for what happened." Another gleeful cackle.

"So as long as you take your medication, they don't really care how many people you hurt—is that it?"

Outraged snarl. "I never hurt anybody!"

"I don't recall giving permission to hold hands, Dietz."

Contemptuous smirk. "Oooooh! Tough girl!"

"When necessary."

Looming over me, Delbert flashed a feral smile. "You're really not scared of me, are you?"

Actually, my knees were doing a lively castanet routine beneath my denim wrap skirt. But I wasn't letting him know that.

Casual toss of the raven hair. "I ran into some *real* crazies in Billsburg. You don't even come close . . . Delbert Dumb Butt!"

His equine face quivered in fury. Spraying spit, he rasped, "That's somethin' else I owe you for, squaw! I had two days in that fuckin' tank, listening' to those motherfuckers call me that! Especially that fucker Kramer!"

Well, no one could ever call me a member of the Dan Kramer Fan Club. But at that particular moment, nothing would've pleased me more than the sight of Fischer's bad-tempered deputy striding down the center aisle.

That's the trouble with real life. Sir Lancelot never shows up to rescue the lovely Anishinabe princess. Meaning I had to handle this lunatic on my own.

Taking the offensive, I suggested, "Why don't you go home, take a Valium and lie down? It'll all seem much better in the morning."

"Don't tell me what to do, you little red-skinned bitch!"

The racist remark made the next part much easier. "You're right, Del. I do get weary using all those one-syllable words."

"What!?"

"One last piece of advice, then. Next time you grab me, try to stand downwind, okay?"

Delbert's pupils resembled dark pebbles in a pair of snowballs.

"Your friends won't tell you, but . . . then again, I'm not really a friend, am I?" Awkward grimace. "Come to think of it, you don't *have* any friends, Delbert. Just psychiatrists . . . and *victims*."

"What are you trying to—!?"

My tirade had him off balance. I struck while he was still reacting, driving my long fingernails into his exposed wrist. The crow's feet near his eyes quivered in agony. He let go at once.

I took off like a startled fawn. Fast but not quite fast enough. Insanity had given Delbert the reaction time of a Wimbledon pro. Backpedaling, he blocked my path.

"Not so fast, An-ge-la! I ain't finished with you!"

"Yes, you are, Delbert." Bracing myself against the stage, I stood on the balls of my feet. Waited for him to come within leg range. "There's the door. Leave!"

Anticipatory giggle. "Game's just started."

"Touch me again, looneytune, and you're going to wish you'd worn a steel jockstrap!"

Boy, did *that* keep him out of range!

Obsidian eyes watched his every move. Shaking a fist, he tried to impress me with his macho. "You owe me, bitch!"

"Owe you what?"

"His fuckin' *address!*" Delbert's bellow turned heads further up the aisle. I hoped one of them would go for a cop.

"Whose address?"

"That asshole who hired you!"

He threw me for a moment, and then I remembered the fantasy I'd spun at Bonnie's farmhouse. "John Goodman?"

"Not *him!*" Delbert raged. "The *other one!*"

That's right. Delbert had been babbling about "the other one" during the farmhouse hostage crisis. I shot an anxious glance up the aisle. Oh, Officer, where are you?

Polite Angie smile. "Uh . . . other one?"

"The one working with Goodman!" His shout stirred a faint echo among the corncob mosaics.

Oh, terrific! Maneuvered into chatting with a mental patient about nonexistent people. It could only happen to me.

Better play along, princess. The cavalry could be awhile.

"I told you before, Delbert." Touch of debutante pique. "I never met him. I only worked with Mister, uhm . . ." *Tayaa!* What name did I give that character? My memory tossed it up. *"Sutton!* Yeah! You know, he—"

"Yeah, yeah, I know," Delbert interrupted, waving an impatient hand. "He paid you cash money down in Sioux Falls. What I want to know is how come the other suit was snoopin' around? How'd he know where to find me? And what was he doin' askin' me all them questions about—?"

Delbert's jaw clamped shut.

"About what?" I asked.

"Somethin' that happened a long time ago," he muttered.

An eerie shiver ran through me. For the past few minutes, Delbert and I had been traipsing through Fantasy Land. Now it seemed as if we'd unwittingly crossed the border back into reality.

Had Delbert been stalked by an unknown man? Or was his paranoia beginning to rub off on me?

How much stock could I put in the word of a madman?

Somethin' that happened a long time ago . . .

I could think of only one incident in Delbert's life that might fit, so I played the long shot. "Holly Larsen?"

Jackpot! Delbert's face blanched instantly. "You liar!" Yelp of betrayal. "You have been in touch with him."

Tread carefully, Angela. "What did he ask you about?"

More tenor bravado. "Why don't you ask *him*, squaw? He's *your* boss."

"You kidding? He never tells me anything." Sympathetic look. "Come on, Del. You can level with me. Why is he after you?"

Warily he stood erect. "Why don't you keep that Injun nose out of my business?"

Showing a demure smile, I laid a dainty hand on his wrist. Sly fingertips sought his pulse. "Maybe it's revenge. Holly had relatives. Maybe one of them wants to know where you live these days."

Ah, a slight fluctuation in the beat. Delbert found that concept most distressing.

"I didn't kill her," he rasped.

"Sheriff Fischer seems to think so."

Sudden ferocious glare. "You know all about it, I suppose."

"Yeah. He told me how you, Oscar, and Marvin played musical chairs during the Q & A session."

"*He* told you that!?"

Actually, it was Jake Norton, but I didn't want Delbert making trouble for the ex-deputy.

"He wasn't just fishing for leads when he stuck you in that chair, Delbert. Somebody saw you in that field."

"That's his story!"

"What's yours?"

"I was nowhere near that cornfield!"

Delbert said it with enough indignation to be convincing, but his pulse beat branded him a liar.

"So where did you go when you left school that day?"

Manic shrug. "Shit, I don't know! Who remembers that far back?"

But, Delbert, you remembered your interrogation at the hands of Fischer.

Switching gears abruptly, I asked, "Did you know Holly Larsen?"

"Sure. I'd seen her around."

True enough. No variation in the pulse.

"Did you ever see her near the creek?"

Malignant glare. "No!"

"Delbert, if you were never in that field, then how did you know about Enemy Creek?"

Flinching, he knocked my hand aside. "I didn't say I was *never* in that field. What are you trying to do to me?"

"Get some straight answers. Did you ever cut brush for Mrs. Ostlund?"

Wary eyes. "On occasion."

Okay, that fit with what I'd learned.

"Did you ever see *anyone else* poking around the creek?"

Suddenly, Delbert's gaze lifted. His expression shifted from surly suspicion to stark terror. Once again his feverish eyes showed white.

I turned at once, wondering what had spooked him so. But the side entryway was deserted. The fire door lay open to the night, admitting stray flakes of windblown snow.

Delbert's fist closed around my padded shoulder. Doing a shaky 180-degree pirouette, I found myself crowded by Delbert's snarling face.

"You go on back to that boss of yours, and tell him to forget it." *Sotto voce* mutter. "I don't know who killed that little girl, and I don't want to know! Tell him to quit botherin' me! I-I had nothin' to do with it."

"Sheriff Fischer has another opinion—"

"Then he can take it up with Fischer!" Delbert gave me a brutal shake. "Just stay away from me . . . *all'a you!*"

Just then, a familiar baritone inquired, "Something wrong here, Angie?"

"*Paul!*" Looking over my shoulder, I blinked in relief.

And there he was. Tall, brown-haired, resolute parole officer, tackily dressed, as usual, in a ten-year-old topcoat, a heather-brown blazer, and khaki slacks. The cavalry, at last!

Delbert kept his grip. "Who the fuck are you?"

"My name is Holbrook. I'm with the Department of Corrections." Paul came to a halt. "Let the young lady go."

Delbert sneered. He'd seen the stiff right arm and mistakenly thought Paul no threat. "Fuck you, pig!"

"If you don't let her go . . ." Paul's voice was deceptively calm. ". . . you're going to end up as one of my clients."

I felt Delbert's grip tighten.

Turning to me, Paul asked, "Angie, where's the bathroom?"

I did an instant double take. Delbert let out an insane chuckle. "You shittin', prison pig?"

"No, I just want to know where to *flush* you."

One good look at Paul's steel-eyed expression, and Delbert let go. Stepping away from him, I heard a polite cough, turned to my right, and spied a Mitchell cop striding our way.

"Well, now! Seems we got us a shortage of good fellowship around here." Neighborly smile. "Rest easy, boys. Let's see some ID."

To make a long story short, Officer Stalburger was very much impressed with my parole officer's Department of Corrections identification. Small brown leather wallet with its laminated photo and ID card and round silvery badge. I made sure I was standing right next to Paul. Official Angie.

Alas, Delbert failed to make a favorable impression. Your standing in society tends to slip when you have no wallet, no driver's license, no Social Security card, and your last known residence was a mental hospital in Iowa.

One hand on Delbert's arm, Officer Stalburger suggested that he come down to the station and use their telephone to call his DMH counselor.

Watching them leave, Paul remarked, "All right, Angie. What was that all about?"

"Long story, *Kemo Sabe.*" Slipping my arms around his neck, I thought of the perfect way to express my gratitude. "Thanks for the rescue."

To be perfectly honest, people, I'd wanted to do this for

months. Up on tiptoes. Sultry smile. Thrill to the warm pressure of Paul's hands on my waist. Pucker up and kiss.

First contact sent a shiver of pure delight through my nerves. I snuggled a bit closer, enjoying the oscillating motion of his warm mouth. Mmm—lovely! There's definitely something to be said for this damsel-in-distress business.

And then an amused female voice shattered our moment.

"Very professional, Paul."

Enraged, I shot a sidelong glance at the center aisle. There she stood—Sarah Sutton—looking as smug as a pampered Siamese. Green eyes glittered in disapproval.

Paul's lips broke contact. Holding me at arm's length, he mustered whatever dignity he had left. "This, uh, took a little longer than I thought, Sarah."

"I can imagine." Irritation altered her serene expression. "I guess Angela needs a *lot* of counseling."

I let her catty remark pass. Any other time, I would've been seething, but not tonight. The sight of the imperious Mrs. Sutton in that expensive Niveau jacket, slingback pumps, and Wrangler blue jeans was just too much. Choking back my laughter, I wondered how much time she'd spent in the OP ladies' room.

Merry Anishinabe grin. "So what brings you out here tonight, *Kemo Sabe?*"

"Just in the neighborhood, Angie." He gave my shoulder a brotherly pat. "I was doing a client check down in the Falls, and Sarah gave me a call. She needed a ride back to Pierre. Since we were passing through Davison County, I figured to check in on you. Trudy told us you were at the meeting here in town."

Needed a ride!? Sudden fussbudget face. Great! Now she's got him playing *chauffeur!*

Facing the lady lawyer, I became Schoolgirl Angie. Smile of total innocence. "Bad hair day, Sarah?"

"You might say that! First those idiots at OP lost my—!" Thoroughly flustered, she cut herself short. "By the time I got to my car, the meter had run out. I found a traffic ticket under the windshield wiper. And then the damned car wouldn't start!"

I clucked my tongue in sympathy. "Poor dear!"

She gave me a look, and Paul chimed in. "You were running off the battery, Sarah. You have to check those alternator cables once in awhile. Make sure they're tight."

Sarah's nose lifted. Her poise was incredible—for a woman who'd lost her skirt.

"Nice jacket," I commented.

Condescending look. "Thank you."

"But I don't know if it goes with those jeans." Impish Angie smile. "Making a fashion statement, Sarah?"

Emerald eyes turned frosty. "Not really."

"What is that look? Retro-Casual or something?"

Ignoring me, she turned to Paul. "Shouldn't we be going?"

Before Paul could reply, I jabbed, "That's a Niveau jacket, isn't it?" Sideways step into interrogation. "Where'd you buy it? Birnbaum's?"

Turning, Sarah flashed me a strange look. "How did you know that?"

Inspired prevarication. "You were wearing a Birnbaum's suit the day we met at the courthouse. Remember?"

Uncertain smile. "Yes . . . of course."

Eyeing her cutaway jacket, I added, "Tailored?"

Nodding, she tugged at her cuffs. "I picked it up the last time I was in Houston."

"I didn't know they had a store in Houston."

"It's in The Galleria. They have stores all over Texas."

Texas! The word rang alarm bells in my memory. But I couldn't be certain why.

"Discount house?" I teased.

"Hardly!" Impatient glance. "Their suits are tailored to order, and they cost twelve hundred dollars." She turned to my parole officer. "Paul, I'd really like to get home before midnight."

"Older women need their beauty sleep," I needled.

Sarah took an angry step in my direction. "I have had all I'm going to take from *you*, miss."

"Come on, Sarah. She was only kidding." Paul stepped between us. "You know how Angie is."

"Little Miss Fun!" I said, giggling.

"And you!" Turning to confront me, Paul added, "Stick around. I'll be back in a day or two. We have to talk."

"What about, *Kemo Sabe?*"

"What happens to you if Sheriff Fischer brings accessory charges in that man's disappearance." Paul was dead serious. "We're meeting with him first thing Monday morning. So stay accessible."

"Will do. Girl Scout's promise."

With a brisk farewell wave, I started up the aisle, grinning as I heard Sarah's furious whisper.

"Now look, Paul, either you do something about that girl's mouth, or, believe me, *I will!*"

Halfway to the exit, I spied Josh and Kristy chatting beneath the basketball hoop. The sharp-eyed farmer spotted me first. "Angie! Ready to go?"

"All set? You bet!"

And I showed them a radiant Angie smile.

Zinging Slinky-dink La Sutton had been fun, but that wasn't responsible for the wall-to-wall grin. No, I'd suddenly remembered why *Texas* had rung a bell.

Three interesting facts. . . .

The Larsen family had moved to Texas following Holly's mysterious disappearance.

Birnbaum's operated many stores in Texas.

My friend, Mister Beach Tan, owner of a Birnbaum's suit, was shot to death in the same field where Holly had vanished thirty years ago.

Time for a few phone calls, princess!

TEN

Saturday morning brought a cloudless sapphire sky and enough cold to glaze over the farmyard puddles. We almost cheered at the sight of that pallid November sunshine. Two more days of sun and the stalled corn harvest could resume.

After the morning milking, Josh and the boys resumed work on the combine. Clem Mutchler showed up to lend a hand, as did Doug Krause, who offered to sharpen its cutting blades. On Saturday, Trudy and Kristy worked first shift at the ShopKo, so I volunteered to do the housework.

That's right. Volunteered! You should have seen the look on my grandfather's face.

So there I was, *Hausfrau* Angela, raven-haired princess in her striped woven shirt and snug-fitting ranch jeans, sponge in one hand, dust cloth in the other. Wiping, scrubbing, dusting, cleaning. No need for my customary aerobic workout today!

By ten-thirty, I had the washing machine humming. Stooping over the washstand, I scrubbed my gritty hands clean. Quick wipe with the towel, then it was off to the parlor.

Swinging my legs over the armrest, I lounged in Josh's easy chair and reached for the telephone.

Fleeting glance at the grandfather clock. Ten past eleven. The men wouldn't be home for lunch for another hour. Plenty of time for me to make a few calls.

"Directory Assistance. What city, please?"

"Houston, Texas," I replied, snuggling into the chair.

Beeping computer sounds serenaded me. Replacing them was a voice as lovely as bluebonnets in March. "Howdy! How are you this mornin'?"

"Could you please give me the number for Birnbaum's at The Galleria?"

"Surely, hon. Hold on a sec."

I memorized the number, hung up, then tapped it out on the phone's keypad. Two short rings, and a woman answered. Her Lone Star accent was just as musical as the operator's.

"Thank you for callin' Birnbaum's. My name's Jennilee, and I'm your store representative. How may I help you?"

I went into my act. "Hi, Jennilee. I'm calling from out-of-state. I read about your store at the beauty parlor, and I'm wondering if you have a mail-order catalog."

"Yes, we do." Sensing a sale, she brightened at once. "Where are you calling from, ma'am?"

"Minnesota," I fibbed.

"Oh! Well, then you'll be interested in our brand-new store in Bloomington. It opened just last month at the Mall of America."

Oho, I thought, so that's where Chief heard the name. He must have seen their ad in the *Duluth News-Tribune*.

"One of these days I've got to get over there." No fib, that. "Could you tell me a little about your store, Jen?"

"Sure! Birnbaum's is almost a hundred years old. We're having our Giant Centennial Sale next June. Ten percent off on all inventory in the store." My, they certainly had Jennilee well trained. "We have forty stores. Located all over the

Southwest, from Rodeo Drive to the Rio Grande. We have a
wide selection of top-quality fashions for women—"

I cut right in. "No tailored clothing for men?"

"No, ma'am. Not in the mall stores. The only place we still
sell men's clothing is at the mother store."

"And where's that, Jen?"

"McLintock, Texas."

"Near Houston?"

"Oh, no, McLintock's a little town in the Panhandle. West of
Amarillo."

"My uncle's birthday is coming up. Could I order a man's
suit through your catalog?"

"I'm afraid not, dear. He'd have to go to the mother store
for a fitting." Hoping to keep me interested, she tried a sales
pitch. "Ma'am, would you be interested in opening a charge
account with us?"

"Absolutely!"

"Okay. Give me your name and address, and I'll send you
our credit application."

"Here it is . . ." I rattled it off from memory. "Carolyn
Wadena, 1571 Twelfth Avenue, Two Harbors, Minnesota
55616." I figured my cousin Carolyn would hold it for me till
my next trip to the Northland. "Thanks again, Jennilee!"

I hung up. Grin of satisfaction. I could feel the pieces coming
together. The missing Mister Beach Tan must have gone to
Birnbaum's mother store for that suit. Meaning he must be a
resident of the Panhandle.

Closing my eyes, I conjured up an image of that navy-blue
suit. Hmm—the shoes were all wrong. Dark brown hand-
stitched oxford brogues. A rancher would wear polished black
Tony Lamas. Okay, he's a city boy. From Amarillo?

Rising from Josh's chair, I made my way to the bookshelf. I
remembered Miss Edna telling me about Holly's family. A
couple of years after the disappearance, Sam Larsen had gotten a job in the oil fields of the Panhandle.

I picked up the phone book, lugged it over to the coffee table, and spread it open to the Yellow Pages. Deft Anishinabe fingers swiftly found the *Motel* section.

My forefinger slid down the page. My grandfather had struck out at the Mitchell motels. And a stranger like Mister Beach Tan would have caused comment in any of the smaller towns. So I decided to test Chief's theory and check the motels in Huron.

Lifting the receiver again, I tapped out the first number. A gruff male voice answered. "Hullo?"

"Good morning, sir!" Perky contralto. "My name is Angela Rasmussen, and I'm with Apex Autos here in Rapid City. How are you today?"

His tone turned surly. "Ain't buyin' anything, sis."

I sensed he was about to hang up. "Wait! You don't understand. We leased a Cutlass Ciera to a gentleman from Texas two weeks ago. It's three days overdue. He listed Huron as a destination, so we thought he might be staying at your motel."

"Sorry, sis. Can't help ya." He warmed a little. "We had a whole passel o' Texans come through last summer. Tourist season, ya know. Ain't seen any since Labor Day. 'Ceptin' this trucker from Beaumont named Harry. He always stops in at the cafe whenever he's makin' a run up to Bismarck. Sorry."

"That's okay, sir. Have a good day today and a better one tomorrow. Bye!"

I pulled my "Angie Rasmussen" scam on three more Huron motels. Strikeout every time. Then I telephoned the Meadowood and made contact with a laconic teenaged female.

"Texas?" she echoed.

"That's right," I purred. "He mentioned staying at the Meadowood when he got to Huron."

"There's a feller from Texas stayin' here. Mister . . . oh, what's his name? Damned if I can remember. He's out gallivantin' somewhere."

My skin prickled suddenly. "Why do you say that?"

"I make the beds, Angie, and I ain't made his for near onto a week and a half." I heard gum popping at the other end. "No problem, though. He reserved clear on through the end of the month. Payin' by credit card."

"Visa?"

"Lemme check." Rustling of registration slips. "Nope! Optima card. That what he used to rent the car?"

"Uh-huh." I ransacked the tabletop, seeking a pencil or pen. "He's a bald man, right? Big guy. Pushed-in knuckles. Narrow ears. Tan like a Florida lifeguard?"

"Yeah, that's Mr. Rankin, all right."

"You remembered the name."

"Oh, it's right here on the Optima slip. L.J. Rankin, Apartment #38, 17827 Osage Street, Amarillo, Texas."

I scribbled in the Yellow Page margin. "Did Mr. Rankin list the business name?"

"Right here. Southwest Sentinel Systems, Inc." Questioning had piqued her own curiosity. "Tell me, Angie, did he rent the car under the company name?"

"Indeed he did," I replied, jotting down the name. "Say, why don't you give me the license number? I'm pretty sure it's him, but we really ought to make sure."

"Okay! It's a South Dakota plate . . . DN-359. Your car?"

"Right on the nose, dear."

After thanking her for her help, I hung up, ripped the page out of the phone book, then put through a call to the Amarillo operator. I had a feeling Rankin's home number would be unlisted. It was! So I tried Directory Assistance again, requesting the number for Southwest Sentinel Systems.

The phone rang four times. *Click!* A mellow bass voice came on line. "Howdy! This here's Southwest Sentinel. Our investigators can't come to the phone right now. But if you'll please leave your name and number, we'll get right back to you."

Hand shaking, I put down the receiver. A cold damp sensation slithered up my spine.

I'll never get used to that, you know. To hearing the victim's voice on tape. You'd think after Mona I'd be accustomed by now. I'm afraid it doesn't work that way, folks. Not for me!

Rankin's pleasant Texan voice stirred up some frightful imagery. Dead body sprawled in Mrs. Ostlund's field, facedown in the stubble, with those two bloodstained bullet craters erupting from his back.

At least now that puzzling physical description made sense. Prominent tan, citified clothing, pushed-in knuckles. L.J. Rankin was a private investigator. Doing pretty good at it, too, if he could afford a suit from Birnbaum's.

Questions, questions. What brings an Amarillo P.I. to South Dakota?

The murder scene answers that question, princess. Rankin was poking about in the Holly Larsen case.

The shooter? Obviously, someone determined to halt this new investigation.

Another interesting question—how did he know that Rankin was looking into the case?

Because he had *already met* Rankin?

Several questions still eluded me, however. For instance, how had a Lone Star private eye become interested in the Larsen case? Even here in Davison County, it was old news. Who had summoned him to South Dakota? And why?

I heard a whirring in the bathroom. The washing machine had begun its spin cycle. Leaning forward, I closed the phone book, folded the torn-out page and slipped it into my pocket. I knew I wouldn't find any more answers here on the farm.

Well . . . maybe after lunch I could interest Chief in a run up to Huron.

The Meadowood was a small, gracefully aging, ground-level motel that had gone up sometime in the Fifties. It squatted on the curb of U.S. Route 14, just across from the state fairgrounds. Red-painted shingles, white unit doors, and sizable picture windows, each one discreetly veiled by a sliding forest green curtain. Tacked onto the right was a breezeway leading into another Colonial building, which housed the motel office and an antique shop called Betty's Bargain Barn.

Tall leafless elms loomed over the miniscule parking lot. I slid Clunky into an empty space in front of the Coke machine, switched off the engine, and told my grandfather what I had in mind. Chief was only too happy to let me do the talking.

Leaving the car, we wandered the lot aimlessly. Expressions of mild confusion. Arms folded, Chief leaned against Clunky's rear fender. I made a great show of checking room numbers.

As expected, my act soon drew an audience. The office door creaked open, and out stepped a tall, rawboned man in his late forties. Thin Scottish face with a high forehead. Sandy hair rapidly turning gray. Hollow cheekbones and a drooping outlaw mustache. Red mackinaw shirt and khaki corduroy pants. Descending the steps, he asked, "Need any help?"

Scintillating Angie smile. "Hi! Mr. Rankin around?"

I didn't need to look at his hands to know he was a farmer. The way he rocked back on his heels, warily cocking his head, said it all. "Who's askin'?"

"I'm Susan Wanagi," The Lakota word for *phantom* made a fine alias. "This here's my Uncle Jack. We have an appointment with Mr. Rankin."

"Today?" He gave my outstretched hand a neighborly shake.

"Yeah, Mr. Rankin's supposed to show us some burglar alarms. See, we own this store up in Milbank. Genuine Native American souvenirs. We've had a lot of trouble with break-ins lately, so we—"

Muscular palms lifted suddenly. "Hold on there, missy. One thing at a time. 'Fraid you folks drove all the way down for nothin'. Mr. Rankin ain't here."

Disappointed Angela. "But we had an *appointment*."

"Who'd you make the appointment with?"

"His office in Amarillo." A nod to Chief. "Uncle Jack saw that Southwest Sentinel Systems ad in *Farm and Ranch*. I called the number. Lady said Mr. Rankin'd be in Huron for a spell. If we could be here Saturday afternoon, we'd get a free demonstration."

"When did you call 'em, Susie?"

"Ten, twelve days ago, Mister—?"

"McParlan. Bill McParlan." Thoughtfully he stroked his unshaven chin. "Sure must've changed his plans, gal, 'cause I ain't laid eyes on him in over a week."

Chief spoke up. "When's the last time you saw him, Bill?"

"Week ago yesterday. Halloween."

The day he got shot in Mrs. Ostlund's field, I thought.

Fastening his top shirt button, Bill tilted his head toward the motel office. "Gettin' a little windy out here. Can I interest you folks in some coffee?"

"That'd be fine, Mr. McParlan. Thanks."

The office lounge boasted a small Formica-topped counter, pastel-blue walls, framed watercolor paintings, a portable color TV, and modern furniture more suited to a dentist's waiting room. Comfortable sofa and padded lounge chairs and an oval cherrywood coffee table.

While we sipped coffee, Mr. McParlan informed us that Huron was the birthplace of Hubert Humphrey and the hometown of actress Cheryl Ladd. If we could get away next August, the South Dakota State Fair was not to be missed.

Turned out Bill wasn't really the owner—he just managed the front desk on weekends. Like every other East River farmer, he had a part-time job that took him away from the tractor.

"Talk much to Mr. Rankin?" I asked.

"Some." Bill's large hands dwarfed the steaming paper cup. "Nice feller. Real affable. Mrs. Talbot wasn't too keen on him, though. Caught him puttin' his foot on the armrest to shine a shoe." Rueful chuckle. "Thought she was goin' to lay him out right then 'n' there."

I took a sip. "Did he try to sell you anything?"

"Me? Nahhhhh! He was out on the road a lot, mostly. Sales trips. Pretty damned good at it, too."

"Why do you say that?" asked Chief.

"Well . . ." Bill put down his empty cup. "There was one feller almighty anxious to make a buy. From Mitchell, he said."

Tremor of excitement. "Mitchell?"

"Yeah, he showed up . . . oh, day or two before Halloween, I reckon." Rotating brawny shoulders, he added, "I tell ya, that feller was the ugliest critter I seen since ol' Pop Wilkinson died." Shake of the head. "Reckon his momma spent too much time out in the stable 'fore he was born."

I could think of only one man in Davison County who matched that description. "Sort of a horsey face, eh?"

"You got it. Skittish as a thoroughbred, too. Did a lot of twitchin' and lookin' around. Nervous as my Aunt Nellie. He got real sore when I told him Mr. Rankin wasn't around. Commenced to shoutin' at me." Dark blue eyes narrowed grimly. "I told him, 'Put a sock in it, mister. You got a message for Mr. Rankin, you give it to him your own self.' So he up and left."

"Light brown hair?" I prodded. "Hickory eyes?"

"That's him." Bill gave me a strange look. "You know the feller?"

You did it again, Princess Big Mouth. Open and insert foot!

Nonchalant shrug. "He barged in on me once. Gave me a real hard time."

"She didn't have the right brand of *flour*," added Chief, a teasing gleam in his obsidian eyes.

I made a tart face at my grandfather.

"More coffee?" Bill asked.

Smiling, I shook my head. I needed a peek at Rankin's telephone tab, and this seemed like the perfect moment, with Bill at his most receptive. No longer were we threatening strangers. By the rules of Midwestern hospitality, drinking his coffee had transformed us into friends. Instant neighbors!

Scratching my knee, I inquired, "Any idea where we might be able to reach Mr. Rankin?"

He poured himself another cup. "Couldn't rightly say, Susie. Them sales fellers . . . usually they leave a business card at the front desk. But Mr. Rankin didn't."

Glancing at the telephone switchboard, I added, "Did he make any outgoing calls?"

"A few." Holding the coffee in his left hand, Bill rounded the counter. Within seconds, he spread a quintet of pink phone messages across the Formica. "Most of 'em are calls to his home office in Amarillo, I reckon. Area code 806, uh, 555-6233." He glanced at me. "That's the number you called, ain't it?"

It wasn't, but I nodded anyway. "Uh-huh." And committed that number to memory.

Bill lifted a single slip. "Then there's this one. Local call—incoming. From Yorktown. Patti took the message." He squinted at the date. "Came in for him, uh, November third."

Instantly I sat erect. "Any name?"

"A woman—*Edna*. No last name."

Before I could react, Chief intruded with, "Could be he's gone there. What's the number?"

"Uh . . . 277-8416."

Chief and I exchanged startled glances. No coincidence and no mistake. It was the *Elderkins'* phone number.

An hour later, we were speeding south on Route 37. A sea of tawny cornstalks rippled in the autumn wind. Off to my right, cottonball clouds masked the sun, splintering the daylight into a regiment of brilliant slanting sunbeams. A pair of combines appeared at the skyline, ready to kick off the harvest.

"It's the same Edna," I commented, both hands on Clunky's steering wheel. "It has to be!"

Chief peered my way. "What makes you so sure?"

"The timing," I replied, keeping a watchful eye on the traffic. "L.J. Rankin was shot in Mrs. Ostlund's field Halloween afternoon. I got to him five minutes later. Four days after that, Miss Edna telephoned Rankin's motel in Huron—"

"If it *was* Miss Edna," he interrupted, drumming his fingers on Clunky's armrest. "Could've been another woman using her name."

Thoughtful grimace. "I don't think so, Chief. The call came from the Elderkins' phone, remember? There were only three other women on the farm that day. Trudy, Carol and, me."

"And Kristy."

I shook my head. "She didn't get back until five. No, it had to be Miss Edna, Chief. She waited until she was alone in the house; then she put through that call to Huron."

He nodded in agreement. "So what does all that tell us, missy?"

"Plenty! Miss Edna knew Rankin was in the area. She expected to hear from him. When he didn't show, she got worried and called his motel."

"How did she know he was in Huron?"

Exasperated glance. "He *told* her, Chief! That much is obvious. McParlan said Rankin's been in the area awhile. What do you want to bet he phoned the farm one afternoon and had a long chat with Miss Edna?"

"I'll go you one better, Angie. Maybe Rankin intended to meet Miss Edna on the thirty-first but got sidetracked—permanently."

"You mean Rankin got killed *because* he was meeting with Miss Edna?"

My grandfather nodded. "Exactly. Remember, Miss Edna was murdered right *after* she called Huron."

"That's crazy!" I protested. "Miss Edna was sitting right at the kitchen table when I described the man I found in the field. Why didn't she say something?"

Mulling it over, Chief replied, "If Rankin made contact by phone, could be she never got a look at him."

"And she never mentioned the call to Trudy?"

"There's a lot Miss Edna hasn't told her family." Dour expression. "She didn't tell 'em about the Enright Trust, did she?"

I shook my head. True enough! I had a hard time reconciling this closemouthed, secretive Edna with the jovial elderly lady I'd come to love. A woman with secrets, our Miss Edna, and one of them might have gotten her killed.

"What have we got?" my grandfather asked.

"A nice blend of hunches and information." Stepping down on Clunky's gas pedal, I passed a hay-laden flatbed truck. "For some unknown reason, L.J. Rankin got in touch with Miss Edna, probably by telephone. Maybe he wanted to set up a meet—maybe not. At any rate, his reason, whatever it was, was compelling enough to convince Miss Edna not to confide in Trudy. It was also urgent enough to worry her when Rankin failed to show. She gave him a few days to make contact, then called his motel in Huron, using the number Rankin had given her." Fussbudget face. "Which brings us right back to the brick wall. Namely, why was Rankin here in South Dakota?"

"We can't very well question a dead man, Angie."

"Maybe we don't have to." My lips turned upward in a coy smile. "There's that Amarillo number McParlan gave us."

"What about it, Angie?"

"It isn't the same number as Rankin's office. Meaning he was in regular contact with somebody back home." I slowed Clunky as we approached the Mitchell airport turnoff. "Maybe that person can tell us a little bit more about him."

"Such as why he was so interested in the Holly Larsen case." Grim chuckle. "He must've been on to somethin'."

"Why do you say that?"

"He brought *Delbert Dietz* on the run, didn't he?"

Scowling, I said nothing. My grandfather was right. Delbert had shown up at the Meadowood Motel *before* Halloween, while Rankin was still nosing around. How come?

Did he visit Huron because Rankin had called Miss Edna?

If that's the case, then what is Delbert's connection with Miss Edna?

I thought back to my chat with Jake Norton, remembering what he'd told me about Delbert's Q & A session. If Delbert really did kill the Larsen girl, then that would explain why he went gunning for Rankin.

After all, Delbert had never been formally charged the first time around. Holly's remains had never been found. Hmm— that's a thought. Had L.J. Rankin located the girl's body, extracting enough physical evidence to convict, he could have put Delbert away for good. Which provides Mr. Dietz with an excellent motive for shooting the Amarillo P.I.

There's just one hitch, princess. Is Delbert rational enough to concoct and carry out such a deceptive scheme?

My mind drifted back to the farmhouse and the Corn Palace. Listless sigh. Nope! I'm afraid no one will ever, ever describe Delbert Dietz as *levelheaded.*

Under the stress of police interrogation, Delbert had manifested two new personalities—Oscar and Marvin. Sounds as if he's suffering from a multiple personality disorder. I wish I knew more about MPD cases. If an alternate personality— say, Marvin—had killed Holly and shot Rankin, would Delbert have any memory of the event?

Chief's gentle nudge jolted me out of my reverie. "Pull in over there, Angie. I've got an idea."

I steered Clunky into an empty space in front of the Video Palace. Sudden inquisitive glance.

Opening the passenger door, my grandfather asked, "Do you still have that scraping you took off Miss Edna's bed?"

"Sure. Why?"

His gnarled hand beckoned. *"Ambe, Noozis."*

Chief waited while I popped a quarter in the meter. Then we sauntered down North Main, turned the corner at Third, and headed east. Clutching my shoulder bag, I asked, "Where are we going?"

"North Kimball. I saw an ad in yesterday's paper. Maybe the owner can help us out."

The store was called Aladdin's Lamp, and it occupied a century-old building on North Kimball. Clutter completely filled the display window. Stand-up lamps and dangling light fixtures. Discount signs and paddle fans and electric garage door openers. Down in the corner was a sun-faded bumper sticker reading BUY SOUTH DAKOTA FARM PRODUCTS . . . WE DO!

Chimes pealed as we walked through the door. I spied the owner behind the walnut counter, ripping open a cardboard box. He was about my grandfather's height, a chubby, durable fellow of indeterminate middle age, wearing a windowpane black-and-white plain shirt. Orange-shaped face, slate-colored eyes, blunt Saxon nose, and a slightly protruding chin. He looked up instantly, then offered a smile brighter than any cinema spotlight.

"Howdy, folks! Have a look around. I'll be with you in a minute. Got to find that damn manifest."

"No hurry," said Chief, and then he turned to me. "Give me that scraping, Angie."

While I dug for the evidence, the owner found his shipment manifest, slapped it on the counter, reached for his calculator, and did some quick arithmetic. He had slightly more hair than L.J. Rankin, a wreath of fieldmouse-brown reaching around the back of his skull from ear to ear. With a grunt of satisfaction, he pinned the manifest to an upright spike.

"All set!" Rounding the counter, he extended a welcoming hand. "Hi, I'm Bob Kittridge."

"Pleasure." A panicky shadow flitted across Chief's face. It took him a second to remember his cover name. "Uh, I'm Jack Wanagi, and this is my granddaughter, uh—"

"Susan," I chimed, standing at his elbow.

"What can I do for you?" Bob asked.

Since it was Chief's *nandobani*, I let him run with the ball. My grandfather removed the dollop of dark material from the little plastic envelope and, palm up, showed it to Bob.

"Found this in the barn," Chief said, his features sober. "Tried the light switch when I went to milk the cows. Nothing. Replaced a pair of fuses and still nothing. Then I come across this on the floor."

With a thoughtful hum, Bob Kittredge adjusted his horn-rimmed glasses. Deep frown. "I'd say you got problems, Jack. Run any wire through the hayloft?"

"Sure, right under the center beam."

Bob nodded in understanding. "It'll have to come out. You've got a bad short in there."

"Short?" I echoed.

"Short circuit, gal." He showed me the scraping. "It melted the insulation."

My fingernail prodded the black material. "You mean you know what this is?"

"Sure!" He brightened at once. "It's *thermoplastic insulation*—AWG Type S, I'd say." Turned to Chief. "What kind of line did you run in there?"

"Standard house line . . . 240 volts, 100 amps."

"You'd better shut down then," Bob advised. "A hundred-amp short circuit is nothing to fool with."

"Dangerous?" I remarked.

"I should say so." His slate-eyed gaze met mine. "Young lady, a one-amp jolt could kill you."

"Are you kidding me?"

"Not at all." Bob's face turned dead serious. "Why, 0.1 amps—that's one-tenth of an amp—could stop your heart."

I stopped slouching instantly, standing erect, feeling a sudden tremor of excitement zipping up my spine. "Really?"

"Word of truth, Susan." His pudgy finger drew a wavy line across his chest. "All it takes is a 0.1-amp wire right here. Whammo! You're getting fitted for your wings and harp."

"Instant heart attack, eh?"

"You've got it. Doctors got a fancy-ass name for it. Ten-letter word." He grinned. "Just like a damn hospital bill. All them big fancy words and numbers even *bigger*."

"Ventricular fibrillation?" I offered.

"Yeah, that's it." He shot me a curious glance. "Susie, how'd you know—?"

"She's a medical receptionist," Chief intruded, helping to allay his suspicions.

"I'm curious, Bob." Somehow I banished the excitement from my voice. "What exactly happens when someone is touched by a live electrical wire?"

"Sort of depends on the voltage, Susie." He scratched his bald pate. "In any case, the heart and the breathing stop. If the voltage is high enough, there may be a burn."

I thought instantly of Miss Edna's discolored wrist. "Like a sunburn?"

He nodded. "Yeah. Voltage drives the body temperature way, way up. Even a low-voltage charge has been known to kill people."

Chief's triumphant gaze found mine, and I knew he'd arrived at the same conclusion. At last we understood the method of Miss Edna's murder—*electrocution*. All that remained now was to find her killer.

"If you want me to have a look at it, I can get out there sometime next week," Bob offered.

Chief had a blowoff ready. "You don't mind coming up to Fort Thompson?"

The electrician hesitated. "Well, that's a little off my trail."

Handing Chief a business card, he added, "Tell you what, I know a couple of ol' boys here in town. They're almighty handy with wiring. They wouldn't mind taking a ride up north. Give me a call in a day or two. That'll give me a chance to get in touch with 'em."

"Good enough, Bob," I said, heading for the door. "And thanks! Believe me, you've been a great help."

"Pleasure's all mine, Susie. Drop in again!"

Fifteen minutes later, Clunky was speeding west on Route 38. I had the wheel. Turning to my grandfather, I said, "You knew that stuff was thermoplastic insulation, didn't you?"

Settling back in the passenger seat, my grandfather nodded. "Sorta had my suspicions, Angie."

"What tipped you off?"

"The melted Number 6 wire," he explained. "If the short circuit turned the wire's exposed end into slag, it must've melted the insulation, too."

A slow-moving green tractor appeared on the horizon. My foot gently pressed Clunky's brake pedal.

"So now we know," I said, passing the tractor on the left. "It really was murder."

"You bet. He exposed one end of the wire, snaked it through the cable TV outlet, maybe poked around until it made contact with Miss Edna. Then he turned on the juice."

"So that was Miss Edna I heard."

My grandfather nodded. "She cried out as she was being electrocuted."

My mind conjured up an image of Miss Edna's darkened bedroom, of the lady herself snuggled under warm quilts. I could see the stiffened cable gliding across the floor . . . unseen hands forcing it up onto the bed . . . the naked metal edge coming to rest against the old woman's fragile hand.

"Whoever it is, he knows wiring," Chief said, glancing at me again. "There's no way he could safely handle a live hundred-amp wire. So he must have had some kind of portable step-down transformer."

Instant double take. "A *what!?*"

"I can see you never worked in construction, missy."

"Mother said I'd do better in an office job."

He chuckled. "She was right! A step-down transformer is a device designed to reduce current and voltage from a primary circuit and feed it into a secondary circuit."

I put it in plain English. "Meaning the killer tapped into another power source and zapped it through the wire into Miss Edna's bedroom."

"You've got it."

"The house system?" I asked, flicking strands of hair away from my eyelashes.

"Could be. We'll check it out when we get home."

"How?"

His smile turned sagacious. "You'll see."

Arriving at the farm, I experienced a sudden tremor. The barnyard looked strangely deserted. Then, as I pulled up beside the white fence, I spotted Kristy coming down the ramp, lugging a pail full of grain.

"Hi, Kris!" I shouted, climbing out of the big green Merc.

"Hi, Angie." Halting, she tried and failed to build a welcoming smile. "Hi, Mr. Blackbear."

As Chief and I joined her, I noticed the tearful irritation rimming Kristy's eyes. She stood with her shoulders drooping, her chin down, a child-woman weighed down with all the cares of the world. Looking around, I asked, "Where is everybody?"

"In the house," she murmured, gesturing with her free hand. "A letter came today. Registered letter from the bank."

"Kristy . . . what's the matter?" I asked, holding her shoulders.

"Th-They're going to foreclose on us." Lifting her chin, she made herself face me, determined not to cry. "M-Mama said we-we're going to lose the farm!"

I looked up. "Chief—?"

"Go on, Angie." He placed a comforting arm across Kristy's tense shoulders. "Here, girl, let me give you a hand with them chickens."

Hastening my stride, I made a beeline to the back door. Kristy was in good hands, I knew. Between me, Mother, and Aunt Della, my grandfather had had plenty of experience dealing with distraught teenaged girls.

I found the Elderkins seated around the kitchen table. Josh looked about ten years older. Trudy's eyes were as red as her daughter's. Brad and Jeremy stared grimly into coffee mugs. In-laws were present, too. Tearful Ronnie looked at the bank's letter as if it were a rattlesnake. Carol sat there, clenched fists on the tablecloth, as if ready to pounce.

The kitchen door slammed. Six pairs of eyes riveted onto me, one angry, the rest glum and defeated.

"Kristy told me." I hooked my thumb toward the yard. "What are the terms, Josh?"

His big, callused hand reached for the letter. He read it yet again. Reminded me of a Death Row prisoner getting the bad news.

"Bank's callin' in the loan," he muttered, his deep voice clotted with emotion. "All of it. A hundred thousand dollars. MBSB wants it by the end of the month."

"Borrow somewhere else," I snapped. "Sioux Falls."

Brad glanced up at me. "What'll we use for collateral, Angie?"

"The farm! Go for a short-term loan. In sixty days, the corn will be sold, and you can pay it off."

Shaking his head, Josh sighed. "It's no good, Angie. We're already carryin' one mortgage. We go in askin' for more money, and the interest rates'd kill us."

"Worse'n that, Angie, we ain't got time to sit around in

banks, renegotiating loans," Jeremy said, frowning. "We've got a crop to bring in."

"He's right." Brad lifted his palms haplessly. "If we miss that harvest, we're finished."

My fist smacked the refrigerator's side. I had a strong feeling Mr. Covington had planned it that way.

Ronnie looked anxiously at her father-in-law. "There must be some way we can raise the money. Maybe we could call the silo. Take whatever we could get."

Josh shook his head slowly. "No one's gonna pay for a crop that's still in the field."

"But you have money!" I blurted.

Instantly the men's eyes swiveled toward me.

Biting my lower lip, I looked away. Sure, I could tell them all about the Enright Trust, and they could use that for collateral. But if I spoke up before the reading of Edna's will, that might alert Sam Covington. And, if Covington really is the murderer, he might get clean away.

No, I could think of a *better* way to handle that swindler Covington.

Instant backtrack, followed by an uncertain Angie smile. "Uhm . . . I mean, the farm itself is worth something. Why, the land alone—"

"Forget it!" Josh snapped. "I've had offers, and I've turned 'em down. I ain't subdividin' my roadside property—puttin' up fancy homes. This is a workin' farm. Always has been, always will be."

Carol made a strangled sound of frustration. "We could at least talk to Mr. Covington—"

"I said *no!*" Josh's green eyes flashed fire. "There is no quit in this family!" Scowl of irritation. "Though I don't expect a Bailey to understand that."

"Dad!" Jeremy cried.

Outraged, Carol stood up. "So we're going to lose it all, is that it? We're going to sit here until the sheriff's auction, and then we're going to leave with our clothes stuffed in Hefty bags!"

"Carol, please . . ." He tugged at his wife's forearm.

Josh refused to look at her. "I'm gonna say this once and only once, so I hope ever'body's listenin'. There is no quit in an Elderkin. We're farmers, and we're gonna stay farmers."

Shaking free of Jeremy's hand, Carol shouted, "You stiff-necked, stubborn . . . *ohhhh!*" Taut fist struck her hips. "Don't you get it yet? It's over! You're finished! You can't make a living like this anymore. No one can. It's senseless. No, it's worse than senseless—it's *stupid!* You're throwing your lives away, and for what? Fifty cents an hour?"

"It's more than just a job, Carol." Brad's features showed irritation. "You ought to know that by now."

Turning on her husband, Carol cried, "How can you be so spineless? Why don't you stand up to them for once in your life? They've already ruined their own lives. Are you going to let them wreck *ours*, too?"

"Don't, Carol!" Jeremy snapped, standing up. "Don't make me choose between you and my family!"

"Well, I'm sorry, but I just can't take it anymore!" she shouted, pointing at her father-in-law. "You've worked for him for ten years or better, and you don't even get a damned paycheck!"

Reaching for his coffee, Josh muttered, "Don't hear anybody bellyachin' about the vegetables in their freezer."

Jeremy stiffened. "Dad, stay out of it, will you?"

"This isn't what I *wanted!*" Carol screeched.

Facing the enraged spouse, Jeremy said, "We all get stuck with things we don't want, Carol. What am I supposed to do about it?"

"Try deciding if you're still married!"

"Carol!" he bellowed.

She flounced right by me on her way to the door. Jeremy rounded the table in pursuit. As she turned, I thought Carol was going to hit me. Instead, she rushed past me and scooped a china saucer off the counter.

"Stay away from me, Jer!"

Eyes glistening with rage, Carol cocked her arm, ready to fling. I chopped her forearm at the last possible second. The saucer cartwheeled through the air, shattering against a cupboard door.

"Bitch!" Shaking all over, she turned her hate-filled glance on me. "That goes for you, too!"

The door whammed shut. We all looked at one another. Josh's eyes narrowed. There was no quit in the Elderkin family . . . and not much room for disloyalty, either. "You'd better get that wife o' yours under control, boy."

"Don't start, Dad!" Jeremy's tone actually made his father blink. His face as hard as stone, the younger Elderkin strode briskly into the parlor.

Brad sighed. "I'd better go talk to him."

We sat in silence for many moments. Josh seemed troubled by our presence there. Finally, he knocked down his coffee and muttered, "Somebody'd better see 'bout the work around here."

Ronnie gave me the high sign, and I helped clean up the crockery. Trudy sat there helplessly, her eyes shiny with tears, fingering the bank's cream-colored letter.

"Trudy?" Ronnie muttered, putting the cups in the sink. "Want to talk about it?"

"Wh-What can I say?" Uncertain eyes found mine. "I-I just don't understand what's happening to my family." Anxious fingers twisted the linen napkin. "Carol's angry all the time now. It comes out every time she's here. It-It's tearing poor Jeremy apart. And Josh—it's like he won't admit there's anything wrong."

I turned on the faucet. "Reckon Carol doesn't like farming, huh?"

Trudy's eyes blinked rapidly. "I—I guess she's always wanted to live in town."

Hoping to comfort the boss lady, I kept the conversation going. "Yeah, Jeremy told me she grew up in Mitchell."

"Her daddy owns an appliance store," Ronnie interjected. "Over on North Rowley. Wish I could remember the name, though."

"Bailey's Electrical Supplies." Trudy handed me her cup and saucer. "I've known Curt Bailey since I was a kid. He installed my washer and dryer."

Sudden preternatural shiver. "Electrical supplies?"

Trudy showed guileless eyes. "You bet! Curt's mighty handy with a lineman's pliers. So's Carol. Why, she worked in that store for years, right up to the day she and Jeremy got married."

ELEVEN

"Anything else?" I inquired.

Josh locked the pickup's rear gate. "Nope. That's about it, Angie."

Smiling in relief, I set the last feed sack on the black plastic toolbox behind the cab. The wind teased my hair. Huddling in my parka, I glanced at the items spread before me. Wired bundles of newspapers, sacks of Pioneer seed, and a wicker laundry basket containing the Elderkins' contribution to the Sunday breakfast at the First Presbyterian Church.

Josh's workaday coveralls had given way to clean dark Western slacks and a denim sheepskin jacket. Instead of his customary seed cap, he wore a brown range hat with a broad brim and a rancher's crease.

"What time will you be back?" I asked, watching Trudy, Kristy, and my grandfather descend the front steps.

"Around one, I reckon." He rounded the truck, halted at the passenger door, and pulled it open for his wife. "Don't forget to look in on that calf, gal."

"I won't." Swinging my legs over the transom, I slid down the truck's side. The landing bounced my hair.

We said our goodbyes as they climbed into the truck. Chief slammed the passenger door. "Drive careful now."

"Sure you don't want to come with us, Charlie?" The closed window muffled Trudy's voice.

"Some other time." Chief raised his hand in farewell. "You tell your medicine man to pray for some more sunshine. Them fields are wet enough to go ricin' in."

We both watched the pickup rumble down the dirt driveway. Then, a brisk breeze plucking at his white hair, my grandfather turned to me. "Where does Josh keep his electric bills?"

"In the computer." My head tilted toward the porch. "He's got all the farm expenses organized into separate files."

Ambling toward the farmhouse, Chief pulled a notepad and stubby pencil from his coat pocket. "Let's get at it."

The OP meter clung to the shingled wall, sprouting metal cable conduits above and below. Behind the glass was an array of five horizontal dials. They reminded me of airport clocks showing the hour in five separate time zones.

Features tensing in confusion, I watched my grandfather jot down numbers. "How do you make sense of that?"

Amused Anishinabe glance. "Aren't you the girl with the Master's degree from MSU?"

Playful nudge. "We didn't cover this in Accounting."

"You should have." Chief's pencil tapped the glass. "You read 'em from left to right. The first dial has the arrow between zero and one. To find out which one it's closest to, check the second dial. If that arrow's on a number lower than five, your first dial is a *zero*. If the second dial's number is above five, then Dial Number One is a *one*. Clear enough?"

Comprehension. "Aha! Each dial to the right is a subset of its neighbor. And this gives us the—"

"Total number of kilowatt-hours, right." Chief kept up his scribbling. "Didn't they cover this at Central?"

Chastened, I shook my head.

Heartfelt sigh. "I've got to have a long talk with that there School Committee."

On our way inside, Chief explained that the farm had used 587 kilowatt-hours since the first of November. He figured to pull the monthly totals for September and October off the computer, divide by thirty, and come up with an average daily usage rate.

Minutes later, I switched on the Elderkins' trusty IBM home computer. Chief stood at my shoulder, content to let me work within my own area of expertise. I booted up the system, dialogued with DOS, gained access to the Q & A program.

A warning prompt winked at me.

Enter Code Phrase

Grimacing at the bright blue screen, I studied the empty box. Hmm . . . four digits. Let's try a word. *Farm.*

The screen flickered. *Access Denied.*

Josh? Aaaaargh! Wrong again.

Corn? Shit! Too obvious.

Milk? Oh, shit! This is going to be a long morning.

Chief's hand rested lightly on my shoulder. "I thought you were an expert with these things."

"You're not helping, Grandfather of mine."

"Sorry." Deep rich chuckle. "This ain't my field. If you need another meter read, let me know."

Typing frantically, I muttered, "I had an easier time breaking into the computer at Jaswell's bank."

Brad? Nope. Stifling an urge to clout the monitor, I closed my eyes and counted to ten—*three times!*

Think, Angela. Looking at everyone in the Elderkin household, who's the most likely candidate to have loaded Q & A on the hard disk?

Sudden triumphant grin. I pecked away madly. *Kris!*

I found myself facing the Main Menu.

Fingertips did a war dance on the keyboard. Might have known, I thought ruefully. Kids are usually the ones who get these things up and running.

Soon I had the family's September and October electric bills on the clipboard. Gripping the spine of my chair, Chief leaned closer. "You got a math calculator handy?"

"Right here," I replied, tapping a flurry of keys.

He had me tally up the daily kilowatt-hour usage rate for each of the previous two months. Next, I multiplied each rate times four to get the estimated usage total for November.

Chief frowned. "Line 'em up and let's see what we've got."

More hasty typing. The computer tossed the numerals onto a blank screen. Here's how they broke out.

September	October	November
596	587	587

"Damn!" Chief muttered.

"What's the matter?" I asked, looking up at him.

"October and November—they're identical." His forefinger tapped the screen. "See? September was a little higher. Figures—they were still using the air conditioner." His blunt head shook stubbornly. "It isn't possible."

"*What* isn't possible?"

"That they're the same," my grandfather explained. "A mammoth power surge killed Miss Edna. That surge should have been reflected on the meter." Bewildered look. "I-I don't understand it."

"Maybe he hooked up to a battery or something."

"Angie! That was better than a hundred-amp jolt. There aren't any backpack batteries with that big a kick. The killer *must* have tapped into the house system." Scratching the back of his head, he murmured, "But why didn't it show on the meter?"

Jumping back to the file menu, I asked, "Could he have hooked up to another house?"

"No way!" Obsidian eyes showed vehement disagreement. "The nearest place is Bonnie's, and that's two miles from here."

Thinking instantly of Delbert, I added, "He couldn't have strung a power cable that far?"

"I don't think so, missy." Laconic smile. "Two miles works out to *ten thousand* feet of cable. *That* comes on a spool the size of a forklift!"

Exiting from the program, I said, "This is crazy, Chief. We have the evidence. We *know* Miss Edna was electrocuted!"

"True." My grandfather nodded slowly. "But where did the electricity come from? There's your mystery."

I gave the matter plenty of thought while I shut down the Elderkins' computer. If Miss Edna's killer hadn't tapped into the house's electrical system, then how did he do it?

Well, I knew how he *couldn't* have done it. He couldn't possibly have run a wire to Bonnie's farmhouse. It was just too far away. And I couldn't see anyone—not even a zany like Delbert—pushing a jumbo-size spool across back pastures in the middle of the night.

You can forget about the backpack battery, too. No way could it generate over a hundred amps.

Wait a minute! I thought, switching off the computer. What about a portable generator mounted on a truck? The killer could have parked in the farmyard, run his lethal cable into the house, and then fired her up.

A fine theory, but it didn't quite fit the facts. I was awake that night. Miss Edna's hushed death-cry had jolted me out of a sound sleep. Had there been a truck in the yard, I would have heard the mutter of its idling engine, the chugging of that portable generator.

Listening to the echoes of memory, I heard the skittering of ice on the windowpane. That had been the only sound.

Then, of course, there was that weird blue corona ...

Suddenly, I heard a truck engine approaching. Rising from the desk, I glanced out the parlor window and spied a dull-red Jeep Cherokee tooling up the driveway. Slipping on my parka, I headed straight for the front door.

Stepping onto the porch, I watched the Cherokee groan to a halt beside the barn. I recognized the driver even before I saw the DOUG'S FIX-IT sign on the truck's door. He was wearing his favorite denim work jacket over a set of khaki coveralls. Turtleneck wool sheathed his Adam's apple.

Cheerful wave. "Hi, Mr. Krause!"

Dull brown eyes gleamed in sudden surprise. "Miss Angie." Slamming the Cherokee's door, he looked around warily. "Where is everybody?"

"Church breakfast." Casually I leaned against a porch pillar. "What brings you out here on Sunday morning?"

Doug Krause displayed an aw-shucks smile. "Oh, I thought I'd drop by and say hello." His bronzed hands flexed nervously, reminding me of a small boy face-to-face with the principal. "Just huntin' up work, I reckon. You wouldn't know if Josh needs anything fixed 'round here, would you?"

I jutted my chin toward the rear shed. "You could have a look at the milking machines. They've been giving us trouble lately."

Doug's smile persisted, but it had a sickly cast. He looked as if he was trying to grind orange seeds with his teeth. "Sorry." Regretful shake of the head. "I don't do electrical work."

"How about cable TV installation?" I asked.

"Beg pardon?"

"You were good friends with Miss Edna, weren't you?"

"Sure." His voice thickened strangely. "She was a fine woman." Sudden suspicious glance. "What's that got to do with cable TV?"

"Miss Edna told me she had cable TV put in a few years

back," I explained. "I thought maybe you did the work for her."

Doug laughed suddenly. "Part of it, yeah. She had me cut a hole through the baseboard." Chuckle of reminiscence. "She stood at my elbow every minute, directin' the work. Lord, I miss that dear old woman."

"You're not the only one," I replied, warming to the sincerity in his voice. "Do you know who installed the little corrugated metallic pipe?"

"The conduit?" Shrugging, Doug remarked, "I ain't sure. Cable company, I reckon. Or maybe it was Carol's daddy. He did a lot of the wiring here on the farm."

Carol's daddy . . .

Filing away that bit of information, I parked my fanny on the porch railing. "You're welcome to wait, Mr. Krause."

"Thanks, Angie." Cracking his knuckles, he started across the yard. "Are you the only one here?"

As if on cue, my grandfather stepped onto the porch. He stood protectively at my side, giving Doug a neighborly nod. "Howdy."

Stopping short, Doug replied, "Howdy. Don't believe I've seen you 'round here before, Mister—?"

"Blackbear. Charlie Blackbear." Chief descended the stairs and took the proffered hand. "I'm Angie's granddad."

"He's staying with us for a bit," I added, all smiles.

"Nice meetin' you." Slowly he shook Chief's hand. My grandfather's sudden appearance had startled him.

Hoping to put him at ease, Chief gestured at the Cherokee. "Rural handyman, eh?"

Doug's smile glistened. "You bet."

"I was one myself a long time back," Chief added. "Got to really hustle to make a buck."

"That's for damned sure." Doug let out a wry chuckle. " 'Course, it helps if you're the only one in a big county."

"Seems to me fixin' combines is mighty seasonal work," Chief commented. "What do you do in the winter, Doug?"

"You kiddin'?" Instant rush of laughter. "That's when I'm workin' my ass off."

"Doing what?" I asked.

"Roof repair, Miss Angie. A prairie blizzard will rip them shingles right off. Most sunny days you'll find me up on a farmhouse roof, pullin' the trigger on a staple gun."

"I'll bet that's pretty chilly work in the wintertime."

"Got that right, miss." Crooked smile. "Why, it gets so cold I've had the staple gun freeze right up on me. Had to put it on the truck's engine block. I'll tell you, Miss Angie. Roofin' in a Dakota winter is no work for a thin-blooded man!"

Chief laughed. As Doug lifted his right hand to straighten his corduroy cap, I spotted a bluish tattoo just above his wrist—the fluke of an old-time anchor.

I spent too many seconds looking at it. Doug reacted to the pressure of my gaze. "Something wrong, gal?"

"Oh, nothing." I clapped my hands together. "Would you gentlemen care for coffee?"

Doug waggled his fingers in refusal. "None for me, thanks. I reckon I'd best be goin'. Josh won't be back for a couple of hours. I've got a quickie repair job to see to. Tell him I'll be back around two."

"No problem, Mr. Krause." Friendly Angie smile. "Take it easy."

As Doug's Cherokee bounded down the driveway, its tires splashing mud, I joined my grandfather at the foot of the steps. Folding his arms, Chief murmured, "Nice enough fella."

Quick shrug. "If you say so."

"And you don't?"

"I'm just wondering what he was *really* doing here, that's all."

Chief's keen gaze zipped my way. "Ain't takin' the man at his word?"

I shook my head. "He wasn't exactly Sunday visiting, Chief."

"What makes you so sure?"

"People tell me Doug Krause was a very close friend of Miss Edna's. Indeed, he just confirmed it."

"So?" my grandfather prodded.

"So . . ." I took a hasty breath. "If he was so friendly with Miss Edna . . . if he's such a frequent visitor to this farm . . . then wouldn't he *know* that the Elderkins are likely to be at the First Pesbyterian Church on Sunday morning?"

Chief grimaced thoughtfully. "Good point."

"So why did he show up?" I asked, facing my grandfather. "You know, he looked awfully surprised to see me. I don't think he expected to find anyone here."

"Yeah, and maybe that explains why he didn't want to stick around," Chief said, stroking his chin. "I don't get it, though. Why come to the farm when the Elderkins *aren't* here?"

Shoulders rising in a puzzled shrug, I sighed. There was an answer, of course, but I didn't have it.

Tugging at my grandfather's sleeve, I said, "Come on. Let's get out of this wind."

Muted chuckle. "You'll never make it as a roofer, Angie."

"I have no desire to become one, Chief."

Midafternoon found me hanging newly laundered bed linen on the clothesline. The morning overcast had burned off, and Trudy wanted to take advantage of all that bright sunshine.

So there I was—Washerwoman Angie—pinning sheets to the line with old-fashioned wooden clothespins. Sunshine warmth felt good on my face. Looking toward the barn, I saw Doug Krause busily installing the tractor's new air filter. Brad, Trudy, Kristy, and my grandfather were hard at work in the garden, gathering the last of the ripe pumpkins and gourds.

There was no sign of Jeremy.

Judging from the dour expression on Josh's face, he was troubled by the younger son's absence. Not that he'd ever say anything. Old farmers are a tight-lipped bunch.

Josh entered the back pasture. Hurriedly I pinned the last sheet to the line, carried the wicker basket back to the porch, and set off in pursuit.

The sun had reduced the pasture puddles to hardpan clay, but the rye grass was still wet enough to soak my jeans at the knees. Hearing my footsteps, Josh halted and turned.

"Hi!" Pert Angie smile. "I thought you'd might like some company."

He plucked a stem of rye. "Suit yourself, gal."

Tilting my thumb back toward the barn, I said, "Doug's doing quite a job on the tractor."

"That's what I'm payin' him for."

Good old Josh—chatty as ever! Well, now that I had him talking, maybe I could fill in the blanks of Doug's background.

"How long have you known Mr. Krause?" I asked.

"Oh, twenty years, I reckon." He led me down the weed-strewn alleyway between two rows of corn. "He set up shop over in Mitchell when he got out of the service."

I remembered the anchor tattoo. "The Navy?"

Josh shrugged. "I don't rightly know, Angie. He don't talk too much 'bout himself."

"Is he a local boy?"

Brisk head shake. "Sioux Falls."

"How old is he?"

"Few years older'n me. Over sixty, I reckon." Josh flashed me a sidelong look. "You're almighty interested in Doug Krause, gal. Mind if I ask why?"

I wasn't yet ready to tell him about Krause's earlier visit, so I came up with a plausible alternative. Languid smile. "I'm intrigued by the business he's in . . . itinerant handyman."

"What's so intriguin' about that?"

"Just wondering how he makes a living at it, that's all."

Josh snorted in mild derision. "He's gotten pretty handy at dodgin' landlords."

I pushed a broken cornstalk leaf out of my way. "You don't like him very much, do you?"

"Doug? He's all right, I suppose. It's just . . ."

"Just what?" I prodded.

Josh's troubled gaze locked with mine. "I don't know. It seems to me . . . well, he'd have a whole lot more if'n he'd stuck with one job 'stead of twenty-five." He seemed wistful. "If Doug had put down roots, he'd have his own farm by now. Driftin' from farm to farm, doin' chores . . . that's a kid's job, Angie. A man that age—he ought to know what he's here on earth to do."

"He's a drifter, then."

"Sorta. Doug never stays in one place too long. He's been here in Yorktown 'bout twenty years. In all that time, I'd say he's spent about seven o' them years right here. Rest o' the time, he was out on the road."

"Where did he go?"

"Iowa, North Dakota, Nebraska—any place he could reach in that truck o' his. Always said he wanted to see more farm country." Low chuckle. "That's been his pattern. One year here, two years gone. There's no holdin' back Doug Krause once he gets itchy feet."

Seeing my cue, I tried to change the subject. "Sort of like Carol?"

Josh's weathered face turned to stone. "Yeah, Carol's another one. Don't care where the road leads so long as it's away from this here farm."

"I hear she used to be really helpful, Josh."

His frown broadened. "Heard wrong, gal."

He was thinking about Jeremy, wondering if he'd alienated his son for good. I swallowed hard. I hated to stir up recent painful memories, but I had to find out if Carol had wired Miss Edna's cable TV outlet.

Schoolgirl Angie. "I heard she did some of the wiring."

Male eyes narrowed slightly. "Who told you that?"

"Doug Krause."

Lowering the seed cap's brim, Josh muttered, "Well-lll . . . I guess she did help out once or twice with the emergency generator."

Emergency generator! The phrase burst in my mind like a skyrocket. Mouth dry, I added, "The one in the barn?"

Dry chuckle. "Only one we got, gal."

Together we emerged from the cornfield. Just ahead lay the barbed-wire fence. A small stand of shelterbelt maples marked the county line. Beyond the treetops, I spotted the steel crossbars of an OP transmission tower.

Plucking some windblown cornsilk out of my hair, I asked, "What kind of generator, Josh?"

"A Hopedale. Came with the farm. Uses diesel fuel."

"What's the power rating?"

"Seven thousand watts, I think."

Watts!? Sudden fussbudget face. Oh, that's a big help. How much is that in *amps?*

I wondered if Carol could have run that wire from the emergency generator into Miss Edna's bedroom. Possible—the barn was less than a hundred feet from the house. Hay bales stacked all around would have deadened the sound of the diesel motor.

"What kind of work did Carol do?" I asked.

"Nothing fancy. Just wired in some new receptacles." Smile of reluctant admiration. "Her daddy taught her well."

"I guess the next time you'll have to call *him,* eh?"

Josh's smile faded. "Sure looks that way, don't it?"

"How did Carol get along with your wife?"

"Okay, I reckon. Trudy ain't like me, you know. She never gave Carol much cause to scrap with her, but . . ." Doleful scowl. "Well, I had the feelin' Carol came out here only 'cause Jer asked her to."

On to the big question, Angela.

"How did she get along with Miss Edna?"

Grimacing, Josh shook his head. "You know, from the way those two used to ruckus, you'd've thought *Miss Edna* was her mother-in-law!"

"Went at it hot and heavy, eh?"

"You bet." Josh surveyed the barbed wire as we strolled along. "'Course, that wasn't all Carol's fault. Miss Edna wasn't the easiest woman in the world to live with. Always did have a tendency to speak her mind. She decided early on that Carol wasn't pullin' her weight. After that, there wasn't anythin' the poor gal could do right."

Josh's sympathetic tone surprised me. Somewhere beneath that denim bib beat a loving paternal heart.

Oblivious to my reaction, he went on. "Miss Edna came down too hard on that gal—said there was no place for a damn debutante on a farm. I told Miss Edna, you shouldn't ought to judge her—she ain't one of us. But Miss Edna felt Carol had made her bed and all." Deep sigh. "Maybe I should've done more, Angie . . . I don't know. Guess I figured a young farm wife needs to fight her own battles."

Touching his sleeve, I murmured, "Sometimes it helps if she knows she has friends."

"Does it?" Frowning, Josh booted a bovine turd out of our path. "Well . . . too damned late now."

Shifting to a less touchy subject, I said, "I hear Miss Edna was pretty chummy with Doug."

Absentminded nod. "Yeah, he was here every Sunday. Whenever he was in the area, that is. We'd come home from church, and there they'd be—out on the front porch."

Perhaps nostalgia had brought Doug to the farm this morning, I thought. "Was he a good friend?"

"Miss Edna sure looked forward to his visits, gal." A smile softened his stony features. "He used to honk his horn whenever he came up the driveway. And Miss Edna—her face'd light up and she'd say, *'Doug's here!'* " Another chuckle. "I used to tease Bonnie and Trudy about it. Hint that their aunt was foolin' around with Doug Krause. Trudy used to get all red in the face. Swat me good and tell me I was a dirty-minded old farmer." Chuckle of reminiscence. "She said that with near on twenty years between 'em, Doug was young enough to be her son!" Sudden crooked smile. "Got to give the man credit, though, Angie. He was almighty kindly to Miss Edna for a good many years."

"What about her other friends?"

"We saw fewer 'n' fewer of 'em every year," Josh said, halting at the pasture's back corner. "Miss Edna was seventy-two when she came to live with us. Most of her friends were the same age or older. Awful hard to get out here to the farm. Every year, we'd see another one o' them names in the paper . . . Lucille Hempstead, Emily Schultz, Birgitta Ostlund—"

"Is that the same Mrs. Ostlund who used to own the field on the other side of Enemy Creek?"

"Used to she did." Brown eyes blinked in amazement. "How'd you know that, Angie?"

"Been talking to people," I replied, hands on my hips. "They tell me a girl named Holly Larsen may have been killed there thirty years ago."

"That's right." He rubbed his whiskered chin. "State trooper's dog found Holly's lunch box by the creek. Lord, we were all jumpin' at shadows back then! Trudy was a nervous wreck. She wouldn't let Brad out of her sight."

That fit with what Trudy herself had told me. Folding my arms, I asked, "How did Miss Edna react?"

After pausing a moment to search his memory, Josh replied, "Miss Edna was damned upset about it. Trudy and I stopped by her farm couple days after it happened. She told me she phoned the Larsens personally, offerin' to help put up a reward."

I wondered how far Miss Edna's curiosity had taken her.

"Do you know if she talked to Mrs. Ostlund?"

Surprise tugged at Josh's rugged face. "Clem Mutchler tell you that?"

"Clem!?"

"Sure! He was there when Miss Edna got back from visitin' Mrs. Ostlund."

"Ah, no." All at once, I found myself in a verbal minefield. One wrong move, and I'd shut up Josh for good. Tread carefully, princess. "I heard it in town." Lick dry lips. "Miss Edna was at the Ostlund place?"

"You bet. Day they found the lunch box," he reminisced. "I don't know what went on over there, but Clem says it sure upset Miss Edna."

"Upset her how?" I asked.

Josh's broad shoulders flexed. "Danged if I know. You'd have to ask Clem." He put his hand against the weathered fence post. "Way he tells it, Miss Edna's car pulled up, but she didn't get out. Clem was workin' hired hand back then. He went over, lookin' to see if she needed any help, and he found her hunched over the steerin' wheel, cryin' so hard she didn't even hear him when he rapped on the windshield."

Fussbudget face. Did Miss Edna have some knowledge of Holly's disappearance? If so, that might explain why L.J. Rankin contacted her.

This was beginning to make a frightening kind of sense. Rankin arrives in search of Holly's killer. Then the killer finds out he's been talking to Miss Edna. Fearful of exposure, he shoots Rankin in that cornfield, then engineers Miss Edna's demise.

Question, Biwaban—if Miss Edna knew the key facts behind Holly's abduction, then why did she keep silent all these years?

I decided to have that little chat with Winifred Gunderson, Mrs. Ostlund's niece. Maybe she could help me fill in the blanks.

Keeping pace with him, I asked, "Are we going to start combining tomorrow?"

Putting his back to the barbed wire, Josh studied the tall stands of ripened corn. "Hardly seems worth it, gal."

His spiritless tone made me heartsick. "What do you mean?"

"Come December first, it all goes to Mr. Covington."

"Josh, you can't *give up!*"

Sorrow darkened his brown eyes. "I haven't got a hundred thousand dollars."

"What are you talking about? You have money. Miss Edna's estate! Trudy's one of the heirs."

Patting my shoulder, he replied, "I've thought of that, gal. I've thought this thing through every which way, but it's just no good. They won't be readin' the will till Thanksgiving. Ain't no way we can line up another loan in time."

"But you have the collateral—"

With a dismal sigh, Josh shook his head. "No, we don't. Those two farms of Miss Edna's—Trudy'll be sharin' title with Clem and Bonnie. If we were the sole owners, we might have a chance." Hands in his jacket pockets, he surveyed the rustling corn. "There's maybe twenty thousand dollars in that field. Twenty thousand . . . if it don't snow, and there's no killer frost, and we can get it all combined and sold before folks hear what Covington's doin' to us. We pick all our fields and get the crop sold and maybe—just maybe—we can pay Mr. Covington his hundred thousand. And then we're stone broke, Angie." His voice turned brittle. "Ain't no way to win this time."

He was wrong. I could think of one way to win. A way to beat Covington at his own crooked game. *Nandobani!*

It's an old word among our people. It means to go on the warpath. To become a hunter of men. To steal up on your entrenched enemy and lay him low with a single well-placed arrow.

Rattle his cage, princess. "I thought there was no quit in an Elderkin."

Josh's angry face resembled a granite cliffside. "There ain't! We're bringin' that crop in, gal. We'll stay workin' farmers till the bitter end!"

"Maybe it doesn't have to be the end."

He gave me a long questioning look.

"If you could get the money, would you stick it out?"

"Bet your ass!"

Placid expression. "Would you accept the money from me?"

Brown eyes goggled. *"You!?"*

"I can get you the money to pay off Covington," I said, adopting a schoolgirl pose. "On one condition, though. There are no questions asked."

"Where are *you* going to come up with a hundred grand?"

"That's a question, Josh."

Minutes passed as he thought it over. Features tensing in uncertainty, he grumbled, "If you can help us, we'd be almighty obliged, Miss Angie."

Broad smile. "Cavalry's on the way, Josh."

"But how—!?"

"Unh-uh-uh!" My upright index finger waggled. "We agreed, remember? No questions!"

It took Josh Elderkin another moment to swallow his considerable pride. "I reckon I'm goin' to have to learn to keep my big mouth shut."

"Our little secret, Josh. Okay?"

Nodding, he headed back to the house. "I just hope we both don't live to regret it!"

With the wire fence on my right, I resumed my country stroll. Tall grass caressed my moccasin boots. Blue jays soared in and out of the wooded shelterbelt.

I thought of my old mentor at Springfield, Toni Gee, the woman who taught me all about "the game." What kind of con works best with small-town Midwestern bankers, Toni? No time for an elaborate hurrah here. It'll have to be a short con. Meet the mark, slip him the hook, make the sting and run.

Hmm—could get hairy, princess. You're putting your ass on the bull's-eye, running a con here in South Dakota. Sure, you may be wanted in three states, but here you're still Angie Biwaban, mild-mannered, well-behaved darling of the Department of Corrections. If the scam fails, you could be taking up long-term residence at the Big Dollhouse.

Worse than that, the FBI might notice the strong resemblance between newly captured con artist Angie Biwaban and the elusive, raven-haired Pocahontas. Remember, you still have that federal bank rap hanging over your pretty head.

But if I didn't spring a short con on Good Neighbor Sam, the bastard would take the Elderkins' farm and drop it in the greedy clutches of Owechahay Power. My friends would be forced off the land that they loved, their lives shattered.

I hadn't been able to save Miss Edna. Maybe if I'd been a little more alert, I might have awakened moments earlier—heard the killer skulking about—done something to save her. Maybe.

So it's *nandobani* time again, princess. Maybe you couldn't save Mrs. Mutchler, but, before you leave Davison County, you're going to guarantee the safety of that woman's family. You're going to pull the teeth of the rapacious banker and make certain the Elderkins are the *last* farm family he ever victimizes!

All at once, I spotted a familiar track in the dirt. Two-inch footprint with five clawed toes. Instant smile of recognition. A raccoon. Among my people, he's known as *Asebou*. His tracks ran the length of the barbed wire fence.

Then I noticed the furry brown mound ahead, and my smile vanished. Bluebottle flies buzzed the small carcass. A breeze carried the stench of decay to my nose.

I hurried over there. It was *Asebou*, all right. A well-fed boar raccoon, twenty-five pounds in weight, with his glossy black mask and stubby banded tail. He lay on his side, his wiry black paws curled at his chest. A fleck of tongue protruded from the corner of his mouth.

Troubled Angie frown. I'd seen my share of slain raccoons on the north shore but never one with his tongue sticking out. What goes on here!?

At first I thought *Asebou* had fallen victim to a coyote or a bobcat. But there were no bloodstains on his glossy coat. No bite marks or torn fur.

Gently I wiggled my moccasin toe beneath *Asebou*'s chubby middle. Flipped him over. Surprised gasp. A slender black stripe ran across his stomach, making him look as if he was wearing a belt.

Ignoring the flies, I knelt beside the dead raccoon. My fingertips brushed the black stripe and came away sooty. The belly fur was charred, as if someone had drawn that line with a blowtorch.

Squatting on my heels, I looked around for telltale footprints. Saw some month-old tracks belonging to itinerant jackrabbits, badgers, and black-tailed prairie dogs. Nothing remotely human, though. Meaning some dull-witted sadist hadn't tortured little *Asebou* for kicks.

So how did he burn himself, Angie?

My gaze drifted toward the Elderkins' fence. The barbed wire strand was the same width as the raccoon's burn mark.

On hands and knees, I scrambled through the tall grass. Rye tufts tickled my face. Pushing the stalks aside, I carefully scrutinized the bottom wire.

Eight or nine bristles of scorched fur clung to the blackened strand.

Grimace of confusion. This fence wasn't *electrified*. Why, I'd seen Josh Elderkin touch barbed wire less than fifteen minutes ago.

Thoroughly bewildered, I decided on a little experiment.

Reach into the jeans pocket. Withdraw a shiny new penny. Hold it suspended over the bottom wire. And . . . bomb's away!

Twang! My penny rebounded off the wire, vanishing into the weeds. No spark of contact. No metallic sizzle. Proof positive that there was no electric current running through this wire.

My gaze darted back to the raccoon. So what happened to you, little friend? How did you manage to burn yourself on a dead wire?

Questions, questions. The young raccoon, dead at least a week, offered no answers. Slow-moving blowflies continued their remorseless feeding.

Brushing the dirt from my denimed knees, I sighed, stood upright, and then sauntered back to the house.

TWELVE

"What makes you think Carol did it?" Chief asked.

We were at Weber's General Store, my grandfather and I, doing some Sunday evening shopping for the Elderkins. I watched as the gangly teenaged clerk bagged each item. Bread, cookies, mustard, relish. Paper-wrapped luncheon meats from the deli. Two six-packs of Coors Silver Bullet.

"Plenty of reasons," I replied, grabbing a six-pack and a bag of groceries. Chief scooped up the remainder.

"How about sharing them?" he muttered, trailing me out of the store.

Clunky was parked right outside, his grille nudging the general store's clapboard wall. As soon as we were out of earshot, I said, "All right. Consider this—Carol is desperately unhappy. She hates farm life and wants out. Killing Miss Edna ensures the farm's demise."

"Pretty thin motive, Angie."

"She hated Miss Edna, Chief. Josh and Jeremy told me so." I levered open the passenger door, then swung the six-pack onto Clunky's front seat. "I thought it was pretty odd when Carol didn't show for the funeral. Now I know why."

"Child, you don't kill somebody because they've criticized your housework."

"Yeah?" Taking the grocery bags from him, I stacked them beside the six-pack. "Tell that to Galatea Marsh."

"Who's Galatea Marsh?"

"Lady I met in Springfield," I replied, rounding the car's rear. "She killed her husband with a six-inch skillet."

Chief slid onto the passenger seat. "I'm afraid I don't see the point."

"She was a lot like Carol," I explained, getting behind the wheel. "One of those cool lady-of-the-manor types. Lot of pride there. Not the kind of woman who takes kindly to criticism, especially from a perfectionist like Miss Edna."

Turning the ignition key, I coaxed Clunky's big engine into a throaty roar. Then, backing into the street, I added, "Carol had the knowledge and the skill. She knew about Miss Edna's earlier heart attacks. She'd worked on the barn's portable generator. And she'd learned enough about wiring from her father to run an electrified cable into the bedroom."

We drove past the gas station and Mom's Auto Body. Buff-colored cornfields pressed both sides of the road. Showing a mild scowl, my grandfather murmured, "What makes you so sure it was the portable generator?"

"Well, we know the killer didn't tap into the house system," I replied, steering Clunky down County Road 7. "And the neighboring farms are too far away. Therefore, it had to be the generator."

"Do you know how much power that generator cranks out?"

"Sure! Josh told me. Seven thousand watts."

Chief shook his head in disagreement. "Not enough, Angie. That's only fifty-eight amps."

"Wait a minute!" My hand waggled in frustration. "How do *you* know how many amps it is!?"

"There's a quick conversion formula. Simple math. The barn

runs off a 120-volt system, right? Seven thousand watts divided by 120 volts equals fifty-eight amps."

"I'll take your word for it, Chief." Wry Angie smile. "You don't think Carol did it?"

He shook his head briskly.

"Why not?"

"Too many links to the Larsen case." Thoughtful Anishinabe frown. "Holly Larsen disappeared thirty years ago. Miss Edna and Delbert were both involved. Our buddy Rankin made contact with both of them. Young Holly has to be the key."

"Where does Carol fit in?"

"She doesn't. She's too young. She wasn't even born when Holly disappeared. I don't think she's mixed up in it." Those shrewd obsidian eyes shifted my way. "You still have that Texan phone number. Going to use it?"

"Absolutely!" I spied four silvery silos beyond the shelterbelt up ahead. "Just as soon as we finish here."

The Gunderson farmhouse was fifty yards off the road, a white, two-story Victorian home with a wraparound front porch and dark green storm shutters. Half a dozen maples surrounded the house, their stark limbs waving in the breeze. Several yards behind the man-made grove were the old and new barns, both bright red gambrel-roofed structures, and the long Quonset-style milking shed. Tall twin silos guarded each end of the farmyard.

As I drove Clunky up the driveway, I spotted a large hand-painted canvas sign flapping against the barn door.

WELCOME, MARS PATROL!
Meeting Tonight

Switching off the engine, I grimaced. "Mars Patrol!?"

"Don't look at me." Chief chuckled. "This was your idea."

As we emerged from the car, a smiling sixtyish lady in a denim jacket and black ranch jeans appeared on the porch. She was about my height, a farm matron with silvery gray hair impeccably coiffed. Huge rimless glasses gave her an owl-ish appearance. Pale blue eyes and fresh lipstick. Thin at the shoulder, broad at the hip, she still moved with the coltish grace of a schoolgirl.

"Howdy!" Her clarion voice reached across the yard. "Are you folks here for the meeting?"

I had a cover story already prepared, but maybe I wouldn't need it. Slamming Clunky's door, I replied, "Sure! Are you Mrs. Gunderson?"

"I sure am." Welcoming smile. "Don't think I've seen you folks around before."

"We're new to the area." My fingers daintily touched my collarbone. "I'm Angie Biwaban, and this here's my grandfa-ther, Charlie Blackbear."

"Sure! You're the ones stayin' with Josh and Trudy." Her smile blossomed even more. "You must've seen my poster at the general store."

"That's right." I tagged along at her side. To tell the truth, I hadn't even looked at the store's bulletin board. "You sort of tweaked our curiosity, Mrs. Gunderson."

"None of that, Angie," she admonished. "Neighbors ain't anywhere near so formal. Make it *Winnie*, okay?"

Just then, my grandfather did a double take. My gaze fol-lowed his into the backyard, and I let out a soft gasp of aston-ishment. Instead of the customary chicken coop stood a small domed building. Peeping through the roof aperture was a rather sizable telescope.

Turning to Winnie, I asked, "Is that an observatory?"

"Uh-huh!" She nodded enthusiastically. "I've got a Celes-tron C5 with a 1,250-millimeter f/10 telephoto lens. Best damn telescope in this end of the state. I bought it a couple of years ago after my husband passed on."

"Must get awful cold in there at this time of year," Chief remarked.

"Sure does, Charlie, but that don't bother me none," she replied, leading us up the back steps. "I do all my skywatching from the comfort of my living room. Got me one of those CCD systems. Watch Mars on the TV."

"CCD?" I echoed.

"Charge-coupled device. You know, electronic imager," she explained, opening the door for us. "See, I've got the telescope hitched up to an Electrim EDC-1000 camera. That takes the image and stores it on my computer's hard disk. It's like a series of snapshots. Great resolution, too. Here, let me show you."

Winnie's rumpus room was an even bigger shock than that backyard observatory. Unusual decor, to say the least. Try to envision a Federation command post with hand-stitched floral upholstery. Needlepoint and star charts competed for space on the oakwood table. Adorning the walls were UFO identification posters and large colorful photos of the planet Mars.

In no time at all, Winnie had her huge desktop computer up and running. She switched on the Panasonic TV. Blue screen abruptly yielded to a startling image of crimson Mars suspended in ebony space.

"I took this one Monday night," she said, her eyes shining with excitement. "See? There's a dust storm in Hellas."

"Astronomy's your hobby?" My gaze drifted toward a framed photograph on the wall. An autographed shot of a wild-haired man in his sixties. Down in the corner was a personal message . . . *To Winnie . . . a tireless searcher for the truth. Best wishes, George Adamski.*

"It's no hobby, Angie." She turned away from the keyboard. "Mars Patrol is serious business. There's eight of us in the group. We use our telescopes to monitor Martian space."

Seeing Winnie's MUFON life membership certificate on the

wall, I guessed at the purpose of the group. "What are you looking for?"

"Unidentified flying objects. We're pretty sure they've got a base on Mars."

"They?" echoed Chief, a bit incredulous.

"The Zeta Reticulans." Complete sincerity. "You know, those little gray humanoids that get involved in all the contactee cases."

Tongue in cheek, my grandfather replied, "Oh, yeah! I saw a picture of them in the *Enquirer*."

"Of course, it could be the Lanulans. They're from the Pleiades." Oblivious to Chief's skepticism, Winnie prattled on. "Or maybe the Naosians. Nobody's heard from Captain Aura Rhanes since 1952. Well, that's no surprise. Naos is 2,300 light years from Earth."

"Aura Rhanes?" Angie the Echo.

"Yes, dear. That was one of the first documented contactee cases. Captain Rhanes commanded a flying saucer that landed near Flagstaff in 1952. She came to Earth with a message for President Truman. Instead she gave it to a truck driver named Truman Bethurum."

Anishinabe whisper. "After a screw-up like that, *Noozis*, she probably became *Private* Rhanes."

"Chief!" I murmured, struggling to suppress my laughter. Somehow I managed to show Winnie a solemn face. "Why do you think they're on Mars?"

"Well, we've had our suspicions since that Russki spacecraft disappeared near Phobos a couple of years back. Then, when NASA lost contact with the Mars Observer, we were certain," she said, her eyes grim. "UFOs are shooting down our space probes. They don't want us taking pictures of their bases on Mars. Something's up—that's for damn sure."

"Like what?" asked Chief.

Glum look. "I don't know. It could be anything, Charlie. Maybe they're building up for an invasion. Maybe they're

starting colonies with all the people they abduct from Earth."
Her veined hand patted the computer. "That's why we're
keepin' an eye on 'em. We're like an early-warning system. If
they try anything, the Mars Patrol is ready!"

"Winnie . . . have *you* ever seen a UFO?" I asked.

"You bet!" Bluish-gray eyes danced in awed reminiscence.
"It was a Sunday afternoon—August 18, 1963. I will never,
ever forget it. My boy Freddie, he was about six then. He was
right there with me. He was playing in the sandbox, and I was
hanging wash on the line. Then I heard this strange noise—
like the humming of a thousand bees. I looked up, and this
huge silver disk floated up from behind our barn." Her face,
brimming with a strange ecstasy, swiveled toward the back
door. "It hovered right out there, dipping a little from side to
side. The rim was rotating real fast." Fingers made a whirling
motion. "Counterclockwise, same as a twister. I grabbed
Freddie's arm and hauled him into the house. Then I took my
husband's binoculars and watched it from the back door.
Didn't see any hatches or portholes. There was an elm tree
nearby, which was sixty feet high, and the saucer was maybe
twenty feet above that, so I guess it was hoverin' eighty feet
off the ground. Bigger than a railroad boxcar! I watched it for
five whole minutes. Then it made a *whooooo* noise and zoomed
straight up out of sight!"

Chief grimaced in disbelief. I motioned for him to keep silent as our hostess wandered over to the TV.

"I still dream about it," she murmured, staring at the image
of Mars. "The saucer, I mean. I dream about it coming back.
But, of course, it never has."

Winnie seemed more than a little disappointed by that.

A fascinating tale, to be sure, and I sure would have liked to
have heard more. But already we'd strayed too far afield.

I tried to put us on track again. "How about your relatives,
Winnie? Have they ever seen a UFO?"

"Oh, no . . . never!"

"How about your aunt, Mrs. Ostlund?"

"Aunt Birgitta!?" Wistful smile. "Lord, no! She had absolutely no use for UFO stories. Every time I raised the subject, she'd cackle 'Little green men!' and laugh like a loon." Doleful expression. "I'm afraid my aunt wasn't the most open-minded of women."

I saw an opening. "Maybe she just disliked notoriety."

"That's for damned sure!" Winnie straightened the lace antimacassar on the easy chair. "Aunt Birgitta detested newspapermen. Why, she wouldn't even subscribe to the paper."

"Was that because of Holly Larsen's disappearance?"

Frowning, Winnie tossed me a curious look. "You're not from around here. How did you know about that?"

Deep breath. "Got talking to an old friend of mine. He used to be a deputy—Jake Norton."

"Oh, I know Jake! He used to be married, you know. Aunt Birgitta told me he came to the house a couple of times. Him and Sheriff Fischer." Turning to face me, she added, "It was those *newspapermen* my aunt couldn't stand." Mild frown. "The day that little girl's lunch box was found, it was a three-ring circus at her farm."

Draw the lady out, princess. "What do you mean?"

"Well, the way Aunt Birgitta explained it, she had a couple of friends over for tea—"

"Edna Mutchler included?"

"That's right." Instinctively she straightened the ashtrays on the rosewood coffee table. "Then . . . oh, I guess it was three-thirty or so . . . someone knocked on the door. My aunt answered it. A state trooper stepped inside and asked if she owned the field near Enemy Creek. Aunt Birgitta said yes. Then he asked some questions."

"What kind of questions?"

"Dozens!" Her hands fluttered in emphasis. "Was she in the field that day? When was the last time she was there? Had she seen a car in the area?"

"Two-toned 1955 Chevrolet sedan?" I blurted, remembering the car reportedly seen by Holly's bus driver.

Winnie flashed an exasperated look. "I-I have no idea. I wasn't there. All I know is what Aunt Birgitta told me—the trooper asked her a zillion questions. Finally, she asked him what it was all about, and he said their dog had sniffed out Holly Larsen's lunch box."

"How did the ladies react?"

"They were stunned—horrified. Aunt Birgitta had children of her own, you know. She told me she burst into tears. It was a mother's worst nightmare come true." Winnie seemed to be reaching back into the vault of memory. "They were all badly shaken by the news. Even Miss Edna. My aunt told me she'd never seen Miss Edna so upset. And Mrs. Weisberger—she cried so hard they had to call her daughter to come fetch her. It was just plain terrible, Angie."

Anishinabe frown. "Miss Edna took an interest in the case?"

Swift nod. "Sure did! Why, the very next day, I was in Mitchell, and I saw Miss Edna and her daddy, Frank Enright, talking to Sheriff Fischer. 'Course, he was still a deputy back then."

"Where was this, Winnie?"

"Oh, right over there on North Main, just down from the Corn Palace. The three of them were havin' a little private talk. Mr. Enright did most of the talkin'."

I fired a glance at my grandfather. Saw that Chief was thinking along the same lines. In his day, Frank Enright had had plenty of clout in Davison County. Why had he and Miss Edna approached Cal Fischer?

Then I saw Winnie looking sadly at a wall-mounted star map. Letting out a mournful sigh, she added, "They never found her, you know. Little Holly, I mean. Sometimes I wonder if she's still out there. If maybe she was one of the first abduction cases." Tears glistened as she looked at me. "Maybe she was one of the Chosen. Could be she's on Lanulos right now, studying at the feet of the Ascended Masters—"

This was too much for my hardheaded grandfather. Aghast, he blurted, "You don't really *believe* that, do you!?"

"Chief . . ." I warned.

Too late! Winnie had too often experienced the sting of derision. She had no tolerance for scoffers. Confronting my grandfather, she snapped, "You *bet* I believe it, mister! I saw that saucer with my own two eyes! I've talked to people who've been abducted. There *is* a Celestial College on Lanulos, and only selected spiritually advanced humans are allowed to attend."

Chief wanted to reply, but I beat him to it. Anishinabe murmur. "Let it drop, *Nimishoo*. We're not here for a debate."

Unable to understand what I was saying, Winnie automatically assumed I was mocking her. Her angry gaze zipped my way. "You don't believe me!" Scowling in determination, she seated herself before the computer. "Well, I'll show you. UFOs are landing all the time, and I can *prove* it!"

Like a crazed concert pianist, Winnie tapped away at her keyboard. All at once, the Martian image faded, replaced by a nighttime shot of the Dakota countryside.

Victorious laugh from our hostess. "See!?"

I nearly reeled at the sight of the image. Even in darkness, the Gunderson barns and the distant OP transmission towers were clearly discernible. What really knocked me for a loop, however, was that pallid blue corona on the horizon, that faint sapphire nimbus casting the tall towers into sharp relief.

Winnie's forefinger jutted toward the screen. "Would you care to explain *that*, Mr. Blackbear?"

Features tense, Chief made no reply.

"Last week a UFO landed in my back forty." Pride seemed to add inches to Winnie's petite stature. "I don't care what that Philip Klass says. A starship landed in my pasture, and I've got the whole thing on videotape!"

Blink of astonishment. Somehow I found my voice. "You took this picture *last week?*"

"Sure did, gal! November the fourth. Sometime around two or three in the morning, I reckon."

My eyes blossomed wide. *November the fourth!* My chest tightened in sudden sick excitement. *That was the night Miss Edna died!*

Ten minutes later, my grandfather and I were heading down County Road 19. Chief did the driving. Brown hands on the wheel, he showed Clunky's windshield his patented warpath scowl.

"Guess I ruined things back there for you, didn't I?"

"Not really." Reassuring pat. "I wasn't exactly interested in sitting through a UFO meeting." Folding my arms, I added, "She sort of got to you, didn't she?"

Chief's shoulders tensed. "A bit." Another sigh. "I've got two daughters. And one granddaughter—*you*. Don't think I didn't worry! You know, it could've just as easily been you or Geri or Della as that poor little Larsen girl." His voice coarsened with anger. "All the goddamned molesters out there! And that damned silly woman thinks it was a UFO!"

"Maybe it's easier for her that way." I brushed my hair back over my shoulder. "Maybe Holly enrolled in some interplanetary college is a whole lot easier to handle than the harsh reality."

Sidelong glance at me. "Which is?"

Closing my eyes, I sighed. "She's probably buried in a cornfield somewhere."

We rode in silence for several minutes. Clunky's headlights painted a yellowish-white splash across the asphalt. Chief's thumb tapped the steering wheel.

"So what do you think, Angie?"

Lifting my arms in a quick stretch, I replied, "I think Miss Edna was Fischer's *confidential source.*"

"And Fischer went after Delbert Dietz." Chief made a thoughtful sound. "Why did Miss Edna finger Dietz?"

"Could be she saw him in Mrs. Ostlund's field."

"You could be right," he murmured, looking straight ahead. "It wasn't enough to convict Dietz, but maybe it was enough to get him tucked away in that mental hospital. I say it's high time we paid a call on Sheriff Fischer."

"What for?" I asked.

"Look at it from Dietz's point of view. What if he only just found out that Miss Edna fingered him? What if he knew Miss Edna had been talking to Rankin?"

My grandfather's words triggered a mild shiver. Pursing my lips, I replied, "That makes Delbert the only one with a motive for both murders."

"Like I said, we'd better have that chat with the sheriff." He turned his thoughtful gaze on me. "What do you make of that picture she showed us?"

"Chief! I *told* you there was a corona blue!" I shifted to face him. "Winnie's TV camera photographed it around three A.M."

"You sure it was the same glow?"

"Positive! Winnie's photo showed the power lines, remember? That puts the corona halfway between her place and the Elderkin farm. I saw it from the Elderkin side."

"Terrific! But what *is* it?"

"Chief, if I knew that, I'd—"

Just then, a high-beam glow caught the corner of my eye. Peering over my shoulder, I saw a pair of headlights coming up fast. Tapping my grandfather's shoulder, I snapped, "Watch it! Hot dog at six o-clock!"

My grandfather nosed Clunky to the right, giving the oncoming driver plenty of room to pass. At the last second, however, the sedan swerved in our direction, its grille connecting solidly with my car's rear fender.

The unexpected impact tossed us both forward.

"Gawanadisid!" Chief hollered, reverting to our language. "What does he think he's doing?"

Bracing myself against the dash, I fired an anxious glance

hrough the back window, just in time to see the sedan's grille
·losing in again. *"Nimishoo—!"*

Kaaa-wham! Clunky shuddered from trunk to headlights. I
heard the tinkle of splintered glass, the agonized shriek of
wisted chrome trimming. Any of today's high-tech-and-
plastic compacts would have crumpled under the impact. But
not my long, fleet, steel-bodied '69 Merc. We were still rolling.

"Takoki, Nimishoo! Step on it! *Ojima!"*

My grandfather's foot stomped down on the accelerator.
Eight cylinders roared in response, and Clunky galloped away
from the oncoming sedan. Down the centerline we hurtled, the
speedometer needle climbing past seventy. Ripe cornstalks
whizzed by on either side, silent witnesses to the chase.

I glanced out the rear window again. Enemy high-beams
strained to keep up. The left one sagged slightly, and I knew
he sedan's front end was out of line. It lacked Clunky's capac-
ty to withstand punishment. Plus my Merc's ability to cruise
at a buck-ten. Hope soothed my jangled nerves. With luck, we
ust might outrun him.

And then I saw the sudden flame wink beside the driver's
window.

Bweeeowww! The ricochet cut through the slipstream's soft
whistle. The gunshot reverberated a second later, and I felt
my car shudder under the bullet strike. Instinctively I ducked
behind the seat's backrest.

Yes, I know that's sort of like turning a paper towel into a
bulletproof vest. But at that moment, sudden panic had just
about wiped out my conscious mind.

"He's shooting!" I yelped.

"Keep your head down, *Noozis!*" Chief hunched over the
steering wheel, his gaze fixed on the deserted road.

Blam! Blam! One shot went wild. The other punched a hole
in my Mercury's rather spacious trunk. Probably lodged itself
in the spare tire. I shot a fearful glance at the speedometer.
We were cooking along at eighty-five plus, but Clunky held

the road like an eighteen-wheeler. Chief's expert driving ha
put us a dozen yards out front.

Another ricochet zinged into the night. Four shots so far. I
it's a wheelgun, princess, he has two left. Then again, auto
matics carried anywhere from ten to fourteen rounds these
days. Practice was bound to improve his marksmanship.

We had to do something, but what? My frantic gaze scurrie
about the front seat. We needed a weapon. A hammer, a
wrench, anything we could throw at his windshield. Even a
handful of tacks would help.

Then my gaze zeroed in on the six-pack. The first surge o
fright had come and gone, freeing up my imagination. On
winked the mental lightbulb.

This has to work, I thought, pushing open Clunky's passen
ger door. The icy slipstream tousled my long hair, blinding
me. I let the door slam shut. No good! I need to *see* what I'm
doing!

Scowling, I reached for my shoulder bag.

Another gunshot sounded behind us.

Frantic fingers dug out my plastic Topsy Tail. Gathering a
handful of tresses, I worked them through the loop.

My grandfather goggled in disbelief. "This is no time to be
doing your hair!"

Ignoring him, I gave my newly wound French braid a firm
tug, then peeled a beer can away from the pack. My free hand
snaked toward the passenger door. Again the slipstream
chilled my face. This time, though, my hair stayed safely out of
the way.

Putting one foot on the door's armrest, I hollered, "Brace
me!"

Puzzled, Chief shouted, "*Noozis*, what are you—?"

I extended my right arm. "No time to explain. Grab my
wrist and hold on as tight as you can."

Gnarled Anishinabe fingers caught and held. Straining

against the slipstream, my left leg pushed Clunky's passenger door all the way open.

Suddenly, there I was, standing *outside* my speeding Mercury Montego, one foot on the door's armrest, the other on my seat cushion. My ponytail fluttered past my cheek like a sailboat pennant. Leg muscles tensed at the strain of holding the door open. The beer can nestled in my left hand.

Oh, sure! I'd done this sort of thing before. Usually horsing around at Park Point Beach with the gang from Central. But never in an automobile zipping down a lonely country road at eighty-five miles per hour. And never with a gunman in the pursuing car.

Behind the headlight glow, I made out the contours of an Oldsmobile Achieva. Shiver of apprehension. Those high-beams made me the perfect target.

Just then, I saw a hand appear above the driver's window. Instant flame wink, punctuated by a loud gunshot. Beside me, Clunky's passenger window shattered.

Yelping, I gave the beer can a vigorous shake. Adrenaline had my forearm churning like a piston. Lifting the can high, I pushed my thumbnail against the poptop ring. Cracked the seal and let fly.

Emitting a fine spray of beer, the aluminum can spiraled through the night. It struck the windshield just above the wipers and exploded.

Milwaukee hand grenade!

A carpet of foam smothered the enemy windshield. Brake pads howled like injured dogs. The headlights veered crazily to the left, then swerved to the right.

I didn't stick around for the show. Quick Angie scramble into the passenger seat. The door bruised my foot as it snapped shut.

My grandfather told me later how the Achieva fishtailed all over the road, brakes squealing, windshield wipers flinging beer foam. He watched the whole thing in Clunky's rearview mirror. By the time I looked out the back window again, th Achieva had already struck the irrigation ditch at the side of the road. Horrifying glimpse of the airborne chassis. Tire spinning. Sparks flying from the manifold. Then it vanishe into the cornstalks.

I cringed at the sound of that hellish crash. Chief repeatedl pumped the brake, slowing Clunky to a crawl. Beads of per spiration littered his craggy face. Breathing in ragged gasps he whispered, "Son of a bitch!"

Once his hands stopped shaking, he put Clunky in reverse and we rolled back to the crash site. I was out the door befor we even stopped. Dew-covered leaves snatched at my jacke as I plunged into the cornfield. My nose wrinkled at the stencl of leaking gasoline.

I found the Achieva on its roof. Three flat tires and one stil spinning. Its cornstalk-encrusted grille had gouged out a shal low muddy trench. Tendrils of thin smoke billowed upwar from the engine. Amazingly, muffled sounds emerged from the interior.

Coming closer, I watched a bareheaded man wriggl through the shattered side window. Grunting and swearing he rose shakily to his knees. Even in that faint headlight back glow, there was no mistaking those angular features. *Delber Dietz!*

Putting his backbone to the Achieva's dented door, Delber let out a pained roar and pushed himself erect. He favored hi right arm, keeping the weight off it, gripping his bloody wris with his other hand.

Anger got the better of me, I'm afraid. Rushing forward, shouted, "Might have known it was *you*, Delbert *Dum Fuck!*"

"Not . . . my . . . *name!*" Hatred twisted his equine features With an agonized snarl, he thrust his left hand into his waist band.

And out it came, the latest addition to Delbert's private arsenal. A .38-caliber Colt Detective Special, the snub-nosed revolver most favored by American private eyes. And, in that instant, I wondered if he'd taken it from Rankin's body.

I tallied maybe twenty yards between me and that rising pistol muzzle. And twice that distance to the nearest solid cover. No choice!

Lightning sprint toward the gunman. Onward the Light Brigade. Was there a woman dismayed? You bet your ass! Despite his injury, and the handicap of shooting left-handed, Delbert was doing an excellent job of lining up that pistol. The Colt's muzzle wavered in increasingly smaller circles. His forefinger whitened on the trigger.

My right foot rose in a flawless Rockette kick. A Radio City masterpiece. My boot smashed the underside of his wrist, knocking his gun hand skyward.

Blam! The gunshot drowned out Delbert's agonized shout. He still had a good grip on that pistol, though. Blued steel flashed toward my face. I ducked instantly, feeling Delbert's hearty swing skim my braid. I grabbed his arm as it passed overhead, dug in my heels, threw my hundred-and-five pounds against it. Shoved his clenched gun hand against the upturned exhaust pipe. Hot metal sizzled masculine flesh.

Delbert howled. The Colt slipped from his fingers, clattering down the chassis into darkness.

"Bitch!" Clawing fingers seized my hair, and he slammed my head against the Achieva's side. Multicolored lights gyrated across my field of vision. Everything took on a dreamy aura. My knees began to sag.

Ohhhhhh! Don't pass out now, Angie! I bit down hard on the web of his hand. Another baritone roar. Feeling his grip loosen, I lashed out with an overhand right. My fist struck him on the injured shoulder. Delbert's yowl traveled upscale into soprano territory. Whitefaced and sweating, he stumbled away from me.

Chief's voice rang out. *"Mi minik, Noozis!"*

My grandfather was right, of course. Delbert had had more than enough. For that matter, so had I.

"You little . . . *aaargh!*" Clutching his shoulder, he grimaced. "It's *broken!*"

"Then you'd better lie still, asshole," my grandfather said, salvaging the snub-nosed Colt.

Chestnut eyes blazed at me. "I'll get you yet, squaw! They can't hold me—"

"Oh, yes, they can!" I cut in. "It's *attempted murder* this time, Delbert. With bullet holes in Clunky to prove it. The Department of Mental Health is going to have a little trouble keeping your sorry ass off the rockpile." My head tilted to the left. "Where'd you get the gun? Did you steal it from Rankin?"

Hateful Delbert snarl. "Fuck you, bitch!"

Hefting the pistol, Chief took a menacing step forward. *"Miskwassabwaj! Gawanadapined!* Don't you talk that way to my granddaughter!"

The outburst startled Delbert. Frightened brown eyes shifted my way. "Wha-What'd he say?"

"He said you ought to apologize for your foul language," I translated, squatting at Delbert's side. "But I'll settle for an explanation, Dietz. Why'd you come gunning for us?"

"Why shouldn't I?" His mouth set defiantly. "You've been trying to set me up!"

"Set you up!?" I repeated.

Vicious nod. "Blame me for that girl's disappearance!"

Nodding slowly, I said, "So you went after us like you did Rankin."

The name triggered a shudder. Still, Delbert managed to fabricate a blank expression. "Who?"

Weary sigh. "Don't play games, Delbert. The motel owner saw you in Huron. He'll make a dandy witness in open court."

"He was *persecuting* me!" Dietz shouted, wriggling like a beached shrimp. "He thought I killed that Larsen girl. I *told* him, I had nothing to do with it. But he wouldn't leave me alone. He kept after me and after me." Hate-filled eyes zeroed in on me. "And *you* helped him! That's why you were snooping around Bonnie's farm!"

I sat back on my heels. Well, I had only myself to blame for that. Running that crazy bluff at Bonnie's had convinced him I was Rankin's accomplice.

"When's the last time you talked to Rankin?" I asked.

Dismal scowl, punctuated by a sullen shrug.

"What did you do with yourself on Halloween, Delbert?"

"I don't remember."

Keeping the pistol trained on him, Chief snapped, "Why did you kill him?"

Confused blink. "Who?"

"Rankin! He was shot to death on Halloween."

Color flooded his face. "You think I killed him!?"

"He was found in your favorite cornfield," I said. "The one where Holly's lunch box was found. Coincidence?"

"It's not *my* cornfield!"

"*Del*-bert, the police had eyewitnesses who placed you at the scene."

Keen outrage. "They're fucking liars!"

"Did you discuss the Larsen case when you visited Miss Edna?" I asked.

Genuine bewilderment altered his expression. "*Miss Edna!?*"

"Edna Mutchler. Your wife's aunt," Chief prodded. "You went to see her."

"I did not!" Indignation deepened his tone. Why, Delbert almost sounded like a solid citizen. I might've been inclined to believe him, too, if not for tonight's assault. "I-I haven't talked to Miss Edna in *years.*"

Sudden frown. I had a feeling he wasn't lying. No one as excitable as Delbert could fabricate such a forthright tone. I stood erect slowly. *What's going on here?*

Chief stepped into the breach. Leveling the pistol, he snapped, "Let's go back to Question One, Dietz. Where'd you get this gun?"

Delbert's mouth hardened, and he looked away.

I thought of something else, too. At Bonnie's farm, Delbert had seen me on horseback. At the Corn Palace, I'd arrived with the Elderkins. So how had he recognized Clunky as *my* car?

"Who told you I'd be out here this evening, Delbert?" I asked, leaning over, hands at rest on my knees. "Same guy who gave you the gun?"

A sudden fearful glimmer brightened his dark eyes. Thin lips compressed even tighter.

Sudden surge of triumph. I'd seen that look in Delbert's eyes before. At the Corn Palace, when he'd looked past me into the departing crowd. Instant shiver.

Go for broke, Angie!

"Same guy who sicced you on me at the Corn Palace?"

"Bitch!" Delbert's good arm lashed out suddenly. "You're gonna get me *killed!*"

I dodged his wild-ass swing. Nothing wrong with Angela's reflexes. And it's nice to know I didn't waste all those childhood hours playing jump rope. My landing left something to be desired, though. I came down on one foot, toppled leftward and landed on some leafy debris.

Encouraged, Delbert rose to his knees, favoring his broken shoulder, ready to pounce. But my grandfather was right there, lifting the Colt pistol high. Steel barrel met skull bone in a noisy crunch. Delbert's pupils twirled skyward. He pitched face-first into the corn, uttering a low-pitched moan.

"Chief!" I protested.

"That'll hold him until the sheriff arrives." He tucked the .38 in his waistband. "*Gawanadapined!*"

"But I wasn't finished asking questions."

"That's a job for the police, missy." Aged features hardened in exasperation. "You'd better start dreaming up a tale for Sheriff Fischer." He gestured at the wrecked Achieva. "Namely, how are you going to explain *this* mess?"

"What's the matter with *you?*" I asked, brushing twigs off my jeans.

"I spent sixty-three days under enemy fire on Okinawa! And I'll tell you something, Angie . . . in all that time, I was never as *shit-scared* as I was *five minutes ago!*"

Grinning, I hugged him from behind. "Couldn't have done it without you, Chief!"

"I can just see the obituary page! SENIOR CITIZEN KILLED IN CAR CHASE!" Puzzled glance. "And *you!* Hanging out the goddamned car! What the hell were you trying to *do?*"

Impish Angie grin. "Milwaukee hand grenade."

Warpath scowl. "Never heard of it."

"Ah, but you never went to Central."

Obsidian eyes blinked in amazement. "Don't tell me you've done this *before!?*"

"Now, Chief, there is such a thing as a statute of limitations—"

"Not in *our* family!"

Years ago, I might have been cowed by that pretense of paternal fury. Not anymore! Giggling, I kissed his leathery cheek. "Do you really want to know?"

"I guess not." Brisk one-armed hug. "Right now, I'd settle for a hot cup of coffee . . . and a good lawyer!"

THIRTEEN

There weren't any lawyers present when I marched into Sheriff Fischer's office the following morning. Just my grandfather, the sheriff, Deputy Dan Kramer, and Paul Holbrook. All were sporting frowns of varying intensity. First prize went to Chief. I don't think he enjoyed spending the first eight hours of Monday in a jail cell.

Charming scene. Cal Fischer, still in *Bonanza* mode, lounged in his swivel chair while the hot-eyed deputy stood nearby. Naturally, it had been Kramer who'd come upon the wreck. I don't think he'd ever enjoyed an arrest so much. There was Chief, yawning against the back of his hand, and Holbrook, listening with interest to my tale of L.J. Rankin's meeting with Miss Edna.

I gave them everything I had. Everything but Rankin's Texan phone number. A woman must have her secrets, you know.

A few hours of fitful sleep had wrinkled my clothes. Loose shanks of raven hair slipped the confines of my life-saving ponytail. I desperately needed a few minutes alone with a mirror, brush, and lipstick. Well . . . perhaps Sheriff Fischer wouldn't keep us *too* long.

Finishing up, I offered an amiable smile, smoothed my wrinkled jacket and said, "That's about it, Sheriff."

"Not quite, Miss Biwaban." One by one, Sheriff Fischer put his boot heels back on the floor. "Now I've got a request for you."

"I'm listening, Sheriff."

His white-knuckled fist pounded the blotter. "Give me one good reason why I shouldn't toss your ass in a cruiser and ship it right straight back to Springfield!"

"Just a minute, Fischer." Stepping forward, Paul took a protective stance at my side. "Angela has been cooperative."

"Why, thank you, *Kemo Sabe.*" Princess Angie.

You know, it was great seeing Holbrook again. Especially without that la-di-da lawyer in tow!

"Cooperative!?" Fischer sat bolt upright. "Damn it, Holbrook, how long has she known the identity of our John Doe?"

"Uh, not long!" I assured him.

Fischer's mustache bristled in disbelief. "I suppose you were on your way to tell me all about it when that fruit loop Dietz bushwacked you."

"Good guess, Sheriff!"

"Bullshit!" Fischer eyed his scowling deputy. "You're the arrestin' officer. What do you think, Danny?"

"I think that smart-mouthed little Injun ought to go straight back to Pussyland!"

Fischer's gaze shifted to Paul. "Counselor?"

"I don't see where Angela's committed any crime," Paul said, one hand on my shoulder. "She's told you everything she's learned about the murder victim."

Kramer hooked his thumb toward the wall. "Yeah? What about that wreck out back?"

Chief flashed his warpath scowl. "Dietz attacked us, Deputy, not the other way around!"

"Take it easy, Blackbear. You ain't goin' to be charged. Why, you've got a self-defense plea that'll stand up in any court." Leaning back in his chair, he added, "May be awhile before it comes to trial, though. I hear Dietz is laid up with a compound fracture."

Paul frowned. "I hear the Achieva was *stolen*, Sheriff."

"Got friends in the Highway Patrol, eh?" Fischer toyed with his letter opener. "True, true. Dietz clouted it off the ShopKo lot." Clucked his tongue. "Sure wouldn't want to be the owner this mornin'." Rueful chuckle. "Grand theft auto. Attempted murder. Shit, they don't put that boy back in the looney bin, he's going to have a rap sheet longer'n *War and Peace*." Another chuckle. "No, I don't think you've got anything to worry about." The letter opener swiveled toward me. "Your granddaughter, though . . . that's a whole other story."

"Not sure I follow, Sheriff," I said.

"It's very simple, Miss Angie." Casually he cleaned his stubby fingernails. "You need a *license* to operate as a private detective in the great state of South Dakota. To get that license you have to be a former police officer who has advanced in rank beyond patrolman." Stern look at me. "I don't have to tell you what happens to parolees found to be in violation of state law."

"Kind of a rotten way to pay her back for her cooperation, Fischer," said Paul, his features showing disapproval.

Kramer made a sound of derision. *"What* cooperation!?"

Leaning against the sheriff's desk, Paul remarked, "Before Angela walked into this room, did you know the victim's name?"

Fischer's eyebrows flickered. "Tell him, boy. It's your case."

"How about it, Kramer?" Paul added. "Did you know he was a private eye named Lawrence Joseph Rankin from Amarillo?"

Crimson rushed upward from the deputy's collar. "We were workin' on it!"

"Kind of taking your time, weren't you?"

"Now, look, city boy—!"

"You know, if police work is too difficult for you," Paul cut in, "then maybe you ought to go back to hauling manure."

Fuming, the deputy took a step forward. Fischer's shout rooted him to the spot. "Dan!"

Kramer's outthrust forefinger quivered an inch from Paul's nose. "I'm getting damned sick of these Pierre hot dogs shovin' their faces in *my* county."

Stone-faced, Paul slowly loosened his tie. "I hope to hell that ain't your trigger finger, Deputy."

"You threatenin' me, hot dog!?"

Paul's good hand patted the desktop. The steel in his tone gave me a momentary shiver. "Put your badge and your piece right here, Kramer. Then we'll step outside and discuss it some."

I caught a gleam of uncertainty in Kramer's eyes. He was weighing the odds, his two hands against Paul's one, and seriously rethinking the whole thing. Something in Paul's Marine sergeant stance, the deadly undertone in that pleasant baritone voice—they'd slaughtered the deputy's appetite for confrontation.

His mouth taut, Kramer turned away. "You want me, Sheriff, I'll be in the squad room."

The door slammed behind us. Reaching for the sheriff's phone, Paul said, "If you're intent on charging Angie, then you won't mind if I arrange legal counsel for her."

"Now, Holbrook . . ." Fischer's hand immediately smothered the receiver. Warm country-boy smile. "There's no need to bother Mrs. Sutton. I'm sure we can all come to a mutually satisfactory arrangement here."

I'll say one thing about Cal Fischer. Like his predecessor, Sheriff Ben, he could read the political winds blowing out of

Pierre. Which explains why he was so eager to please Miss Edna's daddy thirty years ago.

"Then I'm not going back to Springfield?" Pert Angela.

His glance found Paul. "Not today, gal. I'm deferrin' to the Department of Corrections this time."

Paul nodded. "Wise decision, Sheriff."

"But I'll expect you to stick around, Miss Angie," Fischer added, touching his string tie. "Gonna need you and your granddad as prosecution witnesses against Dietz."

"We'll stick around, Sheriff," Chief promised.

Fretful grimace. "And no more of this cloak-and-dagger shit in my county. Understand?"

Demure Angie nod. "Are you going to charge Delbert for the Rankin murder?"

"I'm considerin' it." Frowning, he folded his hands on the blotter. "Trouble is, there ain't a whole helluva lot in the way of physical evidence. Sure help if we knew what happened to Rankin's body."

"That didn't stop you in the Larsen case," I remarked, oblivious to Chief's anxious glare. "Holly's body was never found, yet you picked up Delbert, anyway."

Fischer's beefy face froze. "An informant in that case linked Dietz to the scene."

"Miss Edna," I added, my smile sublime.

Stiffening, he snapped, "How did you know that?"

Conscious of Paul's amazed stare, I opted for a mild prevarication. "Miss Edna told me when I asked about the Larsen case. She said she and her father, Frank Enright, discussed it with you."

The expression on Fischer's face reminded me of a Presbyterian minister caught thumbing through *Penthouse*.

"Maybe you'd better explain yourself, gal."

"Rankin phoned Miss Edna and asked to meet with her at the Elderkin farm. Right after that, he was shot. And then Miss Edna died."

Troubled look. "What are you getting at, Miss Angie?"

"Maybe you ought to take a closer look at the cause of death, Sheriff," Chief advised.

Fischer's lips puckered thoughtfully. "Mrs. Mutchler died of a heart attack."

"Heart attacks can be induced, Sheriff." I groomed a loose wing of hair. "A severe electrical shock shows the exact same symptoms."

"*Jesus!*" The sheriff looked like a man who had just seen his elaborate matchstick castle collapse. "Dietz killed *Miss Edna?*"

"Someone killed her," I said. But I wasn't so sure it was Delbert Dietz. "What did you and she and Mr. Enright talk about that day?"

Fischer gave me a long look, as if wondering if I might use the information against him. Then, deciding that I posed no political threat, he answered, "Miss Edna told me she drove by in her '55 Chevy and saw Dietz hiding in that cornfield. When she heard we'd found Holly Larsen's lunch box, she decided to come forward."

My obsidian eyes widened. *Fifty-five Chevy!?*

Chief picked up on it, too. "Was it a two-toned Chevy?"

"That's right." The sheriff nodded. "I asked Miss Edna what time she saw Dietz in the field."

"Are you sure that was *her* car?" I asked.

He gave me a puzzled look. "Of course! Miss Edna bought it as a second car . . . oh, about two years earlier. Got a ticket for speeding once, as I recollect."

"So what was Frank Enright's interest?" I inquired.

Fischer's color deepened. "Mr. Enright said he wanted his daughter's name kept out of it."

"And Frank being such a big shot, you were just naturally eager to oblige."

"Angie!" Paul snapped.

Too late! I'd tweaked the sheriff's nose once too often. Features reddening, he rose from his swivel chair.

"I'm all through bein' polite to *you*, Miss Ex-Convict." He gave his cowpoke belt buckle a tug. "For your information, I've been an officer of the law for nigh onto forty years, and I have received hundreds of tips from informants. Ain't nothing wrong with that! Everybody does it!" His furious gaze shifted to Paul. "Get her out of here, Holbrook, before I change my mind 'bout that trip to Springfield!"

Out the door we went, with Paul in the lead. One Department of Corrections parole officer and two Anishinabe defendants. Fischer's deputies flashed us hostile looks as we halted at the water cooler.

"So that's how you got all those charge sheets at Springfield," Paul said, pouring himself a cup of water. "We have to do something about that smart mouth, princess."

Fussbudget face. Paul had been hanging around La Sutton too long. He was starting to sound just like Slinky-dink!

"I've been saying the same thing for years." Chief chuckled.

"Oh, did I make a *faux pas* back there?" I replied icily, my fingertips touching my collarbone. "Perhaps I ought to enroll in the Sarah Sutton School of Charm!"

"Leave Sarah out of this, okay?" Paul's tart tone made me flinch. Talk about touchy subjects! Taking a calming breath, he added, "Angela, needling the sheriff is an excellent way to wind up back in the slam!"

"Paaaul!" I bellowed. "Open your eyes! Don't you understand what happened back then? Old man Enright and his daughter rolled over Delbert Dietz. Then Fischer sold the deal to his boss, Sheriff Wirtz."

"There's no proof Dietz didn't kill that girl," Paul said.

"There's no proof he *did!*" I snapped. "The investigation stopped the minute Enright put his foot down."

"You don't know that, Angie."

"Oh, yes, I do." Then I told Paul all about my chat with former deputy Jake Norton.

Nodding, Paul finished his last sip. Nimble fingers crumpled the cup. "Bottom line, Angie?"

"Old man Enright gave the local law a broad hint. Here's your culprit—no need to look any further. And Fischer, eager to curry favor with the old man, put the collar on Dietz."

Paul's handsome face tensed in uncertainty. "But why would Mr. Enright meddle in a police investigation?"

"I don't know, Paul." Although I had my suspicions.

Stroking his chin, he murmured, "I'm going to talk to a few people in the Highway Patrol. It sure sounds as if Wirtz's men botched the Larsen case." Gently he cupped his fist beneath my chin. "Can you stay out of trouble for the next few days?"

"Of course, Paul." I gestured at the corridor window. "We're going to be real busy with the harvest."

"All right. Let's head down to the clerk's office and get you both signed out." He gestured at the public phone. "In a minute, though. I've got to check in with Pierre."

Together my grandfather and I descended the stairs. Chief made the switch to our language. "I notice you didn't share everything with him, *Noozis.*"

"*Kemo Sabe* has this childlike faith in the integrity of rich people. I didn't want to shatter it."

"By telling him that Miss Edna could not have possibly been driving that two-toned '55 Chevy?" Chief added. "Holly's bus driver saw a *man* behind the wheel that day. Also, if Winnie Gunderson is correct, Miss Edna spent that afternoon playing bridge with her aunt at the Ostlund farm."

"True enough, *Nimishoo*. But, according to Fischer, the Chevy was *her car!* How did Holly's killer get ahold of it?"

"Good question." Chief's chin lifted in understanding. "Ah, now I see why you didn't want to tell Holbrook. Miss Edna knew Holly's killer. And so did her father." Sudden curious look. "Do you think they tried to protect him by framing Dietz?"

"Could be." I ran my hand along the smooth oak banister. "I'm wondering if Mr. Rankin knew about the wandering Chevy."

"There's one way to find out, *Noozis*." Chief shot me a questioning glance. "Do you still have that phone number?"

I patted my purse. "You read my mind, *Nimishoo*."

"Well, watch your step." His expression turned wary. "Rankin's killer isn't the only one you have to worry about." Seeing my inquiring glance, he added, "Fischer's deputy . . . that Kramer guy."

Impish grin. "*Kemo Sabe* sure cut him down to size."

"Maybe so, *Noozis*, but that's *twice* he's been humiliated by a friend of yours." Chief's face suddenly sobered. "He wants revenge, girl. He wants it real bad, and you just happen to be handy."

I swallowed hard. No debate from Angie. Kramer could prove a real hazard. Suppose he started a clandestine investigation of his own? A deputy sheriff had access to all sorts of official channels. He might trace my movements all the way back to my release from prison—learn how I'd violated parole.

Sudden icy shudder *Tayaa!* If Kramer fingered me as Pocahontas—!

Squelching the horrible thought, I squeezed my grandfather's hand. "I'll watch out, *Nimishoo*. Girl Scout promise."

"*Mino!*" Stout fingers encircled mine. "Now, where'd they hide that Clerk of Courts office?"

". . . still can't believe Delbert tried to kill you." Trudy planted a bulky chicken-salad sandwich on a square of plastic wrap. "He's just getting worse and worse. He always was kind of mean but never a killer."

"Well, tell Bonnie not to worry about him," I said, reaching for a slice of tomato. "He's going to be out of circulation for a while."

We were at the kitchen counter, Trudy and I, fixing lunch for the men. Chief had left thirty minutes earlier, driving Clunky over to Yorktown. My car had an appointment at Mom's Auto Body.

"Lord, Bonnie'll sure be glad to hear that. She still has nightmares about him coming to the farmhouse." Sympathetic gaze. "You must've been terrified, Angie, when he crashed into your car."

"Sort of!" I replied, reaching for the bread. "We survived, though. Actually, Clunky got the worst of it."

"Don't you fret about that car, Angie. Jeremy will get it all patched up this weekend. Oh! Put some more mayo on Jer's sandwich." Her deft fingers finished wrapping. "He says it really doesn't need much work. Just the back bumper and those bullet holes in the trunk." As she finished, she asked, "Did you fill the thermoses with coffee?"

"Yes, ma'am." I helped her stuff sandwiches into the wicker picnic basket.

"Then I'm off." She added three thermoses to the basket. "Lunch delivery!"

"Don't forget Jeremy's!"

She scooped it off the counter. "I'll be spotting Josh for a spell on the combine. Keep an eye on the place, okay?"

"Will do, Trudy. Take care."

Listening to the family pickup rumble away, I grabbed a dishrag and wiped the Formica. And then it was straight to the parlor for another long-distance telephone session.

Lounging in the easy chair, I lifted the receiver and tapped out Mr. Rankin's mysterious number. Three rings sounded at the other end. Then a pleasant female voice said, "Mornin'! Cavanaugh residence."

Memory conjured up an image of Fischer's honey-haired female deputy. Clearing my throat, I went into my act.

"Good morning. My name is Deputy Lambanek, and I'm calling from Mitchell, South Dakota. Official business. Could I have a moment of your time, ma'am?"

"Mitchell!" Suspicion thickened her voice. "W-Why are you calling me?"

"Ma'am, are you familiar with an Amarillo private investigator named Lawrence J. Rankin?"

"Yes!" Surprised gasp. "What did you say your name was?"

"Deputy Lambanek." Gentle Angie. "Did you know Mr. Rankin, ma'am?"

"Yes, he's hired out to me. I-I've been waiting *days* to hear from him." Suspicion gave ground to anxiety. "I've called his office in Amarillo, but all I get is the answering machine."

"Let's start at the beginning, okay?" Somehow I stifled my own growing sense of excitement. "Your name?"

"Mrs. Laurel Cavanaugh," she said, her accent straight off the Cap Rock. "H-Has something happened to Mr. Rankin?"

"That's what we're trying to find out, Mrs. Cavanaugh." Policewoman Angie. "He disappeared from a motel in Huron at the end of October. We found your phone number in the room." I heard her startled gasp. "Why did you hire him?"

Emotion clotted her lovely voice. "I-I w-wanted him to find out what happened to my sister."

Laurel! The name lit up like a neon billboard. Holly Larsen's baby sister.

"You hired him to reopen the Larsen case?"

"That's right," Laurel replied. "My sister was killed in Yorktown thirty years ago. I-I was little more than a baby then. I've always wondered what *really* happened. Mike—he's my husband—he said, if it's that important to you, go ahead and hire him." Anxious tone. "And now you say he's vanished?"

I avoided a direct reply. The real law would eventually be getting in touch with Laurel. "Mrs. Cavanaugh, when's the last time you heard from Rankin?"

"Oh, uhm, a couple of weeks ago. Day before Halloween, I recollect. 'Bout noontime or so."

The day before he got shot, I mused. "What did he say to you?"

"Well, he told me the investigation was moving right along. Said it had taken a surprising turn."

"Surprising?" I echoed. "How so?"

"Well, he didn't exactly say. Told me he'd have more to report after he talked to some fella."

"Did he mention any names?"

"No, ma'am."

Scowling in frustration, I tried another tack. "Please try to remember, Mrs. Cavanaugh. Did Mr. Rankin ask you anything out of the ordinary that day?"

"Well . . ." Melodious West Texan drawl. "He was curious about my daddy. Asked me all kinds of questions about the move down here. Who helped Daddy sell the farm. Who put him in touch with Wrangler Oil here in Amarillo."

Excitement provided a sudden lilt. "And what did you tell him, Laurel?"

"Same thing my daddy told me. How Mr. Enright sold our farm while Daddy was workin' the field down here."

"Is that Mr. *Frank* Enright?"

"That's him."

Triumphant Angie smile. Bingo! I chatted with Laurel for a couple of minutes more, giving her Sheriff Fischer's number and advising her to contact the Texas Rangers. Then I hung up.

You know, for a retired businessman, Frank Enright had shown a peculiar interest in the Larsen case. He and his daughter had sent Fischer after Delbert Dietz. Enright clout had reined in Deputy Norton's line of inquiry. And then Mr. Enright himself had stepped forward, offering to help relocate the grieving family in faraway Texas.

So who was he protecting, Angela? His daughter, the owner

of the '55 Chevy? Or the person who had been driving it that day—a person known to both Miss Edna *and* her father?

Maybe the same person Mr. Rankin had been so eager to meet on Halloween!

Shortly before eleven on Tuesday morning, I came breezing out of the Middle Border Savings Bank, smartly attired in a long woolen jacket in navy-blue, with a fanny-hugging skirt to match. Long-sleeved pleated-front white silk blouse. Smart lizard-print navy-blue dress pumps.

Keeping an eye out for traffic, I dashed across the street to the waiting Elderkin truck. Chief sat anxiously behind the wheel. Pulling open the passenger door, I grinned. "All set!"

"You sure Covington's going to fall for it?"

"Positive!" I tilted the rearview mirror my way. "Once he sees the cashier's checks in that dummy purse, he'll be very happy to make my acquaintance." Sidelong smile. "Don't look so worried, Chief. It's not like we're robbing the bank."

"Awful close to it, missy! This . . . what'd you call it?"

"*Sawdust game.*" Putting my own purse on my lap, I fished for my lipstick tube. "Don't worry—it'll work. It's tailor-made for a sleaze like Covington." Off with the lid. "Besides, I don't have time to organize a big con. Quick and dirty, Chief. Get in there, sting Covington for a hundred large, then hand off to the Elderkins. It's the only way to save the farm!"

"You're paying off Josh's loan with *stolen money!?*"

"Think of it as *recycling.*"

While I made up my mouth, my grandfather switched on the radio. The KORN weatherman promised another bright, brisk autumn day. Good news for our hardworking harvesters.

"That ain't the only reason you're going in there," Chief said, watching me recap my lipstick.

"We've got to find out more about Mr. Enright, Chief."

"Why not ask Trudy or Bonnie or Clem Mutchler?"

"Because they didn't move in the same financial circles. Covington and his family did. Don't forget—old man Enright served on the board of MBSB."

"I don't follow, Angie."

"It's a pretty fair guess that Rankin was shot by Holly Larsen's killer. The killer then struck at Miss Edna, hoping to completely cover his tracks."

"You're saying Miss Edna *knew* who killed the Larsen girl?"

"Right! And so did her dad. Enright covered up for the killer thirty years ago."

Chief sent me a sharp look. "Why?"

I shrugged, then pulled out my compact.

"What makes you think Covington's mixed up in it?"

"Delbert Dietz," I answered, snapping open the lid. "I think he knows old man Enright had him sent up. You saw him the other night. He's scared of somebody. And it can't be Miss Edna or her father—they're dead."

Chief glanced at the dashboard clock. "Listen, I've got to get back to Yorktown. How long are you going to be in there?"

Four quick dabs with the powder puff. "Go ahead and go. I'll meet you at the Corn Palace at five, okay?"

"Good enough." He switched on the ignition.

"What are you going to do with your afternoon?" I asked, snapping the compact shut.

"I thought I'd have a look at that raccoon you found."

"Any particular reason?"

"Those burn marks. I keep wondering how that little fella killed himself on a nonelectrified fence."

I zipped my bag shut. "How do I look?"

"Just fine . . . 'cept for that dust smudge on your nose."

Alarmed, I glanced at the mirror. My reflection showed no flaws. Mammoth fussbudget face. "Chief!"

Hearty masculine chuckle. "You always fall for that one, Angie."

Asking him to take good care of my shoulder bag, I climbed down from the cab. Giving my skirt a discreet tug, I watched him drive away.

Crossing the street, I quelled my stomach butterflies and mentally rehearsed my speech. I'd had a busy morning. One stop at Geyerman's to buy a new suit. Several more at various small print shops. The guy at Prairie Print had been a little nervous about printing phony cashier's checks. I told him I was playing a birthday joke on my boss and eased his fears with a couple of Ben Franklins.

The Sawdust game is a century old, and it was a favorite of classic American grifters such as Timothy Moore and George Lehman. Like all great cons, it relies heavily upon the mark's greed. In a Sawdust game, the con man pretends to be getting rid of a shitload of *perfect* counterfeit money. The Secret Service is on his tail, and he has to dump it fast. The mark, usually an avaricious businessman, offers to buy the bogus half million for five or ten thousand. The exchange is made. The businessman goes home with his weighty package. Ripping the brown paper open, instead of flawless counterfeit Federal Reserve notes, he finds ... you guessed it ... *sawdust!*

My scam was a subtle variation. Instead of counterfeit cash, I had something else to offer—something I hoped would convice Mr. Covington to give me a hundred grand.

Into the marble-floored lobby I strolled. The bank's old-fashioned interior radiated an aura of permanence. Hand-tooled tellers' counter of black oak. Gilt-framed portraits of past bank presidents. Velour drapery and matching carpets in the same rich shade of evergreen.

I went straight to the teller I'd spoken to earlier. She was a strawberry blonde in her late teens. Classic cheekbones, pale blue eyes, soft mouth, and pixie hairstyle. The instant she spotted me, her mouth made a perfect O. "Ma'am! You forgot your purse!"

"I know. I got all the way to the car before I realized it was gone." Look of utter embarrassment. "I don't know where my head is. Do you have—?"

"I gave it to Mrs. Niewenhuis," she interrupted, pointing out the short, shapely, sharp-eyed brunette at the Auto Loans desk. The lady must have had ears like a bobcat. She looked up at once, saw us staring at her, and hurried right over.

Showing me an apologetic, servile expression, Mrs. Niewenhuis explained that she'd given my purse to Mr. Covington the minute she found the checks. Which was exactly what I'd been hoping for. Swinging open the oaken gate, she offered to introduce me.

Lead on, Nosy Niewenhuis!

Covington's office was surprisingly spartan. Customary managerial desk, a battery of mint-green filing cabinets, and a horseshoe-shaped computer station in one corner. Beside the telephone sat my *hook*, a black leather Worthington handbag crammed with wallet, keyring, toiletries, brush, compact, bogus business letters, and phony six-digit cashier's checks.

"Yes, Barbara?" Covington rose slowly from his chair, nut-brown eyes scanning me curiously.

"Sir, this is the lady who lost the handbag." The loan officer's languid hand swerved my way.

Embarrassed Angie. "Look, I'm sorry to bother you people."

Covington's jowly face broke into a smile. "Why, it's no trouble at all, Miss . . . Nagin, is it?"

"Nah-geen," I corrected. Lakotiya for *shadow*. "Melissa Nagin." Accepting his outstretched hand, I smiled. "You must be Mr. Covington."

"That's right." The banker was at his most charming today. "Barb, why don't you rustle up a cup of coffee for our guest?"

As soon as the lady departed, Covington offered me a plush easy chair. "Barb opened your purse. Hope you don't mind."

"Not really." Smile of relief. "I'm just glad nobody else walked off with it."

Curiosity brightened his frank stare. "If you don't mind my

saying so . . . that's quite a bit of money for a young woman to be carrying."

"Urgent business in the Falls."

Leaning against the desk, he asked, "What sort of business are you in, Miss Nagin?"

"No need to be so formal, Mr. Covington." Cross the nylon-clad legs. Mildly flirtatious smile. "I prefer *Lissa.*"

Toothy male grin. "And I'm Sam."

"Pleased to meet you, Sam." Unzipping my purse, I poked about for a few moments, then produced a newly printed business card and handed it over.

Brown eyes narrowed. "North Central Associates." His gaze zipped back to me. "Don't believe I've ever heard of you, Lissa."

"We opened a branch office in the Falls two weeks ago." Disarming Angie smile. "The home office is in Minneapolis."

"Mutual funds?"

I shook my head. "Real estate. We offer our investors an opportunity to invest in potentially lucrative tracts throughout the Midwest."

The magic phrase—*real estate.* All at once, Covington's eyes gleamed. "What brings you to Mitchell?"

"I understand there are several large tracts available here in the county." Barbara Niewenhuis ferried a tray into the room. Smiling graciously, I accepted a cup of coffee. "I was hoping to talk to a few realtors here in town."

Grabbing the second cup, Covington dismissed her with a taut nod. "Well, perhaps I can be of some help, Lissa."

Toss out the baited hook. "Do you know anyone at Palace Realty?"

"Why, yes!" Sudden eager smile. "As a matter of fact, I'm on their board of directors."

"Really?" I feigned a wide-eyed, surprised glance.

"You bet." Covington put his cup and saucer aside. "Lissa, do you have to be in the Falls today?"

Mild shrug. "I suppose it could wait till morning. Why do you ask?"

"Let me show you a few of those rural tracts," he said, his hands darting about in anxiety. No way was he letting Little Miss Moneybags stroll out of his office, not with that beached whale of a mall development gathering cobwebs out in farm country. "There's one in particular . . . just wait till you see it. Acres and acres just off County Road 22. Zoned commercial—ready to build—permits and everything. I'll drive you out there. What do you say?"

"Thank you, Sam." Ladylike sip of coffee, followed by a coy Angie smile. "I'd like that very much."

In no time at all, we were headed north in Covington's Grand Marquis. On our way, he gave me a glowing description of the county's economic prospects. New industry, new jobs, low taxes, and acres of cheap kilowatts. No wonder he'd been elected chairman of the Industrial Development Commission.

Listening politely, I watched the big red combines grinding relentlessly across the fields, their spouts spilling ripe corncobs into sturdy truck-drawn wagons. Occasionally a grain truck roared past us on the road, making its mad dash to the silo.

Then Covington's failed dream popped into view. Had the money not run out, it would've been known as Midland Mall, a three-story galleria to rival those huge shopping meccas in Sioux Falls. Rusting girders penetrated the bright blue autumn sky. A patchwork mantle of thistle, flaxseed, and rye grass covered the vast unpaved parking lot.

As we left the car, I commented, "Zoned commercial, you said?"

"That's right." Salesman Sam. "All one hundred and twenty-two acres. I figure it'll cost five or six million to finish. Or, if your firm wants to start slow, you can build a roadside minimall over there, rezone the remainder residential, then subdivide and build. Good cash flow over the long term."

I let him talk. I was remembering what Gordon Kolquist of the Office of Thrift Supervision had told me about MBSB's sagging fortunes. Covington waxed enthusiastic about the mall's exciting and profitable future. When at long last he'd exhausted himself, I gently steered him into his own past.

"You know an awful lot about real estate, Sam."

"Yeah." Aw-shucks smile. "Well, I got started early. Used to handle home construction loans for my dad."

"He was a banker, too?"

Covington nodded. "He bought Middle Border off the Wentworths about fifty years ago."

"Wentworths?" I echoed.

A grin appeared beneath his Selleck mustache. "Some of the area's most prominent families have been represented on the MBSB board."

"Like the Enrights?"

Slowing his stride, Covington shot me a quizzical look.

"I recognized Frank Enright's portrait in the lobby." Artful Angela. "Was he ever on the board?"

"Oh, yeah! Right up until his death, as a matter of fact. Mr. Enright was one of the bank's largest depositors. My dad transacted quite a lot of business for that ol' boy."

"There was an Enright daughter, wasn't there?"

Brisk nod. "Miss Edna. She married a local farmer named Kurt Mutchler."

"Did you know Miss Edna?"

"Well enough to talk to." His tone turned frosty. "Our families didn't mix socially." Somehow he just couldn't resist a posthumous dig. "Miss Edna was a Presbyterian . . . although she had some trouble keeping her skirts clean."

My head turned instantly. Strange thing to say, Mr. Covington! I thought. Then I wondered what he knew about Miss Edna and her dad.

Toss out the disquieting name, princess.

"Lived around here all your life, Sam?"

"Just about." He led me past a mound of hardened cement.

"Then you were here thirty years ago," I added. "When that little girl—what's her name—*Holly Larsen*—vanished."

Dead silence. Without breaking stride, Covington let out an uneven chuckle. "I'll say! Just a kid then—twelve years old. I'll never forget it. We had a special deputy riding on the school bus with us. Old Mr. Werremeyer. All the boys wanted to ride in the back so we could see that Colt .45 automatic he had tucked in his belt."

I didn't know what to think. The banker's garrulous reminiscence had the ring of truth. But still he'd taken much too long to answer.

Taut frown. Did he know about the Enright cover-up? And, if so, then *how* did he know?

Delbert was scared shitless of somebody. Could it be Sam Covington?

We halted beside what would have been the mall's main entrance. A mud-caked wheelbarrow stood by attentively. Hands on his hips, Covington cast a proud look around.

"Well, Lissa, what do you think of it?"

"Very impressive, Sam."

Showing me a jovial look, the banker drawled, "How much would you like to buy?"

"All of it."

Covington did an instant double take.

"You heard me right, Sam. The whole kit and kaboodle." I gave my purse a knowledgeable pat. "By the way, do you take cash?"

FOURTEEN

Brown eyes flickered. "You're joking."

"Not at all, Sam." The breeze stirred my hair. I ran a grooming hand through it. "If Palace Realty is ready to sell, my firm is willing to buy."

Covington gave me an odd look, as if I were a dream image that might vanish in an instant. Nervous fingers stroked the knot of his club tie. "North Central Associates must have an excellent line of credit."

"Money's no problem, if that's what you mean."

Country-boy smile. "Now, Lissa, I didn't mean to imply anything. It's just that the purchase price on this here parcel is likely to choke a mule."

"We have ready access to cash, Mr. Covington," I added, tongue in cheek. I didn't tell him it was *his* cash!

Covington stiffened at once, and I knew exactly what he was thinking. *Drug money!* My smile turned rueful. You should choose your words more carefully, Angela.

"Have you ever been to Minnesota, Sam?"

"A few times." Suspicious eyes met mine.

"Ever played the Grand Casino in Hinckley?"

"The Indian casino?" Comprehension filled his pudgy face. "You're involved with them?"

"Uh-huh." Brisk nod. "Grand Portage and Onamia, too. My firm arranged the initial financing for construction."

Now that's the kind of fib I got sent to my room for—back when I parted my hair in the middle like Marcia Brady. Native American casinos are wholly-owned enterprises operated by individual tribal councils. Outsiders just aren't involved.

"As you can imagine, the arrangement has generated a substantial amount of cash," I concluded.

"I see." Avarice colored his tone. Leading me away from the half-finished building, he asked, "But why is your firm so interested in purchasing real estate here in South Dakota?"

I had difficulty suppressing an impish smile. So far, so good. Covington was falling for it. And it was easy to understand why. Few *gitchimookomanag* had a grasp of our tribal politics.

On with the scam, princess.

"It's very simple, Sam. The casinos generate hundreds of thousands of dollars each month. And we'd much rather pay taxes on South Dakota real estate than on capital gains."

"So you're converting the cash directly into equity."

"That's about it."

"I'm curious, Lissa. How much cash are you folks lookin' to invest? Ballpark figure, now."

The question stumped me but only for a second. "Actually, Sam, I couldn't give you an overall figure, but I'd say . . . on the average . . . about seven hundred grand per month."

Covington's sparse brown eyebrows rose a half inch. Humming thoughtfully, he escorted me back to the Grand Marquis.

He said very little on the way back to Mitchell. I squirmed restlessly in my seat, glancing periodically at the banker's soft profile. I knew he was thinking it over. He couldn't afford not to. Seven hundred grand per month would go a long way toward shoring up MBSB's nonperforming home loans.

Okay, maybe I should have opted for the con artist's usual pitch. Maybe I should have suggested he open his bank to North Central's nonexistent millions. But I thought a direct pitch would have warned off a mark as sly as Covington. Sometimes it's better if the pigeon suggests the scam on his own.

Had I guessed wrong?

Ripe cornfields gave way to shorn ones. We were getting awfully close to town. My throat went dry. If Covington didn't buy the scam, the Elderkins were finished. No way would I be able to con the ice-eyed banker again.

Just then, Covington cleared his throat. "Lissa?"

"Yes?" I masked my anxiety beneath a casual smile.

"Where does the firm do its banking?"

"Minneapolis." My heart began pounding. Steady, girl.

An odd note marred his voice, the only clue to the strain he was under. "Has the firm ever considered depositing its cash assets here in South Dakota?"

A joyous shudder ran through me. "We might . . . if we could find the right bank."

"I don't think you'd have to look very far." Smug sidelong look. "Middle Border Savings Bank could offer your firm quite a bit in the way of financial services. Good interest rates on certificates of deposit. Assistance with real estate purchases." He faced forward again. "Most importantly, I can guarantee *privacy.*"

"Privacy, Sam?"

Solemn nod. "A good deal of cash can be secured in our safe-deposit vault."

"Cash balance has to be reported quarterly."

Oily smile. "Reports have been known to go in late, Lissa."

Instant Angie double take. Covington kept right on driving, oblivious to my reaction. I couldn't believe what I was hearing. Samuel A. Covington, pillar of the community, had just offered the use of his bank as a hideaway for untaxed casino cash.

Boy, I thought, he must really be in deep shit.

He awaited an answer, and, feigning an expression of reluctance, I provided one. "Sam, there's an awful lot of risk involved in underreporting cash balance."

"That's a risk I'm willing to take." His expression hardened in determination.

"You are?"

"For a modest fee."

Ahhhhh, I thought, now I get it. Not only is Covington willing to bend federal banking laws to bail out MBSB, he's figured out a way to profit on the deal. Profit twice, as a matter of fact. The "modest fee" from my imaginary company would go straight into his wallet. In addition, as hidden honcho of Palace Realty, he stood to benefit from any sale the realtors made to North Central.

My lips puckered in distaste. What a sleaze!

Then again, they're always the best suckers for an Angie scam!

Knees trembling, I settled back in my seat, while Sam Covington, visions of dollar signs cartwheeling through his greedy brain, chauffeured the big car back to the bank.

When we arrived, Covington opened the passenger door for me. "I hope I can count on you, Lissa."

Showing a warm smile, I made a graceful exit from the vehicle. "For what?"

He thumped the door shut. "Letting your board know about Middle Border's . . . *availability*."

"I'll do my best, Sam," I promised. "But it may take some persuasion."

"Give me a dollar figure on the persuasion."

"Let me make a few phone calls first," I said, my hand affectionately touching his sleeve. "In the meantime . . ." Nervous lick of dry lips. ". . . would you mind if I opened a safe-deposit box here at the bank?"

His head turned instantly. "What for?"

"Checks are one thing." I gave my ersatz purse a gentle pat. "But we'll be dealing in cash. I can't very well keep it at my place in the Falls."

"I think you'll find our security *quite satisfactory*." Hearty chuckle. He liked the idea of sitting on all that bribe money. "Step into my office, gal. This won't take very long at all."

It didn't. In less than forty-five minutes, I was back on the street again, with the key to Box Number 664 jingling in my purse. Heady with success, I breezed down North Kimball, my step as light and carefree as a schoolgirl's.

Turning left at the corner, I made a beeline to the Corn Palace. Not many tourists about. The cleanup crew was hard at work, getting the place ready for the big basketball game that night. Girls' basketball. Mitchell Kernels versus the Sioux Falls Lincoln Patriots. I wished Kristy and her team well.

After digging some change out of my purse, I made a call to the farm. The phone rang and rang. No answer. They were all still out in the fields. Fortunately, I had already memorized the number of Josh's cellular phone. I hung up, listened to coins plinking into the change box, then started dialing again.

"Hullo?" Josh's voice sounded faint and distant amidst the combine's diesel roar and the *bangetty-bang* of cornhusks bouncing down the steel chute.

"Hi, Josh! It's Angie. How's the harvest coming?"

"We're gettin' there. Maybe another quarter mile to go on this field." I visualized him sitting up there in the combine's cab, one hand on the steering wheel, the other holding the phone. "Where are you callin' from?"

"The Corn Palace." Tone of growing excitement. "Green light, Josh. Covington went for it."

"I still say the whole deal sounds loco."

"You want to hang onto the farm, don't you?"

Momentary silence. "Can't do much farmin' in jail."

Sensing the worry in his voice, I asked, "What do you mean?"

"Had me a call from Brad this mornin'. Said Deputy Kramer was nosin' around Enemy Creek, lookin' for you."

My woolen suit was no protection against that sudden fearful shiver. Terrific! I thought. One hell of a time for Kramer to start playing bird-dog . . . just as I'm about to sting Covington!

Voice thickening, I asked, "What did he want?"

"Brad said he wanted to know what kind of work you were doin' for us. If you'd been back to that field."

Fussbudget frown. Why would *Kramer* want to know if I'd been back to Enemy Creek? Surely he was past that point in the Rankin case.

"He showed up *here* 'bout two hours ago," Josh added. "I told him I sent you into town to pick up some spark plugs." Urgent tone. "Think he's on to anything?"

"No." I wished I was as confident as I sounded. "I think he's just trying to bust me for parole violation. Thanks for telling me, Josh. I'll make sure our stories match."

"You still plan to go through with it, eh?"

"You bet! Covington's ripe for the plucking . . . and as dirty as they come. Don't lose sleep over this guy, Josh. He's crookeder than his old man ever was."

"It's still wrong, Angie."

"Uh-huh! And so is taking cash from Owechahay Power to drive you people off your land."

Outraged bellow. "The *bastard* did that!?"

"That's what it's all about, Josh." Briefly I told him about my earlier chat with the planners at OP. "They need your farm for the proposed transmission line. That's why Covington foreclosed early." Muted Angie giggle. "Don't worry. We're not really stealing from him. He'll get his hundred thousand back . . . *as a loan payment from you!*"

"I don't think the judge is goin' to see it quite that way, young lady." Despite his best intentions, Josh chuckled.

Leaning against the wall, I shifted the receiver to my right hand. "Here's what I need you to do. Put on your Sunday best and be at the Middle Border Savings Bank promptly at ten tomorrow morning." I visualized the bank's interior. "Do you know where the safe-deposit vault is?"

"Sure do, Angie."

"Terrific! I want you to stand five feet away from the vault entrance. There'll be a potted rubber plant on your right. You'll see me come out of the vault. Do not, repeat, *do not* speak to me. When the guard closes the door, I'm going to drop a satchel beside the plant. The money'll be inside. Wait till I've left the bank, pick it up, and head for the aggie loans desk." Breathless Angela. "If anybody asks, it was a surprise gift from Miss Edna."

"Wait a minute, Angie! You lost me! Covington's going to *give* you a hundred thousand dollars!?"

"Not exactly, Josh. It's bribe money for my nonexistent board of directors."

"Gal, you ain't makin' a bit o' sense."

"It's an old con game, Josh. We call it the Sawdust game." Licking dry lips, I tried to simplify my explanation. "I've convinced Covington that I represent a group of real-estate speculators interested in buying here in the county. I've told him we have a lot of cash that needs to be salted away. Banker Sam kindly offered me the use of the MBSB vault as a cash laundry."

Josh let out a soft whistle. "That boy ain't one to play by the rules, is he?"

"You've got that right, Mr. Elderkin." Coy Angie smile. "Anyway, I told him I needed some cash to convince reluctant members of the board. And suggested that he make it a hundred grand."

"So he's payin' you a hundred thousand so your phony board will put millions in his vault. That it?"

"An accurate summation of the tale, Josh," I replied. "Of course, there is no board. And when we go in there tomorrow, we're walking off with the hundred thousand." Sly grin. "But only as far as the aggie loans desk!"

He sounded worried. "What if somebody else sees that bag?"

"No problem, Josh. You'll be standing right there, and it'll have your name on it. It's yours."

"Thought of everything, eh?"

Slowly my smile blossomed. "I try."

"You know, your grandfather says he never should have let you watch *Charlie's Angels.*" I opened my mouth to respond, but Josh beat me to it. "But I'm damned glad he did. We're goin' to owe you plenty, gal."

"*If* we pull it off," I reminded. Didn't want him getting too cocky. "Let's just concentrate on getting the bank to issue you that receipt for payment."

The harvest cacophony nearly drowned out his chuckle. "I'll see you back at the house."

"Happy combining, Mr. Elderkin!" And I hung up.

As I strolled down North Main Street, I gave some thought to Josh's warning. Pert frown. What was that pluperfect shit Kramer up to? Was he merely trying to catch Angie out of bounds? Or was there something more sinister behind his visit to Enemy Creek?

Troubled frown. What did I really know about Fischer's hot-tempered deputy? You know, Kramer had gotten to the murder scene awfully quick. Private eye Rankin had been shot with a large-caliber handgun. The deputy toted a .357 Magnum. What if *he'd* shot Rankin? He might have seen me with the corpse, lost me in the woods, and then shown up at the combine, *pretending* to answer the call.

Kramer wasn't making much progress in the case, was he?

I tossed a lasso over my galloping paranoia. Whoa! Think about it a moment, princess. If the murders of Rankin and

Miss Edna are linked via the Larsen case, then how could Kramer be involved? When Holly disappeared, the deputy was all of four years old!

In any event, the deputy's interest seriously compromised my scam. Sooner or later Sam Covington would realize he'd been conned (hopefully not until the bank's next audit!) and he'd go storming into the sheriff's office. Even a lawman as sloppy as Kramer would have no trouble putting two and two together.

My frown deepened. Of course, you realize, Angela, that once the deputy tags you as *Melissa Nagin*, the word will go out to all the other law-enforcement agencies. And won't the FBI be interested to learn that ex-convict Angie Biwaban has been running a *Pocahontas* scam.

Lips puckering, I thought the ramifications all the way back to their source. Somehow I had to prevent Mr. Covington from blowing the whistle after I finished the sting. Yeah ... right! How am I supposed to accomplish *that?*

All at once, my gaze struck Saterlie's front window. Someone had taped a full-page ad against the glass, announcing the big Veterans Day sale. An item leaped out at me. Olympus L400 microcassette recorder. Inspiration turned my frown into a mischievous Angie smile. Clutching my purse, I headed straight for the store entrance.

Don't you just love sales? I certainly do!

"You took your own sweet time gettin' back."

Covington flashed a glance of annoyance. He was seated at his desk, poring through the contents of a manila folder. Probably ready to foreclose on another farm. Making my smile apologetic, I gently closed his oak-paneled door.

"Sorry, Sam. It took a little longer than I thought."

As I crossed the room, I dipped my right hand into the open purse. Switched on the Olympus recorder. To allay any masculine suspicions, I withdrew my compact.

His Selleck mustache bristled impatiently. "So how did it go?"

Peeling open the compact, I gave my mirror reflection a quick, critical glance. "Rather well, I thought." Knowledgeable smile. "They're definitely interested. I'm pretty sure I can convince the majority of the board."

"You did stress the privacy angle."

"Absolutely!" My compact snapped shut. "But there are still a few members who seem to be reluctant."

"Convince them." Covington muttered. He wanted absolutely nothing to ruin his grand scheme.

Timid shrug. "That could take some doing."

"How much?" he asked bluntly.

"Beg pardon?"

"Don't get coy with me, Lissa. You know how the game is played." Leaning forward in his managerial chair, he asked, "How much is it going to cost me to buy their approval?"

I already had the dollar figure in mind, but I put on a little show for his benefit. Cross the lissome legs. Lower the delicate eyebrows. Pout somberly. "Ohhhh . . . I'd say a hundred thousand."

Always the master poker player, Covington's expression revealed nothing. "That's a bit much."

I met his gaze unflinchingly. "Not really. There is considerable risk involved, Mr. Covington."

"Risk for everyone, Lissa." His fingers drummed the blotter's padded edge. "If Uncle Sam finds out I'm holding unrecorded cash in the vault, I'm fucked."

"You made the offer," I said, hoping the recorder caught that. If I went down, I was taking him with me. "A few of the board members want the deal sweetened."

"That's a lot of sugar, gal."

"No argument here." Arch one eyebrow. "Are you still interested?"

He nodded. "I can get the cash. Don't worry."

"Can't help it, Sam. I'm under some time constraints here." I fired a glance at the wall clock. "Can you get that hundred thousand by tomorrow morning?"

Twin forehead wrinkles tensed in a blend of frustration and worry. He was fearful that my imaginary board might back out of the deal. "I'll have to send a courier to Sioux Falls first thing in the morning."

"All right." I hated to change the timing, but I had no choice. "Why don't we get together at eleven?"

"Eleven o'clock is fine." Chair wheels squeaked as he rolled it back. "How do you want the cash, Lissa?"

"Big bills are fine, Sam. My superiors are great admirers of Benjamin Franklin."

"So am I." Covington let out a dry chuckle. Taking my arm, he escorted me through the semideserted bank. Behind their brass nameplates, youthful female tellers rapidly ran through the daily count. Nimble fingers shuffled bills and chastised computer keyboards. An elderly Mexican janitor wheeled his portable bucket across the marble floor.

Covington unlocked the front door for me. Then, offering his hand, he murmured, "Pleasure doin' business with you, Lissa."

Bright Angie smile. "Believe me, Mr. Covington, the pleasure was all mine."

Slinging the purse strap over my shoulder, I set off down the walkway. Reaching the sidewalk, I casually dipped my dainty hand into the bag and flicked off the Olympus recorder. If nothing else, that tape would provide the IRS with hours of listening pleasure.

Leisurely I strolled down North Kimball, heading for my planned rendezvous with Chief. Walking along, however, I suddenly became aware of fine hairs rising on the back of my neck. That old prison awareness of hostile intent. Someone had it in for Angie.

Spend three years of your life behind green chain-link

fences with over a hundred women—some of whom would love very dearly to slice your precious hide with a homemade shank—and you soon learn to trust these sudden atavistic nuances.

Had I not trusted mine, that crazy Elena Varo would now be serving additional time for her *fourth* murder.

Shoulders tensing, I slid my gaze leftward. Studied the store window reflections. Nope. Nobody following me. Then my gaze darted across the street, and I gasped in alarm.

Parked beside the curb on East Third Avenue was a Davison County police cruiser. Shadows veiled the driver's face. I saw only the brown leather jacket and the gloved hands.

Deputy Kramer!

Heart beating madly, I averted my gaze and kept right on walking. Deep soothing breath. Easy, princess, I told myself. You don't know that's the guy.

(Then why is he parked there? Why isn't he out on patrol?)

You can't be certain it's Dan Kramer.

(But what if it is? I'm not exactly dressed for the hardware store!)

I bit the corner of my lower lip. Oh, shit! How long has he been trailing me, anyway? Did he see me leave the bank?

Resisting the surge of paranoia, I wondered if he'd get in touch with Covington. *Tayaa!* If those two ever compared notes, and he clued Covington to my real identity . . .

I willed my hands to cease trembling. Very unpleasant thought, that. Josh Elderkin and I could be walking into a trap tomorrow morning.

On the other hand, I thought, Kramer just might hold off for a little while. Covington's clout could make or break a deputy's career. Kramer might wait for something solid before making his approach.

The famed Covington clout. I remembered what Clem Mutchler had told me about Sam's father. Phil Covington, the miller turned banker, trusted financial advisor to Frank Enright. I was getting sick and tired of these old prairie families and their web of corruption. Too many rancid secrets festered behind their façades of respectability.

Those thoughts led me back to Covington's snide remark. *"Miss Edna was a Presbyterian . . . although she had some trouble keeping her skirts clean."* Fussbudget frown. Strange thing to say about a woman in her eighties. What did he mean by that?

Covington didn't strike me as the type given to outlandish statements. His nasty remark had been off-the-cuff, an unthinking reference to some past event. Had there been some trouble earlier in Miss Edna's life?

Somewhere in a far corner of my memory, I heard Miss Edna's no-nonsense voice. *"You're not the only girl who ever made a foolish choice when she was young."*

My heart began to pound. I couldn't shake the feeling that Miss Edna had told me the truth that night. That she'd been trying to confide in me. That there was indeed some scandal in her past. But what?

Her life seemed so cut and dried. A typical prairie childhood here in Mitchell, a teenaged bout with mono, a stay with relatives in Sioux Falls . . .

My obsidian eyes narrowed suddenly. Wait a minute! Miss Edna told Jeremy that she graduated from high school in the Falls. But Chief had found no mention of her in the city's yearbooks.

Somehow I just couldn't see a girl with Miss Edna's brains as a high school dropout. Yet the teenaged Edna hadn't finished school. *Why?*

I stopped short, resisting the impulse to grind my teeth. Aaarrgh! Angie, you dope! We're talking about 1930, remember? Use your head!

Bout with mono, eh? Could be. But let's expand the reasons

a bit. *Why else* would a girl from a prominent family suddenly up and leave town?

Excitement quickened my stride. My heels pummeled the sidewalk. Veering to the right, I dashed down West Third, heading for the public library.

"Oh!" Soft hazel eyes blinked as I rushed up to the desk. The librarian was wearing an evergreen button-front dress instead of her usual white blouse and cardigan. Frosted light brown hair curled inward at her jawline. "May I help you?"

"I hope so." Breathless Angie. "You serve as the community information center, right?"

Gleam of recognition. "You're the girl who was here last week."

Ingratiating smile. "That's right."

"Did you find your birth announcement on the microfilm?"

I nodded vigorously. "But now I need a copy of the Certificate of Birth. Do you have a computer station here?"

By way of reply, the librarian pointed out the array of desktop computers in the reference section.

"Does your system have access to birth records?" I asked, trailing her across the room.

"Yes, we have a complete listing for the county."

Hopeful expression. "What about the state?"

"We don't have that here," she said, her tone full of regret. "But we are hooked up to the state Department of Health. You can touch base with the main office in Pierre, but you'll have to hurry." Her lacquered fingernail stabbed toward the clock. "They close at five."

Thanking her profusely, I seated myself before the beige computer, switched on and rode the mouse around the pad. Two minutes later, I came face-to-format with an onscreen query from the Bureau of Vital Statistics.

Still trying to catch my breath, I filled in a few selected entries. And prayed that my hunch was correct.

          Year of Birth   1930
          Sex   Male
          Mother's Name   Enright, Edna Jane

Alphanumerics rearranged themselves into an official birth
announcement.

          Date of Birth: August 27, 1930
          Child: Male
          Weight: Six pounds, two ounces
          Place of Birth: Sioux Falls, S.D.
          Mother's Name: Enright, Edna Jane   *Age:* 18
          Occupation: None
          Father's Name: Timmins, Robert A.   *Age:* 19
          Occupation: Farmhand

And there he was—Miss Edna's illegitimate son. Frank Enright's grandson. Now it all made sense—her dropping out of
school, the lengthy stay in Sioux Falls.

So that was Miss Edna's "foolish choice." Giving herself to
Bobby Timmins in love. However, old Frank had used his con-
siderable clout to squelch any tarnishing of the family name.
The wayward daughter had been handed off to relatives in the
Falls, and Frank's mono fable had made the rounds. Miss
Edna had spent a couple of years in the Falls, caring for her
infant son until his eventual adoption.

I switched off the computer, wondering how Sam Covington fit into all this. Could be he knew about Miss Edna's son
and the terms of the Enright Trust. If the son could prove that
he was indeed the last Enright, could he inherit all of old
Frank's money?

Sounds like a question for a lawyer. Oh, Sarah!

Footsteps sounded behind me. "Did you find what you were
looking for?"

"Yes, I did!" I flashed a grateful smile as I left the chair.
"Thanks again, ma'am."

"...goddamndest thing you ever saw!" Scratching the back of his protuberant ear, Clem Mutchler showed us all an irritated look. "I don't know what the hell happened. Picker head kicked up a rock or somethin'. One second I'm fartin' along, twenty rows to go, and next thing you know the goddamned combine's shakin' like a wet dog trying' to dry hisself. One hell of a rattle-de-bang! Sounded like engine parts clangin' around in a spin dryer. So I just rolled her to full stop, grabbed my flashlight and climbed down out of the cab. Shone the beam straight up the picker-head throat. Goddamn if one o' the elephant ears ain't missin'! Snapped right off. Cleanest break I ever saw. Son of a bitch landed on the rasp bar, knockin' the shit out of 'em. Well, I says, that's it for corn-pickin' today." Grimacing sourly, he reached for his coffee mug. "I'm tellin' ya, if a farmer didn't have bad luck, he wouldn't have any kind at all."

We were seated around the Elderkin kitchen table—Clem, the Elderkins, Chief, and I. For the first time in days, we had a full complement of Elderkins. Carol was back, very cool-eyed and subdued, looking as if she didn't want to be there. She refused to acknowledge my presence. No stomach for sassy *hired girls*, I guess.

"I'm obliged to you for lettin' me use the barn," Clem said after finishing his long sip. "Ain't one to leave machinery out in the weather."

"You'd do the same for us, Uncle Clem." Brad closed the top of the milk carton. "'Sides, this way you won't have so far to drive to the field."

"Doug Krause'll have it up and running in no time," Jeremy predicted.

"Yeah? Well, you tell ol' Doug to slap some grease on his ass and move it." Clem made a sour face. "My arthritis is kickin' up almighty fierce. We'll be seein' snow in a few more days. Bet on it."

We talked about the harvest. Josh thought we were in reasonably good shape. Just another two hundred acres to go. We spoke of rumbling combines and stalk choppers spitting out debris, of laboring trucks and overflowing grain carts. The words came slow, the speakers nearly punch-drunk with fatigue, but the tone was one of quiet satisfaction.

After the conversation broke up, I motioned for Clem to pass me his empty dishware. "I'll take that."

"Much obliged, Angie."

Sorting the dishes, I casually remarked, "You've lived in the county all your life, haven't you?"

"Damned right." Hoarse chuckle. "Undertaker'll never get that black soil out from under my nails."

"Ever heard of a man named Bob Timmins?"

"Sure!" His homely face brightened in recognition. "Bob Timmins. He was a few years younger'n my daddy. Family worked a farm out by Union township."

"What ever happened to him?"

Clem gave me an odd look, then shrugged. "Keep forgettin' you're a stranger 'round here. Bob Timmins was a war hero. World War Two."

Mention of his war brought my grandfather on the run. "The Pacific?"

"Yeah. Bob was killed on Bataan. Artillery sergeant." Clem slid his chair back. "He left town back in the Depression. Joined the army. He was in Manila a couple of years before the war started."

"Back in 1930?" I prodded.

"I couldn't say, gal. I wasn't around back then." Letting out a chuckle, he added, "Hey, Trude! Almost had him for an uncle, you know."

Turning off the sink faucet, Trudy looked over her shoulder. Her features wrinkled in disbelief. "Bob *Timmins!?*"

"You bet." His crooked smile doubled in width. "Ma told me once he went to an awful lot of barn dances with Aunt Edna."

"So I've heard." Muffling a wry smile, Trudy slipped a plate into the steaming water. "Shame on you, Clem Mutchler, spreadin' that old gossip around!"

With a hearty laugh, Clem ambled into the living room. Chief's dark eyes showed curiosity. "What was that all about?"

"I'll tell you later, Chief. Come on."

We found Josh in the study. He stood before the file cabinet marking a date on the calendar. Mild expression of surprise. "Angie . . . what's up?"

"Slight change of plan, Josh." I lowered my voice. "Covington won't have the cash until eleven. You'll have to be in the bank at ten-forty-five."

"No problem." He tucked away the manila folder. "Want me to give you a ride into town?"

I shook my head. "It'll be better if we arrive at separate times."

"I'll take her in the Bronco," Chief offered.

"This could get tense," I warned. "The bank'll be busier at that time of morning. You might not have a whole hour to close out the loan. Worse, you might have to wait."

"Don't you worry, gal." Josh squared his shoulders in determination. "I'll make damn sure they process that payment."

Just then, I heard Carol's voice behind me. "Payment?"

Doing an about-face, I spied Jeremy's wife in the open doorway. Curious eyes gleamed. "What's all this about a payment?"

Quick Angie save. "My grandfather was just asking about the down-payment on a tractor."

Carol shot me a lofty look. "Really? Are you thinking of going into farming, Mr. Blackbear?"

The dig was obvious. She didn't believe a word I said. Fortunately, my grandfather did an excellent job of reinforcing my save.

"Not at all, miss. Just wonderin' how the price compares to Minnesota."

Carol masked her reaction behind a bland smile. No way to tell if she'd bought it or not. "Would you people like some squash pie with your coffee?"

"Sure, Carol." With an uneasy smile, Josh escorted his daughter-in-law from the study.

Chief touched my shoulder. Heeding his slight head shake, I dallied awhile. Anishinabe murmur. "How much do you think she overheard, *Nimishoo?*"

"I don't know, *Noozis*. She could've been standing right outside the door for a couple of minutes."

"She's never been a member of the Angie Fan Club," I said, casting a heated glance into the hallway. "Why's she following us around *now?*"

"Good question, *Noozis*. Good question."

But my grandfather had no answer.

FIFTEEN

Friday morning. The tenth of November. Three minutes before eleven o'clock. As expected, a crowd filled the MBSB lobby. Women, mostly, doing some last-minute banking before the weekend. The men were out in the field, hoping to finish the harvest on this brisk sunshiny autumn day.

Strolling through the lobby, I cast a look around and found Josh idling in the alcove that led to the safe-deposit vault. Lifelong farmer turned novice con man, frowning and fidgety in his Sunday best. He looked as if he would much rather be riding a combine.

Avoiding his gaze, I made my way to Covington's office. Corporate Angie once again. Tailored teal double-breasted jacket with slim skirt to match. White satin camisole and patent leather midheeled ornament pumps. Over the suit I wore a long lamb coat, open at the front. A leather bag dangled from each padded shoulder, one my ersatz purse, the other a square navy Gitano shoulder bag with a double handle and latch lock. An item indispensable to today's scam.

Covington's secretary looked up as I approached. She was a

thin-faced strawberry blonde nicely turned out in a pale green jacket and floral blouse. Toothy smile of welcome.

"Hi, I'm Melissa Nagin," I said, slipping off the Gitano bag. "I have an appointment to see Mr. Covington."

"Go right in, Miss Nagin. He's expecting you."

So into the sanctum I went. Covington was not alone. To the left of his desk stood a brawny bank guard, maybe two or three years younger than me. No padding was required to puff his shoulders. Farmboy tan and handsome chiseled features. White shirt, black tie, and neat olive green uniform.

I found the reason for his presence on Covington's desk. A mound of currency two feet wide and twelve inches high sat on the blotter. One hundred thousand dollars. A thousand Ben Franklins in paper-wrapped stacks. Fifty bills to a stack. Twenty stacks in all.

I thought of the items already in my Gitano bag and wondered if I'd have enough room.

"Bang on time!" Flashing a welcoming grin, Covington rounded his desk. "I like that. Good to see you, Lissa."

Shaking his outstretched hand, I aimed my bright smile at the pile of cash. "I'd say we're in business, Sam."

"That's for damn sure." He rested one hip on the edge of his desk. Grinning country banker in his single-breasted worsted wool suit. "So when are you making the first deposit?"

"I'll be back Monday to open the accounts," I fibbed, holding the Gitano bag by the strap. "Then I'd say . . . oh, another week?"

"Excellent!" He rubbed his hands eagerly.

"Do you mind if I count it, Mr. Covington?"

"Not at all!" Expansive chuckle. Snatching a stack from the pile, he tossed it my way. "Be my guest."

Hefting the bills, I feigned a thoughtful grimace. "Uh, not here."

Quizzical gaze. "Why not?"

"It wouldn't do to have one of your employees walk in on us. They do like to chat."

He nodded slowly. "Good point."

"Why don't I count it in the safe-deposit vault?" Helpful Angie. "Your man, here, can lock us in. And when I'm done . . ." I patted my Gitano bag. "I can put the money in the box."

Surprise widened his brown eyes. "You're not taking any money back to the Falls?"

"Not until Monday," I replied. "Besides, this place is a whole lot more secure than my apartment."

"All right." He turned to the guard. "Swanson, escort the young lady to the vault and see that she's not disturbed."

Well, it was a tight squeeze, but I did manage to cram every last stack into my navy-blue bag. And then, with Mr. Swanson following three steps behind, I sauntered off to the vault.

Josh manned his station beside the rubber plant, arms folded, leaning against the pastel blue wall. Even though he knew we were coming, he still flinched as we rounded the corner. Ignoring him, I went straight to the riveted forged-steel door. The guard, however, gave him a neighborly nod. "Howdy, Mr. Elderkin."

"Howdy, Kev. Your daddy back to work yet?"

"Another week or so, I reckon. Cast comes off next Tuesday. Say, how're you boys doin' with the harvest?"

"Oh, comin' along. Got one more field to go south of Yorktown and—"

I wanted to scream. *Josh! Why don't you just get on the public address system and tell everyone you're here!?*

Loudly I cleared my throat. Look of severe irritation. Kevin the Bank Guard trotted down the alcove.

Getting a good grip on the bar, he levered it upward. The armored door swung easily on its oiled hinges. The dark green safe-deposit boxes were set right into the wall. To the rear of the well-lit room stood a large Formica-topped table. Swanson pulled the steel door shut, slammed its deadbolt home, and stood sentry off to one side, looking like a paratrooper at parade rest.

Adrenaline kicked my reflexes up to hyper-speed, but I knew I had to take it slow. Any sudden moves might alert the guard. Heart pounding, I deliberately dallied at the box, slowly choosing the correct key, turning it in the lock, gingerly withdrawing the long steel container.

Over to the table, princess. Slow-ly! That's it. Place the steel box on the Formica. Slide it back. Slip off the Gitano shoulder bag. Set it down in front. Now, step to the left and put your shapely self between the bag and that hunky guard. Can't have you watching when I zip this open, Kevin.

Ziiiiiip! And what have we here? Why, it's a *second* Gitano bag, identical to the first but *one size smaller!*

It fit very nicely within its big brother. And only Mr. Gitano himself could tell the difference. My fingers worked quickly, unzipping the inner bag. One by one I removed the stacks of currency, working my way down to the hefty pair of telephone books at the bottom.

When Covington finally got around to forcing my safe-deposit box open, he'd have no trouble at all making a call to Sioux Falls!

Out came the phone books—filler for my Sawdust game. Heart thumping, I peeled the smaller bag out of the larger. The vault's silence made me jumpy. I imagined that Kevin could hear every little sound—the rasp of the zipper, the hushed whisper of moving fabric. Any second now, I expected to feel his hand on my shoulder. *Just what do you think you're up to, Miss Nagin?*

Quelling my paranoia, I concentrated on the task at hand. My hands moved with the certainty of a Renaissance artist. Tuck the phone books into the larger bag. Slip that bag into the oblong steel container. Snap the latch shut. And now the cash, Angie. Back it goes into the smaller bag. Twenty green stacks tumbling through the aperture.

I gave the zipper a decisive pull, then slipped the strap over my left shoulder. A hundred thousand dollars bumped my slender hip. Mmm . . . lovely feeling!

What a shame I can't keep it, I thought, ferrying the steel box back across the room. Oh, well! It's for a good cause.

Conscious of Swanson's gaze, I put on a little show. Pretended to have difficulty reinserting the metal box. Steel corners dinged the framework.

"Uhhh . . . excuse me." Angie the Helpless. "Could you give me a hand with this?"

"Sure!" Kevin's smile had me wishing I'd met him earlier. My social life could certainly use a boost.

Taking the steel box, he hefted it once, showed me more of his movie-star smile, and slid it into the pigeonhole. The weight of my phone books proved highly convincing.

Turning the small brass key, I grinned. "Thank you very much, Mr. Swanson."

"My pleasure, miss."

Emerging from the vault, I spotted Josh waiting nervously beside the rubber plant. Behind me, the armored door slammed. Walking straight ahead, I deftly I removed my shoulder bag, ready to let it drop.

Suddenly . . . *disaster!* Deputy Dan Kramer stepped into the bank, features grim, wearing his khaki uniform and trademark leather jacket. Doffing his Stetson, he walked over to the nearest desk and questioned the loan agent.

I froze. Panic sent a shudder into the toes of my ornament pumps. I didn't dare let him see me. One look at my tailored teal suit, and he'd know I was up to something. He might even make me open my Gitano bag. And when he saw all that money—!

Hands shaking, I halted. Okay, okay, I am *not* going out in that lobby. Not until the bastard leaves.

The deputy, however, showed no inclination to leave. His hooded gaze zigzagged through the crowded lobby.

Twinge of alarm. What is he doing in here, anyway? Oh, shit! Is he looking for *me?*

Sidling my way toward the rubber plant, I tried to keep out of Kramer's line of sight. Then a loud metallic clang captured my attention.

Anishinabe lips puckered in dismay. *Kevin!* I thought. I forgot all about him! I can't just stand here in the alcove. He's bound to get suspicious.

Sickish expression. Oh, terrific! The deputy out front—the bank guard right behind—and *me* with a hijacked hundred grand in my bag!

Imminent peril boosted my imagination to greater efforts. Nothing I could do or say would sway the deputy. Ahhh, but Kevin . . .

Josh's eyes goggled in alarm. He'd seen the deputy, too, and he was looking to me for guidance.

Hang in there, Mr. Elderkin! We're not caught yet!

Resuming my stride, I veered suddenly to the left. Rubber leaves caressed my skirt. Deliberately my left leg scraped the clay pot.

"Shit!" Scowling, I set down the Gitano bag. Extending my leg, I gave the nylon a critical scan. "Damn it!"

Certain Kevin's eyes were on me, I raised my hem an inch or two, smoothing the nylon with my fingertips.

His appreciative chuckle warmed my heart. "Looking good!"

Aiming a coy glance over my shoulder, I waggled my forefinger in mock reproof. "Naughty boy!"

The guard rushed to my side. Josh and my shoulder bag had ceased to exist for him. "Serious damage?"

"Four dollars down the drain." I stood erect, tugging and straightening my skirt.

"Would you like me to shoot the plant?"

Flirtatious Angie smile. "I'll settle for tea and sympathy."

"We could have dinner with that tea."

"I'd like that very much, thanks."

"Are you busy tomorrow night?"

"Afraid so." Regret laced my voice, and, believe me, I wasn't acting. The sacrifices I've made playing Robin Hood!

Oh, well, it wouldn't have worked out, anyway. Witnesses for the prosecution make poor boyfriends.

Leading him back toward the vault, I introduced myself as Melissa Nagin and asked how long he'd worked at the bank. As we chatted, I maneuvered him so that Josh was facing his rear.

"So when are you heading back this way, Lissa?"

"I'll be back Monday," I replied, shooting a hasty glance over Kevin's shoulder. At last Mr. Elderkin had taken the hint. Eyeing the guard carefully, he stooped and retrieved my money-filled bag. "Will you be on duty then?"

"You bet! Hold next Saturday open for me, will you?"

"I'll definitely consider it." I waggled five fingers in farewell.

With a ragged breath, I halted at the alcove's edge and peered into the lobby. Bag in hand, Josh stood patiently beside a black vinyl settee. My apprehensive gaze darted through the crowd. No sign of Kramer.

Forcing a nonchalant smile, I strolled into the lobby. Coming up alongside me, Josh whispered, "He's gone."

"Thank goodness." I steered my employer toward the farm loans desk. "Let's get on with it."

Josh glanced at the front door. "What do you suppose he was doing in here?"

"Forget about him. Just pay the lady the money and get your receipt." Nervously I straightened my shoulder pads. "Then get the hell out of here, Josh."

"What about *you*—?"

"I'll be running interference," I whispered, smoothing my hair. "I'll keep Covington busy. Just don't take too long at that desk."

We parted company. Seconds later, I looked back and saw Josh patiently waiting for the loan officer to put down her telephone.

My sweaty palm grabbed Covington's doorknob. Show time!

"Hi, Sam!" Polyanna Biwaban.

"Lissa!" He put down his pen, noting the bag's absence. "You're not taking *any* cash back to the Falls?"

I shook my head. "Not today. The board meeting isn't till Tuesday." Neatly folding the lamb coat, I draped it over the back of a guest chair. "Besides, I've been meaning to ask you about that tract over in Mount Vernon. Has it been zoned commercial yet?"

For the next five minutes, Covington and I discussed the properties being listed by Palace Realty. All at once, his desk telephone jangled.

"Wait a minute, Lissa." He scooped up the receiver. "Hello?"

Crossing my legs, I watched Covington's expression harden with annoyance. "All right, all right, I'll talk to her." He listened for a second, then . . . "I asked you not to call here, Carol."

Carol!? Icewater cascaded through my veins. Keenly conscious of my pounding heartbeat, I leaned a little closer.

"Payment?" Covington's expression tensed in disbelief. "Where the hell did he get the money?" Then anger. "Who gave it to him!?"

Apprehension turned my knees into tapioca. The banker listened intently. "Give me that name again." He scribbled on a yellow notepad. "Angela what!?" The pen poised in midstroke. "Spell that . . . what do you mean, *you can't!?* How do you expect me to . . . No, I don't know any Angela *Bih-wah-bahn.*"

Yes, you do, Sam! Fragile Angie smile. Now be a good boy and *don't* ask Carol for a description!

"So where did this Angela character get the money?" Covington's voice brimmed with impatience. "All right, then. When is Josh making the payment?" He threw down the pen. "What the Christ *do* you know!?"

I masked my growing anger behind a languid expression. Very nasty, Carol! Helping the crooked banker foreclose on the family farm. I guess you'll do anything to move back into town.

"All right. I'll keep an eye out for him." Terse mutter. "Call me back when you've got something solid."

Covington hung up. Putting both feet on the floor, I sat on the chair's edge and showed him a winsome smile. "Sam, you wouldn't happen to have the marketing data on that Mount Vernon property, would you?"

"No." Mild shake of the head. "But I can have Palace Realty fax it right over."

Covington put through a quick call to the real-estate office. Afterward, as he rose from his chair, I asked, "Mind if I make a quick call to Sioux Falls?"

"Not at all, Lissa. Just punch nine for an outside line."

While Covington hovered at the fax machine, I did some frantic dialing. My imagination hammered out an impromptu script. In about thirty seconds, Covington would be on his way to the lobby, checking to see if Josh had made that payment. And the instant he saw Josh with all that cash money . . .

My forefinger hopscotched across the touch tabs. Nine-nine-six-five-four-four-four. A cheery voice came on line. "Thanks for calling Roxy Cinema 3. Today's movie lineup includes—"

Tuning out the robot voice, I said, "R.T. Langston, please." That's Paul's boss. I just love taking his name in vain. "Hello, R.T. Lissa here. I'm wrapping things up in Mitchell and—" Dramatic pause. "Really? Hmm, very interesting." Longer pause. "No, I haven't been in contact with him."

Covington sent a curious look my way. I pasted on an expression of mild bafflement. "No, sir . . . No, sir . . . Well, I'll see what I can find out. . . . Thank you, sir."

The fax whine smothered my imaginary conversation. I did some casual head-nodding. As Covington returned to his desk, I hung up.

"Something wrong?" he inquired.

"I'm not sure, Sam."

"What do you mean?"

Puzzled Angie glance. "My boss had a call this morning from Kyle Rasmussen, the head honcho at OP."

Brown eyes flickered in surprise.

"Rasmussen asked him if we were really interested in purchasing farmland here in Davison County." Mystified Angie. "I gather they're interested in a joint venture. Only how did they get onto it so fast? The only person I spoke to was my boss."

Covington grimaced. "Don't look at me. I didn't tell him."

"You know Mr. Rasmussen?"

"Sure!" He couldn't resist bragging a bit. "I've done consultant work for OP for years."

"Real-estate acquisition?"

"That's right. I've found a lot of bargains for them." His chest puffed. "Kyle's a friend of mine."

"Really?"

My smile went rigid. I wondered how many farm families had been evicted to create Sam Covington's pool of *bargains*.

All at once, Covington's forehead creased. He started toward the door. I jumped from my seat, thinking, *The loans desk! Josh is still out there!*

"Uhhh . . . Sam!"

"Yeah?" His hand rested on the doorknob.

I tilted my head toward the phone. "Aren't you the least bit curious?"

"About what?"

"Rasmussen." I joined him at the door. Fleeting sidelong glance through the little glass window. Josh was haggling with the woman at the desk. "Why would *he* be interested in that property?"

Covington's shoulders shrugged.

Suspicious look. "You don't suppose he's trying to undercut us, do you?"

"What do you mean, Lissa?"

"End-run Palace Realty. Cut a separate deal with the owner." I spread my hands in speculation. "Maybe he wants to throw an OP right-of-way across the property."

Covington blanched, his mind conjuring up visions of a power line bisecting the defunct mall's acreage. He knew what that would do to the tract's marketability. To say nothing of future sales commissions!

"R-Rasmussen wouldn't do that." He was having a hard time convincing himself. "It must be a joint venture. Like your boss said."

My gaze shifted to the phone. "There's one way to find out."

Mulling it over, Covington stood motionless. Troubled brown eyes kept glancing at the desk phone. Tiny sweat beads glistened beneath his forehead wrinkles.

Come on! I urged silently. *Get on the phone!*

Nervously fingering his mustache, Covington inched away from the door. I began breathing again as he lifted the receiver.

"I-I'll just be a minute, Lissa."

Saintly smile. "Take your time."

Covington asked his secretary to put through the call to Sioux Falls. While he waited, I folded my hands and peered through the chicken-wired window.

At the loans desk, a wide-eyed lady executive was busily counting all those hundred-dollar bills. Josh sat on the guest chair's edge, looking around anxiously, turning the Stetson in his large hands.

Behind me, I heard Covington's hushed voice. ". . . if he's in the building, then page him . . . Look, this is really important . . . Yes, put me on hold. . . ."

Slightly giddy, I watched the loan agent write out Josh's receipt. Don't dawdle, Mr. Elderkin. Get out of here!

"Well, why didn't you *tell* me he was in conference?" Covington sounded ready to explode. "I've got to talk to him, dammit . . . No, it can't wait till tomorrow. . . . Look, when the meeting breaks, tell him to get in touch with Sam Covington in Mitchell." Tone of exasperated rage. "No, I am *not* Mr. Mitchell. That's Covington, dammit! See-oh-vee . . ."

Broad Angie grin. Out in the lobby, the loan agent stood and shook hands with Josh.

The telephone chimed as he slammed down the receiver. I stifled my mirth, pasted on a sympathetic expression, and did a graceful pirouette. "Couldn't get through, eh?"

Shaking his head, the banker muttered, "He's in a meeting."

"Well, we can always try later," I said, returning to my chair. "In the meantime, Sam, fill me in on the *ad valorem* structure out there in Mount Vernon."

Covington and I discussed rural property taxes for another twenty minutes. Then he tried the OP building again. No luck. Rasmussen must like to gab.

As I reached for my lamb coat, the banker remarked, "You're leaving?"

"Afraid so." I nodded, slipping it on. "I have to be in the Falls by two o'clock." Opening my purse, I searched frantically for a North Central business card. Ahhh, here we are. Handed it over. "Give me a call Monday morning, okay?"

Covington read it aloud. "Three-three-nine-seven-oh-five-nine. That's your main office?"

Actually, it's the Great Plains Zoo, but I'd let him find that out for himself. Showing a radiant smile, I extended my dainty hand. "It's been a distinct pleasure, Mr. Covington."

"Same here, Melissa." He pumped my hand with undisguised enthusiasm. "I'll be seeing you Monday."

Don't bet your OP payoff on that! I thought. And, shouldering my bag, I breezed into the crowded bank lobby.

Twelve-thirty found me at the Town House Cafe, seated at a corner table, serenaded by clinking cutlery and scraping chairs. The large lunchtime crowd raised a noticeable din. Tuning it out, I tucked into my Corn Country Special—jumbo hamburger, cucumber salad, and steamed corn-on-the-cob.

Afterward, sipping black coffee, I gave some thought to our recent successful scam.

Well, that's one problem solved, I thought. So much for the OP threat to the Elderkin farm. Boy, is Sam going to be rip-shit when he forces open that safe-deposit box and finds those telephone books! I can just see him in the vault, red-faced and screaming and jumping up and down. . . .

Mischievous Angie smile. That's the thing about rich crooks like Covington. They can dish it out, but they can't take it.

Then my thoughts turned to Miss Edna. I wondered how Chief was making out at the farm. He'd told me that morning he had some more poking around to do.

Fussbudget face. I still couldn't figure it out. How did the killer electrocute Miss Edna *without* hooking up to the farm's power supply?

He'd have to know a lot about electrical systems to pull that off. And who knew more than Carol Bailey Elderkin, the electrician's daughter?

Sure, it made sense. But only if I ignored the murder of L.J. Rankin and its links to Miss Edna.

Theory—Carol wants her husband off the farm, so she sells the family out to Covington. For the banker, eager to help OP acquire the Elderkin farm, this is a heaven-sent opportunity. Realizing that the hated Miss Edna is the main impediment to success, Carol dreams up her very clever murder scheme. Or perhaps Sam Covington orders her to do it.

Frowning, I put down my coffee cup. Now, *that part* doesn't make sense. If the murder succeeds, Covington grabs the farm. But all Carol gets is a ticket out of Davison County.

Why would she put her neck in the noose for Covington?

And what about Holly Larsen? I knew for a fact that the murdered L.J. Rankin had zeroed in on Miss Edna. And I felt reasonably sure that Miss Edna and her father were somehow involved in Holly's abduction. What did Carol have to do with all *that?* She wasn't even born when it happened.

And Sam Covington had only been twelve years old.

If Carol didn't run that cable into Miss Edna's bedroom, then who did? Who has the technical skill needed to pull it off?

A sudden cry nudged me out of my reverie. "Angie, hi!"

Looking up, I saw Julie Sievert and Scott Hasner threading their way between tables. My smiling teller friend was wearing a single-breasted floral jacket, a burgundy roll-neck sweater, and a long black slit-skirt. Her professor boyfriend got by with a herringbone sport coat, turtleneck, and jeans.

"Mind if we join you?" Julie gestured at the empty chairs.

"Be my guest." Nod of invitation. "So how goes the battle against OP?"

"Ever since the public hearing, we've been swamped with calls." Julie's eyes glittered with enthusiasm. "We've set up a telephone hot line at our headquarters downtown. People are really concerned about the EMF hazard. Just wait till January. We're going to swamp that courtroom."

"Numbers won't impress the judge, honey." Scott took his seat. "Expert testimony will."

Julie squeezed her boyfriend's forearm. "He's been phoning scientists all over the country."

Weary smile. "And organizing fund-raising events for SPSD. And meeting three times a week with Jonas. And carrying a full schedule at the university."

Dimples widened Julie's smile. "I don't know how he does it."

I finished my coffee. "How *do* you do it, Scott?"

"I have four crackerjack teaching assistants." Smiling, he rubbed the back of his neck. "They're running my labs. I could use a couple more, though. My distinguished colleagues on the faculty just elected me chairman of the spring symposium. One more job to do."

"What's the symposium topic?" I asked, putting down my cup.

"Space sciences." He signaled the waitress. "I've got to put together a stable of guest speakers. Well, maybe Carl Sagan is available."

I grinned. "You ought to introduce him to the Mars Patrol. Bet they'd have lots to talk about."

Scott grimaced angrily. *"Those* idiots!"

If there's one thing I can't stand, it's professorial pomposity. I decided to have some fun with him. "Listen, they've done quite a bit of research—"

"Research!?" he echoed, slightly aghast.

"You bet! Winnie Gunderson has a high-powered telescope on her farm. She's out there studying Mars every night." You know, I actually enjoyed sticking up for that nice old lady. "She even has a videotape of a UFO landing. She showed it to me the last time I was there."

Scott's handsome face reflected angry disbelief. "Are you hitting me!?"

"No way. Saw it with my own two eyes, Scott. She really does have a videotape. It doesn't exactly show the UFO—"

"Of course it doesn't! There is no such thing!"

Ignoring the interruption, I went on. "But it does show this strange blue glow out in Winnie's back forty. A weird blue aura near the power lines."

All at once, Scott's expression showed interest. "Tell me exactly what you saw, Angela."

I did, adding my own eyewitness observation. When I fi
ished, Scott let out a hushed groan, lowered his face, rubbe
his brow with his fingertips.

"Angela . . ." He sounded as if he were tutoring a backwa:
child. "That *wasn't* a UFO." An exasperated gaze met min
"It was a *corona!* A natural phenomenon caused by ions r
diating from the power lines."

Julie blinked in surprise. "Transmission lines give off
glow?"

Her boyfriend nodded. "Occasionally. It's an electroma:
netic effect. Mostly it happens in bad weather. When you s
the corona, it means the lines are losing power."

Losing power . . .

The physics professor had my full attention. "Losing pow
. . . how?"

Scott shrugged. "Any number of ways. As I said, ba
weather. A tree limb landing on a high-voltage line. Powe
being diverted off the main line." He warmed to his topic. "
crackling noise is also produced. But the corona itself is us
ally only visible at night."

That was all I needed to know. Standing abruptly, I reache
for my purse. "So long, guys. Enjoy your lunch."

"Angie!" Julie sounded disappointed. "Can't you stay fo
another cup of coffee?"

"Got to run." Regretful glance. "My parole officer is a re:
stickler for punctuality. Take care!"

After paying the cashier, I dashed out the door and heade
down North Main Street. Scott's nonchalant words reve:
berated in my mind.

"Power being diverted off the main line."

I thought of the dead raccoon in the Elderkins' back pa:
ture, of the curious burn stripe across its belly, rememberin
that *Asebou* does his hunting at night. My memory retrieved
vivid image of that blue corona.

So *that's* how he did it, I thought, striding swiftly int

Saterlie Drug. Our friend didn't need the house system or the generator. Somehow he tapped into the OP transmission line. He sent a stream of electrical current a mile or so to the house, using the Elderkins' barbed wire fence as a *conductor*.

Lifting the receiver, I thought of little *Asebou* making his customary nocturnal rounds. Imagined his confusion at the sight of the faint blue nimbus enveloping the wires. He probably remained motionless for a long time, watching the strange aura. Eventually hunger pangs overwhelmed his caution, and he climbed over the bottom wire, as he had so many times before.

Coins tinkled into the phone. Hastily I tapped out the Elderkin number. The phone rang three times, and then Trudy's weary voice came on. "Hello?"

"Trudy, hi! It's Angie. Is my grandfather around?"

"Not right now, dear," she replied. "He came back to the house around ten-thirty. Sure was excited about something."

I bit my lower lip. Ohhhh, Chief, what did you find out there in the back pasture? "Did you talk to him?"

"Not for long, Angie. He was on the phone when I walked in. I asked him who he was talkin' to. Electrical supply, he said. Right after that, Clem showed up, and Charlie bummed a ride into town with him."

Apprehension left a dry taste in my mouth. Chief must've gotten to Mitchell just after eleven. He knew I was at the bank. So why wasn't he there waiting for me when I came out?

"Listen, Trudy, if you see my grandfather, tell him to stick by the phone, okay? I've got to talk to him. It's very, very important."

"All right, Angie. I will if I see him," Trudy promised. "Maybe I'd best leave him a note, though."

"You're not staying?"

"Afraid not. I'm drivin' the grain truck. The boys'll have that combine full in another twenty minutes. I've got to get back out there."

"Leave him a note, then. And thanks."

Hanging up, I did some hard thinking. Chief had said he wa going to have a look at the raccoon. What do you want to be he read some trail sign, as well? If there were any huma tracks in that area, he would have found them. After all, m grandfather is the best tracker on Superior's north shore.

Sudden queasy feeling. Sure! He would have spotted the and then followed them all the way back to the OP transmis sion lines.

And found *what?* Physical evidence?

Clutching my purse, I rushed out of the pharmacy. *That it!* Why else would he call an electrical supply store? Chi must have found something.

All at once, I remembered the store on North Kimball m grandfather and I had visited a few days ago—Aladdin Lamp. And wondered if he had called the owner.

Only one way to find out. . . .

Ting-a-ling! The overhead bell sounded as I pulled ope the door. Bob Kittridge sat behind the counter, watching a afternoon soap on his tabletop color TV. He looked up at onc fluorescent lights gleaming off his bald skull. Slate-colore eyes brightened in recognition. "Hi, Susie!"

Neighborly Angie smile. "Hello, Bob."

"What can I do for you?" Grinning, he rounded the counter' corner. Sudden look of admiration. "Hey, that's a nice coa Don't let my wife see it, though. It's too close to Christmas."

I gladly let him babble. I needed a moment to remember th cover names we'd used on our last trip.

Bob tenderly patted a lightbulb display. "Need somethin for your store?"

"Actually, I'm looking for my . . . Uncle Jack," I said, m curious gaze circling the shop. "We're in Mitchell for the day and I thought he might've stopped in."

Bob shrugged. "Sorry. I ain't seen him."

"I know he wanted to get some replacement wire for the barn," I added, absentmindedly rubbing my coat sleeve. "He didn't call or anything, did he?"

Shaking his head, the storeowner replied, "Nope. And I've been here since eight this morning, too."

His orange-shaped face was perfectly guileless. No signs of prevarication. No nervous wetting of lips. Apparently, he hadn't been the target of Chief's excited phone call.

"I guess he changed his mind." Making my smile apologetic, I retreated to the door. "Sorry to have bothered you, Bob. Have a nice day."

"Oh, it's no bother, Susie . . . *oh!*"

The shout halted me in midstep. One hand on the doorknob, I glanced back at him.

"I almost forgot." Sheepish expression. "I found a guy willing to make the trip up to Fort Thompson."

He threw me for a second, and then I remembered the rest of Chief's *nandobani* cover story. The bit about how we needed a man to repair the hundred-amp short circuit in our barn.

"Yeah? He'll replace the wiring?"

"You bet. He's done it often enough. Sort of a jack-of-all-trades. Folks around here swear by him." Amiable smile. "His name's *Doug Krause.*"

Instant Angie double take. "Krause does electrical work?"

"You bet. Handiest man with a lineman's pliers I ever saw."

In my mind, it was Sunday morning, and I was back in the farmyard with Chief, chatting with Doug Krause. Who had shown up at the Elderkin farm for no apparent reason.

Krause's words floated up from the depths of memory. *"Sorry . . . I don't do electrical work."*

You're too modest, Doug!

I thought of the anchor tattoo on Krause's arm. "Did he learn in the Navy?"

"Yeah." Bob's smile widened. "Doug joined up when he was

twenty. He had fifteen years in. Served aboard aircraft carriers. Electrician's mate."

Fierce Angie smile. "Thanks, Mr. Kittridge!"

"You're welcome, Susie. Bye!"

As I hurried out of the store, I thought of Doug's Sunday visit to the farm. Anxiety quickened my stride.

So that's what Krause was doing there! I thought, my features grim. He came back to the farm, hoping to sneak out to the power lines. He was looking for whatever my grandfather had found.

Minutes later, I was behind the wheel of Chief's Bronco, speeding down West Havens Street. The city limits sign whizzed by on my left. I pushed the accelerator all the way to the mat.

My memory replayed a portion of my Sunday afternoon conversation with Josh. What he'd told me about the handyman.

"Miss Edna sure looked forward to his visits, gal. He used to honk his horn whenever he came up the driveway. And Miss Edna—her face'd light up . . ."

And why not? Miss Edna was always delighted to see her son!

I thought of that state birth record. Miss Edna's illegitimate son had been born in Sioux Falls sixty-three years ago. Which made him the same age as Doug Krause!

That's right. Good ol' Mr. Fixit himself. Miss Edna's son. Frank Enright's grandson.

Now it was beginning to make some sense. Electrician's Mate Krause comes home on leave from the Navy. Drops by to visit his mother, borrows her car, and then assaults little Holly Larsen. Miss Edna, playing bridge at the Ostlund farm, hears the state trooper describe the car the bus driver saw and realizes who the perpetrator is. Which explains her emotional breakdown, witnessed by Clem Mutchler, when she returned home.

So the distraught Miss Edna turns to her father. Once again, Frank Enright uses his considerable clout to engineer a cover-up. This time, though, the scandal is a whole lot worse. His illegitimate grandson is a murder-minded child molester!

Enright's plan works. Jake Norton's investigation is spiked. Cal Fischer is sicced onto ready-made patsy Delbert Dietz. And he banishes the sailor grandson. Indeed, Doug does not return for several years, until the fearsome old man is dead.

I wondered what Krause had done in the meantime. And then remembered what Josh had told me about Doug's periodic long-term trips to neighboring farm states. Sudden surge of near nausea. *Tayaa!* What if Holly *wasn't* his only victim!?

I filled my mind with unanswered questions. About Miss Edna and Rankin and Delbert Dietz. Anything but the one question that haunted me all the way to Yorktown.

What happened to my grandfather?

Rounding the bend, I spied the Elderkin farmhouse, barn, milking shed, and silos through the leafless trees. I sent the Bronco charging up the dirt driveway. Tires bounced through muddy potholes. The Bronco braked to a halt beside the grass-covered root cellar.

Switching off the engine, I scouted the area. The house looked deserted. John Deere tractor in the pasture. Distant forlorn scarecrow. Sealed milking shed. Aging cement water trough. Large barn with its front doors slightly ajar.

Leaving the Bronco, I made my cat-footed way across the barnyard. The wind plucked at my long lamb coat. I tried the house first. Jiggled the doorknob, then peered through the back window. Nothing.

As I turned, I noticed a blue-and-white Ford Ranger tucked away beside the barn. South Dakota plate SB-511. A pickup I'd never seen before.

My gaze found the truck's tread mark in the dirt, and I stopped short, crouching for a closer look.

Tart smile of recognition. I'd seen that tread pattern

before—on the edge of Mrs. Ostlund's cornfield—right after my release from jail. Just to be certain, I snuck a glance at the Ranger's right rear tire. Yup—Goodyear Wrangler, all right. Rankin's killer was definitely in the neighborhood.

I moved toward the pickup's cab, looking for more clues. But something beat me to it. A small object splintering the air at supersonic speed. *Blam!* The gunshot reached my ears just as the truck's door-mounted mirror exploded.

Peppered by tiny shards, I dove to the left. *Blam!* The second bullet skewered my long coattail, its friction heat toasting my thigh. I yelped as I hit the muddy ground, then, quick as a weasel, scrambled behind the cement water trough.

Crawling forward commando-style, I risked a momentary peek around the bottom corner. And there he was—Doug Krause—half-hidden shadow in the barn's doorway, holding a rather large handgun.

"Welcome back, Miss Angie." His hate-filled chuckle raked my ears. "And thanks! You just saved me the trouble of tracking you down."

SIXTEEN

Blam! Beeeyoww! Doug's bullet ricocheted off the trough's rim. A cement chip went spiraling toward the house.

Instantly I withdrew behind solid cover. That was one big handgun—a .44 Magnum, judging from the boom. Two shots at point-blank range had blown the lungs out of Larry Joe Rankin. No way was he getting a clear shot at Angie!

Trapped! I thought. But not for long! Any second now, Krause would leave the barn, moving up and around the pickup's front grille. He couldn't possibly miss at that range.

I had to keep him in the barn. Bluff time, princess!

Shrill Angie yell. "Another step and I'll shoot!"

Flurry of footsteps, followed by Krause's taunting voice. "I don't think you're packin', little gal."

"Willing to stake your life on that?"

"I just might do that little thing!"

"Your funeral, Krause!" Panic raised my voice an octave. "Surely you don't think I was stupid enough to come here without a gun?"

Of course, that's *exactly* what I did. But I didn't count on running into Miss Edna's killer at the farm. Had I not been so concerned about my grandfather, I might've considered the possibility. This was the last day of harvest. What better time for Krause to retrieve whatever evidence he'd left behind in the OP right-of-way?

I heard strange noises coming from the barn. Four metallic *snicks*, punctuated by a roulette clatter. Krause reloading the pistol. Baritone laughter. "Guess we've got us one o' them Mexican standoffs, Miss Angie."

"Asshole! Where's my grandfather?"

"Good question, gal. I figured he was with you." Anger choked the handyman's voice. "Guess he ran off with my stuff. It wasn't there when I checked." Hateful snarl. "I'll take care of that son of a bitch later!"

"What stuff?" Keep him talking, princess.

"That slag under the power lines. All that's left of my cable." I detected an undertone of pride in his voice. "I used THW 4/0 cable. That power surge melted it in less than a minute. No surprise, though. That's a 900-kilovolt line. Talk about a fireworks show! You should've seen it, gal."

"I did! I saw the corona."

"No shit?" Ferocious laugh. "Well, I guess there's just no way I'm going to let you walk away from here."

"I'm surprised you didn't fry yourself, Dougie!"

"Don't be! I've worked with heavier voltages than that."

"In the Navy?"

"You *are* a nosy little thing, aren't you?"

"How'd you hook up to the fence?' I asked.

"Wasn't hard. I put the clamps on the barbed wire, hitched up to my portable step-down transformer, and tossed the rest of the cable over the OP line." More laughter. "Man, that was a lot of juice. Melted the cable and burned out my transformer! I lost most of the amps on the way to the house. But thirty seconds of power was more than enough to do the job."

"Killing *your mother*, you mean!"

Krause went silent all at once.

I kept on prodding. "What happened, Dougie? Did your mother tell you Rankin was on to you? Or did you hear about him from Delbert?"

"My mother!" Years of bitterness flavored those two words. "She told him too damned much. She never should have talked to him at all."

"And that's why you lured him out to Mrs. Ostlund's field and shot him?"

"How'd *you* know that was Ostlund property!?"

Slowly I rose to my hands and knees. "I've been talking to people, Dougie."

Krause made inarticulate sounds of fury. "Shit! I *knew* I should've risked a shot from the road. Didn't figure on losin' you in them woods." Harsh laugh. "Would've gotten you Sunday, though, if that granddad of yours hadn't been here."

Keeping my spine below the rim, I asked, "What did you do with Rankin after you pulled him out of the thicket?"

"Found that, too, eh?" Merciless chuckle. "I guess you did a lot of snoopin' around back there. Don't you worry none 'bout him, Miss Angie. There's an old limestone quarry just south of Wessington Springs. I got him tucked away in there—right next to Holly. And there's more'n enough room for a nosy little Injun gal!"

I didn't doubt him for a second. Firing an anxious glance at the driveway, I hoped my grandfather had more sense than I did. *If you're coming, Chief, bring the sheriff!*

"Why did you kill her, Krause?"

"I told you! She *betrayed* me! My own mother!" Very strange to hear a man in his sixties fuss like a petulant toddler. "And it wasn't the *first* time, either!"

"I'm talking about *Holly Larsen*, Short Eyes!"

Yowl of fury. "Don't you mention that name! That little bitch ruined my life! He-He made me leave—the old fucker! Told me if I ever came back he'd shoot me himself. My grandfather! And *she* let him do it. She stood right there and let him throw me out!" I was stunned by the depth of his hatred. "I-I tried to tell him how it was. I couldn't help myself. S-She *enticed* me—the little bitch. I saw her waiting for the rain to stop. That sweet, innocent face . . . I-I just c-couldn't help myself."

"*Enticed!?*" I echoed, stomach churning in disgust. "You crazy short-eyed bastard! She was eight years old!"

"I'm not *crazy!*" Krause bellowed. "That's what *he* said! You should've seen them all kissing his ass. The great Frank Enright! He never wanted *me* around. You see, I couldn't be allowed to soil the precious family name." Sudden anguished sob. "We-We were happy in the Falls, Mother and I. And *he* made her give *me* up for adoption! Damn him! I-I should've killed him when I was sixteen!"

Another swift glance. The empty driveway mocked me. Hoping to stall him, I tried another tack. "What about Deitz? What's the story, Krause? Meet him in the Navy?"

"'Fraid not, Miss Angie! Bert's been in and out of looney bins for years."

"So what's the connection?"

"He's my cousin." Rage deepened his voice. "I thought he could handle you two. I shoulda known better! That dumb little shit couldn't sit on the john without falling off!"

"He must *really* be crazy, risking a murder rap for a diddler like you!"

"Bert knows better than to cross me!" Krause's laughter raised hackles on the nape of my neck. "He's got a long memory, and he knows I'll hurt him." Sinister chuckle. "Happened often enough when he was a kid."

I did some artful guessing. "That was you who convinced Grandpa Enright to toss Delbert to Sheriff Wirtz!"

"You bet! I saw Bert enter the field as I drove away. *He* thought it was Mother behind the wheel." More lunatic gaiety. "That was my present to the Krause family. I made them *all* suffer!" His voice tightened. "I never wanted to be one of them. I'm an Enright! I was *always* an Enright!"

"You're a rancid little child molester, Dougie!" I crept forward again, intent on a quick peek. "And if you think your life's been rough up till now, just wait till the guys in the joint get their hands on you!"

"You shouldn't have ought to said that, Miss Angie!" Subdued dangerous tone. Was it my imagination, or was Krause's voice coming closer? "A bullet would have been easier. Now I'm going to let you see the quarry for yourself."

Another verbal jab. "Why did you *really* kill her, Dougie? Because she abandoned you in Sioux Falls?"

"Shut up!" he screamed. "I didn't *want* to do it! I had no choice! She-She said she didn't want to die with Holly on her conscience. That's why she talked to Rankin." His voice became noticeably louder. "S-She kept hintin' I ought to turn myself in. She was going to *talk!* She t-thought Holly was the only one. *She didn't know about the others!*"

I peered around the trough's edge. Krause loomed in the barn doorway, his sun-bronzed face contorted by a savage glee. Up came the .44 Magnum revolver, a silvery Ruger Redhawk.

"Go on, Angie. Take a shot." Demented cackle. "I *knew* you weren't packin'!"

My stomach filled with ice-cold slurry.

And then it happened. A stentorian *whoop-whoop* shattered the yard's silence. Glancing to my left, I saw a Davison County cruiser speeding up the driveway.

All-lll right! Anishinabe grin. You know, I must be the first Native-American princess who was ever delighted to see the cavalry arrive.

Krause backpedaled into the barn, closing the door with his free hand.

I broke cover the instant the cruiser skidded to a halt. Dep-

uty Kramer emerged from the driver's side, his right hand o:
his pistol butt. His unzipped brown leather jacket flapped i:
the slight breeze. "Biwaban!"

"Help me!" I ran like a spooked whitetail, head low, tryin;
to give Krause less of a target. "He's here! The man who sho
Rankin! The *barn!* He's got a *gun!*"

The Stetson rested low on Kramer's forehead. Mirrore
sunglasses reflected my approach.

"He killed Rankin and Miss Edna. He just tried to ki
meeeeeeee—!"

Kramer's hand snaked out, gripping my coat collar. With
smooth sweep of his hard-muscled arm, he flung me agains
the cruiser's hood. "Just the gal I've been looking for!"

Thump! My upper torso bounced on the springy metal. Th
impact turned me breathless. Uttering a hushed groan, I trie
to stand. Grabbing a fistful of lamb coat, the deputy slamme
me right back down again.

"Kramer! What are you—!?"

"Now, you be sure to give that blonde in Pierre a full report.
Brutal hands held me rigid. "I'm lookin' forward to seein' tha
bitch again . . . just before I ship your ass back to Pussyland!"

"Listen to me! The barn—!"

Kramer was having none of it. He must have been dreamin;
about this moment for days. Deep-throated chuckle. "I'd rea
you your rights, Injun gal. But I ain't too sure what name t
put on the arrest report. Which one is it? Angie Biwaban?
His smile turned feral. *"Or Melissa Nagin!?"*

Gasp of alarm. The deputy must have returned to the bank
Shown my arrest photo around. Who had he talked to?

Kramer's right hand began an insolent pat-down search. A
I glanced behind me, all thoughts of the Covington scam in
stantly vanished from my mind.

Obsidian eyes went wide. *Kramer, you idiot!* You've pu
our backs to the barn. *We're perfect targets!*

"What were you doin' in that vault, Miss Angie?"

My midheeled pump lashed out, tagging the deputy's knee-cap. Grimacing in pain, he performed a genuflection that would have warmed the heart of any monsignor. Wriggling free, I left him holding a fistful of lamb coat.

And she's off! Anishinabe princess in her smart teal suit and dress pumps, trying to find solid cover before Krause began a second fusillade. I didn't get far, though. The cursing deputy reached his feet in a millisecond. Fifteen feet from the cruiser, his hand snagged my wrist.

"Oh, no, you don't!" Kramer barked, spinning me around. He caught my fist on the downswing, then gave me a shaking. Not in the same class as Miss Carlotta's, but enough to rattle my teeth. "Before I run you in, you're gonna tell me *everything*, Injun gal!"

So intent was Kramer upon getting my confession he never heard the muted rumble coming from the barn. The start-up mutter of a diesel engine. *But I heard it!*

Struggling against the deputy's grip, I hollered, "Let go of me, asshole!"

"No way, gal! We're gonna have us a little dialog, right here and now."

My pumps' pointed toes repeatedly pounded deputy shins. No effect. I might as well have been kicking a combine.

"The barn! He's going to kill us!"

Wry masculine laugh. "Resistin' arrest, eh? Oh, you're gonna be back on the laundry before midnight, gal!"

The diesel rumble grew louder. Hydraulic brakes gave way with a subtle hiss.

"Kramer ... *listen!*"

"I'm listenin', squaw. And I want to hear the whole thing. What were you tryin' to pull on Mr. Covington, eh? What were you doin' in that vault?"

Glancing fearfully at the barn door, I redoubled my efforts. Slender arms swung every which way. No use! I couldn't break the deputy's grip.

A wild swipe dislodged his Stetson.

"Oooooh, you're a feisty little Injun, ain't you? Looks like I'm gonna have to scuff you up some before I turn you over to the sheriff."

Just then, the barn doors exploded off their hinges. The frightful impact shattered wooden beams and panels, reducing them to kindling. Wood screws shrieked as they burst out of the joists.

Kramer's head swiveled toward the barn. My gaze was already there, staring in horror at Clem Mutchler's huge Case International 970 diesel combine. Handyman Krause had gotten the big dull red machine running again. Bulling its way through the wreckage, the combine plunged into the barnyard.

Bewilderment flooded the deputy's face. Far above us, sitting in that glass-walled cab, a maniacal Doug Krause frantically twisted the shift levers. The big machine surged forward at a startling speed. And no wonder! The picker head hovered a foot above ground, its grinders and snappers whirling in hellish clatter.

"Krause!" The diesel roar nearly smothered the deputy's bellow. "What are you doing!? Are you *crazy!?*"

Still pinned in Kramer's grip, I watched helplessly as the harvest teeth of the combine came speeding our way.

Suddenly, Deputy Kramer came to life. Hard-muscled arms hurled me away from him. Flopping backward, I saw him reach for his holstered .357 Magnum.

I hit the dirt hard and kept right on rolling. A tire the size of a barn door thundered past my hip. Hot diesel vapors enveloped me, accompanied by the hissing sound of hydraulic brakes.

I hopped to all fours. Caught a glimpse of the hatless, auburn-haired deputy on his knees, swinging his pistol toward the combine's cab. Glancing my way, he hollered, "Get out of here, Miss Angie!"

Kramer managed to get off one shot. Then, roaring like an enraged grizzly, Clem's venerable combine suddenly reversed direction and charged the deputy. Howling, he vanished beneath the rear tires.

Bump-rumble-thud! Brakes sizzled as the combine halted again. I saw Kramer facedown in the dirt, crushed and bleeding, his legs jutting at an unnatural angle. Somehow he managed to raise himself on one elbow. Nostrils and mouth streaming blood, Kramer took aim at the cab. The .357 Magnum wavered in his grip. Feeble gasp. "Halt!"

The cab's hatch swung open. Krause appeared on the steel porch. His Ruger Redhawk boomed twice. The deputy's body bounced with both bullet impacts. Kramer's features contorted in agony. Slack fingers relinquished his pistol.

The Ruger's deep-throated roar spurred me into motion. Darting to the left, I saw Krause swinging his .44 Magnum my way. Trying to put the cab itself between us, I angled toward the barn. The big gun muzzle kept right on tracking me. My skin turned to ice.

Then the cab's steel framework bumped Krause's wrist, spoiling his aim. Success! Triumph sent a fresh surge of adrenaline coursing through my legs. Rounding the barn's corner, I galloped into the Elderkins' recently harvested field.

If I could get to Bonnie's house, I thought. I just might have a chance.

An industrial symphony erupted behind me. Wheeze of releasing brakes. Throaty rumble of the mammoth diesel engine. Clankety-clank of the gnashing grinders. Shooting a quick glance over my shoulder, I watched the huge combine lumber past the barn. Krause came a little too close. Metal screeched as the dump auger splintered the barn's aluminum drainpipe. The guide wire snapped, and the auger shot upright, looking like an iron chimney right out of Dickens.

Oblivious to the collision, Krause stepped down on the pedal. The big combine hurtled downfield at its top speed of

fourteen miles per hour. Doesn't sound very fast, does it
Well, I've got news for you, gang. That's nearly *twice* as fas
as the average human being runs!

Best I've ever done is ten m.p.h., and that was in th
Grandma's Marathon back home. Ohhhh, what I'd give for
pair of jogging shorts right now! The narrow teal skirt ham
pered my every stride. And my pumps' two-inch heels san
easily into the damp, loose soil.

Behind me, the ominous roar-and-clatter grew ever loude
Barbed wire blocked my path. Gasping in terror, I began t
climb. A steel spur slashed my palm. Another tore my blaze
sleeve. Wire strands bent beneath my wobbly shoes. Anothe
fast glance to the rear. The combine lumbered forward, mash
ing the corn stubble beneath its monster tires. Up in the cal
Doug Krause clutched the wheel and grinned with sadistic tr
umph.

With a cry of despair, I swung my left leg over the top wire
A barb snagged the hem of my skirt. Glancing frantically a
the approaching combine, I tore at the woolen fabric with m
fingernails.

Oh, shit! Hung up on the fence!

"Come *on!*" I hollered, tugging at the stretched wool.

The snappers and grinders raised a hungry clatter.

Riiiiiip! I freed my skirt with a two-handed tug, leaving
long teal streamer on the wire. Gravity yanked me into th
neighboring cornfield. I landed flat on my back in the muc
and stubble, heedless of my now-jagged hem. My nyloned le:
foot waggled its toes. Groping for the missing pump, I peere
over the bottom wire and saw the combine's clattering picke
head coming straight for me.

Slipping my shoe back on, I scrambled once more to my fee
and plunged into the jungly undergrowth of ripened cor:
Grasshopper Angie fleeing the relentless lawn mower.

The fence proved no obstacle to that Case combine. The ma

chine plunged through it as easily as a Panzer tank. Wire strands parted with a musical twang.

By this time, Breathless Angie was twenty yards down-field, shrouded by the tawny cornrows. Dropping to my knees, I drew long gasping breaths. No good, princess! Can't possibly keep up this pace. Krause can keep driving that thing all day.

Huddled beside a cornstalk, I looked around. Hmm, maybe it was time to stop running . . . and to start *thinking!*

Swallowing hard, I shielded my face and dashed across the rows. Stiff leaves sliced at my blazer. Last year's stubble and assorted debris reduced my nylons to shredded yarn. I ran a broken-field pattern through the corn, halted, pivoted ninety degrees to the right, and did it again. And then I dove to the ground.

Off to my left, I heard the clamor of the combine's shifting gears, punctuated by the rumble of diesel acceleration. Tiny grin of satisfaction. My zigzag pattern had rattled Krause. In trying to align the picker head properly, he'd lost me in the corn.

Tense moments passed. Breathing heavily, I rose slowly to my bruised knees. The diesel noise diminished to an impatient idling mutter. Fussbudget face. What was that man up to?

Blam! Krause's bullet kicked up a fount of soil beside my leg. Reacting like a spooked squirrel, I bounded into the tan-colored vegetation once more.

Does that answer your question, princess? I thought, running down the neighboring cornrow. He stopped momentarily to see where you were. Your teal suit really stands out in this monocolor field. And that combine cab, looming eight feet above the corn tassels, offers the ideal gun platform.

No choice, then. I had to keep running, but for *how long?* I couldn't keep this hectic pace up forever. But the moment I collapsed, the picker head would grind me into hamburger!

On and on through the cornstalks I ran, enduring the sharp slash of the leaves, my heartbeat thundering in my ears. And behind me, the relentless *rumble-roar-and-clatter* of the mammoth harvesting machine.

Suddenly, a dark man appeared in my path. Letting out a shriek of alarm, I crashed into him. Cornstalks, field, and sky rotated wildly in my field of vision. I struck something soft and damp. Eyes winking open, I found myself sprawled on top of an Elderkin scarecrow.

The Case combine wheezed into idle. I heard the hatch pop open, followed by Krause's infuriated voice. "You up to your tricks again, little gal!?"

My face pressed the scarecrow's dew-dampened chest.

"You can't hide from me, Miss Angie! No, you can't!" Hate-filled bellow. "I'll get you if I have to trim this cornfield bare!"

Tassels waved in the slight breeze. Beyond them, I spied the gaunt maples of the shelterbelt and the peekaboo steel crossbeams of the OP transmission towers. Any other time of year, and that shelterbelt would have made a dandy hideout. But the maple leaves were all gone, and Krause had that .44 pistol.

Heart thudding against my rib cage, I took a deep breath and considered my options.

Then my gaze found the scarecrow. The legless effigy was perhaps an inch taller than me. Faded long-sleeved Mackinaw shirt stuffed with straw. Someone had sewn his feed-sack head right onto the shirt collar. A Smile face. Tattered raincoat and a black floppy-brimmed hat.

Anishinabe lips pursed in a thoughtful frown. You know, I just might be able to stage a little diversion . . .

The combine's approaching roar made up my mind. I stripped the scarecrow of his raincoat, grabbed his black hat, tucked him under my arm, and dragged him stealthily through the corn.

I had maybe a few minutes before Krause realized he'd lost

me once again. Not much time to set the stage, I know, but it was my one and only chance.

Keeping a wary eye on the combine, I hauled Mister Scarecrow the remaining thirty yards to the back fence. Propped him face-first against a steel post. Peeled off my teal blazer. *We're improving your wardrobe, my straw-filled friend.* Thrust his arms through the satin-lined sleeves. *You'll make the cover of* Gentleman's Quarterly *yet!* I smoothed the hat's floppy brim. Black felt made an acceptable substitute for Angie's raven tresses.

Now . . . right up against the barbed wire, as if I'm trying to sneak through the fence.

Backing away from Mister Scarecrow, I padded through the rustling corn, head low, listening for Krause's combine. The harvest clangor drew closer. I spied the red cab above the tossing tassles. Then, as the engine shifted to neutral, I huddled at the foot of a cornstalk.

The fence, Krause! I fumed. *Look at the fence!*

Miss Edna's murderous son opened the hatch. His surly potato-face moved from side to side. I prayed all those waving leaves overhead would shield me from his searching gaze. His gaze swung my way. Then stopped. I shivered in my blouse, and not from the November chill, either!

Wide-eyed, I held my breath . . .

And then his eyes began moving again. He looked toward the fence, then spat out a bark of triumph. The hatch snapped shut. The diesel engine roared like a Jurassic beast. Gray smoke spurted from its upright stacks, and the big combine lumbered forward.

As the colossal front tire rolled past, I jumped up and ran alongside the machine. Caught a glimpse of Krause's left arm up in the cab. That's right, Douglas. Concentrate on running down Decoy Angie. My right hand snagged the ladder's steel rung. I ran along on tiptoe, trying to double my grip. My left lashed out. Got it!

Trembling all over, I scaled the steel ladder. A sidelong glance showed the picker head closing in on my motionless straw-filled twin. I winced as my knees touched down on the combine's diesel-warmed porch. Licking dry lips, I slowly slid my hand onto the door latch.

Krause's lunatic laughter erupted as "Angie" and the wire fence were snatched into the maw of the picker head. Hellish cacophony of sounds down there. Whirling snappers turned Josh's fence into raw material for paper clips.

I yanked the hatch open. Krause's eyes bulged in disbelief. But surprise didn't stop him from grabbing the .44 Redhawk. As the pistol cleared his belt, I hurled myself into the cab, grabbing him around the neck, knocking him right off the driver's seat.

Krause's pudgy body absorbed most of the impact. Somehow he kept his grip on the pistol. I got both hands around his wrist and slammed it against the steel floor. No luck! His knuckles turned purple, but he wouldn't let go!

Together we thrashed on the floor, baring our teeth at each other, struggling for control of the pistol. His free hand grabbed a fistful of raven-black hair. My fingernails gouged four bloody trails across his face.

Deprived of human guidance, the rudderless combine, its grinders chewing on air, followed the path of least resistance, waddling downslope into the OP right-of-way.

Unaware that we'd crossed the county line—and were about to pass between two lofty OP transmission towers, I gave the molester's chubby face another hearty rake, and, listening to him bellow, sank my teeth into his hairy wrist.

The .44 Magnum skidded beneath the driver's seat.

Howling in anguished rage, Krause hurled me away from him. My shoulder blades smacked the windshield. Then the back of his fist walloped my chin. Shrill feminine yelp. Knees wobbly, I tried to bring my blurry vision back into focus.

Krause gave me no respite. Clutching my arms, he slammed

me repeatedly against the hatch. Screams of mingled pain and outrage. *Thump-thump-thump!* My foot lashed out at him. Missed! His brutal retaliatory shove popped the hatch and laid me out, flat on my back, on the porch.

Long muffled groan. Rolling onto my side, I tried to rise. Swift glance at the cab. Krause's boot sole came rocketing toward my face.

Ducking, I got my shoulder up just in time. That kick knocked me right off the combine. Instant somersault in midair! Letting out a shrill scram, I went limp.

The crushing impact nearly extinguished my senses. Vague sensation of rolling along the ground, of dry grass tickling my face. Momentum kept me turning for several dizzying seconds, and then I landed facedown in the meadow.

Through bleary eyes, I watched Doug Krause, gun in hand, slowly descend the cab's ladder. My claw marks had left reddened stripes all over his face. Brown eyes sizzled with a murderous rage. He had the gun, and he was coming to kill me. And I didn't even have the strength to stand!

All at once, I heard a crisp explosive *pop*—like a gargantuan flashbulb going off. My gaze zipped to the cab roof, and I gasped. The combine's upright dump auger had snared one of the OP high-voltage lines!

Rubber tires began to smoke. A hideous crackle made itself heard over the diesel roar. Intent only on getting me, Krause leaped from the ladder's bottom rung. And then, showing me a predator's grin, he leveled the big Ruger pistol.

His index finger whitened on the trigger . . .

Suddenly, as if by magic, the .44 Magnum leaped skyward, pulling his arm right along with it. Krause's face displayed an expression of ghastly surprise. Even all those yards away, I still heard the rasp of tearing cartilage. *Clang!* The Ruger adhered to the combine's steel side. A slim bluish-white bolt darted out of the ground, striking Krause on the hip.

His eyes gleamed with the terrible realization of what was happening. I have no idea what Krause meant to say, but I really don't think it was the bleating cry that came out—that hellish ululation of *"Fuck meeeeeee!"*

An invisible hand slapped him flat against the combine. More bolts pinned him to the steel. Electric arcs tickled his writhing body, accompanied by the sizzling sound of frying eggs. Krause rose on tiptoe, quivering like an aspen leaf in a stiff autumn breeze.

The scent of roast meat reached my nostrils. Flames burst out of the engine compartment. The giant front tires exploded simultaneously. Mercifully—for me, perhaps—those twin booms masked the sound of Krause's death scream.

And then I heard shouting behind me. Turning, I saw Paul Holbrook and my grandfather running out of the cornfield. Paul's handsome face tensed in horror. "Angie! Get out of there! Get out—*now!*"

Just then, a fiery paddle walloped the soles of my feet. I rose on tiptoe, ready to howl. Rose and stayed there. An eerie paralysis stilled my larynx. Arching my back, I stood for a split instant like a freeze-fried ballerina. And then the quivering started. Quivering and shivering, vibration and pain, a force field of agony that washed over me and swept my conscious mind into complete oblivion.

So cold . . .

I opened my eyes to darkness. Diamondlike stars littered a cloudless winter sky. An icy breeze chilled my face. I heard the snap and crackle of a wood fire. Smelled the sweet scent of burning sage. Sensed the dampness of a March snow.

A warm hand touched my cheek. Turning, I looked into the smiling face of Grandma Blackbear—dead these many years. Familiar contralto voice. "Little one, do you wish to sleep now?"

Then she unhitched my *tikinogan*—my cradleboard—from the maple branch and cuddled me in those loving arms. Strange feeling of *déjà vu*. And then I remembered.

Wendjiduzinzibakwud gabeshiwin. Maple sugar camp. I went for the first time when I was two years old. The maple grove east of Crystal Creek. We camped beside the small beaver pond.

Turning, I spied the familiar *waginogan*. My mother crouched before the campfire, feeding it fresh birchwood. A few feet away, my father stirred boiling sap in a huge iron kettle. The paddle is called a *gackagokweigun*. Daddy had whittled it over the winter from a basswood bough. I listened for the night sounds, and there they were. Wind stirring the leafless branches. Campfire sparks hissing as they struck damp snow. The distant mournful aria of the timber wolf.

Grandma Blackbear carried me into the *waginogan*, lifted me out of the cradleboard, removed my snowsuit, and dressed me in fleece pajamas and knit booties. Then she swaddled me in warm rabbit-skin blankets and put me to bed. Soft Anishinabe lullaby, followed by a feathery kiss to the forehead and her warmhearted murmur. "Go to sleep, *Noozis*."

Sleep . . .

All at once, the *waginogan* flap tore open. My gaze flitted toward the man standing there. One of our people in traditional Anishinabe dress, his hair roached and feathered, his face painted with red-and-white stripes. He vaguely resembled Chief as a young man. Obsidian eyes reflected a blend of affection and kindness. *"Gawiin, Indaanis. . . not yet!"*

"Keep up the pressure!" Paul's anxious voice jolted me into semiconsciousness. "Keep pushing, Charlie!"

An unbearable weight descended on my chest. Masculine fingers pinched my nostrils shut. And then I tasted my parole officer's firm lips. He blew a strong stream of air into my lungs.

Grateful tingle. Nice job on the CPR, Mr. Holbrook!

One by one, my nerve endings switched on. I became aware of the cold ground beneath my spine. My headache came rumbling back, along with painful twinges from all my other bruises. Paul kept up the mouth-to-mouth for a few minutes more. He halted as I began to cough.

Personally, as far as I'm concerned, he could have kept it up *all day!*

"Enough!" Features flooding with relief, Paul sat back on his haunches. "She's breathing again. Thank God!"

Chief knelt on the other side. He took my hand, his dark eyes swimming with tears. *"Noozis . . ."*

"P-Paul?" My throat felt like beach sand. "Wha . . . ?"

His palm tenderly patted my face. "Rest easy, Angie." Emotional rasp. "Oh, God, I thought I—*we'd* lost you." He glanced at Chief. "She's in shock. She needs a doctor!"

My grandfather started to rise. "I'll go."

"No!" Whipping off his stadium jacket, Paul bundled me up. "I'll go! I can run faster. Charlie, keep her warm. If she starts to shiver, put your jacket on her, too. I'll be right back."

He dashed into the cornfield, heading for the Elderkin farmhouse.

Feeling strangely light-headed, I gasped and squeezed my grandfather's hands. *"N-Nimishoo? Wh-What happened?"*

"Don't worry about that now," he murmured, smoothing my forehead. "Just lie still. You're going to be all right."

Sunday afternoon, November twelfth, found me in a semi-private ward at the Methodist Hospital, lounging in bed. Anishinabe princess in her white cotton johnny. Across the room, a man with a bandaged skull watched the Browns play the Bengals on the overhead TV.

Promptly at two P.M., Bonnie Dietz ambled in. Smiling and efficient nurse in her white smock and slacks. Cheery smile. "How are you feeling, Angie?"

Actually, not bad for a woman who had taken an estimated jolt of 3,000 volts. I still had trouble remembering the names of all my teachers at Central, and there were second-degree burns on my heels, where the current had entered my body. That was it for me and country line dancing . . . at least until Thanksgiving!

Other than that, though, I felt reasonably fine. And told Bonnie so, adding, "When are they letting me out of here?"

"Maybe tomorrow." Smile broadening, Bonnie jotted a note on my chart. "Doc Brenning wants to keep you another night. Just to make certain." She rehung the chart at the foot of my bed. "Got some company for you. He's right outside."

Two minutes later, my grandfather walked into the ward. *"Watchiya, Noozis!"* I spied the folded newspaper under his arm. Leaving it on my night table, he sat on the mattress's edge. I sneaked a peek. The weekend edition of the *Daily Republic*. Jumbo headline. DEPUTY KILLED BY ALLEGED MOLESTER.

One eye on my roommate, Chief kept the conversation in our language. "How did your interview with Sheriff Fischer go?"

Fussbudget face. "Sheriff Cal had a lot of questions. He wanted to know what Kramer was doing at the farm. Good thing our deputy friend didn't leave any notes behind."

"What did you tell him?"

I sighed. "A slight variation of the truth. I told him Krause came to the farm hoping to clear out the evidence. That Deputy Kramer had a few more questions about Rankin for me. That Krause saw the two of us talking and came after us in the combine."

"Think he bought it?"

I nodded. Fischer had plenty of supporting evidence. The shattered barn doors and Clem's wrecked combine and the charred body of Doug Krause beneath the OP power lines.

And then there were Krause's two bullets in the deputy's body.

Chief smiled grimly. "So you've made a hero of another deputy."

"With one important difference, *Nimishoo*," I replied, keeping my voice down. "Kramer deserves it. He could have escaped. He could have saved himself—he didn't." Quiet sigh. "Indian-hater he might have been, but he did his best to save me from Doug Krause."

"What happens when that sheriff talks to Covington?"

Pained Angie grimace, followed by a tiny hopeful smile. "I'll think of something, *Nimishoo*." Seeking a less troubling topic, I added, "Paul explained what happened when he was here yesterday, but I still don't believe it. I must have been at least twenty-five yards from that combine."

"Believe it!" Chief nodded decisively. "When that auger hit the power line, the current turned the combine into a giant electromagnet. That's why you saw Krause's pistol go flyin' through the air—"

"With him attached," I interrupted. "Yeah, yeah—Paul explained all that. What I don't understand is, how did the voltage reach *me!?*"

"You got caught in the EMF force field, *Noozis*. The power surge radiated outward through the ground."

Fussbudget face. "How did I get that shock!? I wasn't holding a gun."

Wry grandfatherly smile. "Your shoes, *Noozis*. The tiny nails in your high heels acted as a conductor."

Pursing my lips, I crossed my bandaged feet at the ankle. Many naughty thoughts about OP and their 900-kilovolt transmission lines. I seriously considered a life membership in Safe Power for South Dakota.

Why? Let me put it this way—I have yet to be fricasseed by a *campfire's* force field!

Then Chief told me about the well-wishers waiting in the

hallway outside. Offering instant admittance, I found my hospital bed promptly surrounded by Elderkins—Josh, Trudy, Kristy, Jeremy, and Carol, plus a laconic Clem Mutchler.

When they finished firing questions at me, they turned on Chief. Taking a sip from my glass of lukewarm water, I looked over the *Daily Republic* story. Terrific! Only a very brief mention of Angie.

According to police, Deputy Kramer was questioning Angela Biwaban, a farm worker, when they were attacked by Krause in the stolen combine.

Miss Biwaban was taken hostage by the suspect, beaten and thrown off the combine. She was rushed to the Methodist Hospital where she remains in good condition.

Further down, I found a paragraph that brought a surge of bile into my throat.

Upon entering Krause's trailer, the Highway Patrol investigators discovered dozens of clothing items belonging to little girls, including a winter hat with a white pompom. The hat is said to have belonged to Holly Larsen, who vanished from Yorktown thirty years ago.

From the items found, the number of Krause's victims is estimated at fourteen.

In that moment, I gave a thought to Krause's anguished cry. *"She didn't know about the others."* Pensive frown. Could be you were wrong, Krause. Maybe she did. Or maybe your mother only suspected. Still, that's too much guilt for any mother to carry.

I thought back to my kitchen chat with Miss Edna, to her cryptic reference to a woman's past mistakes, and wondered if she'd been trying to confide in me. And I realized that I could only guess at the depth of that poor woman's guilt. Haunted by the forced abandonment of her illegitimate child, she had used her family's influence to enable him to escape justice. And for the ensuing thirty years, that act had eaten away at her Presbyterian conscience. Perhaps she had been working up the courage to tell me. And perhaps, in telling Rankin, she had taken the first faltering steps toward expiation of her monumental guilt.

All at once, the conversation hushed. Tossing the newspaper aside, I looked up and saw a livid Sam Covington in the doorway. Bristling mustache and fiery eyes. Striding to the foot of my bed, he snapped, "I believe you have something of mine . . . *Miss Biwaban!*"

Cool-eyed Angie. "What might that be, Mr. Covington?"

Through clenched teeth, he muttered, "One hundred thousand dollars!"

"You've got your money, Sam."

He punched the bed's brass railing. "It's not in the vault, young lady!"

"Look again, hoss." Josh took a protective stance at my side. "It's in there. Angie done give it to me, and I used it to pay off the loan."

Covington's face trembled in astonishment. *"You!?"* His gaze zipped from Josh to me and back again. "You used it to— *that's fraud!*"

"So is lending farmers big bucks and then calling in the note early," I added sweetly.

"You'll get your money, Covington," Josh said, folding his arms in determination. "Pay you interest, too. Just as soon as Miss Edna's will's probated." He smiled at my grandfather. "I hear we're all about to come into some dough."

"It's still fraud, Elderkin, and you're both going to answer for it!" Covington reached for the phone on my night table. "I'm calling the sheriff!"

Shaking my head, I sighed. "I don't think so, Sam."

"You can do a lot of thinking in *jail*, Miss Biwaban!"

"Go ahead and call." Scowling, I offered him the receiver. "Sheriff Cal arrests me. We go to trial. I get up on the witness stand. And then I tell it all, Sam." My tone turned deadly. "I'm going to talk my head off. Tell the jury everything. Including how you tried to cheat this family out of their farm on behalf of OP." Sardonic smile. "And I'm sure Uncle Sam will be interested in your offer to turn your bank into a money laundry."

Covington's face trembled.

Tart Angie smile. "But I'll let you explain how a banker on the federal watch list came up with a hundred K in cash overnight."

His features bunched in fury. "You have no proof—!"

"I had a tape recorder in my purse, Sam."

Instantly he turned the color of chalk. "You-you're *bluffing!*"

I waggled the phone receiver. "Call my bluff, then."

Clenched banker's fists trembled.

"I had that tape recorder going every time we chatted." Little white Angie lie. "Let's see if *Kyle Rasmussen* appreciates your taking his name in vain."

When I mentioned the OP honcho, Covington began to look physically ill. Genuine fear altered the gleam of his chocolate-colored eyes. The same fear you see in a wounded animal.

Stepping away from my bed, he tried to put the best face on the situation. "Prison is exactly what you deserve, young woman!"

I glanced at Chief. "You know, the very thought of a witness stand turns me into a chatterbox."

Covington uttered a mild cough. Fiddling with his topcoat buttons, he muttered, "However, a trial would be . . . *inconvenient*—"

"Especially for Mr. Rasmussen," I added.

"It-It seems to me that we'd all be better off leaving the police out of this matter." He cast a conciliatory glance at Josh and Jeremy. "I-I will get my money . . . all of it?"

Slow nod from Josh. "You know we're good for it."

"All right." Covington retreated to the door. "We'll leave it at that for now." Rage-filled glance at Angie. "Im sure I can trust *you* to be discreet."

"One more thing, Covington." I aimed a two-fingered jab at Carol. "Don't forget your pet informer."

The woman's mouth opened wide.

"Don't bother to deny it, Carol." Wearily I slumped against the pillow. "I was right there in his office when you called to tell him about me."

Betrayal swept Jeremy's face. "Carol, you *didn't*—!"

"And what if I did!?" she cried, confronting the family. "This is no life for us. I've told you that for years!"

Covington had already gone. Doing a pert about-face, Carol followed in his footsteps. Halting at the doorway, she looked back at her husband. "Jeremy! Are you coming?"

Josh's younger son shook his head slowly. Handsome features clouded in disillusion. "I-I'll send somebody over for my things."

With that, she flounced out of my hospital room. No backward glances for Mr. Bailey's city-bred daughter.

Clem Mutchler broke the tension with a slap to his denimed knee. A long and hearty guffaw. "Shame on you, Angie! You should've let Sam use your john." Broad silly grin. "When you mentioned OP, I thought sure that ol' boy was going to shit one sideways!"

"And ruin the seat of that pin-striped suit? No way!" I let out a chuckle of my own, then sobered. "Listen . . . I'm sorry about your combine, Clem."

"Don't fret none. It's insured." He scratched at one of his jug-handle ears. "We've got to get you some lessons, gal, and that's a fact. That's *two* you've wrecked!"

Chief grinned. "Three more and you're an ace!"

Enduring the male kidding with a tepid smile, I added, "But the harvest! How are you going to get your crop in?"

"Glad you asked that question." He winked at his in-laws. "Go on and show her, boys."

Josh clapped his son's shoulder. "Give me a hand, Jer."

Together they carried me over to the window. Laughing, I draped my arms across Elderkin shoulders. Trudy darted ahead, peeling back the gauzy drape.

Clem chuckled. "I get by with a little help from my friends."

"Relatives, too!" Jeremy laughed.

Looking down, I saw a parade of empty grain trucks moving slowly past the hospital. Bringing up the rear were a pair of large red combines. I aimed a questioning glance at Clem.

"Folks heard what happened to my combine." Grinning, he gestured at the impromptu parade. "So they're all taking one day off to help me get my crop in. This here's the last bunch headed for Yorktown."

One of the drivers saw us in the window and tooted the truck's diesel horn. In response, I made a fist and pumped my right arm up and down. Grinned at my grandfather.

"Farmers! I love 'em!"

The horns all bellowed at once, blaring in short bursts, filling the streets of Mitchell with a dissonant symphony in D sharp. The din startled a lone eagle circling high in the cloudless autumn sky. I watched his sudden heartstopping turn as he flew north, then smiled as he vanished into the sapphire immensity above the dun-colored prairie.

*"MIND-BOGGLING . . . THE SUSPENSE IS UNBEARABLE . . .
DORIS MILES DISNEY WILL KEEP YOU
ON THE EDGE OF YOUR SEAT . . ."*

THE MYSTERIES OF DORIS MILES DISNEY

THE DAY MISS BESSIE LEWIS DISAPPEARED (2080-5, $2.95/$4.50)

THE HOSPITALITY OF THE HOUSE   (2738-9, $3.50/$4.50)

THE LAST STRAW   (2286-7, $2.95/$3.95)

THE MAGIC GRANDFATHER   (2584-X, $2.95/$3.95)

MRS. MEEKER'S MONEY   (2212-3, $2.95/$3.95)

NO NEXT OF KIN   (2969-1, $3.50/$4.50)

ONLY COUPLES NEED APPLY   (2438-X, $2.95/$3.95)

SHADOW OF A MAN   (3077-0, $3.50/$4.50)

THAT WHICH IS CROOKED   (2848-2, $3.50/$4.50)

THREE'S A CROWD   (2079-1, $2.95/$3.95)

WHO RIDES A TIGER   (2799-0, $3.50/$4.50)